STRUCTURE OF DECISION

WRITTEN UNDER THE AUSPICES OF THE
INSTITUTE OF INTERNATIONAL STUDIES,
UNIVERSITY OF CALIFORNIA (BERKELEY) AND
THE INSTITUTE OF PUBLIC POLICY STUDIES,
THE UNIVERSITY OF MICHIGAN

Structure of Decision

The Cognitive Maps of Political Elites
Edited by Robert Axelrod

PRINCETON UNIVERSITY PRESS
PRINCETON, NEW JERSEY

Published by Princeton University Press
Princeton, New Jersey
In the United Kingdom: Princeton University Press
Guildford, Surrey

Library of Congress Cataloging In Publication Data
will be found on the last printed page of this book

PRINTED IN THE UNITED STATES OF AMERICA
by Princeton University Press, Princeton, New Jersey

To My Students

In a modern society many of the most important decisions affecting the quality of our lives and perhaps even our very survival are made by others. With this in mind, a desire to improve the quality of the decision-making process has been a major research interest of mine for more than a decade. By 1970 I had done work on game theory, the origin of alternatives, bargaining in bureaucracies, the learning of political lessons, and the interrelationships of policy attitudes. In early 1970 I began to turn to psychological approaches, and especially cognitive psychology as a potentially fruitful way of understanding decision making. At that time, Professors Matthew Bonham and Michael Shapiro were at Berkeley with me, and the three of us began thinking about how the beliefs of elite policy makers could be studied in the context of more rigorous systems than were currently available.

My initial work in this direction was the development of a new approach to decision making based on the idea of a cognitive map of a person's stated values and causal beliefs. The framework for this approach was presented as a paper at the Conference on Mathematical Theories of Collective Decisions at the University of Pennsylvania in December 1970, and was later published as a monograph (Axelrod, 1972a). I then sought to apply this analytic framework to a specific empirical study to see what properties the hypothetical cognitive maps would have if they could be derived from the assertions of elite policy makers. I located a high-level policy formation group (the British Eastern Committee) that kept verbatim transcripts of its deliberations, records that were kept secret for almost fifty years and had only recently been released. With these records I derived the cognitive maps of the members of the committee according to coding rules I developed for the purpose, and the resulting analysis was presented to the Peace Research Society (International) at their London conference in August 1971 (Axelrod, 1972b). It appears here in revised form as Chapter 4. A later version of the coding rules drafted with Margaret Wrightson is given in Appendix 1.

Meanwhile, Professor Bonham had left for American University, and Professor Shapiro returned to the University of Hawaii.

Their continued collaboration resulted in a preliminary report of their work (Shapiro and Bonham, 1973), and later in the computer simulation which appears here as Chapter 6.

By this time the project seemed to have a life of its own, as different people found entirely new uses for cognitive maps. Jeffrey Hart, who was then a student at Berkeley, and is now a professor at Princeton, found the cognitive mapping approach useful for one part of his Ph.D. dissertation on the structural aspects of international relations. His empirical study appears as Chapter 8. A second student at Berkeley, Stuart Ross, has also done empirical work extending cognitive mapping techniques into new areas, and his contribution is Chapter 5.

The remaining two contributors initially had no direct contact with the Berkeley group, but their work fits very neatly into this volume on cognitive mapping. Professor Ole Holsti of Duke University wrote a critical review of all the cognitive approaches to foreign policy formation, which is based in part on the organizing principle of my framework paper. This review appears here as Chapter 2.

Professor Fred Roberts of Rutgers University, working completely independently of the rest of us, did research on mathematical and methodological problems in applied graph theory that was strikingly close to my own conception of cognitive maps. His study of transportation policy (Roberts, 1973) provided the basis of an empirical chapter (Chapter 7) and a methodological section (Appendix 2) on the use of a panel of experts to derive a cognitive map.

This book can serve as a primary or supplementary text for a variety of undergraduate and graduate courses in political science, public policy, and psychology. For most purposes, the introductory chapter on the use of cognitive maps (Chapters 1 and 3), the chapter on the British Eastern Committee (Chapter 4) and the conclusion (Chapter 9) are sufficient to teach the basics of the cognitive mapping approach. For political science or public policy courses dealing with a particular policy area, the appropriate empirical chapters can be added: Chapter 5 on the presidency, Chapter 6 on the Middle East, Chapter 7 on commuter transportation and the energy crisis, and Chapter 8 on international control of the oceans. For courses on research methods in the social sciences, the epilogue on limitations (Chapter 10) and projects (Chapter 11) will be especially helpful. In all cases a reading of the conclusion (Chapter 9) will add greater perspective on the significance of the cognitive mapping approach for the improvement of decision making.

With great pleasure I acknowledge the personal and institutional support I received throughout this endeavor. While each chapter includes its own acknowledgements, this is the place to thank those who helped shape the entire volume. First, there are two of my research assistants who treated this project as their own: Margaret Wrightson and Stan Bernstein. Then there are my colleagues whose criticisms always came with the sustaining insistence that the result would be worth the effort: Hayward Alker, Karl Jackson, and Paul Sniderman. Next there are those who helped prepare the manuscript: Phyllis Dexter, Margaret Fletcher, Bojana Ristich, and Claudia Zawacki. And finally there are the contributing authors, who went through draft after draft in responding to my suggestions, and were always ready to do yet one more revision when called upon.

For the financial support of this project I would like to thank the Institute of International Studies of the University of California, Berkeley, its former director, Professor Ernst Haas, and its present director, Professor Carl Rosberg; the Institute of Public Policy Studies of the University of Michigan and its director, Professor Jack Walker; and the National Science Foundation. To all of these people and institutions I say, "Thanks."

ROBERT AXELROD

CONTENTS

xi

TABLES

PART ONE

Introduction

CHAPTER ONE

The Cognitive Mapping Approach to Decision Making

This chapter introduces the cognitive mapping approach to decision making. It describes what cognitive maps are and how they can be empirically derived. Finally, as an indication of how the cognitive mapping approach can help in the understanding, and ultimately in the improvement, of decision making, a chapter-by-chapter overview of the entire volume is presented.

IMPROVING DECISION MAKING

This is a book about how people make decisions and how they can make better decisions. It focuses on an analysis of the effects of policy alternatives upon valued goals. Our approach is to study the cognitive maps used by actual decision makers and policy experts, to see in what ways their performance can be improved. The theme of the book is that although people have to simplify their image of the complexities of the environment in order to cope with it, the number and types of simplifications need not be as great as they usually are. The tools we have used to establish this can also be used to help future decision makers.

This may sound like an ambitious program, and it is. But not impossible. After all, decision makers are typically either experts in a more or less specialized policy domain (such as transportation or foreign policy), or they are "specialists" in aggregating diverse interests (such as Congressmen and the President). Decision makers, however, are not necessarily aware of the specific shortcuts they use in thinking about policy choices. And even if they are sometimes self-conscious about their own cognitive styles, they may not be aware of the limitations these styles impose, and how these limitations could be ameliorated.

Here is a loose analogy. A Roman supply officer employing

3

Roman numerals would not have given much thought to the structure of the system of calculation he was using. He would have thought about the quantity of supplies he was purchasing, their quality, their price, their delivery time, and so on. But he would probably not have considered the fact that his system of arithmetic calculation could be substantially improved by the use of Arabic numerals. If someone had tried to show him that the use of Arabic numerals would make his task considerably easier, his first response might have been that he could already perform all of the calculations he needed to do in his job, and that the new system looked strange and probably was not worth the trouble it took to learn, assuming it worked at all. In a way, the official would be right, because he could already do all that was expected of him ("his best"), and any new system would take some effort to master.

But in retrospect, we can say that the Arabic numerals are a definite improvement over Roman numerals, because they make many tasks, such as long division, substantially easier. Moreover, a person operating with Arabic numerals would have a much better feel for what he was doing. In Arabic numerals, for example, the number with the longer representation is the larger number, but this is not necessarily true in Roman numbers (as in 901 vs 8 and CMI vs VIII). Finally, a place number system such as the Arabic system is superior because it makes it easier to develop more advanced techniques, such as decimals. What lies behind the superiority of the Arabic system over the Roman system is that it better reflects the underlying characteristics of the tens-based number system used by both systems. Indeed, the reasonably skilled user of Arabic numerals might look like a prodigy in a world of Roman-numeral users.

Of course, the evaluation of policy choices is much more complex than the solution of an arithmetic problem, but this is all the more reason why there may be room for improvement. If we had a better idea of the methods people use to analyze and evaluate complex policy choices, then we would be in a better position to design a formalized system to help them do their analysis. Such a formalized system, reflecting the underlying characteristics of the way people actually do evaluate complex choices, could be expected to provide three significant benefits:

1. it would make certain types of evaluation easier;

2. it would expand the range of complexity that a reasonably skilled person could handle; and

4

3. it would promote the development of new ways of thinking that would be logical extensions of the existing methods.

THE ANALYSIS OF CAUSAL ASSERTIONS

This book proposes such a system, based on the notion of causation. The notion of causation is vital to the process of evaluating alternatives. Regardless of philosophical difficulties involved in the meaning of causation, people do evaluate complex policy alternatives in terms of the consequences a particular choice would cause, and ultimately of what the sum of all these effects would be. Indeed, such causal analysis is built into our language, and it would be very difficult for us to think completely in other terms, even if we tried.

The basic elements of the proposed system are quite simple. The concepts a person uses are represented as points, and the causal links between these concepts are represented as arrows between these points. This gives a pictorial representation of the causal assertions of a person as a graph of points and arrows. This kind of representation of assertions as a graph will be called a cognitive map. The policy alternatives, all of the various causes and effects, the goals, and the ultimate utility of the decision maker can all be thought of as concept variables, and represented as points in the cognitive map. The real power of this approach appears when a cognitive map is pictured in graph form; it is then relatively easy to see how each of the concepts and causal relationships relate to each other, and to see the overall structure of the whole set of portrayed assertions.

For added rigor, a mathematical sytsem is presented for the analysis of these cognitive maps. With this system it is possible to derive formal inferences, which can be applied in many ways, such as seeing whether people actually make choices that are consistent with their whole collection of stated causal assertions. Such inferences can also be used to offer advice based on a given cognitive map of the implications of specific choices.

THE DERIVATION OF COGNITIVE MAPS

The analysis of a given cognitive map is one thing, but its actual derivation is another, and often far more difficult, task. For the study of decision making, the methods used to derive a cognitive

5

map should, as far as possible, satisfy four quite demanding requirements.

First, the methods should be unobtrusive. To guard against the possibility that policy makers could not or would not reconstruct the relevant set of causal assertions after the fact, the cognitive map would have to be derivable from whatever materials are left behind in the normal course of a decision-making process.

Second, the derivation should not require advance specification of the concepts a particular decision maker may use in his cognitive map. Ideally, these concepts, as well as the causal links between them, would come from the data and not from any *a priori* assumptions of the researchers.

Third, the derived cognitive map should be closely tied to an evaluation theory of decision making, so that it can be used to advise and even criticize the decision maker. This means that for a given policy issue, the options, the goals, the ultimate utility, and the relevant intervening concepts should all be included in the cognitive map of a decision maker. Moreover, the evaluative theory of decision making that is employed should be sufficiently sophisticated as not to beg the important questions involved in reaching a complex policy decision.

Fourth, the method for deriving the cognitive map should be valid, which is to say that the map should be an accurate representation of the assertions (and relationships among them) used by the decision maker.[1] One important aspect of the validity of such a method is its reliability, that is, the capacity of the method to yield the same results when used by different researchers under the same conditions.

Social scientists have already developed several techniques for the study of people's assertions, so one might well consider these older methods before undertaking the development of new procedures. Survey research techniques, for example, have achieved very good validity by any reasonable social science standards, and they can be tied to an evaluative theory of decision making, as they have in the study of voting behavior. But survey techniques are hardly unobtrusive, and they have only limited capacity to derive concepts that are unique to each respondent. Content analysis, another measurement approach, has achieved very high

[1] Since the term "cognitive map" as used in this volume refers to a particular way of representing a person's assertions, a valid cognitive map does not necessarily have to be consistent with the person's private beliefs.

6

reliability and good validity in certain contexts. Moreover, content analysis techniques can be used unobtrusively, since they are based on documents, and they have considerable flexibility for adopting the categories used by different people. Unfortunately, even the most fully developed form of content analysis is still essentially a counting procedure with limited usefulness for analyzing the structure of the relationships between the concepts.[2] Finally, the open-ended probing interview is an extremely flexible data-gathering method, but it is hardly unobtrusive and has limitations in reliability.

While each of these established methods has its advantages for the derivation of a cognitive map, a new method was necessary to take advantage of the opportunities that arise when suitable documentary material is available. Deriving a cognitive map from existing documents has the advantage of being both unobtrusive and fully able to employ the concepts used by the decision maker himself. Moreover, with the use of the analytic techniques of cognitive maps, the information can be tied to an evaluative theory of decision making. The first three empirical studies of this volume use a coding method for the derivation of the cognitive maps which they analyze. The validity of the documentary coding method is not yet fully established, although the empirical studies that use it offer different kinds of evidence in support of its validity. Reliability, however, *is* fully established. After more than three years of work, the coding rules for deriving a cognitive map from a document have reached a state of precision such that intercoder reliability is fully compatible with the accepted standards of good quantitative work in the social sciences.[3]

An alternative method for the derivation of a cognitive map is used in the remaining two empirical studies. This method employs a questionnaire sent to a panel of judges who are in a position to make informed estimates of causal links. The questionnaire method is necessarily at least one step removed from the decision-making process itself. Its chief advantages are that it allows for the aggregation of individual opinions, and that it may be based on a much wider range of information than research can select for documentary analysis.

These two methods are used to generate comparable cognitive

[2] See, for example, Stone, et al., 1966.

[3] For details of the reliability check, see Chapter 4; for the text of the coding rules, see Appendix 1.

maps, and therefore the same kind of analysis can be used on a cognitive map derived from either method. It turns out that there are interesting differences in the properties of the maps derived by these two methods, and these differences reveal important facts about the cognitive capacities of decision makers.

A third potential method for deriving a cognitive map is the use of an open-ended probing interview. This method could also be used to generate comparable cognitive maps, and it has the advantage of allowing the researcher to interact actively with the source of his data. Work is already in progress by two of the contributors (Bonham and Shapiro) in the use of open-ended interviews to generate cognitive maps.

COGNITIVE MAPPING AND OTHER SYSTEMS

The cognitive mapping approach to decision making uses elements from at least four fields.

1. *Psycho-logic*. The idea that a mathematical system can be specially designed to deal with a person's cognitive processes may be traced to Abelson and Rosenberg (1958), who call their system "psycho-logic." Their system also uses points and arrows, but they give a different interpretation to them. Using Lambert's terminology (1966, p. 126), the points in psycho-logic are " 'thing-like' concepts that for a given subject [person] are relevant to a given object." In cognitive maps, on the other hand, the points are not things, but variables that can take on different values. Thus, for example, in a cognitive map a person is never a point, although some of a person's perceived properties (such as his wealth and utility) may be points. This treatment of points as variables rather than as things makes a cognitive map an algebraic rather than a logical system.

The arrows are also treated differently. In psycho-logic the positive and negative arrows "may be viewed as equivalent, respectively, to the English expressions 'is usefully or desirably associated with' and 'is adversely or undesirably associated with.' " (Lambert, 1966, p. 126). In a cognitive map, the arrows are not representations of attitudinal association, but rather are representations of causal assertions about how one concept variable affects another. Although the interpretations of the two systems are different, from a strictly mathematical point of view, a cogni-

8

tive map can be regarded as a generalization of psycho-logic. In particular, the ideas of ambivalence and balance will be taken from psycho-logic and extended for use in cognitive mapping.

2. *Causal Inference.* The idea that points can be regarded as variables, and that the arrows can be regarded as causal connections between the points, comes from the statistical literature of causal inference, developed by Simon (1957), Blalock (1964), and others. The task of causal inference is to provide a statistical technique to estimate the parameters appropriate to describe a given body of data, subject to a certain set of assumptions about the error terms and the structure of the causal links. That is a long way from the purpose of cognitive mapping, which is to represent what people actually say about causal relationships. While some of the basic ideas of casual inference have been quite useful in this volume, the very complex calculations that are typically involved in causal inference obviously bear little resemblance to what a person is able to do in his head.

3. *Graph Theory.* Both psycho-logic and causal inference employ some of the mathematical ideas of graph theory, as does cognitive mapping. Graph theory provides concepts, such as paths, cycles, and components, that are helpful in the analysis of complex structures of interconnections. Cartwright and Harary (1965) have shown how Heider's (1946) original idea of cognitive balance among three objects can be generalized to any number of objects, and Harary, Norman, and Cartwright (1965) have shown how psycho-logic can be represented in graph theoretic terms. Cognitive mapping uses graph theory, but generalizes it by allowing the points as well as the arrows to take on different values. The resulting mathematical system is similar to the network system developed by Maruyama (1963) to analyze mutual causal relationships in the environment.

4. *Evaluative Assertion Analysis.* The ideal that structural relationships between pairs of concepts can be systematically and reliably coded from a document was taken from evaluative assertion analysis of Osgood, Saporta, and Nunnally (1956).[4]

5. *Decision Theory.* From decision theory have been taken the ideas of choice and utility. (See, for example, Luce and Raiffa, 1957). One of the intended contributions of cognitive mapping

[4] Another system of coding documents for noncausal as well as causal relationships is now under development by Heiskanen (1973, 1974a, 1974b).

9

is to help analyze the decision-making process in terms of the structure of the relationships that a person asserts connect his choices with the expected outcomes of these choices.

The overall research strategy of this volume is to base what is being measured on what is being asserted rather than what is being thought by a person. One basic tactic is to infer things about decision making and cognition from a systematic study of these assertions, and especially from a study of the structural relationships among these assertions.

This research tactic can usefully be contrasted with another recent approach to the study of cognitive processes, namely, the artificial intelligence approach.[5] In the cognitive mapping approach to cognition, the researcher starts with linguistic behavior and makes inferences about cognition. In the artificial intelligence approach, the researcher starts with a model of cognitive processes, uses this model to generate linguistic responses to linguistic inputs, and then evaluates the model in terms of the similarity of its performance with human performance in such contexts. Thus, the cognitive mapping approach requires a good representation of selected features of the assertions made by a person, while the artificial intelligence approach requires a good representation of the internal processes of a person.

A good example of an early artificial intelligence study of cognition is what has come to be called the "Goldwater machine" (Abelson and Carroll, 1965; Abelson, 1968a; Abelson and Reich, 1969). This computer-based model contained a representation of Barry Goldwater's beliefs about the Cold War. The model was designed as an attempt to respond to new assertions much as he might respond to them. Another and more general Ideology Machine sketched out by Abelson (1973) is based on a form of linguistic analysis developed by Schank (1973), which has been adapted and expanded to deal with hierarchical belief systems. This model has literally dozens of different kinds of relationships, such as "possession," "proximity," and "admiration"; "make happy," "achieve," and "enable."

The cognitive mapping approach, in contrast, uses only one basic type of relationship, namely, the causal relationship. While causation is represented as being either positive or negative (i.e.,

[5] For applications of artificial intelligence to cognitive processes see Feigenbaum and Feldman (1963), Minsky (1968), Walker and Norton (1969), and Schank (1973).

promoting or retarding effects), and while it can represent evaluative assertions as well as regular causal assertions, the causal relationship is still the basic building block of a cognitive map. Because the cognitive mapping approach requires an accurate representation of the structural relationships among a set of assertions, the ability to achieve reliable measurement is vital. To achieve this reliable measurement, the use of a single type of relationship is a tremendous help. The fewer the distinctions made among permitted types of relationships, the easier it is to achieve this reliability.[6] And if a single type of relationship is to be used, the causal relationship is a natural candidate, because it is central to the process of evaluating policy.

Thus the artificial intelligence approach, in its desire to stimulate as much as possible of a person's cognitive processes, opts for great variety in the types of relationships it employs. The cognitive mapping approach, in its desire to represent reliably certain selected features of a set of assertions, opts for great restraint in the variety of relationships it employs.

THE PLAN OF THIS VOLUME

Now for a short guided tour of the rest of this volume.

Research on the cognitive processes of elite decision makers has had the greatest impact in the study of foreign policy. Ole Holsti undertakes a critical review of the cognitive approaches to foreign policy decision making in Chapter 2, and notes that the approach by this volume, namely, cognitive mapping, can be readily placed in this tradition, and its difficulties and problems assessed in this context—even though the applications of cognitive mapping already go far beyond the subject of foreign policy.

After Holsti's review, I explain in Chapter 3 how cognitive maps can be analyzed once they are constructed, with special assertions and can be used to generate the consequences that follow from this structure. The chapter explains how such cognitive maps can be analyzed once they are constructed, with special emphasis on inferring the properties of a cognitive map from its parts and the laws of their interaction. In particular, it is shown how a person might use his or her map to derive explanations of

[6] Two additional reasons for limiting cognitive mapping to causal imagery are discussed in Chapter 10, section D. In Chapter 11, section E, some possible expansions are considered.

the past, make predictions for the future, and choose policies in the present.

The heart of the volume is the collection of five empirical studies in five different policy areas:

—neocolonialism;
—the Presidency;
—Middle East policy;
—the energy crisis; and
—international cooperation.

Each of these studies first derives one or more cognitive maps of elite decision makers with respect to specific policy problems, then analyzes these cognitive maps for a particular research purpose to learn more about how people make decisions and how they can make better decisions.

In the first empirical study (Chapter 4), I pose some of the basic research problems and report some intriguing findings. I also provide a short explanation of how cognitive maps are derived from documentary materials, a procedure also used in the following two empirical studies.

This empirical study poses what might be called the *decision-making problem*. Given a cognitive map that includes a set of proposals and the causal relationships linking them, however indirectly, to utility, which proposals should be selected and which rejected? Under certain conditions, there is a simple mathematical answer to this question, but an empirical question is whether decision makers actually act consistently with their own assertions.

To deal with this question I have been fortunate in finding some extraordinarily detailed documentary materials. These are the verbatim transcripts of the cabinet-level British Eastern Committee in 1918, records that were kept secret for almost fifty years. The answer to the empirical question I just posed is that although the cognitive maps derived from this material are quite large, the decision makers took stands on the policy issues in ways that were consistent with their large cognitive maps. This chapter also reports the finding that although the maps are quite large and interconnected, they are structurally simple in several identifiable ways, and these simplifications happen to be ones that make the decision-making problems easy to solve, even for large maps. Whether these simplifications are due to the speakers' desire to explain and justify to others their own policy positions, or whether they reflect

12

cognitive limitations of the speaker, is a difficult question, but there is reason to believe that both factors are operating.

Madison's notes on the American Constitutional Convention in 1787 provide the materials for the empirical study by Stuart Ross (Chapter 5). Ross selected a very complex delegate, Gouverneur Morris, and derived his cognitive map on a very complex subject, the new institution of the presidency. Ross found that under these extreme conditions of complexity, one of the structural simplifications found in the maps of Eastern Committee members was still present, while another of those simplifications was not observed. The analysis of the details of Morris's map yields some new insights into the critical features of Morris's rather intricate arguments about the proper balance of power between the President and the legislature. By comparing the cognitive map of Morris with what his contemporaries said about Morris's style of thought, Ross opens up the field of cognitive mapping to the investigation of cognitive styles.

The next study (Chapter 6) capitalized on a fortuitous circumstance. Matthew Bonham and Michael Shapiro set out to construct a computer simulation of how a foreign policy expert uses his causal beliefs to explain events. They sought to answer what might be called the *explanation problem:* how can a person's cognitive map be used to predict his explanation of new events? In June 1970, in order to generate suitable documentary material, they asked several experts to play the roles of advisors to the President in a crisis game based on a scenario about Russian missiles being discovered in Syria. Bonham and Shapiro used the transcripts from this game to derive the cognitive map of one of the players, a Middle East expert. Three months later came Black September, when Palestinian commandos were attacked and defeated by Jordanian forces. Syria intervened with her army and air force, but withdrew after three days of combat with Jordan and pressure from Israel and the United States.

Bonham and Shapiro took the cognitive map derived from the hypothetical crisis and applied it to the actual situation of the related but quite different crisis to make predictions about how the Middle East expert would explain the actual events and how he would respond to them. Three years later they *asked* the same Middle East expert questions such as "What United States interests were being threatened in this situation? Why?" They found a striking correspondence between the answers they predicted using the three-year-old cognitive map and the actual answers about the real crisis. This demonstrates that not only are the structural properties of a person's cognitive map quite stable, but even the specific concepts and causal links between them can be quite stable. Even more important, it demonstrates that a cognitive map derived in one context can be useful in predicting the response of a decision maker in a new and even unanticipated context. This suggests the possibility of using cognitive maps for predicting behavior in new situations. Thus, a decision maker might be interested not only in advice based on his own cognitive map, but also in predictions based on the cognitive maps of the actors with whom he must interact.

Being able to give advice based on the most accurate possible cognitive map is the long-term task chosen by Fred S. Roberts. To be in a position to do this he needed to develop a method of getting the consensus of a number of experts on a given policy domain, rather than the causal description that a single person might give. Therefore, in his pilot study of transportation and energy demands (Chapter 7), he used a panel of experts: first to assemble a list of the relevant concepts and then (after narrowing the problem to commuter transportation) a consensus of the experts on the causal links between the relevant concept variables.

Roberts is interested, not in selecting among a set of identifiable policy alternatives in a given cognitive map, but in going further and seeing which causal links should themselves be changed to give better outcomes. This is what might be called the *strategic problem,* in contrast to my decision-making problem and Bonham and Shapiro's explanation problem. In his empirical study Roberts finds that the energy demand in intraurban commuter transportation will be stable only if commuter ticket prices go down as ridership goes up. This fascinating result should be regarded as tentative, but it does indicate yet another use of cognitive map analysis, namely as a way to develop answers to the strategic problem of what *changes* in the causal links in our environment we should try to attain.

The emerging potential for international cooperation in the control of the oceans is the subject of Jeff Hart's empirical study (Chapter 8). International ocean regime policy includes such current issues as the exploitation of offshore oil, conservation of fisheries, innocent passage of shipping, and the width of territorial waters. The six relevant actors that Hart selects for his com-

14

parative analysis of cognitive maps are the United States, the Soviet Union, the developed and "satisfied" allies of the United States, the oil exporters, the other developing countries, and an important nongovernmental actor, the oil industry itself. Hart uses a panel of judges to estimate the causal linkages asserted by each of these actors, since documentary analysis is impractical for such a variety of actors in a quickly emerging field. He also used his panel of judges, as Roberts did, to get a consensus judgment about the causal links that actually exist among the relevant variables.

The principal question of Hart's empirical study is what might be called the *sociological problem:* how do the objective characteristics of an actor affect the actor's cognitive map? For example, are the larger nations more likely to take positions consistent with their cognitive maps because they can devote more attention to the entire range of issues involved in a complex policy domain such as ocean regime policy? The results show that, on the contrary, the larger nations often take positions inconsistent with their stated beliefs, probably for domestic political reasons. Sometimes these national actors even alter their stated causal beliefs to make them consistent with their positions, rather than changing their positions to conform to their stated beliefs. Another finding is that although the separate types of actors have quite distinct goals, international cooperation on a multipurpose ocean regime will be easier to attain if they come to share more accurate perceptions of the other causal linkages. This suggests that cognitive map analysis can be used to explore how the conflicts of interest between actors are affected by the alteration of perceptions of specific causal links.

The last three chapters comprise my own assessment of the results, the limitations, and the possibilities of the cognitive mapping approach. Chapter 9 integrates the findings of the separate empirical studies in order to extend our knowledge about decision making. In it, I discuss the different ways cognitive maps can be used in decision making, what can be inferred about individual decision making, and how belief systems of collectivities differ from those of individuals.

One finding is particularly curious. In the three studies of spontaneous cognitive maps that were derived from policy discussion, no recognition of feedback was observed. By contrast, in the two studies using the forced-response questionnaire method, feedback was frequently found. After a series of alternative explanations

15

are examined, I conclude that this pattern is due to decision makers' having more relevant beliefs than they can handle. Based on this conclusion, I then discuss what can be done to enlarge the ability of decision makers to make use of their own beliefs.

In Chapter 10, I explore the limitations of the cognitive mapping approach. Among the problems I consider are the potential for insincerity in policy discussions, the slowness of the documentary coding method, the absence of any types of relationships in cognitive maps other than causal or value relationships, and the lack of quantification in the relationships that are represented. For each problem, I explain the origin of the problem, assess the nature of the limitation, and make suggestions on how to alleviate its effects.

In the last chapter (Chapter 11), I offer fifteen suggestions for research projects using the cognitive mapping approach to decision making. These projects are built upon the findings and the state of the art represented by previous chapters. They are motivated by the desire to learn more about the decision-making process and the desire to improve that process. These suggestions include projects on cognitive processes of individuals, functioning of groups, improvement of decision making, advance of methodology, and description of specific policy settings.

A set of five appendices is offered for those researchers who may wish to use the cognitive mapping approach for themselves. The first two provide instructions for the derivation of cognitive maps. The rules for the derivation of cognitive maps from documentary material are set forth in Appendix 1 in the form of a manual for coders drafted by Margaret Wrightson. The procedures used by Fred S. Roberts for the derivation of cognitive maps from questionnaires are given by him in Appendix 2.

The next two appendices deal with the principles for the analysis of cognitive maps once they have been derived. Appendix 3 is my formulation of the mathematical aspects of cognitive maps. This is followed by· Appendix 4, by George Nozicka, Matthew Bonham, and Michael Shapiro, which is an explanation of the simulation techniques employed in Chapter 6.

For those researchers seeking source material for the documentary derivation of cognitive maps, I offer in Appendix 5 a wide variety of suggestions on suitable source material, including many specific citations of verbatim records of policy meetings.

THE GIVING OF ADVICE

Policy makers have learned to be skeptical of academic advice about how they ought to go about reaching decisions, and with good reason. Many academic theories of decision making begin with an armchair specification of certain ideal standards that a decision maker is supposed to meet, and the theory is developed from there. Such approaches can be useful for seeing how far below such an ideal standard decision makers actually fall. That is to say, they can be useful in emphasizing how difficult the decision-making task really is for a complex policy issue. But often such idealistic theories are also used as the sole basis for exhortations to "do better." When this happens, the specific advice is often ignored, because the advice bears little recognizable relationship to the task at hand as seen by the decision maker himself.

The cognitive mapping approach promises to be more helpful to the decision maker for two reasons. First, since the advice can be expressed in terms of the person's own cognitive map, it can be solidly based in his own experience, using his own concepts, his own causal beliefs, and his own values.[7] Equally important, when the cognitive map approach offers advice, it takes explicit account of the finite capacities of people and the way in which they simplify their images when dealing with a complex policy issue. Thus, with the cognitive mapping approach, a better understanding of how decisions are made can lead to the making of better decisions.

[7] This idea is developed in Chapter 9, section F. The question of whether it is really a good idea to help high-level decision makers become more sophisticated is considered in Chapter 9, section A.

CHAPTER TWO

Foreign Policy Formation Viewed Cognitively
—Ole Holsti

Research on the cognitive processes of elite decision makers has had the greatest impact in the study of foreign policy. This chapter undertakes a critical review of the previous cognitive approaches to foreign policy decision making, and notes that they have yet fully to prove themselves. The particular cognitive approach offered by this volume, namely cognitive mapping, can readily be placed in this tradition, and its difficulties and problems assessed in this context, even though the applications of cognitive mapping go far beyond the subject of foreign policy. This chapter concludes with the challenge that cognitive approaches should be integrated with broader themes, especially interpersonal processes within and between organized groups of policy makers.

Foreign policy analysis has been dominated by approaches that conceptualize the acting unit as a "unitary rational actor," but many of the more interesting studies of the past few years have pointed to several limitations and inadequacies of such models. Norms and interactions within the decision-making group may serve certain needs (emotional support, feelings of solidarity, and the like) of group members. But group dynamics may also have some dysfunctional consequences for the quality of decisions by inhibiting search or cutting it off prematurely, ruling out the legitimacy of some options, curtailing independent analysis, and suppressing some forms of intragroup conflict that might serve to clarify goals, values, and options. Organizational norms, routines, and standard operating procedures may shape and perhaps distort

I am grateful to Hayward Alker, Robert Axelrod, and Matthew Bonham for useful comments and suggestions on a previous version of this paper, and to the Ford Foundation and the Center for Advanced Study in the Behavioral Sciences for support during the period that early drafts were written.

the structuring of problems, channeling of information, use of expertise, and implementation of executive decisions. The consequences of bureaucratic politics within the executive branch or within the government as a whole may significantly constrain the manner in which issues are defined, the range of options that may be considered, and the manner in which executive decisions are implemented by subordinates.

Although these studies of decision processes have identified important limitations of rational choice models (at least as general-purpose frameworks that can be employed for all types of analyses), there are also other constraints on decision making that may warrant investigation. The existence of "cognitive constraints on rationality" is well established in the literature on decision making, with implications that may be especially relevant for foreign policy analysis. It may be useful to recognize that the decision maker's orientation to and interpretation of the political environment is mediated by his beliefs about social life. Thus, his psychological environment may only imperfectly correspond to the "real" or operational political environment.

Nor is it always fruitful to adopt the assumption of homogeneous beliefs among decision makers (that is, the premise that for purposes of foreign policy analysis the nation may be conceptualized as a unitary actor). Some beliefs may be widely shared by top officials within the polity, but even in an authoritarian state with a highly structured official ideology (for example, China or the USSR), there may be significant variations within the elite group with respect to others.

BELIEFS, COGNITIVE PROCESSES, AND FOREIGN POLICY[1]

It is generally recognized that an individual's behavior is in large part shaped by the manner in which he perceives, diagnoses, and evaluates his physical and social environment. Similarly, it is recognized that in order to experience and cope with the complex,

---

[1] Observations and examples throughout this chapter tend to be drawn from studies of foreign policy decision making. Although circumstances under which cognitive process models are useful may occur with greater frequency in the issue-area of foreign policy, many of the observations on the utility, problems, and prospects of this perspective would apply with equal force to decision making in other issue-areas, or in other political contexts (cf. Converse, 1964; Bennett, 1971; Cobb, 1973; Kirkpatrick, 1975).

confusing reality of the environment, individuals have to form simplified, structured beliefs about the nature of their world. This point was made in a striking manner by the philosopher Joseph Jastrow in the statement that the "mind is a belief-seeking rather than a fact-seeking apparatus" (quoted in Rokeach, 1968). An individual's perceptions, in turn, are filtered through clusters of beliefs or "cognitive maps" of different parts of his social and physical enivronment. The beliefs that compose these maps provide the individual with a more or less coherent way of organizing and making sense out of what would otherwise be a confusing array of signals picked up from the environment by his senses.[2] Foreign policy officials are no different in this respect. Because foreign policy situations are often characterized by "structural uncertainty,"[3] the cognitive maps of decision makers may be expected to be of more than passing interest.

The central role of cognitive factors in decision making has long been recognized (Simon, 1947; Snyder, Bruck and Sapin, 1954, 1962; March and Simon, 1958). Nevertheless, progress toward incorporating them into empirical research has been relatively slow and uneven; students of international politics and foreign policy have not achieved consensus about the central relevance or utility of research on the belief systems and cognitive processes of foreign policy leaders. Analysts whose research designs either focus upon or at least leave room for the possible importance of the cognitive aspects of decision making have been in a minority. Although there are some indications of a change in this respect, to date there has been a relative neglect of systematic research focusing on the relationship among: belief systems; the manner in which such complex cognitive tasks as diagnosis of the

[2] Belief systems and cognitive processes should be distinguished from ideology or mere policy preferences. "Belief system" refers to a more or less integrated set of beliefs about man's physical and social environment. In the case of political leaders, beliefs about history and the nature of politics may be especially important. "Cognitive processes" refer to various activities associated with problem solving (broadly conceived), including perception, appraisal, interpretation, search, infomation processing, strategies for coping with uncertainty, decision rules, verification, and the like. These cognitive activities are assumed to be in an interactive relationship with the individual's belief system, as well as with the environment.

[3] "Structural uncertainty" describes circumstances in which "not only are probability distributions not known (as in the constrained rational theories), but even the possible states of the world are imperfectly specified" (Steinbruner, 1968, p. 216).

20

situation, search for policy options, and evaluations are undertaken; choice behavior; and coping with feedback resulting from the selected policy.

This assessment can be documented in several ways. In many of the most prominent data-based research projects—for example, Dimensionality of Nations, WEIS, Correlates of War, Studies in International Conflict and Integration,[4] and Comparative Foreign Policy [5]—input-output models and those that emphasize attributes of the nation and the international system are clearly dominant. Empirically, the research is heavily dependent on "events data" and aggregate data of various kinds. Relatively few include analyses of decision making—the internal political process is usually "black boxed"—much less of belief systems and their effects on policy outcomes.

Limited systematic investigation of the linkages between beliefs and decision making characterizes not only the discipline as a whole, but also the research of those who have found a congenial intellectual home in the interstices between political science and psychology. A perusal of two reviews of the literature on foreign policy and international politics, undertaken from a social psychological perspective (Kelman, 1965; Etzioni, 1969; see also the extensive bibliography in Knutson, 1972, pp. 283–325), reveals that public attitudes, images, and stereotypes, the effects of travel or personal contacts, and other forms of cross-national interaction have received considerable attention. The impact of such variables

---

[4] Although past studies of crises were concerned with cognitive and perceptual variables, more recent ones have been devoted to technology, population, and resources. "Our earlier analyses have focused on individual leaders' perceptions and cognitions. At this point we are not at all sure that such a focus represents the best possible choice. Our strategy now is to explore the capabilities of longer-range models to their fullest" (Choucri and North, 1972, p. 99).

[5] A consortium of scholars at various universities under the intellectual leadership of James N. Rosenau. Rosenau's extensive work on comparative foreign policy (1970, 1971) neglects neither internal political processes nor idiosyncratic variables, but most of those associated with the project have placed their emphasis elsewhere. A notable exception is the CREON project (Ohio State), which is concerned with the effects of beliefs, attitudes, and decision styles on information processing and on foreign policy outputs. Data have been gathered for such variables as cognitive complexity, dogmatism, and belief in internal control of events (M. Hermann, 1972, 1974). For a summary of CREON research, see Rosenau, Burgess, and C. Hermann (1973); and Rosenau and C. Hermann (1973).

21

on decision making and policy outputs, however, may be somewhat limited and difficult to trace. Research on foreign policy leaders and their beliefs, perceptions, styles of information processing, strategies for coping with uncertainty, and the like have been a secondary area of concern, even among those whose investigations are informed by theories, concepts, and data of a psychological nature. Although in recent years a cognitive approach to foreign policy analysis has emerged as a vital area of inquiry,[6] it is nevertheless useful to consider the basic arguments against this approach, for they may identify a number of genuine difficulties that stand in the way of developing rigorous theories and a cumulative body of empirical findings.[7] Several theoretical, methodological, and practical problems may have inhibited extensive application of cognitive process perspectives to foreign policy decision making. These include: disillusionment with some previous efforts of related kinds; skepticism about the relevance of psychological theories, insights, and evidence to analysis of political phenomena; the canon of parsimony; problems of linking beliefs to foreign policy actions; and difficulties of access to data, the laboriousness of coding, and related methodological problems.

Critical Reactions to Earlier Approaches

Possibly contributing to the relative neglect of research on foreign policy officials and their cognitions and perceptions is the con-

[6] Signs of growing interest include the International Conference on Cognitive Models of Foreign Policy Decision Making, the results of which will be published in a forthcoming book edited by Matthew Bonham and Michael Shapiro, as well as a number of projects in progress, some preliminary results of which are cited throughout this paper. Recent studies advocating greater attention to decision makers' beliefs and decisional premises, *and doing so on the basis of empirical evidence,* include: Art (1973), Steinbruner (1968; 1974), Stassen (1972), Krasner (1972), Ball (1974), Cottam (forthcoming), and Lowenthal (1972). See also the essay by Cottam (1973). Among broader assessments of alternative approaches to international politics, compare Alker (1973) and Boulding (1972).

The prominent foreign policy role played by Henry A. Kissinger appears to have heightened interest in decision makers' beliefs. Among studies that deal with Kissinger's beliefs are those by Brenner (1973), Graubard (1973), Isaak (1975), Landau (1972), and Walker (1975). Other studies of this nature are being undertaken by Albert Eldridge and G. Warren Nutter.

[7] Critiques of the premises, methodologies, or specific research results that have been employed in or have emerged from various cognitive process studies include: Haas (1967), Hilton (1969), Jervis (1969), Mueller (1969a and 1969b), Goldmann (1971), and Brodin, Goldmann, and Lange (1972).

22

tinuing influence of critical reactions against previous efforts to deal with the individual and his psychological traits as the central focus of analysis. Three examples illustrate this observation.

1. The "war begins in the minds of men" approach achieved some following after World War II, especially among behavioral scientists who sought to apply the insights of their own disciplines to the eradication or amelioration of international conflict. The optimistic vision of an almost infinitely malleable human nature and the tendency to ascribe conflict largely to misunderstanding, lack of communication, inadequate knowledge, or misperception were inviting targets for critical reaction (e.g., Waltz, 1959).

2. Some approaches focused on the manner in which psychological aberrations or pathological needs of decision makers were projected into the international arena. The examples of Hitler and Stalin seemed to provide special relevance to this perspective. But, without denying that attention to nonlogical aspects of personality may provide some insight into the behavior of individual leaders, critics (e.g., Verba, 1961) questioned whether such explanations were either sufficient or necessary for understanding important international phenomena.

3. The "power school," which reached a position of dominance following World War II, was also rooted in psychological theories of political man. It portrayed him as ambitious and egoistic or, in some versions, as touched with original sin. This is not the place to evaluate these visions of homo politicus. Suffice it to say that global psychological properties such as those posited by the "first image pessimists," to use Kenneth Waltz' term, did not lend themselves very well to rigorous empirical research.[8] As in the case of the "war begins in the minds of men" school, the "realist" approach was subject to trenchant critiques (e.g., Waltz, 1959; Hoffmann, 1960) that cast doubt not only on the specific theories, but also on the more basic proposition that our understanding of international politics and foreign policy could be significantly enhanced by including the decision maker, his belief system, and his cognitive processes at the core of our analyses.

4. Decision-making approaches (e.g., Snyder, Bruck, Sapin, 1954, 1962; Frankel, 1963) were in part a reaction to deficiencies

---

[8] Moreover, if it is axiomatic that all men seek power, then we are left without interindividual variations of real consequence; for explanation we are therefore forced to cast our attention elsewhere—for example, to the structure of the international system and power relations within it.

of earlier theories. The most prominent of these, the framework developed by Snyder and his colleagues, placed the individual decision maker—with his values, attitudes, information, perceptions, and definitions of the situation—at the center of a complex network of organizational and other influences. After an initially enthusiastic reception, this approach came under considerable criticism. There is no need to rehash here the familiar arguments of the critics (e.g., McClosky, 1956; Hoffmann, 1960; Rosenau, 1967), but one point is perhaps worth noting. The major empirical application of the framework—the American decision to resist the invasion of South Korea (Snyder and Paige, 1958; Paige, 1968)—made fairly extensive use of the organizational and information variables of the scheme. It also explored in some detail the internal and external setting of the decision. But less attention was devoted to the belief systems and cognitive processes of those involved in making the decisions. Put somewhat differently, although the original decision-making framework drew upon both sociological and psychological theories and insights, in its application to the Korean decision the former seemed to outweigh the latter by a considerable margin.[9]

The Relevance of Psychology

It is no secret that many political scientists consider the analyses of foreign policy and international politics undertaken by some psychologists to be well-intentioned, but often of dubious realism and relevance.[10] Questions have also been raised about the value

[9] The fact that there was relatively little disagreement within the policy-making group on the decision to resist aggression does not necessarily reduce the relevance of cognitive factors, nor need it imply that a "unitary rational actor" model would provide the most potent and parsimonious explanation. The analyst might, for example, wish to examine the decision makers' beliefs about the nature of international politics, the adversary (for example, who, if anyone, was behind the North Korean invasion, and why), and the like. High consensus on both goals and the means of achieving them within a decision group representing diverse agencies within the government would, however, seem to diminish the relevance of the perspective of "bureaucratic politics," a point developed in more detail by Art (1973).

[10] Debate over the relevance of psychology to political subjects cuts across the so-called "traditionalist-behavioralist" controversy. For example, Morton A. Kaplan, an outspoken critic of traditional approaches, has also written, "when most psychologists, psychiatrists, or psychoanalysts turn to political subjects, they employ the maxims of psychoanalysis as patent nostrums and are thus indistinguishable in manner from the itinerant hucksters of Indian

24

of introducing the premises, theories, concepts, and to some extent the methodologies of other disciplines into the core of foreign policy analysis (e.g., Hoffmann, 1960, p. 172). These objections take several forms. One is that the relevant literature in psychology has emerged from the artificial setting of the laboratory, using subjects who are in some important respects quite unlike foreign policy officials. Moreover, the laboratory subjects have usually been engaged in problem-solving activities that bear only a faint likeness to the complex cognitive tasks that occupy political leaders, especially when they are faced with awesome crisis decisions.[11]

Some critics also question the wisdom of borrowing theories and concepts from another discipline when psychologists them-

---

snake oil" (Kaplan, 1968, pp. 694–695). Prominent efforts by psychologists to deal with problems of foreign policy and international politics include: de Rivera (1968), Frank (1967), Janis (1972), Kelman (1965), Klineberg (1964), Milburn (1972), Osgood (1959b; 1962), Stagner (1967), and White (1970). Psychologists are themselves in less than complete agreement about the relevance of their theories, concepts, and insights to analyses of international politics and foreign policy. See, for example, the exchange between Ralph K. White (1971) and Fred Arnstein (1971).

Similar doubts have been expressed about the relevance of models and concepts drawn from economics. See, for example, various assessments of the field by Hans J. Morgenthau (e.g., Morgenthau, 1968).

[11] The vast experimental literature on stress is highly suggestive, and it can serve as an important source of insights and hypotheses. For several reasons, however, it must be used with caution by the student of political decision making. Research ethics limit the range of stress-inducing stimuli that may be employed in the laboratory. The situations must of necessity be relatively benign and of short duration. Many studies limit themselves to a single type of stress in order to isolate the effects of the independent variable. The tasks undertaken by subjects who have been exposed to stressful stimuli have tended to be either psychomotor problems, such as repairing field telephones, or cognitive problems for which there is a clearly defined correct answer. Relatively few of these laboratory studies have involved more complicated cognitive processes or highly intellectualized tasks that often confront the policy-maker. Subjects have usually been students, who differ by virtue of age, experience, knowledge, and other important attributes from political leaders. Finally, many experimental studies isolate the subject, rather than place him in the context of groups or organizations—both of which may provide the political leaders with supports and/or constraints in performing the required decision-making tasks.

It is interesting to note in this respect that a leading cognitive psychologists has recently suggested that "the best strategy for such research (on cognitions, emotions, and coping processes) is ideographic and naturalistic rather than monothetic or normative and experimental" (Lazarus, n.d., p. 42).

25

selves have failed to achieve consensus on important questions about belief systems, attitude change, and related concerns. Even prominent formulations, such as various "cognitive consistency theories"—approaches that share the premise that man seeks congruence between his behavior, beliefs, and attitudes—have been the source of vigorous debate among advocates of competing explanations (Abelson, et al, 1968; Insko, 1967). Why, then, should students of foreign policy, rarely trained to deal critically with the results of experimental research, add to their own burdens by introducing the controversies of other disciplines into their work? Doing so may render them no less vulnerable than the psychologist who assumes that the world of international politics is merely his research laboratory writ large.

Although these criticisms may overstate the difficulties, they are quite correct in suggesting that indiscriminate borrowing from psychology is no panacea. The starting point and the criterion of relevance should be the substantive concerns of the foreign policy analyst rather than those of the experimental psychologist. It is probably no accident that among the most insightful studies of foreign policy by psychologists (e.g., de Rivera, 1968; Janis, 1972) are those that have started with problems that emerge in a real foreign policy setting and then worked back toward the psychological literature, rather than vice versa.[12]

Parsimony

Perhaps the most widely articulated arguments against cognitive approaches to foreign policy decision making focus on theoretical parsimony and research economy. One can, it is asserted, account for more of the variance in international behavior by starting with —and perhaps limiting oneself to—other levels of analysis. The predominance of the "unitary rational actor" ("Model I") approach to the study of foreign policy and international politics has been documented by Allison (1969, 1971). Advocates of Model I acknowledge that it is, like every model, an oversimplification of reality, but they assert that it nevertheless provides as good an explanation as we are likely to achieve at any reasonable cost. Even severe critics of the "power school," "Sovietologists," or de-

[12] Robert Jervis' forthcoming study of perception and international relations is highly suggestive in this respect. Drawing broadly on both experimental and historical evidence, he develops (but does not subject to definitive test) a number of hypotheses on the scope and limitations of psychological explanations.

terrence theorists—three of the major groups that share a Model I approach to the subject—do not necessarily reject the premise that it is uneconomical to focus much research attention on the individual decision maker. Such analyses are often deemed superfluous for one or more of several reasons. One view is that role, institutional, and other constraints limit the area within which a leader's traits can affect policy. Another is that there is, in any case, little variance among leaders with respect to their decision-making behavior in any given circumstances; that is, whatever their individual differences, they will tend to respond in similar ways. The following paragraphs illustrate, but by no means explore exhaustively, the thesis that explanations centering on the cognitions and perceptions of even the highest-ranking leaders are unlikely to extend our understanding in a significant way.

1.) Foreign policy decisions are made within complex bureaucratic organizations that place severe constraints on the individual decision maker. Organizational memory, prior policy commitments, parochial vested interests, standard operating procedures, normal bureaucratic inertia, and conflict resolution by bargaining, all of which are deeply entrenched within the bureaucratic organization, serve to restrict the impact on the policy output of the leader's beliefs or other cognitive traits and processes. It should perhaps be noted, however, that a focus on bureaucratic politics need not exclude a concern for belief systems. That is, conflict and bargaining may develop as a result of divergent diagnoses and prescriptions that derive, in turn, from different beliefs about the nature of politics, the character of opponents, and the like; and these differences may not be correlated perfectly with bureaucratic position. The recent literature on "bureaucratic politics" perhaps over-emphasizes the notion that intragovernmental conflict arises almost solely from parochial interests ("where you stand depends on where you sit"), to the exclusion of genuine intellectual differences that may well be rooted in broader concerns than the narrow interests and perspectives of one's bureau or agency. Finally, a focus on bureaucratic politics may be especially useful for understanding the slippage between an executive decision and foreign policy outputs that emerge from the process of implementing decisions, but it may be less valuable for explaining the decision itself.[13]

[13] More detailed critiques of some aspects of the recent bureaucratic politics literature appear in George (1972), Rothstein (1972), Art (1973), Krasner (1972), and Ball (1974).

domestic
level

2. Foreign policy is the external manifestation of domestic institutions, ideologies, and other attributes of the polity. The notion that political, economic, and other internal institutions determine the nature of foreign policy is an old one, extending back to Kant and earlier. Contemporary advocates of this position include, among others, "hard line" analysts, who attribute all Soviet or Chinese foreign policy behavior to the imperatives of Marxism-Leninism and communist totalitarianism. Many revisionist American historians adhere to a comparable position—that the institutional requirements of capitalism are not only a necessary but are also a sufficient explanation for the nature of American foreign policy. Theirs is usually a Model I (unitary rational actor) analysis par excellence. Individual decision makers and their attributes are of little concern, as they are allegedly merely the agents of the "system," and faithfully reflect the needs of the dominant ruling class. Names and faces may change, but interests and policies do not, because they are rooted in more or less permanent structural features of the polity.[14] It is assumed that there is a homogeneity of beliefs not only within but also between organizations, because the processes of political recruitment and political socialization effectively suppress or eliminate all but the most trivial differences in politically relevant beliefs. Thus, those whose work is informed by what Waltz (1959) has called "second image" theories—that the causes of international conflict can be located in the malignant institutions of certain polities (it should be noted that their numbers are not limited to Cold War "superhawks" or revisionist historians)—clearly have little reason to introduce into their analyses such concepts as bounded rationality, cognitive dissonance, information processing capacity, coping with stress, and related concerns of cognitive process models. These are regarded, not merely as unnecessary embellishments that complicate the investigator's task, but as diversions that cloud the analyst's insight into the fundamental sources of international behavior.

[14] For a critique of these theories, see Holsti (1974). The criticism is not that national attributes are unrelated to external behavior, but rather that this premise has often been applied in a simplistic manner. Thus, one needs to distinguish between single-factor explanations (e.g., that foreign policy directly reflects Marxist ideology or capitalist power structure), and systematic multitrait analyses of the kind found in the work of Rudolph Rummel, Jonathan Wilkenfeld, James Rosenau, Charles Hermann, Maurice East, Charles Kegley, Patrick McGowan, Stephen Salmore, Ivo and Rosalind Feierabend, and many others.

3. Structural and other attributes of the international system shape and constrain policy choices to such an extent that this is the logical starting point for most analyses (Singer, 1961). Many who adhere to this position would concede that in order to explore the dynamics of the system it may, at times, be desirable and necessary to conduct supplementary analyses of political processes within the nation, or possibly within its major institutions; few would extend the argument to the point of analyzing cognitive processes of even the highest-ranking leaders.[15]

In summary, the argument is that by the time one has taken into account systemic, societal, governmental, and bureaucratic constraints on decision makers, much of the variance in foreign policy making has been accounted for; attributes of the individual decision maker are thus often regarded as a residual category that may be said to account for the unexplained variance. Although many contemporary students of foreign policy and international politics accept some variant of one or more of these arguments, it is not wholly unfair to suggest that they are often the initial premises that guide, rather than the considered conclusion that emerge from systematic research. There are few comparative studies that might reveal the circumstances under which alternative premises—for example, that "beliefs of foreign policy decision makers are central to the study of decision outputs and probably account for more of the variance than any other single factor" (Shapiro and Bonham, 1973, p. 161)—might be applicable. In many cases, and for many analytical purposes, it is clearly unnecessary to undertake detailed investigations of decision makers' belief systems in order to achieve an adequate explanation of policy choices. But there is a growing body of empirical research that indicates that to do so may prove rewarding in one or more of the following circumstances: [16]

[15] A case for this position is summarized by J. David Singer: "I urge here a clear and sharp distinction between behavior and the intrapsychic processes that precede and accompany behavior of the individual; let us simply equate behavior with action. By doing so, we are free to speak of the behavior or acts of any social entity, from the single person on up, and need never be guilty of anthropomorphizing our social system. To use the metaphor of the S-R [stimulus-response] psychologists, we can treat all the psychological and physiological processes that occur within an individual as if they unfolded in a "black box" which cannot be penetrated, and try to understand external behavior (or output) strictly in terms of its empirical association with external stimuli (or input)" (Singer, 1971, pp. 19–20).

[16] Empirical support for this list may be found in many studies, including, among others: Art (1973), Ball (1974), de Rivera (1968), C. Hermann

situations where individual traits of leaders matter ✳

1. Nonroutine situations that require more than merely the application of standard operating procedures and decision rules; for example, decisions to initiate or terminate major international undertakings, including wars, interventions, alliances, aid programs, and the like.

2. Decisions made at the pinnacle of the government hierarchy by leaders who are relatively free from organizational and other constraints—or who may at least define their roles in ways that enhance their latitude for choice.

3. Long-range policy planning, a task that inherently involves considerable uncertainty, and in which conceptions of "what is," "what is important," "what is likely," "what is desirable," and "what is related to what" are likely to be at the core of the political process. In answering these and related questions we might expect considerable variation among policy makers.

4. When the situation itself is highly ambiguous, and is thus open to a variety of interpretations. Uncertainty may result from a scarcity of information; from information of low quality or questionable authenticity; or from information that is contradictory or is consistent with two or more significantly different interpretations, coupled with the absence of reliable means of choosing between them.

5. Circumstances of information overload in which decision makers are forced to use a variety of strategies (e.g., queuing, filtering, omission, reducing categories of discrimination, and the like) to cope with the problem (cf. Holsti, 1972, pp. 81–118, as well as the literature cited therein).

6. Unanticipated events in which initial reactions are likely to reflect cognitive "sets."

7. Circumstances in which complex cognitive tasks associated with decision making may be impaired or otherwise significantly affected by the various types of stresses that impinge on top-ranking executives (Davis, 1974; Schneider, 1972; Broadbent, 1971; George, 1974; Hermann and Hermann, 1974; Holsti and George, 1975, and the literature cited therein).

These categories are not mutually exclusive or exhaustive; nor

(1969a), C. Hermann (1972), Holsti (1967), Holsti (1972), Janis (1972), Jervis (1968), Jervis (forthcoming), Krasner (1972), Lowenthal (1972), May (1973), Milburn (1972), Paige (1968), Schick (1975), Snyder and Paige (1958), Stassen (1972), and Steinbruner (1968, 1974). More extensive discussions of the circumstances under which individual traits of leaders are likely to "make a difference" may be found in Greenstein (1969, pp. 42–62) and M. Hermann (1974).

is it suggested that they are of relevance only for foreign policy decisions. It has been noted, however, that "structural uncertainty" often characterizes important foreign policy choice situations (Steinbruner, 1968, pp. 215–216; cf. Snyder, Bruck and Sapin, 1962, p. 104). To the extent that this is more frequently the case in international than in domestic situations, we might expect that cognitive approaches would more often be applicable in issues of the former type.

As Allison (1969, 1971) has persuasively demonstrated, any given level and units of analysis serve as beacons that guide and sensitize the investigator to some bodies of data and potential explanations; they may also be conceptual blinders, desensitizing him to evidence that might support competing explanations. It is not altogether satisfactory to assert that the choice of levels and units of analysis is merely a matter of taste or theoretical preference. Nor is it always sufficient to assume that the higher (that is, systemic) levels of explanation establish the limits within which choices are made, whereas lower ones serve to fill in the finer details; the different foci may lead to significantly different explanations. What is needed is rigorous comparative research that addresses itself to the issue, not in the spirit of evangelism on behalf of one theoretical position or the other, but rather in response to the question, for what range of research and policy problems is any given perspective or combination of perspectives likely to prove necessary? or sufficient? What is the relative potency of various clusters of independent variables on not only the decision-making process (Rosenau, 1966), but also on the substance and quality of the policy output?

We have relatively few such studies, but of the examples that come to mind a number seem to provide support for greater attention to the belief systems of policy makers. Rosenau's (1968) research on the behavior of United States senators toward Secretaries of State Acheson and Dulles indicated that it was governed largely by role rather than personal or idiosyncratic attributes. An imaginative re-analysis of the data revealed, however, that preferences and "belief-sets" of the senators in fact yielded a *more powerful* explanation for their behavior than did role (Stassen, 1972). Although role and belief-sets provided equally good explanations in many cases, by reference to beliefs Stassen was also able to explain the actions of senators whose behavior did not conform to the role theory.

Allison's study of the Cuban missile crisis did not extend the

31

analysis to a consideration of a cognitive process model, but the potential value of doing so was suggested in the conclusion (1971, p. 277). It seems a reasonable hypothesis that such a study would have illuminated further several aspects of the decision-making process in Washington; for example, the early consensus that the Soviet missiles must be removed; the lineup of "hawks" and "doves" on the most appropriate and effective means of doing so; or the shifting of policy positions as new information became available and new interpretations were adduced.

Such a study might be especially useful because Allison's work—the most complete analysis of the missile crisis to date—did not reveal any significant correlation between bureaucratic role and decision making. That is, neither in the diagnoses of the situation created by the emplacement of Soviet missiles in Cuba, nor in their prescriptions of how best to cope with the problem, did all members of the "Ex Com" act in ways that are readily predictable from the assumptions of the literature on bureaucratic politics. For example, it is not clear that Robert McNamara's initial diagnosis of the Soviet emplacement of offensive missiles in Cuba ("a missile is a missile"), a judgment not widely shared by his colleagues, could be predicted from his bureaucratic role in the Kennedy administration; thus, whether or not a leader defines a situation as a "crisis" perhaps depends at least in part on basic beliefs about the political universe, and these will not always correspond to or be predictable from his role. Moreover, with the possible exception of members of the Joint Chiefs of Staff and UN Ambassador Adlai Stevenson, there did not appear to be an evident and consistant relationship between role and policy prescriptions. This would appear to suggest at least some limitations to the core premise of the literature on bureaucratic politics: "Where you stand depends on where you sit."

Steinbruner's study of the proposed multilateral force (MLF) for NATO tested four alternative conceptions of decision making: the rational, adaptive rational, bargaining, and cognitive process models. He concluded that, "The handling of multiple objectives and the response to structural uncertainty required explanations at the level of the individual decision maker, and it was the cognitive process model which provided the best fit with the phenomena observed" (Steinbruner, 1968) p. 538). As multiple objectives and uncertainty characterize many occasions for foreign policy decisions, the implications of the Steinbruner study would appear to extend well beyond the MLF case. Trotter (1971), examined the Cuban missile crisis from the perspective of nine different models, and concluded that a cognitive perspective provided the best explanation for American decision making during that episode. The latter study failed, however, to develop its models as fully as Steinbruner, Allison, or Stassen, nor is it as persuasive in demonstrating critical differences in the outcome that could be derived from each. Lowenthal's (1972) analysis of the Dominican intervention rejected three competing explanations of American actions in favor of one that emphasized the beliefs, attitudes, and analogies that came into play in the decision-making process. Finally, in a more anecdotal survey of some recent episodes in American foreign policy, Art (1973) concluded that the more important decisions are better explained by the "mind-sets" of top leaders than by a bureaucratic politics perspective.

Relating Beliefs, Decisions, and Foreign Policy Actions

Some studies have been criticized for a failure to distinguish between official and operational ideologies, and for being vulnerable to the charge of having made unwarranted assumptions about direct linkages between official ideologies and foreign policy actions (Singer, 1968, p. 145). These criticisms are appropriately addressed to the danger that a cognitive perspective will be employed in a somewhat simplistic manner—assuming, for example, that beliefs constitute a set of rules that are applied mechanically by policy makers when they make a decision. The concern is not wholly misguided, because some analysts do, in fact, tend to assume a one-to-one relationship between belief systems or operational codes and foreign policy actions (cf. Strausz-Hupé, et al., 1959). Put somewhat differently, Singer's concern is that foreign policy analysts may inappropriately assume a model of foreign policy making like that in Figure 2–1.

FIGURE 2–1.

A Simplistic Model of Foreign Policy Formation

33

The actual relationship is considerably more complex. First, in any political system there will be a set of shared beliefs or "shared images" (Halperin, 1974, pp. 11–16). But, especially in a pluralistic polity, there may also be variations in beliefs, and these differences may take on considerable importance as they are operative in any given decision-making situation. This is precisely the reason for focusing on the individual policy maker, rather than assuming a homogeneity of beliefs among them. It is thus possible to determine empirically the range of core beliefs that are widely shared, as well as those on which there may be substantial variation.

2) Second, it is not very fruitful to assume direct linkages between beliefs and actions in foreign policy, because the role that beliefs may play in policy making is much more subtle and less direct (Figure 2–2). Rather than acting as direct guides to action, they

FIGURE 2–2.

A Conceptual Model of Decision Making

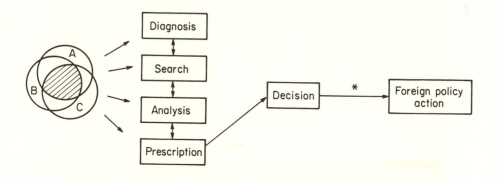

form one of several clusters of intervening variables that may shape and constrain decision-making behavior. They may serve the policy maker as a means of orienting him to the environment; as a lens or prism through which information is processed and given meaning; as a diagnostic scheme; as one means of coping with the cognitive constraints on rationality; as a source of guidelines that may guide or bound—but not necessarily determine—policy prescriptions and choices. Thus, attention should be directed to the linkages between beliefs and certain decision-making tasks that precede a decision—definition of the situation, analysis, prescription, and the like. The manner in which these tasks are performed is likely to establish the boundaries within which the decision is made; for example, the definition of the situation or the focus and extent of search and analysis will eliminate from serious consideration certain policy options, as well as highlight others.

3 Third, it is important to recognize the distinction between decisions and actions. The literature on bureaucratic politics has illustrated the many potential sources of slippage between executive decisions and the implementation of policy in the form of foreign policy actions.

Research Difficulties

Finally, not the least potent constraint has been the very real and persistent problems of undertaking systematic empirical research. At a time when the discipline itself was becoming more self-consciously scientific, applying more stringent standards of theoretical rigor and methodological sophistication, these problems have become increasingly visible. One obvious difficulty is access to data. Unlike the analyst who can index his variables with such measures as GNP per capita, arms budgets, trade figures, votes in the UN General Assembly, or public opinion polls, those interested in the beliefs of decision makers have no yearbook to which they can turn for comparable evidence, much less quantitative data presented in standard units.[17] One result is relatively limited agreement on the appropriate categories into which to code whatever data are available. A no less potent difficulty concerns transformation of available biographical, documentary, and other evidence into data that are both replicable and directly relevant to the theoretical question at hand. Moreover, such data are usually in a form that does not lend itself easily to sharing or depositing in archives. Hence, unlike figures on budgets, trade or voting, each set of data developed for a cognitive process study is likely to be used only once. In a later section of this paper we shall return to some of these research problems.

Although these arguments against expending considerable research resources on the cognitive attributes and processes of

---

[17] It is well established that social background indicators, for which "hard" data are readily available, are imperfect indicators or predictors of beliefs.

decision makers are not without some merit, the tentative conclusion is that their universal validity is open to serious question.
The existing literature is insufficient to provide a definitive and
compelling assessment, but there appears to be a reasonable case
in support of the following proposition: For important classes of
decisions (such as those cited above), a cognitive process perspective is necessary—*and not just as a way of filling in details*—
although probably not sufficient. Put somewhat differently, the
proposition is that for some decisions a cognitive process perspective is fundamental and should be at the starting point of the
analysis, rather than a luxury to be indulged in order to reduce
some of the variance unexplained by the other, more powerful,
approaches.

EXISTING FOREIGN POLICY RESEARCH: DIVERSITY IS THE RULE

Existing studies are characterized by diversity in conceptualization,
sources of theory, research site, subject, and "data-making"
(categories, coding rules, data analysis procedures) operations.
They range from rather traditional single-case analyses of specific
leaders to efforts aimed at developing computer simulations of
cognitive processes (Abelson, 1971). The landscape of cognitive
studies is also littered with possibly useful "models" that have
failed to generate empirical follow-up studies (e.g., D'Amato,
1967), but there are some preliminary signs that this may be
changing. For example, in recent years the operational code construct has been employed in several studies of historical and
contemporary leaders, including Ramsay MacDonald, Getulio
Vargas, Mackenzie King, Dean Acheson, John Foster Dulles,
Dean Rusk, Arthur Vandenberg, Lyndon B. Johnson, Mao Tse-
tung, Liu Chao-chi, Willy Brandt, Kurt Schmacher, Lester Pearson, Pierre Elliot Trudeau, J. William Fulbright, and Henry A.
Kissinger.[18] It is also currently being used in a full-scale study of
the Arab-Israeli conflict (Heradstveit, 1974).[19] A content analysis
coding scheme, developed to extract materials for the construction

[18] Anderson (1973a and 1973b), Ashby (1969), Dye (n.d.), Gibbins
(n.d.), Malone (1971), Gutierrez (1973), Holsti (1970), Johnson (1973),
Kavanagh (1970), Lawrence (forthcoming), McLellan (1971), Thordarson
(1972), Tweraser (1973), Walker (1975), and G. White (1969).

[19] Although our concern is with the role of belief systems in foreign policy
decision making, the operational code should also prove useful for other
purposes—for example, in the study of developmental leaders in choice

of "cognitive maps" from documents, has been employed in a number of studies, including Axelrod (1972b), Shapiro and Bonham (1973), Bonham and Shapiro (forthcoming), and Chapters 4, 5, and 6 in the present volume. Nevertheless, research on belief systems and cognitive processes to date is suggestive and electic rather than focused and cumulative. For an enterprise that is of relatively recent interest within the discipline, and is still essentially in the "pre-takeoff" stage, diversity is probably desirable, and, in any case, inevitable. To expect anything other than a broad range of approaches would be to imply nothing less than the existence of a paradigmatic theory of cognition and choice.

Underlying the variety, however, are two shared premises. First, there is a general suspicion that simple S–R or "black box" formulations are insufficient bases for understanding decision outputs, either of individuals or nation-states. That is, intervening processes are often the locus of powerful explanations of choice behavior. Second, it is assumed that the content and structure of belief systems, information processing styles, strategies for coping with stress, and the like, are systematically related to the manner in which leaders perceive, diagnose, prescribe, and make choices, especially in situations of uncertainty. Both shared and idiosyncratic attributes and processes are of interest. For example, the premise that most, if not all, persons experience predecisional and postdecisional pressures for cognitive consistency, and for congruence between beliefs and behavior, informs many studies. But the propensity to favor one or another strategy for coping with discrepancies between elements of the belief system, attitudes, and behavior can vary widely across individuals, with potentially important implications for decision-making behavior.

Diversity in the existing foreign policy literature can be described briefly along several dimensions.

---

situations (Almond, Flanagan, and Mundt, 1973). The author of one such study has written: "In August 1931, several of MacDonald's most salient beliefs and personality needs seem to have been highly sensitive to certain aspects of the crisis. I have reconstructed an 'operational code' of MacDonald's philosophical and instrumental beliefs that suggests how he related political ends and means. Such a code is useful in enabling the observer to reconstruct the way in which MacDonald was likely to structure and identify the choices available to him in 1930–31." (Kavanagh, 1973, p. 207).

Also, two students of Soviet foreign policy have suggested that the George reformulation of the operational code construct provides an especially useful way of analyzing the political beliefs of Soviet elites, individually and collectively (Hoffmann and Fleron, 1971, p. 96).

Theory. There is a wide range of "models" which, in turn, are informed by different theoretical literatures, and even different disciplines. These include, but are not limited to, various "cognitive consistency" theories, personality theory, communication theory, decision theory, as well as many others.

Scope. Much of the existing research is focused on a single leader, but some of it also deals with relatively large samples of elites (e.g., Burgess, 1967; Putnam, 1973; Mennis, 1972; Semmel, 1972; Garnham, 1971; see also the studies described in Raser's 1966 review article). Moreover, some studies are concerned with a single concept, cognitive task, or stage in policy making, whereas others can be described as efforts at developing or exploring the entire decision-making process, encompassing various types of cognitive activities (Axelrod, 1972a, 1973; Shapiro and Bonham, 1973; Holsti and George, 1975; Jervis, forthcoming).

Categories and concepts. Not only do analytical concepts vary widely; even the language for describing them ranges from ordinary prose to the formal notation of set theory.

Data. The studies draw upon vastly different empirical domains for data and illustrations. At one end of the spectrum are detailed analyses of a single decision maker, based on interviews and/or content analyses of primary documents, and supplementary secondary sources. Jervis (forthcoming) draws on the voluminous record of diplomatic history, as well as reports of experimental research, to illustrate the relevance of existing hypotheses, to generate new ones, and to demonstrate the limitations or inapplicability of other explanations. Still other studies combine data from real decision makers with those from surrogates, including man and machine simulations (Hermann and Hermann, 1967; Zinnes, 1966; Bonham and Shapiro, 1973 and forthcoming).

Analytic procedures. There is no less variety in this respect, a point to be discussed further in the next section.

It should not be necessary to belabor the point further. A somewhat oversimplified summary of some existing studies appears in Table 2–1. Although it is illustrative rather than comprehensive, the table may serve some useful purpose in illustrating the relationship between conceptions of the decision maker,[20] stages or tasks in the decision-making process,[21] theories, and concepts. It also suggests a number of other points.

[20] Columns 1 and 3 of this table were suggested by, but differ somewhat from, the framework provided by Axelrod (1972a).
[21] Drawn from Brim, et al. (1962, p. 1).

1. Decision making, encompassing several stages or tasks, is a shorthand label for a number of different cognitive activities, a fact that may be insufficiently recognized in much of the literature on foreign policy decisions.

2. As might be expected, given the diverse theoretical roots of existing studies, the literature abounds with a plethora of concepts which, taken together, are marked by considerable overlap and something less than complete consistency in usage.

3. There is a small but growing empirical literature (note that most cited studies have appeared since 1965) that provides some basis for optimism about research of this genre.

Not depicted in table 2–1, but of potential relevance at all stages of decision making, is another concern: The impact of cognitive processes on choice behavior may vary according to the nature of the situation; for example, the degree of uncertainty and the number of objectives (Steinbruner, 1968, 1974; Axelrod, 1975). The distinction between circumstances of high and low stress is also likely to be of special interest.[22] The literature on decision making under stress is far too voluminous to review here.[23] Suffice it to say that research in both experimental and natural settings indicates that intense and protracted stress may have a considerable impact on those qualities of cognitive structures and abilities that are most needed to cope with the complex intellectual problems posed by many decision-making situations.[24]

SOME PROBLEMS OF EMPIRICAL RESEARCH[25]

Access to Data

Occasionally the investigator will have direct access to his subjects, although rarely until they leave office. Examples include

[22] For other ways to conceptualize situations, see C. Hermann (1969b).

[23] Summaries may be found in Lazarus, Deese and Osler (1952); Horvath (1959); Janis and Leventhal (1968); Lazarus, Averill and Opton (1969); Broadbent (1971); Holsti (1972); Milburn (1972); Hermann and Brady (1972); Holsti and George (1975).

[24] There is a dissenting note in the literature on bureaucratic organizations. Some, including Wilensky (1967), Verba (1961), and Lowi (1969), suggest that the pathological impact of distorted information, bureaucratic politics, and decision making by bargaining among representatives of parochial vested interests is reduced in crisis, and that, in fact, decision making in such circumstances more closely approximates a rational choice model.

[25] The comments in this section are addressed primarily to research on real rather than surrogate decision makers.

TABLE 2–1

SOME "COGNITIVE PROCESS" APPROACHES TO DECISION MAKING

Predecision: conceptual baggage that decision maker' brings to decision-making tasks

Decision maker as	Stage of decision making	Theoretical literature	Illustrative constructs and concepts	Illustrative studies of political leaders
Believer	Sources of belief system	Political socialization; Personality & politics	First independent political success; Mind Set	Barber (1972); Glad (1966); George and George (1956); Etheredge (1974)
	Content of belief system	Political philosophy; Ideology	Image; Operational code; World view; Decisional premises	Operational code studies; Brecher (1968); Cummins (1974); Stupak (1971)
	Structure of belief system	Cognitive psychology	Cognitive balance/congruity; Cognitive complexity; Cognitive rigidity/dogmatism; Cognitive "maps"/style	Axelrod (1972b); M. Hermann (1974); Osgood (1959a); Shneidman (1961, 1963, 1969)
Perceiver	Identification of a problem	Psychology of perception; Cognitive psychology	Definition of situation; Perception/misperception; Cognitive "set"; Selective perception; Focus of attention; Stereotyping	Jervis (1968); Jervis (forthcoming, chs. 5, 11, 13); Zinnes (1966); Zinnes, et al. (1972)

Information processor	Obtain information	Cognitive consistency theories	Search capacity	Abelson (1971)
		Theories of attitude of change	Selective exposure	Holsti (1967, 1972)
		Information theory	Psycho-logic	Jervis (forthcoming, chs. 4, 6)
		Communication theory	Tolerance of ambiguity	
	Production of solutions		Strategies for coping with discrepant information (various)	
	Evaluation of solutions		Information overload	
			Information processing capacity	
			Satisficing/maximizing	
			Tolerance of inconsistency	
Decision maker/strategist	Selection of a strategy	Game theory	Utility	Jervis (1970)
			Risk-taking	Jervis (forthcoming, ch. 3)
		Decision theory	Decision rules	Stassen (1972)
		Deterrence theory	Manipulation of images	Burgess (1967)
			Ends-means links	
			Bounded rationality	
Learner	Coping with negative feedback	Learning theory	Feedback	Jervis (forthcoming, ch. 14 and unnumbered ch. on "learning from history")
	Learning (post-decision)	Cognitive dissonance theory	"Lessons of history"	Lampton (1973)
				Lowenthal (1972)
				May (1973)

Note: The following books deal with all these categories: Axelrod (1972a, 1972b); Bonham and Shapiro (forthcoming); Shapiro and Bonham (1973); Steinbruner (1968, 1974).

research on the Korean decision (Snyder and Paige, 1958; Paige, 1968), the MLF case (Steinbruner, 1968, 1974), the Dominican intervention (Lowenthal, 1972), McLellan's (1971) analysis of Dean Acheson's "operational code," Gutierrez' (1973) study of Dean Rusk, and Brecher's studies of Israeli foreign policy (1973; see also Brecher, Steinberg, and Stein, 1969). These are, however, exceptions; as a rule documentary evidence of various sorts will serve as a primary source of data.

Whether the investigator relies on interviews, questionnaires, or documents, the situations for which he is most likely to incorporate cognitive process models into his analysis are precisely those in which access to relevant data is most difficult. Moreover, documentary materials that are available in such situations may be contaminated in one way or another. The "color books" issued by various European governments immediately following the outbreak of World War I are notorious examples but, unfortunately, far from unique. "Credibility gap" may be a contemporary phrase, but the phenomenon it describes is far from a recent invention.

Research that is heavily dependent on documentary evidence must almost always be conducted in circumstances of data scarcity, but this does not, of itself, distinguish it from other types of inquiry. Perhaps of greater importance is the fact that available materials may not represent an unbiased sample. Two types of biases may occur. First, the available evidence for any given case may be skewed; for example, formal documents may be overrepresented, whereas verbatim reports of debates within policy-making groups are underrepresented. Second, the cases for which sufficient evidence is available to permit systematic investigation may not represent an unbiased sample of foreign policy decisions. The sample is likely to be skewed toward those that are:

1. at least N years old, N being determined by the rules that govern each archive;

2. from nations losing major wars, such as World War I and World War II, that result in the destruction of the existing regime (often the most salient archival evidence becomes available following major wars, but even then it is usually the losers' documents that become available first; only later, if ever, do we gain access to those of the winning nations);

3. at least in the short run, from "successful" decisions rather than from disasters that may reflect adversely on the competence of those responsible for them; in the longer run, we may gain access more readily to data from the "disasters";

4. from "modern" governments in which vast foreign offices maintain equally vast archives;

5. from democratic rather than authoritarian governments, because the former seem more willing eventually to open their archives voluntarily. They are usually less likely to rewrite history retrospectively to meet the needs of the regime in power, an enterprise that requires tight control over even seemingly innocuous or trivial archival materials.

For many purposes, reports of group discussions represent the most desirable category of evidence, especially when the group is divided not only on preferences about possible outcomes, but also in beliefs about causation. Such data would also enable us to examine the often complex interaction between individual cognitive processes and the supports provided and constraints imposed by the decision-making group. Although we have resumes or retrospective reports about discussions in such groups as those that formulated policy on the decision to attack Pearl Harbor (Ike, 1967), the Bay of Pigs invasion, and the Cuban missile crisis, Axelrod's (1972b) analysis of the British Eastern Committee is one of the very few for which actual verbatim records were kept and eventually made public. This study appears in slightly revised form as Chapter 4 of the present volume. Other transcripts and records that might be analyzed are listed in Appendix 5.

Inference from Documentary Data

Aside from access to the most relevant data, there are other difficulties in working with documentary evidence, especially public documents. One problem concerns the logic of inference. Barring the use of older materials that have worked their way through governmental declassification procedures, or fortuitous circumstances, such as publication of the "Pentagon Papers," analysts will be forced to rely on documents that are in the first instance intended to convey information to the public, to legislatures, or to foreign governments. As likely as not, they are also intended to persuade, justify, threaten, cajole, manipulate, evoke sympathy and support, or otherwise influence the intended audience. Words may convey explicit or implicit clues about the author's "real" beliefs, attitudes, and opinions; they may also be intended to serve and advance his practical goals of the moment. Consider, in this connection, former Attorney-General John Mitchell's comment to observers at the beginning of the first Nixon administration: "Watch what we do, not what we say."

The issue being raised here centers on alternative models of communication—the "representational" and the "instrumental"—and the validity of inferences about the communicator that may be drawn from his messages.[26] The representational model assumes that verbal expressions are valid indicators of the communicator's beliefs, motivations, and the like, whereas the instrumental view begins with the premise that words may be chosen to have an impact on the target of communication. According to the latter position, the analyst must therefore take into account a good deal of the context of communication in order to make valid inferences from verbal behavior.

If we could always assume that the representational model is valid, research life would thereby be greatly simplified. It seems safer to treat it as a tentative hypothesis, the validity of which is better left to empirical confirmation than to untested premise. At minimum it would appear useful to take some elementary precautions to determine whether, in fact, the premises of the representational model are valid for the particular case in question. A comparison of private and public messages (Glad, 1966), interviews with the subject or his colleagues (Steinbruner, 1968, 1974; Zacher, 1970; Putnam, 1973) or, possibly, use of an expert panel, might offer some means of doing so. If only public messages are available, comparing results across audiences (Holsti, 1962, pp. 150–154, 183–187) could provide estimates of which are core beliefs, and which are sufficiently elastic to change according to the target of communication. Even private documents may need to be used with caution. Pressures for "instant history" and leaks of confidential papers may inhibit some decision makers.

---

[26] These problems have been explored at some length in de Sola Pool (1959), George (1959a and 1959b), Jervis (1969), and Mueller (1969a and 1969b). A variant of the "representational-instrumental" debate occurs in a criticism of the "operational code" approach, which is charged with inappropriately equating official and operative ideologies (Singer, 1968). The criticism may or may not be valid in the case of any given study, but the problem is not an inherent attribute of operational code research. That is, such investigations need not be tied to a single data source (such as official pronouncements or doctrinal "classics"), nor need they assume that operational code beliefs remain unchanged either for an individual or an elite group.

Authorship

Establishing authorship may also pose difficulties for the student of cognitive processes. Government documents are often prepared by unidentified bureaucrats, or they are the product of the committees, going through various drafts and passing through many hands before appearing over the signatures of their nominal authors. Widespread use of ghost-writers raises comparable questions about public addresses, statements to legislative committees, and even autobiographies and memoirs.[27]

One way of coping with the problem of authorship is to use only materials drawn from interviews and press conferences (M. Hermann, 1972). Given penetrating questions, spontaneous responses can be a rich source of evidence about beliefs, but there are also some drawbacks to this method. Interviews or press conferences are rarely granted during crises and other nonroutine circumstances in which cognitions of leaders are most likely to have a significant impact on policy choices. Indeed, there is no guarantee that they will be granted at all; note, for example, the wide disparity among recent American Presidents in the frequency with which they engaged in direct contact with the press. It is possible that the structure and content of a belief system are relatively stable attributes, and that measurements taken in one set of circumstances are therefore likely to be valid in others. But for some purposes this assumption introduces a static quality to the analysis. Moreover, many of the most interesting research questions center on the interplay of situation and cognitive processes. There is, finally, considerable evidence that cognitive traits and abilities do not necessarily remain unchanged under varying levels of stress.

Exclusive reliance on interviews and press conferences also tends to rule out examination of initial reactions to a situation, when it may be relatively unstructured, and when there is the greatest latitude for cognitive "set" to have an impact on the definition of the situation and on the subsequent cognitive tasks associated with decision making. Consider, for example, first

[27] Propensity to use ghost-writers seems to vary according to the individual, and probably according to the situation. For example, John Foster Dulles is reputed to have written many of his own speeches, and all ten drafts of Richard Nixon's speech on the Cambodian invasion in 1970 are reported to have been handwritten by the President (Barber, 1972, p. 430).

reactions to the news of Pesident Kennedy's assassination in Dallas. Some liberals, predisposed to associate Dallas with extreme conservatism, jumped to the conclusion that John Birchers or other radical groups of the political right had been responsible. On the other hand, Lyndon Johnson, a Texan, feared that the assassination was part of a larger communist plot to destroy the American government.

By this point it should be evident that there are no easy rules of thumb by which the investigator can overcome problems of access to and inference from documentary data. Those who undertake this type of research have recourse to one of two broad strategies. The first is to work with materials that have passed through the critical scrutiny of skilled archivists and historical detectives (e.g., the various collections of documents relating the outbreak and conduct of World War I and, increasingly, World War II). Alternatively, should they wish (for normative or other reasons) to undertake research on more contemporary situations, they will themselves have to approach available documentary evidence with the same skills and skepticism as the well-trained historian.

Data Analysis

When the research goal is to formulate hypotheses, rigor in techniques of data analysis is rarely the top priority. Anecdotal evidence skillfully used may suffice to inspire creative speculation, to develop and test the face validity of hypotheses in a preliminary way, or to serve as examples. For hypothesis testing, more explicit methods of coding and data analysis are usually required. Most studies of belief systems and cognitive processes are heavily dependent on documentary evidence—whether produced by diplomats in foreign offices or by surrogates in laboratory simulations—systematic analysis of which implies some form of content analysis.

Using a sample of recent studies as a base, Table 2–2 relates some techniques of content analysis (recording units and systems of enumeration in which the results are presented) to the types of inference that are drawn from the data. The recording unit refers to the specific segment of content that is characterized by placing it in a given category. These range from units as small as the word to such complex ones as causal assertions. Once the appropriate content units have been identified, there are various ways of counting them. Frequency measures tabulate each appearance; it is assumed that repetition indicates salience or importance, and that each item should be given equal weight. When these premises

46

appear inappropriate, the analyst may choose merely to record the content attibute as present or absent (appearance), or to adopt some type of weighting scheme (intensity). Contingency analysis assumes that inferences may be drawn from the proximity of two or more content attributes within a specified context (sentence, paragraph, 100 words, etc.).[28] Table 2–2 reveals that, even when the purposes of inquiry are similar, there has been little uniformity of methods, much less development of standard categories into which the content units are to be placed. An important gap is the paucity of studies that examine the same body of data using two or more methods with a view to assessing the strengths and costs of each. A few of the many alternatives include evaluative assertion analysis (Osgood, Saporta and Nunnally, 1956), value analysis (R. White, 1951), contingency analysis (Osgood, 1959a), and various types of causal or structural analyses (Axelrod, 1972b; Abelson, 1973; Shapiro and Bonham, 1973). A definitive assessment of research methods is beyond the scope of this paper, but a few observations may be in order.

There has been heavy reliance on qualitative content analysis in studies that focus on the *content* of belief systems. Qualitative or nonfrequency content analysis is not, as is sometimes asserted (e.g., Berelson, 1952), a contradiction in terms, nor need it imply the absence of systematic methodology. Indeed, as George's (1959a, 1959b) explication of the methods used to analyze Axis propaganda during World War II makes clear, qualitative methods may involve very sophisticated rules of inference linked to an explicit model of the communication process. Nevertheless, the various "operational code" studies reveal some of both the benefits and costs of qualitative analysis. George's (1969) reformulation of the operational code construct developed by Leites (1951, 1953) had guided all of the studies. Using this framework, analysts have been able to range widely across whatever materials were available for the given subject. It is doubtful that even a small fraction of the same material would have been coded using the more rigorous and time-consuming methods of quantitative analysis.

However, freedom from some of the more onerous chores of coding for quantitative analysis has also reduced the immediate imperatives for explicating the rules for inclusion in each category,

---

[28] For a further discussion on coding content data, see Holsti (1969, pp. 94–126).

TABLE 2–2

SOME SYSTEMS OF CONTENT ANALYSIS AND TYPES OF INFERENCE ABOUT DECISION MAKERS IN SELECTED RECENT STUDIES

Recording Unit	System of Enumeration			
	Appearance	*Frequency*	*Intensity*	*Contingency*
Word/symbol		Cognitive complexity (M. Hermann, 1972)		Cognitive structure (Osgood, 1959a)
		Personality traits (M. Hermann, 1974)		
		Values (Eckhardt & White, 1967; Cummins, 1974; Eckhardt, 1967).		
Theme/sentence	Philosophical and instrumental beliefs ("Operational code" studies; Thordarson, 1972).	Perceptions of alternatives (C. Hermann, 1969a, 1972; Holsti, 1972)	Attitudes (Stein, 1968)	
			National images (Holsti, 1967)	

	"World view" (Brecher, 1968) Perceptions of IR (Stupak, 1971) "Strategic image" (Burgess, 1967).	Perceptions of threat, hostility, etc. (Zinnes, 1966).	Perceptions of threat, hostility, etc. (Zinnes, et al., 1972).
Logical idiosyncracy		Cognitive "style" (Shneidman, 1961, 1963, 1969).	
Causal assertion	"Cognitive map" (Axelrod, 1972b; Bonham and Shapiro, forthcoming; Shapiro and Bonham, 1973) "Script" (Abelson, 1971, 1973)		
Sentence paragraph item	Not used in research of this type; too crude to be of very much value.		

and delineating the boundaries between them. As a result, although there appears to be wide agreement that the questions about history and politics encompassed in the operational code construct are central to any leader's belief system, not all of the case studies have given sufficient attention to the issue of category definitions. Thus, individual studies are not always easily compared and, as a result, they are less cumulative than they might otherwise be. A possibly useful development would be to combine the theoretical and substantive richness of the operational code with some other forms of content analysis, either quantitative or with a focus on causal linkages.[29] Continuing interest in operational code studies, including efforts directed at further explication of the construct itself,[30] gives rise to some optimism about future developments on this aspect of research on cognitive processes and decision making.

Research on specific personality or cognitive traits (e.g., cognitive rigidity) that may be relevant to decision making tends to be at the other end of the qualitative-quantitative continuum. Inferences are often derived from various measures of word frequencies. These methods offer several clear advantages. They draw on a rich, although not especially cumulative,[31] literature on theory and method. Dividing the data into units poses no diffi-

[29] For many types of research on belief systems, the case for developing systematic and replicable sampling, coding, and data analysis schemes is quite compelling. Consider the following case. We wish to examine linkages between X's decision-making behavior and his belief system. But often we already know a great deal about his decision-making behavior, and there is the danger that the analysis of beliefs will be contaminated by that knowledge. For example, we know that Richard Nixon visited China and the USSR, placed controls on the American economy, and dismantled parts of the poverty program. There is no way of avoiding that knowledge. There may be a very natural, even if not conscious, tendency to search for and interpret materials on Nixon's beliefs in light of that knowledge, especially if one is working under the hypothesis that there is in fact a close relationship between beliefs and decision-making behavior. Rigorous and explicit methodologies can provide a partial safeguard against this type of contamination.

[30] A further discussion of some aspects of this problem will be found in Anderson's (1973b) dissertation on Senator Arthur Vandenberg, as well as in a shorter paper based on that study (Anderson, 1973a). David Dye, a doctoral candidate in political science at Stanford, has done useful work toward developing typologies of belief systems. Dye's efforts draw upon a number of the previously-cited operational code studies.

[31] See the critical reviews in Auld and Murray (1955) and Mardsen (1965).

50

culty, and quantification is relatively easy. Moreover, developments in computer content analysis programs, theoretically-oriented dictionaries (Stone, et al., 1966), and disambiguation routines (Stone, 1969) offer the promise of freedom from some of the more mechanical tasks of content analysis. Offsetting these obvious attractions are some problems that are less than completely resolved. These techniques have tended to prove more suitable for research in which inferences are to be drawn from either word/symbol frequencies, or from contingency analysis. However, the validity of many constructs based on word frequencies remains to be firmly established.

Methods that yield data about the structure of belief systems generally involve onerous tasks of unitizing and coding, and relatively limited opportunities to use computers, at least without considerable precomputer syntax identification. Coding difficulties have no doubt been a deterrent to further use of Shneidman's (1966) method of drawing inference from logical fallacies; it does not appear to have been employed beyond the original studies of John F. Kennedy, Richard Nixon, and Nikita Khrushchev.

In speculating about the prospects for and likely payoffs from the various approaches to documentary analysis, very safe answers are that diversity will only slowly give way to much standardization of method, and that the choice of methods will, in any case, depend on the purpose. A somewhat more venturesome guess is that, despite the laborious coding involved,[32] the methods listed under "causal assertions" in Table 2–2 appear promising for various purposes:

1. to explicate in detail the belief structure of a leader as it is operative in a given situation;

2. to compare a leader's belief system in different circumstances. For example, this might permit testing hypotheses such as those predicting that cognitive structures become simpler, or less logical and more "psychological," in circumstances of intense and protracted stress.

3. to compare the belief systems of two or more leaders in a given situation.

This method may also be adapted to a variety of other research problems centering on both the content and structure of belief

[32] The coding scheme developed for cognitive mapping (Appendix 1) appears much more manageable for large bodies of data than that described in Abelson (1973).

systems and, where deemed useful for the problem at hand, causal linkages may also be analyzed in such quantitative terms as frequencies and intensities.

The Dependent Variable

The student of foreign policy is interested in beliefs and cognitive process because these are assumed to be among the independent or intervening variables that are systematically related to the substance and quality of decision outputs. But linkages to, or even conceptualizations of, the dependent variable are not always satisfactory.

This problem is by no means confined to studies of belief systems; it may be found in several areas of a discipline that has fared somewhat better in dealing with the inputs to the political process than in conceptualizing decision making or developing performance measures for the outputs. Many studies that focus on the content of belief systems seem somewhat vulnerable on this score. It is not uncommon to find in the conclusion a statement to the effect that, "the preceding analysis of X's belief system established its utility for understanding X's political behavior." Less often do we find an explicit and compelling demonstration of why this is the case.

In part, the problem may be attributed to a problem discussed earlier. It is not necessarily fruitful to attempt to link decision-makers' beliefs directly to foreign policy actions. A more clearly differentiated conceptualization of decision making, emphasizing not only the resulting action, but also the cognitive tasks or activities that precede the decision, may be necessary to explore fully the role of beliefs in policy making (see Figure 2–2). Put somewhat differently, it is in these tasks that the individual's beliefs about social life are most likely to play a significant role—or at least to have an initial impact. This does not, of course, rule out the possibility of also tracing out the process through the decision and the ultimate foreign policy actions.

CONCLUSION

Aside from developing precise, communicable concepts and methods of inquiry that ultimately lead to a cumulative literature, there remains the longer-term task of integrating research on cognitive processes with other conceptualizations of foreign policy decision making. Exaggerated claims on behalf of these models are likely to be even less convincing than those made on behalf of competing frameworks. It will not suffice to assume that foreign policy decisions merely reflect the beliefs of any given leader, or even group of leaders. Hence research on belief systems must ultimately be embedded in a broader context, and the problems of linking and interrelating theories and concepts that are oriented to the individual decision maker—as are most of those in columns 3 and 4 of Table 2–1—to the behavior of groups and organizations need to be addressed directly. Put somewhat differently, a cognitive process model of foreign policy decision making will not represent a great step forward if it simply becomes another "Model I" analysis, assuming that foreign policy is the product of a unitary (subjectively) rational actor. Thus, even those who focus on crisis decisions that are made by a small and relatively autonomous group of top-ranking leaders are likely to profit by exploring possible linkages with models of group dynamics (Janis, 1972; George, 1974), and bureaucratic organizations (Allison, 1971; George, 1972; Allison and Halperin, 1972; Halperin, 1974). Some of the more theoretically oriented approaches to comparative foreign policy also suggest a broader context within which relative potency of leadership variables—including the cognitions of decision makers—can be assessed systematically (Rosenau, 1966, 1970; M. Hermann, 1972, 1974).

Integration across levels is not an end in itself, however, nor is it likely to occur unless we can identify specific questions, the answers to which will require the analyst to focus directly on the linkages between processes in various decision-making contexts. For example:

1. How does the decision maker define his cognitive tasks and needs, and how are these satisfied, modified, or constrained by the small group or bureaucratic organization?

2. What tensions exist between the decision maker's cognitive style and role requirements, and how does he attempt to cope with them?

3. What are cognitive concomitants of organizational differences? (Steinbruner, 1968, p. 500.)

4. What group processes are associated with a premature bolstering of shared beliefs? With systematic examination of decisional premises?

Similar questions may also be couched in normative or prescriptive terms. For example: Given an executive's cognitive

53

style, what types of interventions at the group or organizational level will increase the probability that his cognitive needs are met? Will increase the likelihood that beliefs and decisional premises are subjected to critical analysis?

This list is by no means an exhaustive one. It merely illustrates a few of the questions that relate to cognitive processes in decision making, but which can only be answered by considering also the broader context within which policies are made.

CHAPTER THREE

The Analysis of Cognitive Maps
—Robert Axelrod

A cognitive map is a specific way of representing a person's assertions about some limited domain, such as a policy problem. It is designed to capture the structure of the person's causal assertions and to generate the consequences that follow from this structure. This chapter explains how such cognitive maps can be analyzed once they are constructed, with special emphasis on inferring the properties of a cognitive map from its parts and the laws of their interaction. In particular, it is shown how a person might use his cognitive map to derive explanations of the past, make predictions for the future, and choose policies in the present.

PURPOSE

A person's beliefs can be regarded as a complex system. According to Herbert Simon (1969, p. 86), a vital and perhaps even defining characteristic of a complex system is that "the whole is more than the sum of the parts, not in an ultimate, metaphysical sense, but in the important pragmatic sense that given the properties of the parts and the laws of their interaction, it is not a trivial matter to infer the properties of the whole."

The purpose of this chapter is to explain how cognitive maps can be thought of as a particular type of complex system with two kinds of parts and two basic laws of interaction among the parts. Then, once the properties of the parts and the laws of their interaction are explained, a number of inferences will be drawn about the properties of the whole cognitive map. More specifically, this chapter will deal with questions such as these: given a person's concepts and beliefs, and given certain rules for deducing other beliefs from them, how would a person make a choice among alternatives? How would he make predictions about the

55

future? How would he explain the past? How could he anticipate the effects of changes in his environment? This chapter will discuss how cognitive maps can be analyzed to answer the above questions. Those readers seeking a more rigorous exposition are referred to Appendix 3.

THE COGNITIVE MAP AS A MATHEMATICAL MODEL OF A BELIEF SYSTEM

A cognitive map is a particular kind of mathematical model of a person's belief system; in actual practice, cognitive maps are derived from assertions of beliefs. The relationship between assertions and beliefs is discussed at length elsewhere (Chapters 2, 4, 9, and especially Chapter 10, section A). For the purposes of this chapter, it is easiest to assume that a person's cognitive map correctly reflects his belief system.

Like all mathematical models, a cognitive map can be useful in two quite distinct ways: as a normative model and as an empirical model. Interpreted as a normative model, a cognitive map makes no claims to reflect accurately how a person deduces new beliefs from old ones, how he makes decisions, and so on, but instead claims to show how he should do these things. Interpreted as an empirical model, a cognitive map claims to indicate how a person actually does perform certain cognitive operations, in the sense that the results of the various operations that are possible with the model do, in fact, correspond to the behavior of the person who is being modeled.

The laws of interaction of the parts of cognitive maps are intended to be rational, so a cognitive map does, indeed, have a straightforward normative interpretation. The interpretation is simply that a person whose concepts and beliefs are accurately represented in a particular cognitive map should rationally make predictions, decisions, and explanations that correspond to the predictions, decisions, and explanations generated from the model. For this reason, the cognitive mapping approach has potential as an aid to decision makers who may know what they believe, but who are not always able to make correct deductions from the full complexity of their many interrelated beliefs.

The model also has an empirical interpretation, but whether this is useful depends on the answers to two empirical questions: Is it really the case that individuals operate in accordance with the laws of cognitive maps? And even if they do, is it possible to measure accurately a person's beliefs in such a way that a model can be applied? These questions are the subjects of later chapters, but a preview of their answers can be offered now. In a variety of situations, it will be demonstrated that individuals do operate in accordance with the laws of cognitive maps. In particular, the empirical studies in Chapters 4, 5, and 6 find significant evidence that individuals do express choices, predictions, and explanations that are consistent with the functioning of the cognitive map corresponding to their assertions about their beliefs.

Is this due to unlimited rationality? Not at all. The basic result is that the expressed set of beliefs produces a cognitive map from which it is relatively easy to make correct deductions. Thus, the limitations in a decision maker's ability show up not so much as failures in his ability to draw correct inferences from the beliefs that he does state, but rather as limitations in the structure of the beliefs he presents as an image of the policy environment. Put simply, limited rationality appears in policy settings not as a limited ability to solve problems, but rather as restrictions in the types of problems that are even addressed. It will later be argued that these self-imposed restrictions actually lead to serious distortions of the external policy environment. This suggests that there are two possible cognitive bottlenecks to improved performance: in the complexity of the structure of the separate beliefs, and in the ability to take advantage of such complexity even if it were to be part of the person's belief system. Later empirical work (reported in Chapters 7 and 8) provides direct evidence that, when the conditions are right, the complexity of the set of beliefs needs not be a bottleneck. But that still leaves the other problem, which is how to make correct inferences from a set of beliefs that has a complex structure. Fortunately, precisely this can be done with mathematical models. Thus cognitive maps hold the promise of eventually helping a person make greater use of his own beliefs.

Even if people do operate in a manner consistent with the cognitive map that corresponds to their belief system, can this cognitive map be constructed in a valid way? This question will be discussed at length elsewhere (especially in Appendices 1 and 2), but the short answer is yes, there are valid methods of determining the cognitive map that corresponds to a person's stated beliefs.

This question of construction of a model suggests an important two-way relationship between the mathematics of cognitive maps and the measurement of belief systems. In one direction, the state of the art of measurement constrains the mathematical system, which must not rely on any characteristics of the cognitive map that cannot be measured. In the other direction, the state of the art of the mathematical system sets the requirements for what must be measured to confirm the empirical accuracy of the system's predictions. When measurement problems are severe, as they certainly are in the domain of the structure of belief systems, one of the important properties of the mathematical system is that it will be able to make interesting predictions from relatively little information.

This brings us to the whole point of using a mathematical model of a belief system (or of anything else, for that matter). A mathematical model is a tremendous simplification of what it represents. But it does not simplify everything about its object, or there would be nothing left to model. Instead, it simplifies everything that is *not* to be examined, and leaves in the model what *is* to be examined. Contrary to what many scholars think, the value of the model is not determined by how little it simplifies, but rather by how well it reflects those aspects of the object which it is designed to help study.

In our case, the cognitive map is a mathematical model of a belief system. It does not try to capture every aspect of a person's belief system. That would be a hopeless, and even a worthless, task since it would leave us with something just as complicated as the original object. *A cognitive map is designed to capture the structure of the causal assertions of a person with respect to a particular policy domain, and generate the consequences that follow from this structure.*

What a cognitive map is not designed to study, and hence what is greatly simplified in a cognitive map, are the nuances of the individual causal beliefs, and the nature of the beliefs that are not causal by even a very wide interpretation of causality. The critical question, then, is whether the simplifications are done in such a way that the cognitive map usefully reflects what it purports to reflect, namely, the causal aspects of the structure of the belief system.

BASIC ELEMENTS OF A COGNITIVE MAP

A cognitive map has only two basic types of elements: concepts and causal beliefs. The concepts are treated as variables, and the causal beliefs are treated as relationships between the variables.

A concept variable is something like "the amount of security in Persia"; something that can take on different values, such as "a great amount of security" or "a small amount of security." A cognitive map allows great flexibility in the variables. They may be continuous variables, such as an amount of something; they may be ordinal variables, such as more or less of something; or they may be dichotomous variables, such as the existence or non-existence of something. But whatever type of concept is represented, it is always regarded as a variable that can take on more than one value.

Cognitive maps frequently contain concept variables for utility. Utility means the unspecified best interests of an actor, such as a person, organization, or nation. Thus when an American says that "security is in best interests of my country," his statement is interpreted as including two concept variables, namely "(amount of) security" and "(amount of) American utility."

The second type of basic element in a cognitive map is a causal assertion. Causal assertions are regarded as relating variables to each other, as in the assertion that "the amount of security in Persia augments the ability of the Persian government to maintain order." Here the causal variable is "the amount of security in Persia" and the effect variable is "the (degree of) the ability of the Persian government to maintain order." The relationship between these two variables is indicated by the word "augment."

A word such as "augments" indicates a positive causal relationship between the cause variable and the effect variable. This means that an increase in the amount of security will cause an increase in the ability of the Persian government to maintain order. But it *also* means that a decrease in the amount of security will cause a decrease in the ability of the Persian government to maintain order. Thus a positive causal relationship means that changes occur in the *same* direction, but not necessarily positively.

A causal relationship can also be negative, as in the assertion "the ability of the British to put pressure on the Persian government inhibits the (extent of) the removal of the better (local) governors in Persia." In this assertion the cause variable is "the ability of the British to put pressure on the Persian government" and the effect variable is "the extent of the removal of the better governors in Persia." The word "inhibits" indicates there is a negative causal relationship between these two concept variables. This means that an increase in the ability of the British to apply pressure will cause a decrease in the removal of the better governors. Likewise, with this negative causal relationship a decrease in the ability of the British to apply pressure will cause an increase in the removal of the better governors.[1]

To see the structure of a cognitive map, it is helpful to draw a picture of it with points and arrows. The concept of variables is represented as points and the causal relationships are represented as arrows from the cause variable to the effect variable. A plus sign is attached to the arrows that show positive relationships, and a minus sign is used to indicate negative relationships. Thus, the two causal assertions discussed above can be represented as a positive and negative arrow, respectively, as in Figure 3–1.

FIGURE 3–1.

Examples of Positive and Negative Causal Relationships

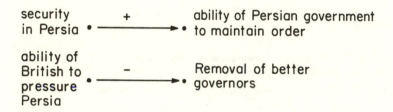

This type of picture is called by mathematicians a signed directed digraph, or *signed digraph* for short.[2] It is very helpful for displaying the structure of a whole set of interrelated beliefs. It frequently happens, for example, that the effect variable of one causal belief is the cause variable of another belief. An example is given in Figure 3–2, which displays two causal arrows that form a single path from the "policy of withdrawal" through the amount of "security in Persia" to the "ability of the Persian government to maintain order." It often happens that causal beliefs are inter-

[1] Positive and negative are the most basic values a relationship can have in a cognitive map. See Chapter 4, and especially Appendix 3, for an expansion of this two-valued system to a somewhat more sophisticated eight-valued system.

[2] Mathematicians frequently use other terms for points and arrows in graphs. Points are sometimes called nodes or vertices. Arrows are sometimes called arcs or edges.

FIGURE 3–2.

Example of a Two-Step Path

related in quite complex ways, with several beliefs all coming out of the same cause variable, and several other beliefs all going into the same effect variable. The next section discusses how even such a complex cognitive map can be systematically analyzed to determine what structural properties it has and what inferences can be drawn from it.

PATH OPERATIONS

In order to keep the discussion on a concrete level, consider the signed digraph in Figure 3–3. This is part of an actual person's cognitive map, taken from my empirical study of the British Eastern Committee (Chapter 4). It is drawn with the usual conventions followed in this book:

FIGURE 3–3.

Example of Part of a Cognitive Map

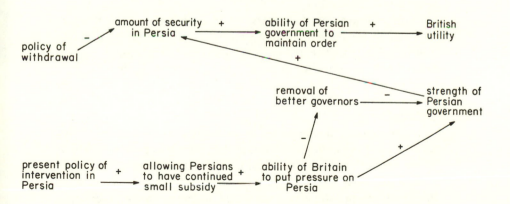

1. whenever possible the map is drawn so that the arrows flow from left to right;

2. the points are arranged so that there is little or no crossing of arrows over each other;

3. if there are variables that represent policy choices for the person or his organization, these policy variables are displayed on the left side of the cognitive map, since typically they have no arrows going into them, and

4. if there is a variable representing the person's, or his organization's overall utility, it is displayed on the right side of the cognitive map, since typically it has no arrows coming out of it.

In Figure 3–3 there are two policy variables, the "policy of withdrawal" (from Persia), which may or may not be adopted, and the "present policy of intervention in Persia," which may or may not be continued.

The first step in analyzing such a cognitive map is to trace out the causal paths. A *path* is a sequence of distinct points that are connected by an arrow from the first point to the second point, another arrow from the second point to the third point, and so on, until there is also an arrow from the next to the last point of the path to the last point of the path. For example, in Figure 3–3 there is a three-step path from the policy of withdrawal to British utility, involving four points:

1. the policy of withdrawal *inhibits* the amount of security in Persia;

2. the amount of security in Persia *augments* the ability of the Persian government to maintain order; and

3. the ability of the Persian government to maintain order *augments* British utility.

Putting these three statements together gives the indirect causal relationship for the entire three-step path that the "policy of withdrawal *inhibits* British utility." Why is that? The easiest way to derive such an inference from a path is to suppose that the first variable undergoes an increase, and then to trace out the effects until arriving at the last point. In this case we have the following sequence of effects:

1. An *increase* in the policy of withdrawal (i.e., a change from not choosing the policy to choosing the policy) leads to a *decrease* in the amount of security because this relationship is negative.

2. A *decrease* in the amount of security leads to a decrease in the ability of the Persian government to maintain order because this relationship is positive.

3. A *decrease* in the ability of the Persian government to maintain order leads to a *decrease* in British utility because this relationship is positive.

Thus an *increase* in the first variable leads through a negative and two positive relationships to a *decrease* in the last variable of the path. The negative relationship reversed the direction of change (from increase to decrease), and the positive relationships preserved the direction of change. The result is that a path with a negative and two positive relationships yields an indirect negative relationship between the first and last point of the path.

In a path with two negative relationships, there is a double reversal, which is equivalent to no reversal, which is an indirect positive effect. An example of this in Figure 3–3 is the following three-step path:

1. the ability of the British to put pressure on Persia *inhibits* the removal of the better (local) governors;

2. the removal of the better governors *inhibits* the strength of the Persian governors; and

3. the strength of the Persian governors *augments* the amount of security in Persia.

The inference that can be drawn from these three assertions is that an increase in the ability of the British to put pressure on Persia increases (through this path) the amount of security in Persia. Thus a path with two negative relationships and one positive relationship yields an indirect positive relationship between the first and last points of the path.

All of this suggests the following general rule about paths of any length:

Rule 1. The *indirect effect of a path* is positive if the path has an even number of negative arrows, and it is negative if it has an odd number of negative arrows.

As an illustration of this rule, notice that there are two long paths from the "present policy of intervention" to "British utility," one path going through the concept "removal of better governors" and consisting of seven arrows; the other path, which does not go through that concept variable, consisting of six arrows. Both of these paths are positive: the longer one because it contains exactly two negative paths, and the shorter one because it contains no negative paths.

This illustration suggests the question of how the indirect effects of separate paths between the same two points can be combined into a single total effect. The answer is quite simple:

Rule 2. The *total effect of point A on point B* is the sum of the indirect effects of all the paths from A to B. If all such indirect effects are positive, the sum is positive; if all are negative the sum is negative; if some indirect effects are positive and some are negative, then the sum is indeterminate.[3]

Whenever there are paths with opposite indirect effects from some point A to some point B, the cognitive map is said to be *imbalanced.* Otherwise the map is *balanced.*[4] For example, in Figure 3–3 the map is balanced because the only paths that might introduce imbalance are the ones that go from "ability of Britain to put pressure on Persia" to "strength of Persian government," and all of these paths are of the same sign, whether or not they go through the point entitled "removal of better governors."

INFERRING THE PROPERTIES OF A COGNITIVE MAP

Now that we have seen the properties of the parts of a cognitive map (the points and arrows), and the laws of their interaction (for determining the indirect effect transmitted by a particular path and for determining the total effect from one point to another), we turn to the question of inferring the properties of the whole cognitive map. To do this we will present four problems and their solutions. These problems correspond to different things a person with a set of beliefs might want to do with his own cognitive map, such as derive explanations of the past, make predictions for the future, and choose policies in the present.

Problem 1. The Decision-Making Problem. Given a cognitive map with one or more policy variables and a utility variable, which policies should be chosen and which policies should be rejected?

Solution. Those policies that have a positive total effect on utility should be accepted, and those policies that have a negative total effect should be rejected. The means for performing this calculation are contained in the two rules. Rule 1 tells how to determine the effect on utility of each path from a given policy variable. Rule 2 tells how to determine the total effect of a given

---

[3] This rule will later be expanded to handle cycles.

[4] In the mathematical literature of graph theory, there are several different types of balance. The definition given here and used throughout the volume refers to the type known as path balance.

policy variable on utility by combining the effects of all the different paths from that policy variable to utility.

Problem 2. The Forecasting Problem. If certain given variables increase, and certain others decrease, what will happen to each of the points of the cognitive map?

Solution. This is just a generalization of the decision-making problem, which asked what would happen to the utility point if the policy variables increased (were chosen) or decreased (were rejected). The answer is that any given point will be affected by the combination of the total effects transmitted by all of the other points that have paths leading to it. The total effects from the separate points are given by Rule 2, and the combination of these effects takes place in accordance with Rule 2, as well. Thus, if all the incoming effects are positive, so is their sum; if they are all negative, so is their sum; and if some are positive and some negative, then the sum is indeterminate.

Problem 3. The Explanation Problem. Given a cognitive map, and given some observed changes in some of the points, what explanations are consistent with these observed changes?

Solution. This question is like the forecasting problem in reverse. It involves tracing the paths backwards to see where the required effects might have come from. For example, if the "amount of security in Persia" were observed to have decreased, but there was no change in either policy variable or in the "ability of Britain to put pressure on Persia," then for the change to be explained by this cognitive map, it must have come through a decrease in the "strength of the Persian government." This, in turn, must have been due to an outside (a so-called exogenous) change in this variable; or the change in this variable might have been due to an exogenous change in "the removal of better governors." But given the observed conditions and the given cognitive map, these are the only two explanations consistent with that map, except for the null explanation that the decrease in the amount of security in Persia was due to an exogenous factor not represented in the map.

Problem 4. The Strategic Problem. Given a cognitive map, what would be the consequence of changing the sign of a given variable? For example, which changes in the causal links would change an undesirable policy into a desirable policy?

Solution. The solution to this problem is simply to examine the cognitive map that would result from each proposed change in a causal relationship. As an illustration, consider what would happen if small subsidies to the Persians actually boomeranged and inhibited (rather than augmented) the ability of the British to put pressure on Persia. In that case, both paths from the "present policy of intervention in Persia" to "utility" would be negative rather than positive, and that policy should be rejected. Notice that the change in that one causal link would have no effect on the evaluation of the other policy, the "policy of withdrawal," since the altered link is on no path from that policy to utility. The consequence is that if subsidies inhibited the ability of the British to put pressure on Persia (but all the other causal beliefs were accurate), neither policy would help the British.

The solutions to these four formal problems are used in the empirical studies as guides to evaluating the way in which people operate within their belief systems, and as guides for making inferences from sets of beliefs, even if the person who has the beliefs does not draw the inferences himself. The decision-making problem is of special interest in my own empirical study (Chapter 4), and also in Ross's study (Chapter 5). The forecasting problem is applied by both Bonham and Shapiro (Chapter 6) and Roberts (Chapter 7). Bonham and Shapiro also use the solution to the explanation problem to predict how a person will explain an unanticipated event (Chapter 6). Finally, both Roberts (Chapter 7) and Hart (Chapter 8) use the solution to the strategic problem to explore how outcomes could be improved through the selected alteration of causal links, assuming the rest of the cognitive map in question to be an accurate reflection of environmental contingencies.

CYCLES

So far, we have considered examples of graphs in which causation flows in a single direction. An example of a graph with two-way (so-called reciprocal) causation is provided by Maruyama (1963) (see Figure 3–4). In this graph there are a number of paths that have an arrow from their last point to their first point. This is called a *cycle*. For example, there is a path from the "number of people in a city" through "modernization" to "migration into city," but there is also an arrow back from "migration into city" to "number of people in a city."

The behavior of such a cycle is easy to determine. All three

66

FIGURE 3–4.

A Directed Graph with Cycles

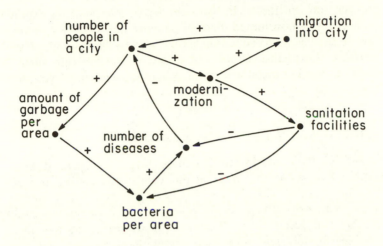

arrows are positive. Thus, if the number of people in a city goes up, modernization will go up, then migration into the city will go up, and this in turn will lead to more people in the city. The result will be that any increase in the number of people in the city will yield a further increase in the number of people in the city. Similarly, a decrease in the number of people in a city will lower modernization, which in turn will lower migration, which in turn will lower the number of people in the city, again amplifying the original change.

A different kind of cycle says that the "number of people in a city" augments the "amount of garbage per area," which, in turn, augments the "bacteria per area," which augments the "number of diseases," which inhibits "the number of people in the city." The result will be that an increase in the number of people in a city will lead to an increase in disease and thus a decrease in the number of people. Conversely, a decrease in the number of people will lead to less disease, and thus, to an increase in the number of people in the city. In other words, this cycle, with its three positive and one negative arrows, tends to counteract any initial change that might be introduced.

The general rule for the behavior of cycles is that a cycle with an even number of negative arrows is deviation-amplifying, and a cycle with an odd number of negative arrows is deviation-counter-acting.

When working with graphs that have cycles (so-called cyclic graphs), some of the effects of a change in one point on another point might be transmitted through paths as well as cycles. Therefore, Rule 2 needs to be expanded to refer to "paths and cycles" instead of just paths. Of course, a deviation-amplifying cycle is simply a positive cycle, and a deviation-counteracting cycle is a negative cycle.

FUNCTIONAL VERSUS SIGNED DIGRAPHS

So far we have considered cognitive maps as signed directed graphs. But saying that a particular causal relationship is positive (or negative) does not say very much about it. It simply means that, other things being equal, an increase in the cause variable will result in an increase (or decrease) in the effect variable. It only tells about the direction of change, and says nothing about the magnitude of the effect which is caused by a given change in the cause variable.

If we wish to be more specific, we could replace the plus and minus signs with actual positive and negative numbers. For example, if we knew that a given change in variable A resulted in three times as much change in the same direction in variable B, we could represent this causal connection by assigning the number $+3$ to the arrow from A to B. Similarly, if we knew that a given change in B resulted in twice as much change in the opposite direction in variable C, then we could represent this causal connection by assigning the number -2 to the arrow from B to C. The indirect effect of the path from A to C would then be -6, because a given change in A transmitted through B would result in 6 times as much change in the opposite direction in C. If there were one other path from A to C whose magnitude was, say, $+1$, then the total effect of A on C would be the sum of these two path effects, which is -5. This would mean that for every unit A increased, C would decrease five units.

We could go even further and specify a specific function for each causal relationship to represent how different amounts of change in the cause variable would be reflected in the effect variable. Indeed, this is similar to what Forrester (1971) and Meadows, et al. (1972) did in their various computer-based models. Both of these models have over a hundred causal relationships between their variables, each with an assumed functional relationship. For example, the relationship in Forrester's World 2 between "material standard of living" and "death rate from material multiplier" is assumed to be the negatively sloped function shown in Figure 3–5.

FIGURE 3–5.

A functional relationship from Forrester's World 2 Model (Reprinted with permission, from *World Dynamics,* 2nd ed., by Jay W. Forrester. Copyright 1973, Wright-Allen Press, Inc., Cambridge MA 02142, USA, as cited by Page, 1973, p. 29).

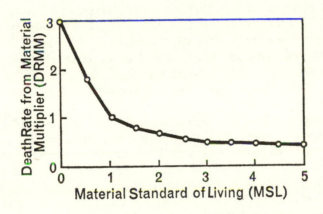

In this volume cognitive maps are represented as directed graphs with signs on the arrows rather than either numbers or functions on the arrows. There are both advantages and disadvantages to this approach. An examination of these advantages and disadvantages will help the reader to see more clearly the capacities and limitations of the signed digraph approach to cognitive maps.[5]

There are two main advantages of using signed digraphs: decision makers themselves usually do not use anything more specific than the signs of the causal relationships they discuss; and signed digraphs are easier to analyze than the other two kinds (called,

[5] A more thorough discussion will be presented after the empirical studies. See Chapter 10, sections D and E.

respectively, weighted and functional digraphs). Let us consider these ideas in turn.

Decision makers usually do not talk in more specific terms than "the more A, the more B," or "B will lessen C." This has several important consequences. First, if we wish to determine cognitive maps from documents, we will have a difficult time measuring much more than the sign of the relationship between the variables. Aristotle said in the *Nicomachean Ethics* that one should look for precision in each class of things just so far as the nature of the subject admits. Put in more modern terms, this suggests that we should not rely on measurements that cannot be made with validity and reliability. But the signs, at least, of a cognitive map can be measured.[6]

The second advantage of signed digraphs is that they are somewhat easier to analyze than weighted digraphs, and much easier to analyze than functional digraphs. Even with a complex signed digraph, it is easy to make inferences about which policies should be selected, what the effects would be of given changes in the variables, what could account for given observed changes, and what would be the implications of changing certain causal relationships.

These problems are slightly more difficult to solve for a large functional digraph. Indeed, it is this very difficulty that led the Forrester/Meadows group at MIT to resort to computer simulation of their own images of reality.[7] The disadvantage of having to resort to computer simulation is that it is more difficult to get the "feel" of the system. This means that it becomes more difficult to understand which aspects of the system account for a given feature of its behavior. The examination of the system thus becomes a matter of trial and error. For example, one of the main concerns of the Forrester/Meadows group is whether population and capital can grow without limit, or whether there are "limits to growth" in their model. The strongest conclusion they report for their world model is that when it is assumed "that population and capital growth should not be deliberately limited but should be left to 'seek their own levels,' *we have not been able*

[6] See Chapter 4 and Appendix 1 for the details of deriving a cognitive map from a document. See Chapter 7 and Appendix 2 for deriving a cognitive map from a questionnaire.

[7] Their images also included multiplicative interactions between variables, a feature that adds still more structural complexity to their models.

to find a set of policies that avoids the collapse mode of behavior" (Meadows, et al., 1972, p. 150; italics added). Had the causal connections been represented as merely positive or negative relationships, as in a signed digraph, it would have been easy to prove conclusively whether a given set of assumptions did or did not *have to* lead to a specific result.

While signed digraphs are closer to the way decision makers talk, and are easier to use than weighted or functional digraphs, they do have several important limitations. One major limitation is that signed digraphs often give indeterminate results. Thus, if there are two paths from A to C, one transmitting a positive effect and one transmitting a negative effect, it is impossible to determine from this information alone whether an increase in A will yield an increase in C, a decrease in C, or even no change in C. With a weighted digraph, its indeterminacy would be resolved. In the example discussed earlier, where one path has a weight of -6 and the other a weight of $+1$, we can infer that an increase in A will definitely result in a decrease in B. In a completely balanced signed digraph, this indeterminacy will never arise, but there is no guarantee that any particular digraph will be completely balanced.

Another limitation of signed digraphs (and weighted digraphs, as well) compared to functional digraphs is that signed digraphs cannot represent nonmonotonic causal relationships, that is, relationships in which changes in the cause variable sometimes augment and sometimes inhibit the effect variable. An example of such a nonmonotonic causal relationship is one in which small increases in A lead to increases in B, but large increases in A lead to decreases in B.

To overcome to some extent these limitations in the signed digraph approach to cognitive maps, a number of avenues are explored in this volume.[8]

[8] To resolve indeterminacies, the following approaches are explored in later chapters:

1. examining separately the consequences of each possibility (Roberts in Chapter 7);

2. assuming that shorter paths have greater weight than longer paths (Bonham and Shapiro in Chapter 6, and Nozicka, Bonham, and Shapiro in Appendix 4);

3. attempting to measure the relative strength of the arrows that go directly into the utility point (Hart in Chapter 9, Bonham and Shapiro in Chapter 6, and Nozika, Bonham, and Shapiro in Appendix 4).

To summarize, there are three reasons why the signed digraph rather than the weighted or functional digraph has been chosen to represent a person's belief system:

1. measurement of causal assertions more precise than the sign of the relationship is very difficult at this stage of our knowledge;

2. for many purposes, more precise measurement is not needed, since many important properties about a cognitive map depend only on the structure of the relationships and their signs, rather than on more detailed knowledge; and

3. the very simplicity of signed digraphs has its own virtue in terms of allowing the researcher to analyze more easily a cognitive map and to communicate more easily with actual decision makers.

WHAT TO REMEMBER

For the sake of understanding the rest of the volume, here are the seven ideas that should be remembered.

1. *A cognitive map* is a certain way of representing a person's assertions about his beliefs with respect to some limited domain, such as a given policy problem. The representation takes the form of a directed graph of points and the arrows between those points.

2. A *point* represents a concept variable, which may be a policy option, the utility of the person (or his organization), or any other concept that may take on different values.

3. An *arrow* represents a causal assertion of how one concept variable affects another. A positive arrow from point A to point B means an augmenting relationship, that is, other things being equal, an increase in A will result in an increase in B, and a decrease in A will result in a decrease in B. A negative arrow from point A to point B means an inhibiting relationship, that is, other things being equal, an increase in A will result in a decrease in B, and a decrease in A will result in an increase in B.

4. A *path* is a sequence of distinct points which are connected by an arrow from the first point to the second point, an arrow from the second point to the third point, and so on, until there is

---

To represent nonmonotonic relationships, Hart shows how signed digraphs can be extended without losing much of their characteristic simplicity.

For more on the indeterminacies of signed digraphs, see Chapter 10, section E.

also an arrow from the next to the last point of the path to the last point of the path. The indirect effect of a path is positive if the path has an even number of negative arrows, and it is negative if it has an odd number of negative arrows.

5. A *cycle* is a path together with an arrow from the last point of the path to the first point. A positive cycle (one with an even number of negative arrows) is deviation-amplifying because any change in one of its points will eventually be reflected back at that point as an additional indirect effect in the same direction as the original change. Conversely, a negative cycle (one with an odd number of negative arrows) is deviation-counteracting.

6. The *total effect* of point A on point B is the sum of the indirect effects of all the paths and cycles from A to B. If all such paths and cycles are positive, the sum is positive; if all such paths and cycles are negative, the sum is negative; and if some are positive and some are negative, then the sum is indeterminate.

7. A *balanced graph* is a graph that has no indeterminate total effect between any pair of points.

PART TWO

Empirical Studies of Cognitive Maps

Decision for Neoimperialism: The Deliberations of the British Eastern Committee in 1918
—Robert Axelrod

This chapter is the keynote of the book because it explains the basic principles of the cognitive mapping approach, it shows how cognitive maps can be derived from documentary materials, it poses some of the basic research problems to be studied throughout the volume, and it reports some important empirical findings.

Using the verbatim transcripts of a high-level policy group discussing whether or not to continue the British intervention in Persia, the cognitive maps of the participants are derived and then analyzed. The results show that although the cognitive maps are quite large, the decision makers did, indeed, take stands consistent with their large cognitive maps. The results also indicate that although the maps are large and highly interconnected, they are structurally simple in several identifiable ways, and these simplifications happen to be ones that make the decision-making problem relatively easy to solve. Whether

For their help I wish to thank my colleagues, Carolyn Ban, Matthew Bonham, Martin Landau, Merrill Shanks, Michael Shapiro and Paul Sniderman; my research assistants, Thomas Hammond, Jeffrey Hart, and Nicholas Miller; and my coders, Michael Foster, Raymond Minella, and Margaret Wrightson. I also wish to thank those institutions whose collective faith was expressed in terms of financial support: the Institute of International Studies and the Committee on Research, both of the University of California at Berkeley; and the post-doctoral fellowship programs of the Council on Foreign Relations and the National Science Foundation. Finally, I wish to thank the Public Record Office, London, for access to the records of the Eastern Committee.

An earlier version of this chapter appeared under the title, "Psychoalgebra: A Mathematical Theory of Cognition and Choice with an Application to the British Eastern Committee in 1918," in *Papers of the Peace Research Society (International)*, 18(1972), 113–131. The author gratefully acknowledges the permission of the Peace Research Society (International) to revise the paper for inclusion here.

these simplifications are due to the speakers' desire to explain and to justify to others their own policy positions, or whether they are due to the cognitive limitations of the speakers, is a difficult question, but later chapters will show that there is reason to believe that both factors are operating.

A decision maker must simplify the manifest complexities of the external world. He must be able to construct a manageable representation of the external world so that he can describe and cope with his environment. The use of this representation for the purposes of making reasoned decisions requires some beliefs that link possible choices with potential outcomes.

The major characteristic of a belief linking choice and outcome is that it is usually indirect; a person is usually unable to make a single deductive leap from a choice to an outcome. Instead, he breaks this process into a series of steps. A decision maker might think, for example, that if a certain choice is made, and the other actors do such and such, and the characteristics of the external world are such and such at the time, then certain consequences will be the immediate results. These immediate results will have certain expected repercussions, which will in turn have certain anticipated effects, which will have other effects, and so on. These direct and indirect results of a choice can be regarded as determining the expected value of the outcome. Thus, in order to understand the decision-making process one must examine the whole structure of the concepts and linkages that are used to bridge the gap between choice and outcome.[1]

It is hoped that the study of these cognitive maps will illuminate some of the capabilities and limitations of actual policy makers. We know that there are limits to man's ability to think rationally. His memory is limited, for example. To aid his limited memory, a high-level policy maker can consult the written records that he keeps in his office, or the expert specialists whom he brings to meetings. But what methods does a policy maker use to cope with the large number of causal connections that can occur among the set of concepts relevant to a given proposal? This study of some policy makers in action seeks to answer this question.

[1] Game theory typically avoids this issue by assuming that the payoff matrix is known, and, therefore, does not examine the intermediate links between choice (strategy) and outcome (payoff entry).

THE EXAMPLE OF THE BRITISH EASTERN COMMITTEE

The Eastern Committee of the British Imperial War Cabinet was a cabinet-level standing committee that had responsibility for British policy in the area from the Mediterranean Sea to the frontiers of India. It met about twice a week during its existence from March 1918 to January 1919.[2]

An unusual feature of the Eastern Committee is that verbatim transcripts were made of a series of its meetings.[3] In early November 1918, the Allies finally won the First World War, and immediately started to think about postwar policy. Apparently in order to allow a few high officials of the government to keep up with the deliberations of the Eastern Committee, the discussions of ten meetings in November and December 1918 were taken in shorthand and transcribed verbatim.

The British records of this period were kept secret in both theory and practice for almost fifty years. They were released only in 1966. The frankness of the discussions provides ample evidence that the participants did not worry about appealing to a broader public.

Being a standing committee of the cabinet, the Eastern Committee was a top-level decision-making group. Its chairman was Lord Curzon, and its other members were General Smuts of South Africa (who, with Curzon, was a full member of the six-man Imperial War Cabinet), Balfour (the foreign secretary, who was usually represented by his deputy, Lord Cecil), Montagu (secretary of state for India), and General Wilson (chief of the Imperial General Staff). Expert specialists were also invited to attend the meetings, and frequently gave their views on specific topics. The scope of its authority and the magnitude of its decisions indicate that the Eastern Committee was an important locus of decision making.

How should one interpret the assertions made in such a setting? It is certainly true that the assertions made by a participant repre-

---

[2] The committee is described by Ullman (1968), and I am indebted to Professor Robert Jervis for this reference, which led me to the Eastern Committee.

[3] The doucmentary coding method is not dependent on the availability of such verbatim records. For a discussion of desirable properties in a document, see Chapter 10, section C. For suggestions on specific documents suitable for coding, see the guide to source materials in Appendix 5.

79

sent the view of the environment which is presented by that participant for consideration by the others. The assertions are probably believed to be true by the speaker, but they may not include all of his relevant beliefs. It is also possible that the participant may have made the assertions to justify a policy preference which he himself arrived at on different grounds. Nevertheless, the assertions made by a participant do form the view of external reality that he presents for consideration by the others.

Each participant's cognitive map is derived from his assertions. Together, these cognitive maps form alternative articulated images of the environment, which are available to the committee members in their collective task of selecting a governmental policy.

The part of the deliberations of the Eastern Committee that have been analyzed in detail are the discussion of British postwar policy toward Persia, which is now called Iran. These discussions occupied all of the meeting of December 19, and half of the meeting of December 30, 1918.[4] During the war, Persia was a nonbelligerent, but military actions between the British and the Russians on one side and the Turks on the other took place on her soil. In December 1918, more than a year after the Bolshevik revolution, the territory to the north of Persia was still a scene of conflict between the central government under the Bolsheviks and a kaleidoscopic collection of anti-Bolshevik forces and newly proclaimed republics, supported to a considerable extent by the British and the French. To the west of Persia lay Mesopotamia (Iraq), which the British had just taken from the Turks. To the east was the jewel of the British Empire, India.

Curzon, as chairman, opened the discussion with an argument that Britain must play an active role in Persia. As he put it:

> Every one of us knows full well, although perhaps the Persians would be reluctant to admit it, that at the bottom we have no other desire, in our own interests as well as in the interests of the Persians themselves, than to build up, establish and fortify the independence and integrity of Persia, even though we have been compelled by the exigencies of the case to take steps which are capable of being represented as the very antithesis of that policy and principle.

No wonder that Curzon was called by his detractors "his royal pomp" (Beaverbrook, 1956, p. 304n). By the term "fortify the

---

[4] The transcripts are in Cabinet document 27/24. Smuts and Wilson were not present at either meeting.

independence and integrity of Persia," Curzon made clear that he meant, among other things, the insistence upon British citizens being in charge of the finances and army of Persia.

Montagu and his foreign policy aide, Grant, argued the India Office position that Britain was partly to blame for the suspicious attitude of the Persians, and that Britain should only intervene if asked by the Persians or by the forthcoming peace conference. Cecil, who at this time was Britain's leading advocate of the formation of the League of Nations, did not think that intervention could be carried out as a half-way measure, and was reluctant to establish what amounted to a British protectorate over Persia. Almost thinking aloud, Cecil said; "You may either go away and let the Persians have a try at governing themselves or you may take them over. I do not think, personally, that there is any [other] alternative that is reasonable. I confess that I am a little inclined to think that we ought to go away; but I am not sure." The meeting ending without a decision.

When the committee returned to the Persian question a week and a half later, Curzon reiterated his interventionist position, putting special emphasis on the point that if Britain did not fill the vacuum caused by the weakness of the Persian government, then someone else would. Cecil came around to Curzon's view because he feared that if Britain let Persia "stew in her own juice," the pro-Czarist Russian commander of the only organized force in the capital, known as the Cossack Division, would take over the country. Grant continued to plead for at least giving a chance to the softer policy of "the velvet glove," but Curzon insisted upon showing the Persians that "within the velvet glove is an iron hand." The official minutes noted that Curzon's recommendations were adopted, and minimized the remaining disagreement by saying, "The only difference between Lord Curzon and the Government of India appeared to be in regard to the manner of our communications to the Persian Government—not the substance." [5]

Incidentally, the subsequent events illustrate the gap that so commonly separates the intended outcome from the actual outcome. Lord Curzon became foreign secretary the following year (1919), and in August an Anglo-Iranian Treaty was concluded that gave Britain control of the Iranian treasury and army. So far so good for the British. However, the Iranian nationalists were opposed to the arrangement, and the Iranian parliament never ratified it. The Iranians managed to remove the pro-Czarist

[5] Cab 27/24, December 30, 1918.

officers from command of the Cossack Division in 1920, and in 1921, a bloodless coup d'etat took place. The new government concluded a Soviet-Iran treaty and repudiated the Anglo-Iranian treaty. The new Persian commander of the Cossack Division, Reza Khan, used his position to gain complete power, and in 1925 started a new dynasty by declaring himself Shah of Iran (Lenczowski, 1949). Today, half a century later, Reza's son rules Iran as the current shah.

THE DERIVATION OF A COGNITIVE MAP FROM A DOCUMENT

The derivation of a cognitive map from a document requires the coding of a given text, sentence by sentence or even phrase by phrase. The first stage of the coding process generates two lists, a list of the concept variables in the text and a list of the causal assertions. In the second stage the assertions made by a given person are put together to construct that person's cognitive map. The rules governing the coding process are too detailed to describe here in full, but a brief example will illustrate the main features of the coding process. For the complete rules, see Appendix 1.

Table 4–1 shows the steps in the construction of a part of Cecil's cognitive map. The text is taken from the second meeting, and consists of Cecil's explanation of his own position before he changed his mind and adopted Curzon's view. Below the text is the list of variables, giving the abbreviation and definition of each variable. Then comes the list of assertions, in their raw form on the left, and in the arrow notation on the right. Figure 4–1 shows the fragment of Cecil's cognitive map which is derivable from these assertions.

The listing of the concept variables is reasonably simple. Notice that they are all variables in the sense that they can take on different values. For example, the first variable is "the amount of money spent in Persia by Britain." The second variable is the utility of Britain, which is the representation of what Cecil has in mind as the goal of any governmental action. The last variable, D, has two equivalent definitions. One is the existence of British interference in Persia, and the other is the opposite of the adoption of the policy of letting Persia "stew in her own juice." These two definitions are equivalent, because the meaning of letting Persia "stew in her own juice" is tantamount to nonintervention.

TABLE 4–1

THE CONSTRUCTION OF A COGNITIVE MAP

Text

CECIL: I was very much attracted at one time by the suggestion that it was not really justifiable for us to go on spending this amount of money in Persia, that we had very little interest in the place, that it was not at all certain that the good government of Persia really mattered to us, and further that apparently our interference had not so far, for various reasons, conduced to the improvement of the government of Persia, but that, on the contrary, the government had become decidedly worse than it was when we had relatively less to do with them. Therefore I was disposed to think that there was a good deal to be said for the "stewing in their own juice" policy.

List of concept variables

Abbreviation	Definition
A	Amount of money spent in Persia by Britain
B	British utility
C	Quality of government in Persia
D	Existence of British interference in Persia (=opposite of policy of letting Persia "stew in her own juice")

	List of causal assertions		*List of arrows*		
Cause	Connector	Effect			
A	Not really justifiable	B	A	—	B
C	Not at all certain really matters	B	C	0	B
D	Not conduced to improvement in	C	D	0 or —	C
D	Since . . . became worse	C	D	—	C
D	Requires	A	D	+	A
—D	Good deal to be said for	B	D	—	B

FIGURE 4–1.

Fragment of Cecil's Cognitive Map

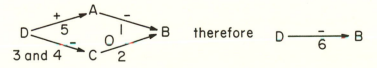

83

The assertions are listed first in the form of cause/connector/ effect. The connectors use words similar to the ones in the original text, but occasionally this becomes awkward, as in the fourth assertion. Notice that the sixth assertion employs the second of the two equivalent definitions of variable D. The fifth assertion is derived from the context of the quotation and states that interference will require money, a fact that is understood from the preceding discussion. When the sixth assertion is translated into arrow notation, the sign of the concept variable is made positive, which makes the sign of the arrow negative. The notation "0 or −" in the third arrow means that the arrow is either zero or negative, but the connector does not specify which.

Shown in figure 4–1 is the fragment of Cecil's cognitive map which is formed by the six assertions coded in table 4–1. The sign is given above each arrow and the corresponding assertion number or numbers are given below each arrow. Assertions 3 and 4 have already been combined.[6] By using this cognitive map, one can conclude that Cecil's position is that the path from D to B through A (money spent) is a negative one, while the path from D to B through C (quality of Persian government) is of no weight. Therefore D lessens B, which means that intervention lessens British utility. The deduction to be drawn from these two paths is that Cecil was against British interference (and for the "stewing" policy), which is the conclusion Cecil himself drew in the sixth assertion.

This method of coding a person's remarks obviously loses a good deal of their subtlety. But it is not the fine texture of each assertion that is being studied here, but rather the structure of the interconnections between the assertions.

THE RELIABILITY OF DOCUMENTARY CODING

Translating a given document into a cognitive map requires a large number of subtle coding decisions, so it is no wonder that getting two coders to agree on each of these decisions is not an easy task. Now, after more than three years of work, the coding rules have reached a state of precision such that intercoder reliability is fully compatible with the accepted standards of good quantitative work in the social sciences.[7]

[6] See Appendix 3 for the formal rules of combining assertions.
[7] The coding rules are given in full in Appendix 1.

84

Here are the details. Two coders, working independently, learned the coding rules and applied them to an extensive text of 7,300 words with over 100 causal assertions. The text was Madison's notes on Gouverneur Morris speaking about the presidency in the Constitutional Convention of 1787.[8] The text was deemed to be unusually difficult because (as Madison himself noted) Morris is "fickle and inconstant, never pursuing one train of thinking, nor ever regular."

The reliability calculations are made by conceptualizing the coding process as four different tasks: identifying the number of codable assertions in each sentence, specifying each of the three parts of the codable assertion that have been identified, determining the identity of the concept variables between different assertions, and determining the relationship of each variable to utility.

The first task is the hardest. The agreement score on the number of codable assertions in each of the 226 sentences was .80 according to Robinson's measure of agreement (1957).[9] This seems adequate, but not exceptional. The main problem was in the coding of parts or wholes, and examples. For example, Morris was fond of using the phrase "intrigue and cabal." One coder regarded this as one concept variable, and the other coder regarded it as two, and hence they disagree on how many assertions there would be in a sentence containing this phrase. While such discrepancies cannot be completely eliminated, a rule can be (and has been) added to the coding instructions to give the coders a reasonably precise criterion to follow in deciding whether to code such a phrase as one variable or two. Had the coders not had disagreements on such problems of parts/wholes and examples, the measure of agreement on the number of assertions in each sentence would have gone up from .80 to .88.

The next three tasks are independent, but were compared only for those assertions that were identified by both coders. For each task the appropriate measure is the common coefficient of reliability: twice the number of coding agreements divided by the total number of coding decisions made by the two coders.

Agreement on each of three parts of a codable assertion was all very good:

[8] The resulting cognitive map is analyzed by Ross in Chapter 5.

[9] This means that 80 percent of the variance in the 226 pairs of observations is accounted for by the within-pairs sums of squares.

85

a. 96 percent on which part of the sentence contained the cause variable; [10]

b. 96 percent on which part of the sentence contained the effect variable; and

c. 97 percent on the sign of the relationship. Counting all three gives the result that cause, effect, and sign were in complete agreement 92 percent of the time.

Agreement on identification of the variables across assertions was also very good. Here the question was whether the coders agreed on their decisions to equate concept variables that appear in different assertions. The calculation is based on a comparison of the lists of merging decisions the two coders made, with a typical merging decision being that the cause variable in a given assertion is the same variable as the effect variable in another given assertion. The two coders agreed on 88 percent of about 150 such merging decisions.

Finally, determining the relationship of each variable to utility also had good reliability. The coders agreed on the direct relationship to utility of a given variable in a given assertion 91 percent of the time.

This test of reliability demonstrates that the coding rules are adequate to the task of reliably measuring the components and relationships in a cognitive map. In the one task where success was only marginal, a single type of problem accounted for a large proportion of the discrepancies, and this problem can presumably be greatly alleviated by the addition of more precise rules to cover that single type of problem.

EMPIRICAL RESULTS

When the cognitive maps are constructed for each of the participants in the Eastern Committee, there is a striking result. Despite our knowledge about the severe limitations on people's cognitive ability, the maps are all quite large and intricate. The set of causal beliefs connecting choices with outcomes seems to be so large as to be quite beyond the ability of people to use. And yet they did use these beliefs, and their conclusions were consistent with their cognitive maps.

The maps were certainly large. One standard of measurement

[10] Whether there was agreement on the exact identity of the variable itself is evaluated as part of the next task.

is to compare the number of variables and arrows used in a given time span. The time devoted to discussions of Persia in the 45th and 48th meetings of the Eastern Committee generated just over 20,000 words. A thorough coding of these words uncovered more than 500 causal assertions, or an average of more than one every 40 words. At that rate, it did not take a person very long to describe his beliefs on a specific proposal in terms of literally dozens of concept variables and the causal beliefs connecting them. Furthermore, repetition accounted for only a small proportion of these assertions, because only a few of the assertions were repeated for emphasis.

As an illustration of a person's cognitive map, figure 4–2 gives the map of Marling, who was the British representative in Persia, and who had returned to London to take part in the deliberations of the Eastern Committee. In the course of being questioned about British interests in Persia, he was able to express his policy preferences and the beliefs upon which his preferences were based. The figure is drawn so that the three policy proposals being discussed are on the left side and the variable representing Marling's conception of British utility is on the right side. In many ways, this is a particularly simple map. It has many arrows of zero magnitude, corresponding to statements that one concept variable does not affect another. It is also much smaller than the maps of the main participants in the Eastern Committee, because Marling spoke a total of only a thousand words. To simplify it even more, the concepts have been arranged in the figure so that the causal flow is easy to follow, and the few assertions that are not relevant to the proposals have been left out. Despite all this, the 31 concept variables and the 43 causal beliefs in Figure 4–2 form an interconnected graph that requires a fair amount of calculation to use.

Not only were there a great many causal beliefs stated in the meeting, but these causal beliefs seem to have been used by the participants in their own decision-making process. When the committee members were explaining their positions, they used cause-effect statements to elaborate the implications of their proposals. When they were collectively exploring the problems of British policy, they used cause-effect statements to trace out the consequences of the alternatives. And finally, when they were obviously trying to persuade each other of the merit of their own position or the drawbacks of some other position, they used arguments that could usually be coded in terms of causal assertions.

FIGURE 4-2.

Marling's Cognitive Map

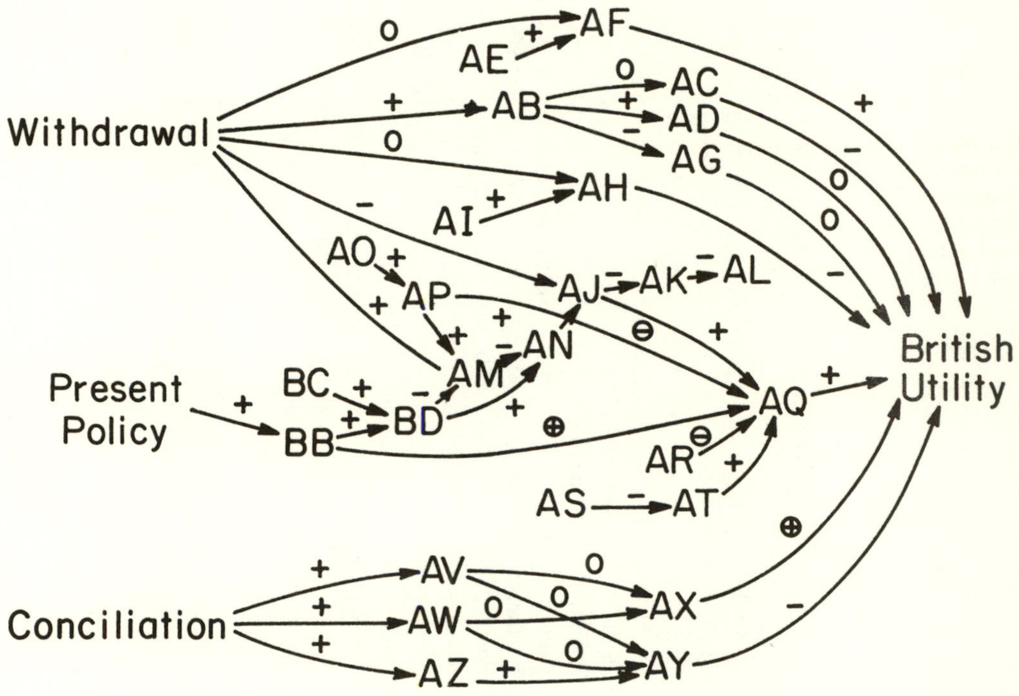

The arrows represent causal assertions about how one concept variable affects another. The symbols indicate the type of relationship:

+ positive
0 zero
— negative
⊕ zero or positive
⊖ zero or negative

The three instrumental (or policy) variables are placed on the left and the utility variable on the right. The other concept variables are represented by two-letter symbols.

The map is derived from Marling's assertions about Persia made in the Eastern Committee on December 19, 1918.

Key to Figure 4-2

Concept Listing for Marling's Cognitive Map

AA Policy of complete British withdrawal from Persia
AO Establishment of Persian constitution
AB Withdrawal from NW districts
AC Probability of occurrence of serious disturbances in NW
AD Amount of chaos in NW districts
AE Presence of Bakhtiari
AF Maintenance of status of Anglo-Persian Oil Company
AG Maintenance of telegraph
AH Probability of invasion of Persia by Bolsheviks
AI Amount of feeling in Persia for Bolsheviks
AJ Amount of security in Persia
AK Amount of blackmail on trade caravans
AL Utility of Persian tribesmen
AM Removal of better governors
AN Strength of Persian governors

AP Lack of quality of the kind of Shah at present
AQ Ability of British to put pressure on Persia
AR Ability of Persian government to maintain order
AS Absence of reformers in Persian parties (=no reformers)
AT Amount of control of reformers by their friends
AU Strength of reformers
AV Policy of conciliation with Persia
AW Abrogation of 1907 treaty with Russia
AX Revision of customs tariff
AY Conciliation of Persian public opinion
AZ Amount of Persian desire to go their own way
BA Amount of British interference with Persia
BB Present policy of intervention in Persia
BC Allowing Persians to have continual small subsidy
BD Amount of Persian debt to British

Not only were the cognitive maps large, and not only were the causal assertions that compose the maps generated at all stages of the committee discussions, but the conclusions that the individual members of the committee drew were, in fact, consistent with the relevant portions of their own very large maps. This is a significant result, because the conclusions that can be drawn from a large and interconnected map are highly constrained by the functional interdependence among the various causal assertions a person makes. This high degree of constraint in the belief systems of the members of the Eastern Committee is in sharp contrast to the looseness of constraint found by Converse (1964) in the members of the mass public when they were asked about their preferences on questions of public policy.

The participants themselves did not find deductive errors in each others' assertions, although they were not shy about pointing out factual mistakes.[11] Not only were the participants unable to find deductive errors in each other's causal statements despite the high level of constraint in the large maps, but a close reading of the transcript fifty years later reaffirmed the very high level of deductive consistency between the conclusions drawn by the individuals and their own set of causal assertions. This was so, even though there were literally hundreds of assertions, which in many cases were connected to each other in rather intricate patterns. For example, Marling's cognitive map is completely consistent with his stated preference for continuing the present policy of "dragging along," and his disapproval of the policies of either complete British withdrawal or conciliating the Persians.

Unfortunately, the process of coding the causal assertions is still as much an art as a science. Therefore, the empirical results must be put in qualitative rather than quantitative terms. It is hoped that the coding process can eventually be specified in terms of precise instructions that will allow two different coders to arrive independently at a nearly identical list of cognitive variables and causal assertions in any given document. Such a high level of reliability has not yet been attained, and the results must therefore be regarded as tentative. Nevertheless, it is quite clear that the

---

[11] For example, when Grant said that the telegraph lines through Persia were important for communications from India to the West, Marling pointed out that "the cable could carry all that now. The Persians' lines are of no value for those purposes." Eastern Committee, Cab 27/24, December 19, 1918.

members of the Eastern Committee expressed a very large number of causal beliefs, used these assertions in all stages of the group decision process, and were able to make deductions that were consistent with their entire set of expressed beliefs.

What is not clear is just how general these conclusions from the Eastern Committee are. It is possible that the English language, with its basic subject-verb-object syntax promotes the use of causal thinking. It is also possible that other factors, such as the British educational system, account for the presence of so many causal assertions in the Eastern Committee. A reading of documents from other times and places leaves the question open. Documents that are as suitable for the present purposes as the Eastern Committee transcripts are hard to find, but the following less satisfactory documents have been read with an eye to placing the results from the Eastern Committee in a broader context:

1. Thucydides' accounts of the public debates in Athens on what should be done with the inhabitants of the conquered cities of Mitylene (416 B.C.) and Melos (427 B.C.).[12]

2. Madison's notes of the secret debates in the American Constitutional Convention on the subject of the length of the term of the President (July 17, 19, 24 and August 24, 1787).[13]

3. The captured verbatim transcripts of the meeting under Goering's chairmanship on the financial and legal problems for the Nazi government arising from a huge pogrom (November 12, 1938).[14]

4. The captured records of the deliberations of the Japanese Privy Council meetings to consider the ratifications of the London Naval Treaty in 1931, the ratification of the Japan-Germany-Italy Tripartite Treaty in 1940,[15] and the notes of a participant in the sixty-seven liaison conferences throughout 1941 between the cabinet and the Supreme Command.[16]

As a tentative conclusion, it seems that the Athenian debates and the American convention are quite similar to the British Eastern Committee in the very great use of causal assertions. The Japanese meetings seem to make less use of causal assertions, with

[12] From Thucydides (1960).

[13] From Madison (1966). Madison's notes were also used as the source material for Ross's study in Chapter 5.

[14] From *Nazi Conspiracy and Aggression, Vol. 6* (1946).

[15] From International Military Tribunal for the Far East (1946–1948).

[16] From Ike (1967).

the Nazi meeting being somewhere in between. It therefore appears that the heavy use of causal assertions of the Eastern Committee is neither unique nor universal. The question still remains as to how the members of the Eastern Committee, with their presumably limited cognitive abilities, could express literally hundreds of inter-connected causal assertions, use them in all stages of the group decision-making process, and still be able to make deductions con-sistent with their entire set of their expressed causal beliefs.

EXPLANATION OF THE RESULTS

Several possible answers to this question are suggested by the literature on decision making under bounded rationality. Simon (1957) suggests that decision makers do not maximize their utility, but rather they "satisfice." This theory asserts that decision makers search through the alternatives only until they find one that is sufficiently promising to satisfy their current aspiration level. In the deliberations of the Eastern Committee, however, the different participants presented different alternatives that they seemed to think were the best of all possible policies under the circumstances, and not merely adequate policies.

Another possible answer is that decision makers do not maxi-mize all of their goals at once, but rather pay selective attention to one goal at a time (Cyert and March, 1963). Actually, however, there was a very broad range of goals considered in the Eastern Committee meetings on Persia. The Eastern Committee itself was set up in order to assure interdepartmental coordination of policy, and it was quite successful at bringing together a wide range of British interests that were to some extent bureaucratically divided among the Foreign Office, the India Office, and the War Office.

A third possible answer is that decision makers used a lexico-graphic decision rule (Taylor, 1970). This means that one goal is assumed to be supreme, but if two policies are equally good with respect to that goal, then they are compared with respect to a second goal. If they are tied on the second goal, the one that is better with respect to the third-ranking goal is chosen, and so on. Actually, the members of the Eastern Committee did not make this kind of comparison, nor did they place in order the multiple goals that were served by the alternative policies. Instead, they asserted that their favorite proposal served many goals, each of which presumably had some importance in itself.

If the members of the Eastern Committee did not make their cognitive task easier by using satisficing, selective attention to goals, or a lexicographic decision rule, how did they manage to generate and consistently use such large cognitive maps? The answer seems to be that although the actual maps were indeed large and highly interconnected, they also had two structural properties that made them easy to use despite their size. First, they contained very few cycles. Second, they contained very little imbalance. An examination of these two properties will show how useful they are in simplifying the cognitive task of the decision maker.

In graph theoretic terms, a cycle is a collection of points and arrows which, when taken in order, return to the initial point. For example, three beliefs that constitute a cycle are "A causes B," "B increases C," and "C lowers A." Such a cycle is formed by Cecil's beliefs that if the British gave no subsidy to the Persians this might cause a breakdown in the Persian government, which would in turn cause them to ask for British aid, which would result in the British giving some aid. A cycle can obviously also be formed with longer chains of causal beliefs, and if there are dozens of points and arrows in a cognitive map, there are a huge number of possible cycles that can be formed. Nevertheless, cycles are very rare in the cognitive maps of the participants of the Eastern Committee. For example, Marling's cognitive map (shown in Figure 4–2) has no cycles at all.

This absence of cycles is a tremendous help in the use of the cognitive map, because it means that in tracing out the effects of a change in a concept variable one will make steady progress through the map and not have any of the causal chains return again to the initial variable. The absence of cycles means, in effect, that the person conceptualized the causal flow as a uniform one from the policy choices, through the mediating concepts, to the outcomes and the utility, with no causal feedback anywhere in the flow. This type of cognitive map certainly represents a simplistic view of the world. The lack of cycles does, however, have the advantage that it helps to eliminate the need for one kind of cognitive sophistication in one's calculations.

The cognitive maps of the participants in the Eastern Committee also had very little imbalance. As defined in Chapter 3, a cognitive map is completely balanced if there is no indeterminate total effect between any pair of points. For example, in Figure 4–1 the sum of the negative and zero paths from point D to point B is negative, which is not indeterminate. The sum of a negative and a positive path would be indeterminate, however, since the sum of a negative and a positive number could have any value: negative, zero, or positive.

The structural property of balance has been employed in systems other than cognitive maps, but the empirical meaning of the property has always been different, because the interpretation of the points and arrows has been different.[17] In a cognitive map, balance means that a person's causal beliefs are related to each other in a particularly simple way. In effect, it means that he never has to worry about the possibility that one chain of deduction will lead him to think that a given concept variable will indirectly work to increase his utility, while another chain of deduction will lead him to think that the same concept variable will indirectly work to decrease his utility. With a balanced set of causal beliefs, the cognitive abilities needed for the decision-making task are not very great even for a rather large and intricate cognitive map. To maximize expected utility with a balanced cognitive map, the decision rule is simply to maximize the instrumental variables that promote utility and minimize the other policy variables.

The cognitive maps of the participants were almost completely balanced. Marling's map in Figure 4–2 is totally balanced. Even the exceptional instances of a causal belief inconsistent with complete balance emphasize the reliance on balance. For example, when Cecil changed his mind, he made assertions that were imbalanced when taken together with his old cognitive map. Yet at no time was there much imbalance, because both the "before" and "after" cognitive maps, taken separately, were almost completely balanced.[18] As another example, here is a representative of the War Office under pressure to admit that the tough policy favored by the military would cost more than the current policy:

GENERAL MacDonogh. Certainly the policy put forward by the War Office was to get the control of Persia generally, and really

[17] For balance in psycho-logic, see Abelson and Rosenberg (1958) and Abelson (1968b); for balance in cognitive dissonance, see Festinger (1957); for balance in evaluation of attitude objects, see Osgood and Tannenbaum (1955); and for balance in communication processes, see Flament (1963).

[18] Cecil's change from one balanced map to another presumably took place in two steps. First, his cognitive map became unbalanced when he somehow became convinced of the danger from the Cossack Division if Britain withdrew. Second, Cecil's cognitive map was rebalanced when he changed other arrows that were functionally related to his new belief.

get something for our money. . . . That is a definite policy—that we should take control in Persia both financially and otherwise.

LORD ROBERT CECIL. What will it cost?

GENERAL MACDONOGH. I do not think that it would cost very much more than what we are spending at present.

LORD ROBERT CECIL. It would not cost any less?

GENERAL MACDONOGH. No. We do not know why we are spending money.[19]

General MacDonogh was reluctant to admit that his preferred policy might not be ideal for some of his goals, even though it was good for others. Indeed, all the participants of the Eastern Committee presented nearly balanced cognitive maps, which means that they rarely stated causal beliefs that could be put together to yield a chain of consequences that would imply either a single disadvantage to their own policy preference or a single advantage of another alternative. Of course, one motivation for doing this was to avoid giving other participants a lever to use against one's own preferences. The lack of cycles, however, is less easy to explain in terms of an instrumental desire to strengthen one's own arguments. Alternative explanations for the lack of cycles will be considered in detail in Chapter 9. For now, the key points are that decision makers such as Marling do employ simplified images of their environment, and that the nature of these simplifications can be specified.

The complexities of the external world must be simplified in one way or another in order for a person to be able to describe and cope with his environment. The tactics used by the participants in the Eastern Committee included describing the causal relationships in the external world in terms of almost completely balanced and acyclic cognitive maps, and thereby avoiding the use of trade-offs or feedback. Further research presented in the following chapters demonstrates the extent to which other decision makers in other contexts use these same tactics.

[19] Cab 27/24, December 19, 1918.

CHAPTER FIVE

Complexity and the Presidency: Gouverneur Morris in the Constitutional Convention
—*Stuart A. Ross*

This analysis of a cognitive map derived from an unusually complex man speaking on an unusually complex subject shows one of the structural simplifications found in the maps of the members of the Eastern Committee (Chapter 4), while another of those simplifications is not observed. The analysis of the details of the map for Gouverneur Morris yields some new insights into the critical features of his rather intricate arguments about the proper balance of power between the President and the Legislature. By comparing the cognitive map of Morris to what his contemporaries said about Morris' style of thought, this chapter opens up the field of cognitive mapping to the investigation of individual cognitive styles.

This study applies the technique of cognitive mapping to the speeches of a delegate to the Constitutional Convention, on resolutions pertaining to the presidency. That delegate was a complex man and matched to a complex topic, he provides fertile material for analysis. This study consists primarily of an application of Axelrod's approach in Chapter 4 to the decision-making situation at the convention, and yields interesting comparisons to the results that were obtained for the British Eastern Committee.

The man being studied is Gouverneur Morris, one of the delegates from Pennsylvania. Although he was less influential in the rest of American history than such men as Washington, Hamilton, and Jefferson, and although he had asked not to be appointed as a delegate, he played a crucial role at the convention.[1] He joined

The author wishes to acknowledge the patience and assistance of Robert Axelrod, Margaret Wrightson, James Beniger, and Priscilla Ross. The paper had its origins as part of a seminar on mathematical models conducted by Professor Axelrod, who in each of innumerable conversations had prodded the author's understanding further.

[1] For a general background on the convention and on Morris, the reader

Madison, Wilson, and others in the drive to provide a strong central government. He served on the committee to which was referred, toward the end of the sessions, important unfinished portions of the Constitution. He is credited with the final rewriting of the Constitution before it was signed. He spoke more often than any other delegate—in spite of a month's leave of absence (Mintz, 1970, pp. 181–185).

Morris was highly admired by his contemporaries, but not always trusted (Farrand, 1921, p. 112). He was a man of known aristocratic beliefs who occasionally rallied to the democratic cause; he was a rich man who could declare that "wealth tends to corrupt the mind" (Madison, 1898, p. 383). This description of him was provided by one of the other delegates:

> Mr. Gouverneur Morris is one of those Genius's in whom every species of talents combines to render him conspicuous and flourishing in public debate: He winds through all the mazes of rhetoric, and throws around him such a glare that he charms, captivates, and leads away the senses of all who hear him. With an infinite stretch of fancy he brings to view things when he is engaged in deep argumentation, that render all the labor of reasoning easy and pleasing. But with all these powers he is fickle and inconstant, never pursuing one train of thinking, nor ever regular (Prescott, 1941, p. 29).

A few years later, Madison wrote in more appreciative tones: "It is but due to Mr. Morris to remark, that to the brilliancy of his genius, he added, what is too rare, a candid surrender of his opinions, when the lights of discussion satisfied him, that they had been too hastily formed, and a readiness to aid in making the best of measures in which he had been overruled" (cited in Mintz, 1970, p. 182).

The arrangement of the executive branch of the government was one of the most troubling problems for the convention. The difficulty arose not so much from the opposition of clearly separate factions, such as the large states and the small states, as from the lack of adequate models in history and experience. The delegates wanted a freely chosen executive for a federal republic: more than a clerk, more than a governor, but less than a monarch. History had no clear parallels to offer.

As a result, the delegates seemed at times during that summer

---

is referred to the works by Dahl (1967), Farrand (1913, 1921), and Mintz (1970).

of 1787 to flounder among many different proposals. Should the executive be chosen by the legislature or by the people? Should he serve for seven years once or for two years as often as reelected? Should there be only one executive, or an executive council of three? Many of the decisions about the presidency, including his term and mode of election, were not settled until the closing days of the convention. It was in these deliberations about the executive, in fact, that Morris made his "most penetrating and enduring contribution" (Mintz, 1970, p. 192).

Thus the topic and the man invite investigation. The first order of business in the investigation is to see, in conventional terms, what materials we have to work with. Then the cognitive map and its properties will be examined. That done, the significance of the results will be discussed.

THE MATERIALS FOR ANALYSIS

No formal records were kept at the convention, and no publication of any deliberations was permitted, because the delegates wanted to consider all possibilities, and change their minds, if appropriate, without committing themselves publicly. Although there are extant many letters and other documents surrounding the convention, the principal source of information now available is the detailed set of notes kept by James Madison and published posthumously in 1840. The notes are written in paraphrase and in the third person. The notes for a single day were typically between 2,000 and 3,000 words in length. The analysis done for this study, including all the quotations from Morris, is based on Madison's notes of Morris' speeches, in the edition by Scott (Madison, 1898). Comments on the use of documents as source materials for cognitive analyses are offered by Holsti (Chapter 2) and Axelrod (Chapter 10 and Appendix 5).

Coding was done for Morris' speeches on motions and amendments that pertained to the impeachment, the term of office, the mode of election, and the reeligibility of the President, as these were written and considered together in drafts from the Virginia Plan through to the completed constitution. The relevant article in each draft contained other provisions as well—the president's stipend, for example—but these issues were rarely spoken to by Morris. The debates coded here occurred on July 17 to 25, August 24, and September 4, 6, 8, and 12, 1787.

What Morris had to say on the four policy questions just mentioned may be given in conventional summary before going on to the mapping analysis. He had these views on the four policy questions:

1. Morris strongly favored having the President elected by the people and not by the national legislature. In Madison's notes we read of Morris, "He considered an election by the people as the best, by the legislature as the worst mode" (Madison, 1898, p. 432), and in another speech Morris states, "Appointments made by numerous bodies are always worse than those made by single responsible individuals or by the people at large" (Madison, 1898, p. 367). He opposed election by the legislature because he feared such a process would make the executive dependent on the legislature; he feared that cabal and legislative tyranny would be the result. In favoring an election by the people, of course, Morris was siding with men of more democratic views in other matters, men such as James Madison and James Wilson.

2. Morris wanted to have the executive be reeligible for a second term; indeed, he thought the provision essential to the national safety: "Shut the civil road to glory, and he may be compelled to seek it by the sword" (Madison, 1898, p. 383).

3. Morris' views on the provisions for impeachment were more complicated. His position throughout most of the early debate was that impeachment "is a dangerous part of the plan. It will hold him in such dependence that he will be no check on the legislature, will not be a firm guardian of the people and of the public interest" (Madison, 1898, p. 384). In the midst of these early proceedings, though, he supported a motion that the President serve "during good behavior" (Madison, 1898, p. 370), which would imply the availability of impeachment proceedings. Still later, after an announced change of mind on July 20, he asserted that "impeachments must be provided for, if the appointment was to be of any duration" (Madison, 1898, p. 423).

4. Morris favored a short term of office for the President. He once moved that the term be only two years long. He wanted the term to be short so that frequent reelection or displacement by the vote of the people would obviate the need for impeachments. Thus both his support of reeligibility and his opposition to impeachment were conditional upon the length of the executive's term, and Morris so expressed himself in explicitly conditional statements.

MORRIS' COGNITIVE MAP

The concept variables identified in Morris' speeches on the presidency are given in the key to Figure 5–1; for each is given the code

FIGURE 5-1.
Morris' Cognitive Map

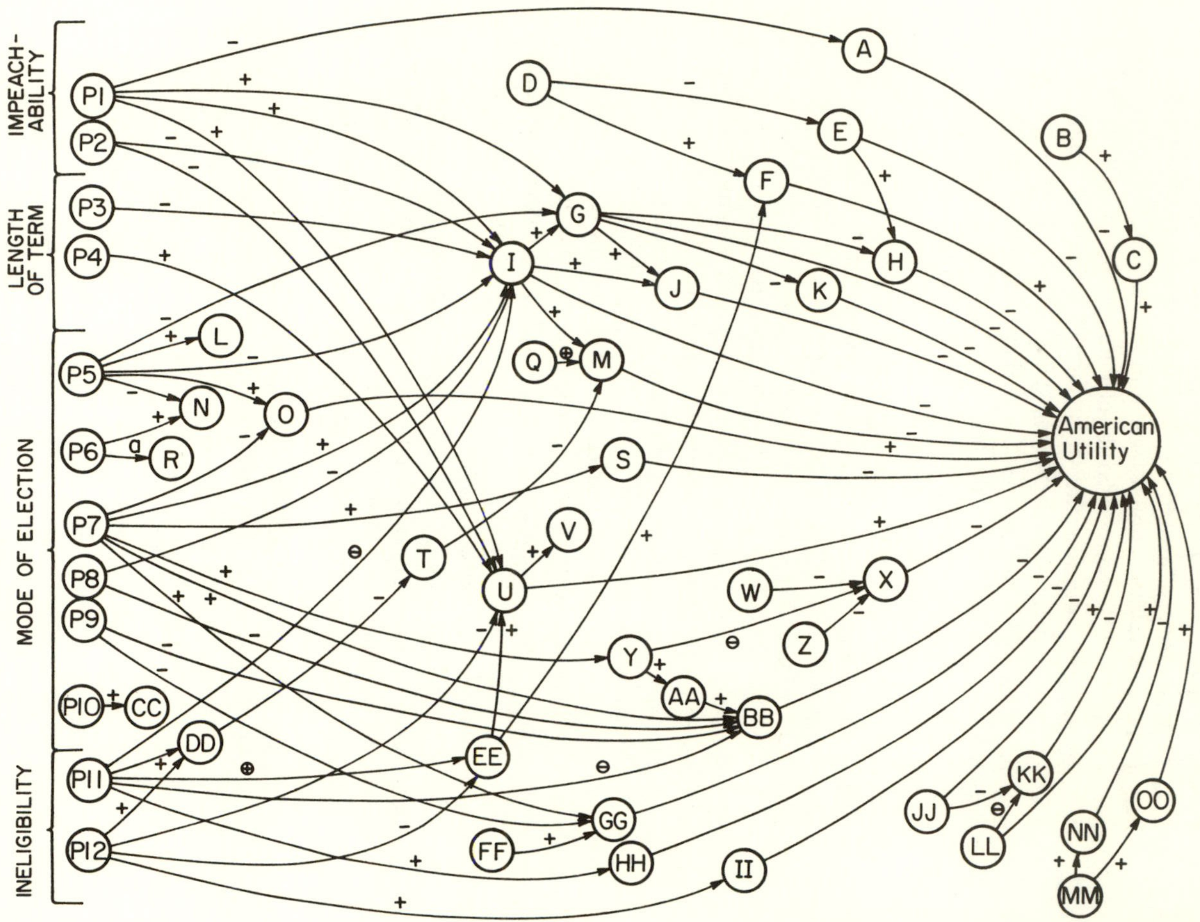

Key to Figure 5–1

P1 Policy of impeachability of the executive by the legislature
P2 Policy of not suspending the executive upon impeachment
P3 Policy of giving the executive a term for life
P4 Policy of electing the executive every four years
P5 Policy of having the executive elected by the people at large
P6 Policy of having the Senate choose the President and Vice President from among the five highest candidates chosen by the electors, if none has a majority of electoral votes
P7 Policy of having the executive elected by the national legislature
P8 Policy of choosing the electors by lot from among the legislators
P9 Provision for the electors to vote at the same time and in separate places
P10 Policy of having each elector vote for two persons, one not from his state
P11 Policy of rotating the executive's period of eligibility—not to serve more than six years in any twelve
P12 Policy of making the executive ineligible for a second term
A   Event of the first magistrate's being bribed by foreign interests
B   Degree of coincidence of the legislature's interest with the general interest
C   Trustworthiness of the legislature
D   Amount of executive's love of fame
E   Performance by the executive of illustrious military actions
F   Performance by the executive of illustrious civil actions
G   Weakness of executive in resisting legislative encroachments
H   Event of a despot in America
I   Degree of dependence of the executive on the legislature
J   Usurpations of the legislature on the executive
K   Usurpations of the executive on the legislature
L   Palatability of the Constitution to the people
M   Existence of tyranny by the legislature

N   Combination by the most populous states to control the election
O   Appointment of a man of real merit
Q   Amount of checking power of the second branch of the legislature
R   Existence of excessive Senate power
S   Difficulty of finding a suitable court of impeachment other than the Senate
T   Executive's objection to an extension of legislature power
U   Amount of good behavior by executive
V   Event of a majority of electors voting for an incumbent executive
W   Amount of combinations and lies in a popular election
X   Amount of undue influence on the choice of an executive
Y   Degree of division of the legislature
Z   Existence of factions and discontents of particular states
AA Executive's being closely associated with one party in the legislature
BB Amount of cabal in the legislature
CC Event of half of the electors' votes going to characters eminent and generally known
DD Executive's looking forward to being in the legislature
EE Executive's hope of being rewarded with a reappointment
FF Amount of wealth held by the legislators
GG Amount of corruption in the legislature
HH Instability of councils of government
II Occurrence, in the future, of violations of the Constitution
JJ Successfulness of republican government
KK Event of a monarchical government
LL Correctness of formation of the executive
MM Geographical extent of the country
NN Renouncement of the blessings of union
OO Provision of an executive with sufficient vigor to pervade every part of the country

abbreviation used and the wording of the concept, worded as closely to the text as possible. The map itself is shown as Figure 5–1.[2] The map contains every causal assertion coded from the text.

At first glance, the map looks forbidding, but after a few tries, tracing out the arguments is not hard. Arrayed along the left side are the various policy options, that is to say, motions in debate, about which Morris constructed arguments—for example, P7, the policy of having the national legislature elect the executive. On the far right, the variable "American utility" refers to America's best interests, or the good of the country.[3] In between are what can be termed intermediate concepts, posed by Morris as steps in his argument.

It should be noted again that the arrows relate *changes in* the variables, even though reference will usually be made to the variables themselves. An arrow from one point to another is an assertion about the relation between changes in the two variables, whatever absolute values the variables may take. Increases in the amount of corruption (GG), for example, always decrease the country's utility, regardless of the absolute levels of corruption or utility.

A path of arrows connecting several points is a line of argument constructed from various assertions made by Morris. The assertions along any one path may not have been made together as one argument at one time, but the argument as a whole is nonetheless here imputed to Morris. Putting diverse pieces of a policy maker's

[2] For information on the coding process as applied to documents, see Chapter 4 and Appendix 1. For the mathematical properties of a map, see Chapter 3.

[3] There is, of course, some room for questioning whether the delegates really had "American" utility in mind. It could be argued that all of the delegates represented only narrowly defined commercial interests, or that each delegate or class of delegates inescapably represented only certain distinct interests. For our purposes here, however, this problem is not a serious one. We are analyzing the evaluations of a single actor, who spoke as if he had only one overall interest in mind. No problem is raised, then, by using only one utility variable in the map. Even if the utility meant by Morris was "really" that of some special group rather than of the country, correcting for that problem could only change the name of the variable, and not the structure or analysis of his argument, which is our principal subject. We may as well call the variable "American utility," since, for whatever reasons, Morris did phrase his arguments in terms of the public interest, and we can leave any argument about his motives to be settled at some other time.

speech together is fairly standard in political analysis; mapping is simply a formalized way of doing it.

As an example, the map shows that in Morris' view adoption of the policy of choosing the executive by the legislature (P7) causes dependence on the legislature (I), which in turn causes legislative usurpations (J), which in turn are bad for the country (American utility). The result of this line of argument, of course, is that having the executive elected by the legislature is bad for the country.

Take, for example, the effects on American utility of variable G, the weakness of the executive. The weakness of the executive encourages legislative usurpations (J), but it also discourages the emergence of a despot (H). One path gives a reason for supposing that a weak executive would be bad, and the other path gives a reason for supposing that a weak executive would be good. The sum of these is indeterminate, so no clear summary opinion about whether the executive should be weakened or strengthened can be inferred from Morris' cognitive map.[4] It is worth noting that he was not alone in this particular ambivalence; uncertainty about the optimal strength of the executive was a major problem during the whole convention.

The variable "American utility" and the arrows drawn to it are inferred from the source material. Morris did not, any more than the rest of us do, explicitly calculate his or America's utility function. But he clearly had opinons about what was good or bad for the country, and like the rest of us he used evaluative expressions to make his opinions known. For this map, the inferences and assumptions about American utility are based on those specified in the coding rules provided in Appendix 1. Any statement in which Morris applied clearly evaluative attributes to a variable was inferred to be an assertion connecting that variable to utility, and variables with a clear evaluative meaning, such as "legislative tyranny," were presumed to have the apparent relation to utility.

For the purposes of this map, all the assertions are shown to have known, definite values. In fact, however, Morris made several of his assertions conditional upon the state of other factors. For

---

[4] The language Morris used in this passage suggests he was possibly thinking of an intermediate range of strength that would be just right for the executive; an executive either too weak or too strong would be bad. In order to handle this interpretation, we would have to have a means for treating simple non-monotonic relationships.

example, he felt that reeligibility would be appropriate only if the term of office were short. Some of the conditioning variables were outside factors that can be presumed to have a certain value—for example, that the country is large rather than small. Others were policy variables, such as the length of the President's term. For these latter variables the values were assumed to be those that Morris himself wanted them to be.[5]

One obvious characteristic of the map is that it can be drawn to have a left-to-right flow throughout. Thus drawn, it shows no backward arrows, no feedback loops. In graph theory terms, the map is *acyclical*.

Another characteristic is that in many cases there are obviously two or more paths between points. Thus the policy of having the President elected by the people (P5) affects American utility by strengthening the President (G), by leading to the election of a man of real merit (O), and by other paths as well. In this map there are hundreds of such pairs of alternative paths—a measure of Morris' complexity.

What happens if two alternate paths show different relations between the same two concepts? Cognitive mapping handles the problem in a way that reflects ordinary logic. For example, the two arguments "A promotes B" and "A does not inhibit B" can plausibly be combined for the conclusion "A promotes B," and this is what the mapping system would conclude. But two arguments like "C promotes D" and "C discourages D" leave any answer possible, and the mapping conventions adopted here register the result as ambivalent (denoted by "a"). Resolving the ambivalence would require some knowledge of the relative magnitudes of the relations, but that is not incorporated into the present coding system.

If a pair of alternate paths does not yield an ambivalent result, then this is said to be a *balanced pair of paths*. By definition, a single pair of paths is either balanced or not, but the map or some part of it may be characterized by various measures of overall or local balance.

---

[5] Alternative assumptions are of course possible—for example, the values that Morris thought prevailed among the members of his audience, or the values that the convention finally chose. For the first, little evidence is available. The search for evidence would require a reanalysis of all the arguments for a differentiation between what Morris thought and what he was merely saying to please others. As for the second assumption, Morris could not have known those values. The assumption made here has at least some plausibility to it, and the evidence for the values is readily at hand.

A measure of the balance in Morris' map has been made here by counting alternative paths between each pair of points on the map and noting how many of the possible pairs of paths are balanced. There are 428 pairs of paths; of these, 239, or only 56 percent, are balanced.

Another way of seeing the pattern of balance is to analyze not the relations between all pairs of arguments, but rather the relation of stated direct policy conclusions to the patterns of intermediate argument. A delegate's policy conclusions could best be measured by how he votes on various issues, but, unfortunately, there is no certain evidence as to how Morris voted, since individual votes were not recorded. The votes were recorded only by state. The votes were by voice, however, so it may be assumed that straightforward statements of support or opposition made during the discussion would be the same as the votes. Therefore, such statements by Morris have been taken as the indicator of his conclusions for purposes of comparison with his supporting argumentation. Each such statement would appear on the map as an arrow from a policy variable directly to American utilty, but these statements have been left off of the map for simplicity.

There were only six policy variables for which Morris expressed both a direct policy position and intermediate argumentation. (Those for which he expressed only a direct position, without argumentation, have also been left off of the map.) One of these six, the impeachment provision, cannot be used for the comparison, since Morris made inconsistent position statements about it. The calculation was therefore made for the remaining five policy variables, and the results are shown in Table 5–1.

There seems to be more balance by this measure. Some 74 percent of the intermediate arguments are in agreement with the stated policy positions to which they apply. In each case, Morris took the policy position he had supported with the higher number of causal paths. However, he clearly did see difficulties, or trade-offs, that had to be made for most of the policies; and only one of the five policy conclusions is free of contrary argumentation.

These figures and the earlier figure of overall balance are influenced somewhat by the artifacts of the mapping process itself, but this influence was quite small. For example, the putting together of arguments from speeches on different days seemed to have little effect. The balanced and the imbalanced combinations alike contain statements made on the same day and statements made on different days, in no recognizable pattern. Nor did problems arise

105

TABLE 5–1

AGREEMENT OF POLICY CONCLUSIONS WITH INTERMEDIATE
ARGUMENTS

Policy variable	Stated policy position	Number of paths in agreement with stated position	Number of paths not in agreement with stated position
Having the people elect the President (P5)	for	8	4
Having the legislature elect the President (P7)	against	10	3
Having the electors chosen by lot from among the legislators (P8)	for	6	2
Having a rotation of periods of eligibility (P11)	against	8	4
Having the President ineligible for reelection (P12)	against	5	0
		37	13
		74%	26%

through combining or differentiating concept variables that were
close in meaning. Although combinations of paths were created
or destroyed with each such recoding, the numbers were small,
since the context and intent of Morris' remarks was usually clear.
No net effect toward balance or imbalance was noted.

INTERPRETATIONS

How can a map like this one be used and interpreted? Without
going further into the mathematics of graph theory, one can still
make several useful observations. These pertain to the usefulness
of the map in summarizing Morris' arguments and their interrelationships, and its significance for further informing the analysis of
decision-making processes. In both areas one finds an admixture
of elements that may simply reflect a personal style of argumentation.

Any political or historical review of a person's work—be it a career or a speech—tries to put separate elements together for comparison, contrast, and summary. Cognitive mapping can be used as a systematic complement to other such modes of analysis, providing its own particular insights and convenience of summary.

For example, an inspection of the map reveals that some variables are obviously more central, or important, to the logical structure than others are. The concept of the dependence of the executive on the legislature (I) and the concept of the weakness of the executive (G) are good examples. Concept I is affected by more variables than any other intermediate variable; it is the only intermediate variable that is a primary factor in all four areas of policy; a higher number of alternative paths to utilty stem from it than from any other intermediate concept. Only variable G directly affects as many variables. The concept of good behavior by the executive (U) and the concept of cabal in the legislature (BB) stand out as other intermediate concepts of importance. Analysis by other modes—say by measuring the strength of the language used, or by counting the frequency with which a concept is mentioned—might give different perspectives on what Morris said, but the detailed logical structure is best seen by this kind of mapping.

When a central or much-used concept is seen to have conflicting impacts on utility, the repercussions for the rest of the argumentation can readily be examined by the mapping procedure. This is certainly the case for variable G, the weakness of the executive. The uncertainty about how strong or weak the executive should be unbalances the other arguments about impeachment, about dependence on the legislature, about the mode of election, as well as other arguments. Over one-third of the imbalanced pairs of paths counted above may be attributed to this conflict. Another concept that leads to important problems of imbalance is the degree of division in the legislature (Y). Morris fears that such division will lead to intrigue between the factions (BB), the intrigues being bad for the country. Yet he argues elsewhere that the legislature could not have much influence on an election by the people (X) because it would be divided against itself (Y). Faction, it appears, makes the legislature both fearsome and impotent.

Mapping will also systematically bring out the various individual sources of imbalance. For example, look at concept variable P11—the suggestion by another delegate that the President be allowed to serve only six years out of any twelve. Morris introduces two possibilities: either the executive will look forward to being in office again (EE), or he will look forward to being in the legislature (DD). These are not mutually exclusive for a President facing six years of forced retirement. Connected with what Morris said on other occasions about currying favor with the legislature (T, a variable with negative impact on utility), and hopes for reappointment (EE, a variable with positive impact on utility), they yield a mixed picture of what Morris thinks will happen.

How is the imbalance found here to be interpreted? To charge all of it up to outright inconsistency is too harsh, although appropriate in a few instances. In most cases, as with the dilemmas about the strength of the President, the imbalance reflects, rather, Morris' awareness of trade-offs: simultaneous advantages and disadvantages of a given concept. The term "inconsistency" might better be restricted to cases in which a policy conclusion goes against all of the intermediate argumentation.

It will be noted that almost all of Morris' assertions have simple positive or negative values. The values "$\oplus$" and "$\ominus$" were used only 4 times and 2 times, respectively, and the value "u" was used only once;[6] while the values "$+$" and "$-$" were used 40 times and 37 times, respectively. Here Morris seems to present quite a contrast with Marling, the policy maker analyzed in Chapter 4; a glance at that map reveals how much more Marling used the indefinite signs. This result could conceivably have several sources and interpretations. It is possible that differences in the coders' interpretations of the signs of linkages led to the result, but this is unlikely, since the rules and procedures used here were originally developed for work on Marling and give a reliability measure of 97 percent for the signs (see Chapter 4). It could also be that the result stems from the difference between direct and indirect discourse—that is, the difference between the verbatim transcripts

[6] The one ambivalent value occurred as the combination of two contradictory statements made by Morris. On September 4, he concurred with Madison that the Senate would have de facto control over the election if it were allowed to choose from among the highest five candidates chosen by the electors. But on September 6 he declared, in response to James Wilson, that the Senators "were limited to five candidates, previously nominated to them, with a probability of being barred altogether by the successful ballot of the electors. Here surely was no increase of power" (Madison, 1898, p. 670). Morris' approaches to opposing conclusions were generally more intricate.

for Marling and the summary notes for Morris. Perhaps the difference reveals a difference in style of argumentation between eighteenth-century Americans and twentieth-century Britons, or between small operating committees and large political assemblies, or between Morris and Marling as personalities. Given Morris' reputation for oratory, the latter possibility seems rather likely.

Cognitive mapping was used in Chapter 4 to suggest how policy makers like those on the British Eastern Committee simplify the complex world in which they must make decisions. Axelrod suggests that they may simplify their complex world by using cognitive maps that are acyclic and balanced. He also notes that several other hypotheses about cognitive simplification do not explain the British Eastern Committee results as well. The work elaborated here can help flesh out the role of cognitive mapping in studying the situation of the policy maker.

The completely acyclic nature of Morris' arguments was already commented upon; this result is in strict agreement with Axelrod's finding for the members of the British Eastern Committee. Note that this result, like Axelrod's, refers to a policy maker presenting his views aloud and spontaneously. It would be of great interest to determine more exactly under what other conditions those who set policy think only acyclically, especially since the cyclical nature of causal chains in the real world has been amply demonstrated.

The finding of nearly complete balance for the members of the British Eastern Committee is not replicated here. The supposed advantage of balance as a simplifying device is that no more than one path from a policy variable to utility need be kept in mind, since it will automatically express the same value as the other paths. For Morris this advantage was lost for about 80 percent of his policy conclusions, as Table 5–1 shows. The advantage seems lost in the overall figure of 56 percent, too. Although more imbalance in this map would be possible mathematically (the maximum possible will vary with the structure of the map), nonetheless it must surely be a complication for Morris to have roughly half of all the possible pairs of arguments between various concepts coming up in disagreement.

In the absence of other maps for other speakers, it is hard to suggest why there is less balance for Morris than for the members of the British Eastern Committee. Some of the factors adduced earlier—such as cultural and personal differences—could hold the explanation. It needs to be kept in mind, surely, that the choice of Morris as a subject was in part a deliberate search for imbalance. Pending further studies, then, the conditions that govern the presence of balance in this kind of policy situation remain an open question.

Another interesting feature of the map is that every policy variable can be related to utility in as few as two steps, and no path from a policy variable to utility is more than four steps long. Only a few of the intermediate variables require more than two steps to be related to utility. The map is extensive "vertically," in that a great many topics and policies are considered, but to each of them are attached only short chains of argument. In that sense, Morris' arguments are revealed to be rather simple ones. The same property can be found in the map for Marling, in Chapter 4. It would be worth considering whether this is a simplifying mechanism used by other decision makers as well.

Any exhaustive comparison with other arguments made in the now huge literature on decision making would be presumptuous, but a few comments may be ventured about the alternative hypotheses considered by Axelrod in Chapter 4. What evidence do the convention and Mr. Morris provide with respect to those hypotheses?

One hypothesis, argued by Cyert and March (1963) in their analysis of decision making in the firm, is that executives focus selectively on one goal, or a few goals, at a time, as circumstances thrust first one goal and then another into prominence. Conflict between goals and the complexity of multiple goals are avoided because simultaneous consideration of the goals can be avoided. However, at the convention each proposal—the reeligibility of the President, for example—was weighed in terms of all goals at once. Consider this excerpt from a speech by Morris on the subject of goals: "The evils to be guarded against in this case are—first, the undue influence of the legislature; secondly, instability of councils; thirdly, misconduct in office. To guard against the first, we run into the second evil. We adopt a rotation of executive office which produces instability of councils. To avoid Scylla we fall into Charybdis" (Madison, 1898, p. 431). He goes on to argue that the policy of rotation (no President to serve more than six years out of any twelve) wouldn't even solve the first evil as supposed, and that the impeachment power necessitated by the third goal, avoiding misconduct, made election by the legislature undesirable. This line of argument is hardly the work of a man who focuses on one goal at a time.

110

A second hypothesis is that decision makers choose among alternatives on the basis of their contributions to some one goal that is considered most important, and they resort to the consideration of other goals only if two or more alternatives rank the same with respect to the primary goal. The process is like arranging words alphabetically in a dictionary, and the term "lexicographic" has come to be applied to this form of decision making. Bonham and Shapiro assume lexicographic decision making of their individual subjects, in Chapter 6. Taylor (1970) has written more fully and more mathematically on the consequences of this assumption for collective decision making, such as would obtain on a civic board of some kind. Certainly one can find this kind of decision making in the convention. The delegates did explicitly consider "fundamentals" (reported out July 26) before moving on to the consideration of the special committee report on "detail" (taken up August 6). Morris did state at one point that he was indifferent to how the executive might be chosen, so long as he served for a term of "good behavior." But again, the more frequent impression (short of an exhaustive categorization and computation) is that the delegates were weighing, for each alternative, all their objectives at once.

A third hypothesis is put forth by Herbert Simon (1957) as part of his consideration of "the principle of bounded rationality." Simon argues that decision makers do not try to optimize among all alternatives, for that process entails a substantial effort and cost. Rather they "satisfice," by establishing criteria of what is "good enough" and ceasing to examine alternatives as soon as one is found that meets the criteria. Agreements at the convention were by majority vote; delegates chose among policies in part by taking cues from the satisfaction level of other delegates to whom they deferred. These are predetermined satisficing criteria, to be sure. Yet Madison's notes of the meetings, and letters written by others years afterwards, are filled wth testimony of the delegates' desires to do the very best job they could, and their awareness of their important role in history. Propositions already voted on were often brought up again for reconsideration, for example—a procedure provided for in the rules established at the outset of the convention. So a drive to achieve the optimum solution, and not merely a satisfactory one, seems to have characterized the convention.

Thus these three hypotheses are not much help in explaining the nature of the deliberations at the convention. It seems safe to concur in this case with the negative report on the applicability of the hypotheses made by Axelrod in Chapter 4.

Granted, the Constitutional Convention was by no means an ordinary decision situation, such as those most of the literature is struggling to understand. This gathering was not an ongoing business firm, or a standing policy committee, or the office of a city official. This convention was rather (as James Wilson claimed afterwards, with excusable hyperbole) the first time in six thousand years of history that a people had assembled to decide calmly and deliberately the form of government by which they would bind themselves (Farrand, 1913, p. 62). However it is described, the convention was an unusual instance of decision making. That the three hypotheses about simplification just reviewed fell victim to the complex needs of that situation is thus perhaps understandable. That the hypothesis about the absence of cycles, put forth in Chapter 4, survived this test as well as the more routine situation reported there, is perhaps some estimate of its importance.

A summary view is in order. The first two hypotheses just reviewed assert that the decision maker simplifies by keeping all but a few goals out of his thinking. The third hypothesis asserts that he may have many goals in mind, but simplifies by not pursuing maximum satisfaction of all of them. The balance hypothesis claims that he may have many goals, but simplifies by not admitting that any one policy may involve opposing effects on utility. None of these hypotheses seems to hold fully for the case of Gouverneur Morris.

A previous hypothesis that does hold for Morris asserts that a policy maker simplifies by not thinking about the possibility of cyclical interactions among the variables that make up his world. In more fashionable terminology, he ignores the possibility of feedback.

A further hypothesis has been suggested here, namely, that the decision maker also simplifies by keeping only short paths of argument in mind. This hypothesis is consistent with the map for Marling in Chapter 4, as well as the map for Morris.

Cognitive mapping as an exercise, and a map itself as the final product, thus permit a systematic analysis of the causal arguments in a text, leading to an awareness of structural aspects of the arguments and of the decisions that would not otherwise be clear.

CHAPTER SIX

Explanation of the Unexpected: The Syrian Intervention in Jordan in 1970—*G. Matthew Bonham* and *Michael Shapiro*

This study capitalizes on a fortuitous circumstance. The authors set out to construct a computer simulation of how a foreign policy expert uses his causal beliefs to explain events. They sought to answer what might be called the explanation problem: how can a person's cognitive map be used to predict his explanation of new events? In June 1970, in order to generate suitable documentary material, they asked several experts to play the roles of advisors to the President in a crisis game based on a scenario about Russian missiles being discovered in Syria. The authors used the transcripts from this game to derive the cognitive map of one of the players, a Middle East expert.

Three months later came the real crisis of Black September, when Palestinian commandos were attacked and defeated by Jordanian forces. Syria intervened with her army and air force, but withdrew after three days of combat with Jordan and pressure from Israel and the United States. The authors took the cognitive map derived from the hypothetical crisis and applied it to the actual situation of the related but quite different crisis. They found a striking correspondence between the predicted explanation of the expert and the explanation he gave when asked about the actual crisis three years later. This demonstrates that not only are the structural properties of a cognitive map quite stable, but even the specific concepts and causal links between them can be quite stable. It also demonstrates that a cognitive map derived in one context can be useful in understanding the response of a decision maker in a new and even an unanticipated context.

An earlier version of a paper delivered at the International Studies Association Meeting, San Juan, March 1971. This research was supported by grants from the Institute of International Studies, University of California, Berkeley, and the National Science Foundation (Grant GS–36558). The authors are grateful to Robert Axelrod, Steven Brams, Ernst B. Haas, George Kent, George Nozicka, and Stu Ross for their helpful suggestions.

In June 1970 a group of foreign policy specialists participated in a gaming exercise that had as its focus an imaginary crisis in the Middle East. We intended to use the exercise as a source of data for constructing a computer simulation model of policy decision making, which was in the early stages of development. In September 1970, however, a real crisis occurred in the Middle East, the Syrian intervention in Jordan, which had some resemblance to the imaginary crisis: both crises involved Syria's relations with its neighbors, and in both crises the United States was uncertain about the intentions of the Soviet Union. The timing of the crisis in Jordan was fortunate for our research, because it enabled us to use the data from the gaming exercise not only to develop the computer model, but also to test the model's ability to predict and explain the reaction of a foreign policy advisor to a real situation.

In this paper we will use this totally unexpected crisis of September 1970 to compare the results of a computer simulation of a policy advisor's reactions to his actual reactions in that crisis. First, we will summarize the main elements of the simulation model. Second, we will explain how we used the gaming exercise to obtain data for the simulation. Third, we will describe the operation of the model in a simulation of a foreign policy advisor's reactions to the Jordanian crisis, using only data collected in the June gaming exercise. Fourth, we will compare the results of this computer simulation to an interview we conducted with him shortly after running the simulation. Finally, we will discuss the next steps we plan to take in the development and further testing of the model, as well as possible policy applications.

MAJOR ELEMENTS OF THE MODEL

The major theoretical presupposition of our research is that beliefs of foreign policy decision makers are central to the study of decision outputs, and probably account for much of the variance in international politics. Beliefs represent both the congealed experiences of the decision maker and his expectations about the decision environment. In the former sense, they are his decisions about the significance of past "events," and, in the latter sense, they orient him to present and future "events." In the decision-making process the belief system as a whole acts like a template for receiving and channeling information, and for relating possible policy

114

options to perceptions about the intentions and behavior of other nations, as well as to the policy objectives of the decision maker.[1]

Representation of Beliefs

A decision maker's cognitive map is represented in our simulation model as a map of causal linkages between four types of concepts: "affective concepts" (A-concepts) refer to immediate policy objectives of a decision maker; "cognitive concepts" (C-concepts) denote beliefs of a decision maker about events that occur in the international system; "policy concepts" (P-concepts) reflect possible alternatives or options from which a decision maker selects policy recommendations; and "value concepts" (V-concepts) are abstract values, such as national security, that a decision maker tries to satisfy. The linkages between concepts carry either positive or negative valence, which distinguishes the nature of the causal relationships that are perceived by the decision maker. Taken together, the concepts and the causal linkages between them form a "cognitive map" of a decision maker's belief system.

Our method of representing beliefs of decision makers reflects the proposition that decision makers tend to believe that international events are related causally, and thus try to infer causal relationships underlying these events and the actions of other nations, even when there is little or no evidence of a causal nature. A decision maker's motivation to exercise control over his environment leads him to attribute causal relationships to the behavior of others in the international system.

Amplification of Beliefs

In our model of foreign policy decision making, five processes are invoked when a decision maker is confronted with a new international situation that may require a response from his government: initial amplification, a search for antecedents, a search for consequences, a search for policy alternatives, and policy choice. These processes will be explained in a nontechnical fashion. For a more precise description of our simulation procedures, see Appendix 4 by Nozicka, Bonham, and Shapiro.

During the *initial amplification* process, the decision maker attempts to place a novel international event or series of events

[1] For further discussion of our theoretical approach, see Shapiro and Bonham (1973).

115

into the context of his experiences. This is a process of relating various components of an international situation to existing beliefs about the nations and actions involved, so that the situation can be understood. It is similar to the cognitive problem that Abelson (1969b, pp. 136–139) has studied with his ideology machine, a computer simulation that makes novel events understandable by referring them to a structure that has interpreted them in the past: a set of beliefs about past events, beliefs that are stored at different levels of abstraction.

At the initial amplification stage of our model, new international developments are introduced into the simulation in order to activate concepts in the decision maker's belief system. When a new situation is introduced, concepts in the decision maker's cognitive map which most closely correspond to that situation are "highlighted," and this information is stored for further use. Operationally, initial amplification is accomplished externally through the intervention of the researcher, who codes the event in categories contained in the cognitive mapping. The event is then represented in the form of a list of concepts to be highlighted in the cognitive map.

The second decision-making process is a *search for antecedents*. After the initial amplification, the decision maker searches his cognitive map for prior causes of the current international situation; for example, the intentions of another state that led it to pursue a policy that caused the new situation confronting our decision maker. These prior causes appear in cognitive maps as "antecedent paths," consisting of concepts and arrows, which lead *to* initially highlighted concepts. Once the first concept of an antecedent path has been located, we look for the concept directly prior to it, and so on, until at last we reach a concept with no prior causes—the beginning of the antecedent path. At this point we store the antecedent path, suppress the portions of the cognitive map unique to this path, and repeat the process to obtain other antecedent paths.

Operationally, the search for antecedents is accomplished by the use of an *adjacency matrix,* which is a square matrix with one row and one column for each concept in a cognitive map (Harary, Norman, and Cartwright, 1965). A non-zero entry in an adjacency matrix indicates that two concepts are directly connected by an arrow. For example, Figure 6–1 shows the adjacency matrix A for digraph D, a cognitive map consisting of four concepts,

FIGURE 6–1.

A Directed Graph and Its Adjacency Matrix

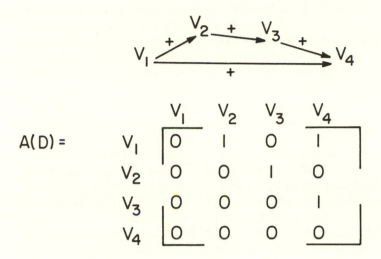

V_1, V_2, V_3, V_4. The non-zero entry in the first row and second column of the adjacency matrix A tells us that there is an arrow from V_1 to V_2. The zero entry in the first row and third column of the matrix tells us that V_1 and V_3 are not directly connected by an arrow.

After the decision maker's cognitive map is transformed into an adjacency matrix, the computer searches for antecedent paths of initially highlighted concepts by working its way through the columns of the adjacency matrix. For example, suppose that a concept represented by point V_4 in Figure 6–1 becomes highlighted by a new situation. Looking at the column for V_4 in the adjacency matrix, we find that there are arrows leading to V_4 from V_1 and V_3. Inspection of the column for V_1 reveals that there are no other arrows leading to V_1; hence the arrow from V_1 to V_4 is one antecedent path. The non-zero entry in the column for V_3, however, indicates the presence of an arrow from V_2 to V_3. By checking the column for V_2, we find an arrow from V_1 to V_2. Hence, the path from V_1 to V_4 by way of V_2 and V_3 is another antecedent path in this cognitive map.[2]

[2] When the sign of the relationships computed over one antecedent path differs from the sign computed over another antecedent path which shares

117

Once all of the antecedent paths have been found, the computer searches for antecedent paths with some plausibility. A plausible antecedent path contains at least one relationship that has "historical support." In constructing a cognitive map, we tag the relationships a decision maker has supported with a historical analogy or reference, so the computer can discover whether or not a path is plausible, in terms of historical support, by simply checking for tagged relationships. Those paths that have historical support are highlighted and stored, while the remaining, implausible, antecedent paths are not used for the remainder of the simulation.

A decision maker's belief system is usually dense enough for him to find plausible antecedents of a policy situation, but there are occasions when he does not. If all of the antecedent paths in a decision maker's belief system are implausible, then the decision maker begins searching for inductive support. The simulated decision maker scans his memory and attempts to find similar past events that might provide some insight about the current situation. During the search the relevance of historical events is determined for the decision maker by the categories or constructs through which he views the international system. He scans his memory and chooses the historical event with the most concepts in common with the new situation. If more than one historical event has the same number of shared concepts, the most recent event is selected. The search then proceeds lexicographically. If the first historical event leads to the selection of a plausible antecedent among two or more possible paths, the search is ended. If this event does not successfully continue or terminate the decision process, a second historical event is selected, using the same decision rules, and so on, until an event is found that overcomes the uncertainty that led to the inductive search process.[3] This procedure can also be

---

two or more concepts, imbalance is said to exist. In Figure 6–1, for example, the two antecedent paths V_1–V_4 and V_1–V_2–V_3–V_4 are balanced, since a positive relation exists between V_1 and V_4 over either path. Had the sign of the relation between V_1 and V_4 been negative on one of the paths, however, imbalance would have existed between the two paths. We resolve imbalance by suppressing the antecedent path that is less "central" to the decision maker's belief structure; that is, the path that has fewer arrows coming into it. The cognitive centrality for each antecedent and consequent path located is computed as the sum of the total degrees of its component concepts. For further discussion, see Shapiro and Bonham (1973, pp. 167–168) and Appendix 4.

[3] Alker and Greenberg (1971) use a similar inductive search mechanism in their simulation of U.N. decision making. The situational characteristics of a dispute lead to a search for precedents and then to the choice of dif-

invoked at later stages of the simulation; for example, if the decision maker needs to find additional consequent paths or policy alternatives.

The third process of the simulation, *a search for consequences,* is an attempt by the decision maker to anticipate where a situation will lead, if his government does not act. Once the decision maker has an idea about the prior causes of a situation, he searches for possible consequences for the behavior of other states and his own policy objectives. In a cognitive map, consequences appear as paths leading to a decision maker's policy values from concepts that were highlighted during the first two processes, initial amplification and the search for antecedents. The procedure for locating "consequent paths" is parallel to the process followed for antecedent paths, except that here the direction of the search is reversed, and we try to find all paths leading *from* the highlighted concepts rather than paths leading *to* such concepts.[4]

Operationally, the search for consequences is also accomplished by working through the adjacency matrix, although, in this instance, the model looks along the rows of the matrix, instead of the columns. A non-zero entry in the row for a given concept indicates the presence of an arrow to a concept that is a consequence of the first one.

Policy Search and Choice Processes

The fourth process of the model is a search for relevant policy alternatives. At this point in the simulation, the decision maker looks for policy alternatives that are embedded in his explanation of the situation and that might give him some control over events in the international system. He hopes that the choice of a policy alternative will lead to changes in events, which, as a result, will have a favorable impact on his policy values. If the decision maker is unable to find any policy alternatives that will give him some leverage, then he resorts again to an inductive search of past events, in order to find an analogous situation.

Operationally, the search for policy alternatives is quite easily accomplished. After a decision maker's explanation of a situation has been sorted out, the process continues with a search for all

---

ferent levels of U.N. involvement. Learning takes place in the simulation as the result of the success or failure of the level of involvement selected.

[4] Although consequent paths are checked for imbalance, as in the case of antecedent paths, no attempt is made to eliminate paths that lack historical support, since consequences refer to developments that might occur at some point in the future.

P-concepts (policy alternatives) that are directly connected to all antecedent and consequent paths. This information is then stored for the next stage.

The *choice of a policy alternative* from among a number of possible options is the final decision-making process in our simulation. At this point, we follow the paths from the possible policy alternatives to the policy values of the decision maker, and calculate which alternative or combination of alternatives will result in a maximum gain in values. The signs of the causal linkages are important here, because we must calculate how each policy alternative will affect every policy value to which it is connected. There are, of course, a variety of decision models one can employ to make such calculations. Presently, we employ a lexicographic decision calculus, which assumes that the decision maker first uses his most important policy value to see if the alternatives affect it differently. If this value does not distinguish between alternatives, he then moves to his second-ranking value, and so on, until he gets a value that distinguishes one alternative as better than the others.[5]

Operationally, we use a matrix of direct effects or *valency matrix* to trace the connections between policy alternatives and policy values. A valency matrix, by preserving the signed relationships between concepts, makes it possible to determine whether or not there is a positive or negative path from a given policy alternative to one or more policy values. By successively raising the valency matrix to powers 2, 3, 4, . . . , n−1, where n is number of concepts in the acyclic cognitive map, the computer can search for the signed relationships between policy alternatives and policy values. Once this is accomplished, it is easy to use the lexicographic decison calculus and print out the policy alternatives in order of decreasing importance.

THE GAMING EXERCISE

In June 1970, we formed two groups of foreign policy specialists, confronted them with an imaginary international crisis, and asked them to make policy recommendations about the crisis situation. During the deliberations of these specialists, we observed how they

[5] The assumption that high-ranking values are so important that there can be no trade-offs makes some sense in the field of foreign policy decision making. For example, if a given alternative does not satisfy national security values, then it must be rejected, regardless of any other values it may satisfy.

brought their beliefs to bear on the crisis, and how they decided on a course of action. The games also provided us with an information base: elements of a belief system for our computer simulation of foreign policy decision making. We used transcripts of the discussions that took place in the games and interviews with game participants to discover some of the substantive concepts of the specialists, construct maps of their cognitive systems, and make rank-order lists of their policy objectives.[6]

Our foreign policy specialists participated in a game developed by Steinbruner (1970), called EXCON III, for the purpose of demonstrating experimentally that individuals who use a "rational" approach to decision making would make policy choices predictably different from individuals who use a "cybernetic" approach. While this game was developed for hypothesis testing, it was also ideally suited to our needs, since the scenario was designed to force the decision makers to make a careful assessment of the intentions of their adversaries before weighing alternative courses of action. In addition, the game materials were sufficiently plausible and rich enough in detail to insure the involvement of senior foreign policy specialists.

Steinbruner's game was designed for an experimental setting, so it differs in important respects from the traditional political game. The participants in the game were organized into teams, as has generally been the case, but the teams were not allowed to communicate or interact in any way with other teams, since such interaction would have reduced experimental control. In addition to removing the interaction among teams, Steinbruner prepared the scenario materials in advance and kept them constant for all teams, except for differences introduced to test the hypothesis. The game was divided into two move periods, which were supposed to take place six months apart (scenario time). Each team acted as a group of special advisors to the President of the United States, and received instructions (in the form of written memoranda) from the "President," who asked for their recommendations and then informed them of his "decision."

[6] Jensen (1966) is one of the few political scientists who has made use of interviews to explore the beliefs of decision makers. He interviewed 89 policy makers in the State Department and Department of Defense, in addition to 82 newspaper correspondents and academicians, to investigate the relationship between the backgrounds and assumptions of decision makers and their ability to predict future events. In addition, Hveem (1972) conducted interviews with 100 members of the foreign policy "elite" in Norway.

The setting of the game was the Middle East in June 1970 (first decision period) and in January 1971 (second decision period):

The first period scenario began with the presentation by the French of a proposal for a Middle East settlement involving Israeli withdrawal to the borders of May 1967, a demilitarization of border areas, and an international force patrolling border areas. All states of the area in unspecified manner were to be guaranteed the right to exist and passage through the Straits of Tiran. There was no mention of Suez.

In the first period the teams were asked to recommend whether or not the French proposal should be accepted as a basis for formal negotiations involving the four powers (U.S., U.S.S.R., Britain, France) and the states of the area.

After the teams made their recommendations they were told that the "President" rejected the proposal as a basis for negotiations on the grounds that since it was completely unacceptable to Israel, it did not offer a serious chance of improving the situation.

In the second decision period the teams were given evidence that the Soviet and the Syrian regimes had collaborated to introduce tactical nuclear weapons systems into Syria. The teams were given three alternative courses of action based on the assumption that this was true: (1) an air strike against the Syrian bases where the weapons were deployed, (2) military aid to Israel involving "dual-key" control of nuclear weapons and build-up of the U.S. Sixth Fleet, (3) a negotiated settlement along the lines of the French proposal from the first period with a temporary deployment of U.S. forces to guarantee Israeli borders (and, upon withdrawing, to secure similar withdrawal of Soviet weapons). The teams were instructed to choose among these three options and to state the rationale for their choice (Steinbruner, 1970, pp. 41–42).

The major uncertainty in the scenario involved the intentions of the Soviet Union. In the scenario documents provided to the participants, some intelligence experts argued that the Soviets were trying to precipitate a crisis in order to get something like the French proposal accepted, while other experts contended that the Soviet moves signalled a more aggressive period of Soviet policy, and cited as evidence the removal of Kosygin from power in the Soviet Union.

Since we were interested in how decision makers generate policy alternatives, we made one major change in the format of the game. Instead of presenting the three alternatives for dealing with the Soviet missiles at the beginning of the second period, we supplied this information toward the middle of the second period, after the participants had an opportunity to formulate their own alternatives. Moreover, our teams were smaller (three participants instead of five), the amount of time allowed for team discussion was less (two hours instead of three), and our participants were more familiar with Middle East politics (senior scholars with international relations, foreign policy, and area specializations, instead of social science graduate students), than was the case in Steinbruner's experiment.

During and after the two runs of the game that we completed, we collected information from the participants to provide insights into their decision-making behavior. Before the team discussions of the first period we asked the participants (1) to indicate what additional information they would like to have about the objectives and actions of other nations, (2) to state, in order of importance, the objectives the United States ought to pursue in the Middle East and how each objective could best be achieved, and (3) to list the major objectives of France, Israel, Jordan, the Soviet Union, Syria, and the United Arab Republic with respect to the Middle East. Before the team discussions of the second period, we repeated the information question to permit the participants to request further information about the introduction of Soviet nuclear missiles into Syria. Finally, at the end of the second decision period, after the teams had chosen a policy alternative, we asked the participants to recall each of the U.S. objectives they had listed in the first questionnaire, and to estimate how acceptance of the various policy alternatives that they had discussed (including the three alternatives that were contained in the scenario materials) might affect those objectives. In order to facilitate this task we provided rating scales for the policy alternatives, running from +5 (completely achieve the objectives) to −5 (completely block the objectives). These questionnaires, along with complete transcripts of the team discussions and open-ended interviews with the participants after the game, provided the major empirical input into our computer simulation.

COMPUTER SIMULATION OF A FOREIGN
POLICY ADVISER

We are now ready to use the gaming data to simulate responses of a foreign policy specialist to a real, but totally unexpected, crisis. In this simulation we will use only the information obtained in the Middle East game to predict the behavior of the specialist in the Jordanian crisis of September 1970. Then, in the next section, we will compare the results of the simulation to a postcrisis interview with our specialist.

The Cognitive Map

For the simulation of the Jordanian crisis we chose a gaming participant whose area of specialization is the Middle East and who is also an adviser to high officials in the United States Government. In the Middle East game he viewed the missile crisis as part of a pattern of developments in the Middle East resulting from the Arab-Israeli conflict. Arab regimes, he felt, looked to the Soviet Union simply because no other nation or international organization seemed sympathetic to their weakened position resulting from the 1967 War. His policy recommendations were oriented toward a more general, long-term settlement of the Arab-Israeli conflict. He advocated the immediate start of negotiations and use of international auspices to effect a settlement that would touch upon all the relevant sources of grievances in the area:

> Consequently, if we could do something to reassure the Arabs that our policy is not hostile to them and that we do not contemplate, in this century of self-determination, a permanent subjugation of a million or so Arabs to an alien rule, and if we could also reassure the Israelis that the method of their survival and security is not through the continuous occupation of Arab territories, but through reliance on other methods, perhaps we could defuse the situation somewhat, and remove, therefore, the incentive Syria had in inviting the Soviet presence on its territory.
>
> With proper provisions for the security of Israel, through the stationing of U.N. forces with international guarantees, the French proposal might open the road to more dialogue and to less saber-rattling. Consequently, my own recommendation to the President would be, "Mr. President, please reconsider your stand on the French proposal under the present circumstances,

because we can't deal with an illness only by applying ointment to the externals, but by diagnosing the first and real cause of the disturbance."

Statements of the Middle East specialist, such as these, were coded by us using an earlier version of the coding given in Appendix 1. Then, we combined these assertions with data from a questionnaire giving the Middle East specialist's policy values and their rank order. This gave the large digraph, shown in Figure 6–2, which is a representation of the Middle East specialist's cognitive map. This digraph consists of 73 concepts and 115 arrows. P-concepts, or policy alternatives, can be identified on the digraph by the letter "P," e.g., P10; C-concepts, or cognitive concepts, begin with the letter "C," e.g., C21; A-concepts, or specific policy objectives, can be identified by the letter "A," e.g., A44; and V-concepts, or more general policy values, are denoted by "USA" and a number that indicates the relative importance of the value, as perceived by the Middle East specialist, e.g., USA6.[7] See the key to Figure 6–2 for a complete listing of the concepts and their identification numbers. Each arrow in the digraph represents a belief that there is a direct positive or negative causal relationship between two concepts.[8] For example, the positive arrow from concept C4 to concept C37 means that the Middle East specialist believes Arab feelings of frustration are a cause of revolutionary ferment in the Middle East, and the negative arrow from concept C37 to concept C28 means that revolutionary ferment is perceived to have a negative effect on stability in the Middle East.

Clearly, the total number of concepts and linkages in a decision maker's cognitive mapping of the international environment of nations is enormous and difficult to manage at the operational level. In graphing the beliefs of the Middle East specialist, however, we were able to include enough beliefs that are relevant to the Arab-Israeli conflict to provide the basis for a nontrivial simulation. The graph that we show in Figure 6–2 is, of coure, only a subgraph of a much larger digraph representing many other concepts and causal beliefs about international politics.[9]

[7] These policy values, as well as the rankings, were obtained from a questionnaire that was completed by the Middle East specialist.

[8] The digraph for the Middle East specialist is completely balanced.

[9] Some concepts in the decision makers' cognitive mapping play less complex roles than others. Using digraph terminology, concept C29 is a "transmitter," in that it only causes other events. Concept C25 is a "receiver," in

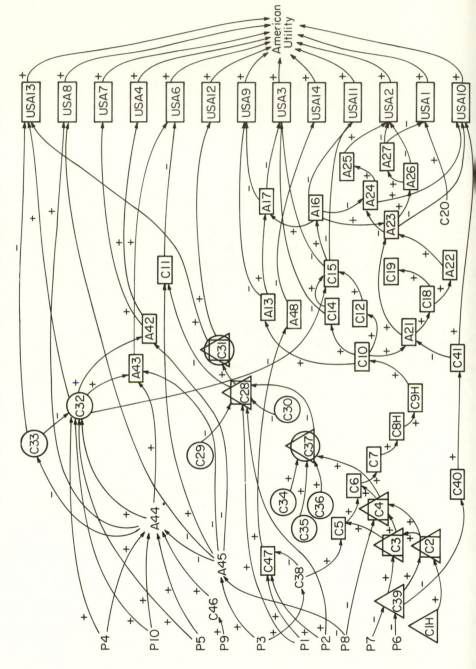

FIGURE 6–2.

Cognitive Map of Middle East Specialist

showing the concepts that were: (1) initially highlighted (circles), (2) part of the highest-ranking
explanation (triangles), and (3) part of the highest-ranking implicatory path (rectangles)

Key to Figure 6–2

P-Concepts

P1   Commit U.S. land forces in Middle East
P2   Commit U.S. naval forces in Middle East
P3   Supply military aid to Israel
P4   Reduce political support for Israel
P5   Reduce military aid to Israel
P6   Convince Israel that security can't be achieved by occupation
P7   Support stationing of U.N. forces
P8   Reassure Arabs that U.S. policy is not hostile
P9   Offer military aid to Arab states
P10 Project a friendly image to Arab states

C-Concepts

C1H Weakness of Arabs
C2   Defeat of Arabs by Israel
C3   Occupation of Arab territory by Israel
C4   Arab feelings of frustration
C5   Arab perception of threat
C6   Arab openness to offers of military aid
C7   Arab requests for military aid
C8H Offers of military aid by Soviet Union
C9H Acceptance of Soviet aid by military-minded generals
C10 Arms supplied by Soviet Union
C11 Soviet presence in Middle East
C12 Friendly relations with Soviet Union
C14 Soviet penetration in Middle East
C15 Close alignment with Soviet Union
C18 Introduction of nuclear weapons
C19 Pattern of proliferation in world
C20 Balance of power in world
C28 Stability in Middle East
C29 * Intraregional feuds
C30 * Militant Pan-Arabism
C31 * Internal law and order
C32 * Moderate Arab regimes
C33 * Radical dictatorships
C34 * Nationalist radicalism
C35 * Indecisive leadership
C36 * Communist radicalism

C37 * Revolutionary ferment
C38 Israeli military strength
C39 Israel's conception of security through occupation of territory
C40 Evacuation of Arab territory by Israel
C41 Dialogue between Israel and Arabs
C46 Acceptance of American aid by military-minded generals
C47 Direct U.S. entanglement in Middle East

A-Concepts

A13 Arab dependence on Soviet Union
A16 Polarization in Middle East
A17 Virtual satellization of Arab states
A21 Escalation of conflict in Middle East
A22 Likelihood of a spark
A23 Possibility of war in Middle East
A24 Peace in intraregional relations
A25 Peace in international relations
A26 Brink in world situation
A27 World War III
A42 American assets in Arab world
A43 American influence in Arab world
A44 Friendly relations between Arabs and United States
A45 Alienation of Arabs from United States
A48 Dissension in United States

V-Concepts

USA1   United States security
USA2   Avoidance of World War III
USA3   Prevention of Soviet penetration in Middle East
USA4   Access to oil
USA5   Access to air/sea routes
USA6   United States presence in Middle East
USA7   Protection of American cultural interests in Middle East
USA8   Governments in Third World friendly to United States
USA9   Political independence of Middle Eastern governments
USA10 Peace in Middle East
USA11 Avoidance of polarization in Middle East
USA12 Progressive development of countries in Middle East
USA13 Democratic political structures in Middle East
USA14 Avoidance of dissension over foreign policy in United States

* Highlighted concept.

The Jordanian Crisis

According to press accounts in the *New York Times,* the Jordanian crisis developed in the late summer of 1970, when Jordanian army units and Bedouins loyal to Hussein moved against the Palestinian commandos, who apparently wanted more freedom to make attacks on Israel. In early September, the commandos struck back at army posts in Amman and northern Jordan. On September 16, King Hussein installed a new military government and ordered it to cope with the situation "with appropriate effort, firmness, and fortitude to restore security, order and stability," and from September 17 to 19 the Jordanian army carried out an assault against the positions of the commandos. This attack by the king's forces triggered limited intervention by Syria, one of the most vocal supporters of the commando movement. During a three-day assault, a force reported to consist of 250 Syrian tanks, backed by heavy artillery, crossed the border between Syria and Jordan and engaged Hussein's army. On September 20, with Syrian forces continuing to invade Jordanian territory, King Hussein appealed to the United States and Great Britain for support. On September 22, the Jordanian army and air force launched a counterattack against the commandos and Syrian tanks, and shortly afterwards, the Syrian vehicles withdrew across the border.

The first reported concern about the Jordanian situation in Washington was on September 16. At this time President Nixon's Special Action Group met and decided that forceful support to Hussein was not necessary because the Jordanian army was loyal to the king and was sufficient to cope with the commandos. Nevertheless, on September 18, President Nixon warned that the United States "is prepared to intervene directly in the Jordanian war, should Syria and Iraq enter the conflict and tip the balance against Government forces loyal to Hussein." On the same day, the Department of Defense announced a move to bolster naval forces in the Eastern Mediterranean and to deploy more C–130 transport aircraft at strategic points in Europe. On September 20, the Secretary of State warned Syria to end immediately its intervention in Jordan, and U.S. naval forces were moved into position in the Eastern Mediterranean and airborne troops in Europe were put

---

that it is caused by other concepts but causes nothing itself. Most other concepts in Figure 6–2 are ordinary points in that they are both causes and effects, and there are no "isolates" or concepts that are completely unrelated to others in the cognitive mapping.

"on notice." On September 21, these forces were put "on alert" for two possible actions: (1) the evacuation of U.S. citizens in Jordan, and (2) an air attack on Syrian tanks operating in Jordan. On September 22, with the Jordanian counterattack under way, the United States announced no new movement of forces already alerted, and on September 23, the United States confirmed the withdrawal of the Syrian tanks, thus ending the crisis.

In addition to a show of force, the United States undertook other initiatives during the crisis. On September 20, Washington asked the Soviet Union to impress on the Syrians the dangers of the situation and the necessity for withdrawing their forces. Moscow responded the next day that it was already urging the Syrians to withdraw their forces, and asked the United States to restrain Israel. The United States was concerned about the possibility that Israel might intervene with tanks and troops to repel Syrian forces. American officials believed that air intervention by Israel was not likely to trigger a reaction from Egypt, but they felt that ground intervention would raise the spectre of another "land grab" and result in an expansion of the war. Apparently in order to forestall Israel's use of ground forces in the conflict, the United States supported a plan for a coordinated air action:

> The plan envisioned an Israeli attack on the Syrian tank forces that had entered Jordan, if it appeared that King Hussein's army was incapable of stopping them. In this event the United States would have used the Sixth Fleet and other units to safeguard Israel's rear and flanks from Egyptian or Soviet attacks from the Suez Canal area. The plan was not put into effect because the Syrian tanks, harassed by King Hussein's jets and armor, began retreating into Syria (*New York Times,* October 8, 1970).

Brandon (1973, p. 167) also reports that the preferred alternative "was to let the Israelis undertake the air strikes, with U.S. air power protecting their rear against possible Egyptian and Soviet intervention."

Amplification of Beliefs

Although our computer simulation is capable of processing larger and more complex cognitive maps than the one we have constructed for the Middle East specialist, we consider his map to be adequate for a preliminary test. We will proceed by working

129

through the model to see how this foreign policy adviser would, on the basis of the cognitive map we have constructed, respond to the Jordanian crisis.

The simulation begins in the middle of the Jordanian crisis, on September 20, 1970, the day when it appeared that King Hussein was in serious trouble. At this point, our simulated Middle East specialist receives information that Jordan is under attack by Palestinian commandos who are being aided by tank forces from Syria, and is asked to recommend to the President of the United States possible courses of action in the Middle East.

In the first stage of the simulation, information about a new situation is used to highlight concepts in the cognitive map of the decision maker. This procedure is accomplished externally by the researcher, who selects the concepts on the basis of their relevance to the situation. In the simulation of the Jordanian crisis we selected nine concepts for initial highlighting because they best describe the events of the crisis: intraregional feuds (C29), militant pan-Arabism (C30), internal law and order (C31), moderate Arab regimes (C32), radical dictatorships (C33), nationalist radicalism (C34), indecisive leadership (C35), Communist radicalism (C36), and revolutionary ferment (C37). In Figure 6–2 these initially highlighted concepts are enclosed by circles.

The amplification of beliefs also involves the discovery of antecedents or prior causes that are part of the decision maker's explanation of the new situation. At this point, there is a search for antecedent paths that lead into the initially highlighted concepts. In our simulation of the Middle East specialist, there are three distinctive antecedent paths of the Jordanian crisis. Antecedent Paths I and II are based largely on the Middle East specialist's analysis of events surrounding the 1967 war in the Middle East: The weakness of the Arabs (C1H) and Israel's conception of security through occupation of territory (C39) caused defeat of the Arabs (C2), and the occupation of Arab territory by Israel (C3), thus increasing Arab feelings of frustration (C4) and revolutionary ferment (C37), which had a negative effect on stability on the Middle East (C28)—a concept which is positively related to internal law and order (C31). These paths are indicated in Figure 6–2 by triangles, and are also listed in Table 6–1. Antecedent Path III, on the other hand, focuses on relations between the United States and the Arabs as a cause of the Jordanian crisis: alienation of Arabs from the United States (A45), which is pre-

130

TABLE 6–1

ANTECEDENT PATHS AND MAJOR CONSEQUENT PATHS OF THE
MIDDLE EAST SPECIALIST FOR THE JORDANIAN CRISIS [a]

		Antecedent paths
I.	C1H	Weakness of Arabs
		+
	C2	Defeat of Arabs by Israel
		+
	C3	Occupation of Arab territory by Israel
		+
	C4	Arab feelings of frustration
		+
	* C37	Revolutionary ferment
		−
	C28	Stability in the Middle East
		+
	* C31	Internal law and order
II.	C39	Israel's conception of security through occupation of territory
		+
	C2	Defeat of Arabs by Israel
		+
	C3	Occupation of Arab territory by Israel
		+
	C4	Arab feelings of frustration
		+
	* C37	Revolutionary ferment
		−
	C28	Stability in the Middle East
		+
	* C31	Internal law and order
III.	A45	Alienation of Arabs from USA
		−
	A44	Friendly relations between Arabs and USA
		−
	* C33	Radical dictatorships
		−
	* C32	Moderate Arab regimes

		Major consequent paths
I.	C39	Israel's conception of security through occupation of territory
		+

[a] Consequent paths II–V, VII, and IX–X are not shown because of space
limitations.

131

TABLE 6–1 (Continued)

C2	Defeat of Arabs by Israel
	+
C3	Occupation of Arab territory by Israel
	+
C4	Arab feelings of frustration
	+
C6	Arab openness to offers of military aid
	+
C7	Arab requests for military aid
	+
C8H	Offers of military aid by Soviet Union
	+
C9H	Acceptance of Soviet aid by military-minded generals
	+
C10	Arms supplied by Soviet Union
	+
C14	Soviet penetration in the Middle East
	+
C15	Close alignment with the Soviet Union
	+
A16	Polarization in the Middle East
	+
A23	Possibility of war in the Middle East
	−
A24	Peace in intraregional relations
	+
A25	Peace in international relations
	+
USA2	Avoidance of World War III

II.	C39	Israel's conception of security through occupation of territory
		+
	C2	Defeat of Arabs by Israel
		+
	C3	Occupation of Arab territory by Israel
		+
	C4	Arab feelings of frustration
		+
	C37	Revolutionary ferment
		−
	C28	Stability in the Middle East
		+
	* C31	Internal law and order
		+
	USA12	Progressive development of countries in the Middle East

132

TABLE 6–1 (Continued)

VIII.	C39	Israel's conception of security through occupation of territory
		+
	C2	Defeat of Arabs by Israel
		+
	C3	Occupation of Arab territory by Israel
		+
	C4	Arab feelings of frustration
		+
	* C37	Revolutionary ferment
		−
	C28	Stability in the Middle East
		+
	* C31	Internal law and order
		−
	C11	Soviet presence in the Middle East
		−
	USA6	United States presence in the Middle East

* Initially highlighted concepts.

sumably caused by American support for Israel, harmed friendly relations between the Arabs and the United States (A44), which are negatively related to radical dictatorships (C33), such as Syria, which, in turn, are negatively related to moderate regimes (C32), such as Jordan. This path is not indicated in Figure 6–2, although it is listed in Table 6–1.

Of the three paths identified by the model, the first two are regarded as more plausible. Four of the relationships in Antecedent Path I are historically supported (C1H–C2–C3–C4), three of the relationships in Antecedent Path II are historically supported (C2–C3–C4), while none of the relationships in Antecedent Path III has historical support. Hence, we store the first two paths as part of the Middle East specialist's explanation of the Jordanian crisis and move to the next process.

Once a decision maker's perception of antecedent causes has been determined, the model further amplifies his beliefs by searching for consequences of the situation for the behavior of other states and for his own policy objectives. In the Jordanian crisis, there are ten distinctive consequent paths.[10] The first consequent

[10] In this simulation of the Jordanian crisis, the consequent paths are balanced; hence, they are all kept as part of the Middle East specialist's explanation of the crisis. If imbalance had existed between two or more

path begins with four antecedent concepts: Israeli conception of security through the occupation of territory (C39), defeat of Arabs by Israel (C2), occupation of Arab territory by Israel (C3), and Arab feelings of frustration (C4); and it continues along the following route: Arab openness to offers of military aid (C6), Arab requests for military aid (C7), offers of military aid by the Soviet Union (C8H), acceptance of Soviet aid by military-minded generals (C9H), arms supplied by Soviet Union (C10), Soviet Union penetration in the Middle East (C14), close alignment with the Soviet Union (C15), polarization in the Middle East (A16), the possibility of war in the Middle East (A23), threat to peace in the Middle East (A24), threat to peace in international relations (A25), and a possibility of World War III (USA2). This path is listed in Table 6–1 as Consequent Path I. In addition, there are two paths that are essentially variations of the concern about Soviet involvement in the crisis. Consequent Path II, which is not listed in Table 6–1, for example, focuses on the possibility of the Arab states becoming virtual satellites of the Soviet Union, while Consequent Path IV, also not listed in Table 6–1, is a concern that the crisis may lead to the introduction of nuclear weapons and increase the chances of nuclear war.

Consequent Path VI, which is listed in Table 6–1, begins with four concepts of the first antecedent path (C39–C2–C3–C4), but then emphasizes the concern that the crisis might increase revolutionary ferment (C37) that would threaten stability (C28), a concept that has a positive effect on internal law and order (C31) and the progressive development of countries in the Middle East (USA12). A related path, Consequent Path VIII, contains the implication that internal law and order has a negative effect on Soviet presence in the Middle East (C11) which in turn has a positive effect on American presence in the region (USA6).

The remaining consequent paths are much shorter than the first two paths. Consequent Path IX focuses on implications of the Israeli conception of security (C39): refusal of Israel to evacuate Arab territory (C40), harm to the dialogue between Israel and the Arabs (C41), and a decrease in the chances for peace in the Middle East (USA10). Consequent Path X suggests that radical dictatorships (C33) threaten moderate regimes (C32), thus de-

---

antecedent paths, then the path (or paths) that was less central to our specialist's cognitive system would have been excluded.

134

creasing American influence in the Arab world (A43) and threatening U.S. presence in the Middle East (USA6).

Policy Search and Choice

Once the beliefs of a decision maker have been amplified, the computer searches for all policy alternatives that are connected to the explanatory structures selected at previous stages. If it finds some of these alternatives, the computer uses a lexicographic criterion to construct a preference ordering.

In some cases, however, the decision-making situation is such that the decision maker does not possess a set of policy alternatives that are tied to his cognitive mapping, ready to be evoked when a relevant situation arises. In a situation like this, alternative courses of action proposed by others must be supplied as inputs to the simulation, which the decision maker responds to after he has assessed their implications by calculating their relationships with cognitive and affective concepts. For example, two of the policy alternatives considered by the United States in the Jordanian crisis were: (1) encouragement of Israel to intervene with air power to save the Jordanian regime, and use of the Sixth Fleet to protect Israel from outside attacks; or (2) direct American intervention to rescue Americans living in Jordan and to safeguard King Hussein and his government. These two alternatives could be treated in the simulation as inputs and, using the process parallel to the amplification of beliefs processes, the links between the policy alternatives and the rest of the cognitive mapping would be discovered.

Since the cognitive mapping of the Middle East specialist does include many policy alternatives that are relevant to the Jordanian crisis, it is not necessary to inject policy alternatives that have been proposed by others. A search of the antecedent and consequent paths reveals five adjacent policy alternatives: P1 (commit American land forces in the Middle East), P2 (commit American naval forces in the Middle East), P6 (convince Israel that peace cannot be achieved by occupation of territory), P7 (support stationing of U.N. forces), and P8 (reassure the Arabs that American policy is not hostile). Since the other P-concepts in the cognitive map, such as P3 (supply military aid to Israel), P4 (reduce military support for Israel), P5 (reduce military aid for Israel), P9 (offer military aid to the Arab states) and P10 (project a friendly image

135

to Arab states) are not directly connected to the Middle East specialist's explanatory network, they are excluded from the policy choice stage of the simulation.

The final results of our simulation, the rankings of the five policy alternatives, as well as their impact on each of the fourteen policy values that we asked the Middle East specialist to rank, are displayed in Table 6–2. This table suggests a clear preference for

TABLE 6–2

RANKINGS OF POLICY ALTERNATIVES AND THEIR EFFECTS ON
AMERICAN POLICY VALUES

Policy alternatives	American policy values (V-Concepts in Figure 6–1)													
	1	2	3	4	5	6	7	8	9	10	11	12	13	14
P8 Reassure Arabs that U.S. policy is not hostile	1	1	1	1	0	1	1	1	1	1	1	1	1	0
P6 Convince Israel that security can't be achieved by occupation	1	1	1	0	0	1	0	0	1	1	1	1	1	0
P7 Support stationing of U.N. forces	1	1	1	0	0	1	0	0	1	1	1	1	1	0
P1 Commit U.S. land forces in Middle East	0	0	0	0	0	1	0	0	0	0	0	1	1	−1
P2 Commit U.S. naval forces in Middle East	0	0	0	0	0	1	0	0	0	0	0	1	1	−1

diplomatic over military approaches to the Jordanian crisis. For example, the most preferred alternative is to reassure the Arabs that American policy is not hostile. The second and third options, which are tied in rank, are efforts to convince Israel that security cannot be achieved by occupation of territory, and to support the stationing of U.N. forces in the area. The low rank of the two options that involve the use of American military forces suggests a reluctance on the part of the Middle East specialist to resort to force. However, it should be noted that the use of American military force is not believed to harm any U.S. interests, except for avoiding dissension, the lowest-ranking value. Hence, given a severe threat to King Hussein, the Middle East specialist might recommend U.S. military intervention to deal with the immediate problem, along with assurances to the Arabs, pressure on Israel to withdraw from the occupied territory, and support for stationing of U.N. troops in the area.

A TEST OF THE PREDICTIONS

In late 1970, shortly after we used the model to simulate the Middle East specialist's reaction to the Jordanian crisis, we asked him to tell us what he would have recommended to the President, if the forces opposing King Hussein had not been defeated. As predicted by the model, he indicated a preference for diplomatic over military alternatives, although the diplomatic approaches he favored were not the same ones suggested by the model. Instead of reassuring the Arabs, pressuring the Israelis, and supporting the stationing of a U.N. force, as predicted by the model, he proposed the use of diplomatic pressure on Syria, and, if necessary, on Iraq, to stop the invasion. Although we are not certain why the model failed to predict the exact nature of the diplomatic measures recommended by the Middle East specialist, we suspect that the model was relying too heavily on the historical precedent of the 1967 war between Israel and the Arab states, when the Middle East specialist did support measures to reassure the Arabs. However, he did say at a later point in the interview that had diplomacy failed in 1970, he would have recommended the intervention of American forces to secure the Amman airport and protect Hussein, despite possible further loss of support for the United States in the Arab world. These actions are similar to the military measures predicted by the model (P1 and P2).

Although in the postcrisis interview we did not ask the Middle East specialist to specify the implications of the conflict in Jordan, we did get in touch with him three years later in order to make a comparison with the model's predictions about possible consequences. His written responses to our questions were as follows:

Q1. Why did the United States think the situation in Jordan was so dangerous?

Back in 1957 Secretary Dulles declared on behalf of President Eisenhower that the continued sovereignty and integrity of Jordan was of vital interest to the U.S. King Hussein is one of the few remaining pro-Western Arab leaders. The destruction of Jordan would have brought about a considerable political and territorial disarray in the Middle East. This was a real danger.

Q2. What United States interests were being threatened in this situation? Why?

The threat to Jordan was coming partly from the Palestine fedayeen and partly from Syria, a country with substantial Soviet connections. Destruction of Jordan as we know it today would thus have paved the way either to the military and extreme Arab elements or/and to Soviet influence. It might have, moreover, provoked Israel into action and thus caused a new enlargement of Israeli occupied territory with attendant various reactions in the Arab world and international complications.

Q3. What might have happened, if Israel had decided to intervene militarily? Why?

If Israel had decided to intervene militarily, it might have produced a second round of the 1967 war, involving unpredictably one or another Arab State and possibly plunging both the U.S. and the Soviet Union into the fray. Any one of these alternatives would have aggravated the situation in the Middle East and strengthened the radical anti-American trends.

The most striking thing about these answers is the close correspondence to both the structure and content of the consequences discovered by the model. For example, the answer to the second question contains two paths, "Destruction of Jordan as we know it today would thus have paved the way either to the military and extreme Arab elements or/and to Soviet influence." This statement corresponds closely to implications of Consequent Path II, revolutionary ferment (C37), and Consequent Path VIII, Soviet presence in the Middle East (C11). Furthermore, the next sentence, "It might have, moreover, provoked Israel into action and thus caused a new enlargement of Israeli occupied territory with attendant various reactions in the Arab world and international complications," is very similar to Consequent Path I, which contains the same prediction. The implications of Israeli involvement are further elaborated in our specialist's answer to question 3, where he argues that it could lead to possible U.S. and Soviet involvement in the conflict. The correspondence in the content of the implications is also close. Table 6–3 shows that eight of the

TABLE 6–3

COMPARISONS OF THE ACTUAL RESPONSES OF THE MIDDLE EAST
SPECIALIST TO THE PREDICTIONS OF THE SIMULATION

Consequences of the destruction of Jordan	
Actual responses	Predictions of the simulation
Political and territorial disarray in the Middle East	Threat to stability in the Middle East (C28)
Pave the way for extreme Arab elements	Increase revolutionary ferment (C37)
Pave the way for military Arab elements	Acceptance of Soviet aid by military-minded generals (C46)
Soviet influence	Increase Soviet penetration in the Middle East (C14)
Provoke Israel into military action	Increase the possibility of war in the Middle East (A23)
New enlargement of Israeli occupied territory	Occupation of Arab territory by Israel (C3)
Reactions in the Arab world	Increase of Arab feelings of frustration (C4)
International complications	Threat to peace in international relations (A25)
Second round of 1967 war, involving one or another Arab state	Defeat of Arabs by Israel (C2)
Both U.S. and Soviet Union plunge into the fray	Increased polariaztion, with U.S. aiding Israel and aiding the Arabs (A16)
Aggravation of the situation in the Middle East	Threat to peace in intraregional relations (A24)
Strengthen radical anti-American trends	Reduction of American influence in the Arab world (A43)

concepts used by the Middle East specialist to describe the dangers of the crisis are similar to concepts in Consequent Path I, and four other concepts he used are similar to those concepts in Consequent Paths II and X.

We also asked our specialist, "How far was the United States willing to go in September 1970?" and he replied: "I have no authoritative knowledge as to how far was the U.S. willing to go in September 1970. I understand that it was willing to intervene militarily should the Syrian thrust, presumably with the Soviets backing them, be not contained. In view of the earlier described dangers to the U.S. and to the area as a whole in such a situation, the American willingness to commit force to defend Jordan does not appear surprising."

This response corresponds closely to the model's prediction that the Middle East specialist might recommend direct American intervention in Jordan. In short, the model, using data generated in an imaginary crisis game, is able to predict many responses of a policy adviser in a subsequent, real international crisis, although it was not able to generate the exact ranking of the policy options he favored.

THEORY DEVELOPMENT

Our simulation of the Jordanian crisis is not meant to stand as a test of the model. There are many possible reasons why the model's predictions were similar to responses of the Middle East specialist. The simulation exercise has helped us to illustrate, however, some of the major processes of our model of foreign policy decision making. Our research can now proceed to experiments with a model that is capable of simulating the behavior of real decision makers.

By constructing a computer simulation model of decision making, we are combining a number of hypotheses in a rigorous and formal system. This serves not only as an integrating device for a body of knowledge, but also adds up to a theory of decision making that has predictive power. While no single hypothesis can be expected to account for all evidence, a number of interrelated hypotheses, by explaining different aspects of behavior, provides a framework for making predictions about decision makers. Furthermore, the collection of data for running the simulation may help to increase our understanding of how information processing by governmental officials in actual decision situations, such as international crises, leads to policy decisions. In order to determine the degree to which the model can be generalized, we have collected primary data from the government officials in the United States and two small countries, Austria and Finland, which occasionally play the roles of buffers in European politics. Cognitive maps and rankings of values obtained in these interviews should provide us with much information about relationships between perceived policy options, beliefs about international events, and policy values.

Another possible contribution of the simulation to the development of theory is more oriented toward policy; it is an attempt to advance and improve the theories about international politics held by the decision makers we are trying to study. Our discussion of decision making has been grounded in a view of the policy maker as an "applied scientist," or a person who is concerned about applying his knowledge of causal relations in order to exercise control over his environment. Both scientists and policy makers try to develop theories from ambiguous data and must interpret information in light of those theories. We are interested in using our simulation to help foreign policy critics improve their theories about international politics by translating their verbal theories into causal models that can be more easily restructured. Moreover, we want to use the simulation to illuminate the kinds of information processing and choice behavior that could be employed to achieve conflict resolution decisions that are less costly in terms of human lives and resources. By confronting simulated decision makers with current and future international situations, we can predict some of their responses and explore likely effects of new commitments and policies. Ultimately, we want to be in a position to make machine-aided policy recommendations that are congruent with the way real decision makers use concepts and justify choices.

CHAPTER SEVEN

Strategy for the Energy Crisis: The Case of Commuter Transportation Policy
—Fred S. Roberts

Being able to give advice based on the most accurate possible cognitive map is the task of this chapter. To do this requires getting the consensus of a panel of experts, rather than relying on the causal description that a single person might hold. Therefore, a panel of experts is used in this pilot study of transportation and energy demands first, to get a list of relevant concepts, and then (after narrowing the problem to commuter transportation), to get a consensus of the experts on the causal links between the relevant concept variables.

This chapter is also concerned with what might be called the strategic problem, in contrast to the decision-making problem of Chapter 4 and the explanation problem of Chapter 6. The strategic problem is to determine how the causal links themselves should be changed to give better outcomes. For example, in this empirical study the author finds that the energy demand for intraurban commuter transportation will be stable only if commuter ticket prices go down as ridership goes up. This

An earlier version of this paper appeared under the title "Building and Analyzing an Energy Demand Signed Digraph," in *Environment and Planning,* 3 (1973), 199–221. The author gratefully acknowledges the permission of Pion Press, Ltd., the publishers of *Environment and Planning,* to revise the paper for inclusion here.

The author's work on signed digraphs and energy demand has been supported by NSF Grants GI–44 to the Rand Corporation and GI–34895 to Rutgers University, and by a grant from the Alfred P. Sloan Foundation to the Institute for Advanced Study, Princeton, New Jersey.

The author gratefully acknowledges the helpful comments of J. Baird, T. Brown, N. Dalkey, H. Marcus-Roberts, C. Morris, R. Norman, J. Rolph, R. Salter, J. Spencer, and P. Velleman. He would especially like to thank J. Bigelow and J. DeHaven for the ideas on feasibility in the section on strategies. Finally, he would like to acknowledge the cooperation of the Rand NSF Energy Project Team who responded to the questionnaires.

fascinating result should be regarded as tentative, but it does indicate yet another use of cognitive map analysis, namely, as a way to develop answers to the strategic problem of what changes in the causal relationships in our environment we should try to attain.

SIGNED DIGRAPHS AND ENERGY DEMAND

In this chapter, I shall be concerned with constructing a cognitive map for use in decision making, rather than with describing a particular person's cognitive map. I shall explore how to build the "best" or most accurate cognitive map possible for use in making decisions. Specifically, I shall concentrate on decision problems involving energy.

The problems of energy supply and demand have recently become more and more important as the seriousness of the "energy crisis" is revealed. In making decisions about energy, one would like to do such things as:

(1) pinpoint the factors underlying the rapidly growing demand for energy;

(2) forecast future demands for energy;

(3) forecast the effect of new technologies or social changes on energy demand and supply;

(4) identify strategies or policies for modifying growth of energy use and meeting various environmental constraints on that use; and

(5) identify alternative strategies for obtaining new energy supplies, and evaluate their potential.

In Roberts (1971), I introduced the idea of studying energy demand by means of a signed digraph, and outlined methods for handling tasks such as (1) through (5). The signed digraph is thought of as an accurate cognitive map to be used in decision making. Additional work on the signed digraph methodology is contained in the works by Brown, Roberts, and Spencer (1972), Roberts (1972a, b, 1973, 1974, forthcoming a, b), and Roberts and Brown (1974). In this chapter, I illustrate the application of signed digraphs to problems of policy making about energy, specifically about energy use in intraurban commuter transportation. I will describe how to construct a signed digraph with which to analyze this area, and illustrate some techniques for analyzing this signed digraph.

One builds a signed digraph for studying energy demand by using as points a collection of variables relevant to energy demand. Then, one draws an arrow from variable x to variable y if a change in x leads to a change in y. As discussed in Chapter 3, one puts a plus sign on the arrow from x to y if a change in x is reflected in y and a minus sign on this arrow if a change in x is reversed in y. (A similar idea is described in Maruyama, 1963.) For illustrative purposes, Figure 7–1 gives a hypothetical example of a signed digraph for energy demand. There is an arrow with a plus sign from population to use, because an increase in population leads to more energy use. There is an arrow with a minus sign from energy use to quality of the environment, because increased use of energy leads to a degradation in environmental quality. I give more details on the construction of signed digraphs after discussing in the next two sections how to analyze them in a policy-making context.

STRUCTURAL ANALYSIS

Once a cognitive map or signed digraph has been built, there are many methodologies for analyzing it. It is useful to divide these into two types, the arithmetic and the geometric.[1] *Arithmetic methodologies* tend to be numerical and precise, and usually aim at the optimization of a few parameters involved in a cognitive map. They tend to be present-oriented and relatively insensitive to change or modification of the basic parameters making up the map. *Geometric methodologies* tend to be rather nonnumerical, and they can take account of variables that are not readily quantifiable. Their aim is an analysis of structure and shape, and especially of changing patterns of structure that may have different ramifications for the future. A typical geometrical conclusion is that some variable will grow exponentially, or that some other variable will oscillate wildly in value. The numerical levels reached are not considered important in such predictions.

Many problems in decision making involve extremely complex cognitive maps with many variables that are not easily quantified, such as environmental quality, freedom, and sovereignty. The use

[1] Cf. Kane (1972), Kane, Vertinsky, and Thompson (1973), and Coady, et al. (1973).

of arithmetical methodologies for studying these problems, though useful and important, will necessarily omit such factors, which at times are of underlying significance. Thus, geometric methodologies must be developed to deal with many important decision-making problems in society. These geometric methodologies should be used in conjunction with arithmetic methodologies.

The need for geometric analysis has given rise to a series of new methodologies that are coming to be called, loosely, *structural analysis*. In structural analysis, there are two problems, first the construction of as accurate a cognitive map as possible, and then its geometric analysis, preferably relating geometric conclusions to structural properties of the map. I shall describe both steps of this procedure with regard to problems of energy demand. Similar techniques, with somewhat different approaches to both the construction and the analysis segments of the methodology, are being applied to a wide variety of problems. For example, the Organization for Economic Cooperation and Development (1974) has been applying structural analysis to study the world-wide levelling off of support for scientific research. Coady, et al. (1973) have studied coastal land use, and Antle and Johnson (1973) have studied the effect on inland waterway traffic of large-scale conversion to coal for energy. Health care delivery, transportation, and international sale of water are among the problems studied by Julius Kane and his colleagues (Kane, 1972; Kane, Vertinsky, and Thompson, 1973; Kane, Thompson, and Vertinsky, 1972. Kruzic (1973a, b) has used structural analysis to study deep-water ports and to study naval manpower decisions. Ecologists in the U.S. Forest Service and elsewhere are studying simple ecological food webs, the effect of phorphorus on a lake, the effect of insecticides on cultivated fields, and so on (Levins, 1974, and forthcoming; R. Leary, personal communication).

ANALYSIS OF AN ENERGY DEMAND SIGNED DIGRAPH

Having built an energy demand signed digraph, there are a number of possible uses that can be made of it. Making use of the signed digraph structure, one can identify feedback loops. This is an analysis of *structure*. Feedback loops correspond to cycles in the signed digraph, for example, the cycle in Figure 7–1 that goes from energy capacity to number of factories to energy use, and

FIGURE 7–1.

Signed Digraph for Energy Demand
(Adapted from Roberts, 1971)

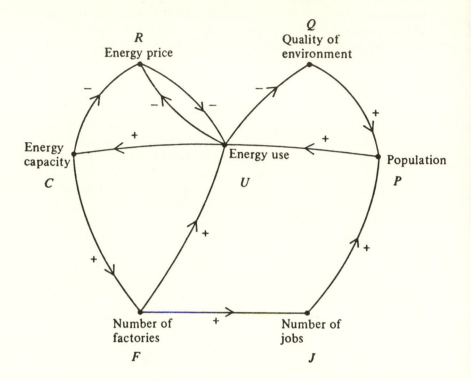

back to energy capacity. If energy capacity increases, this leads to an increase in energy use, which in turn leads to further energy capacity. The initial deviation was amplified, and we say there was positive feedback through the system. If there are many positive feedback loops such as this cycle, they will often lead to instability, as small initial changes can be amplified well beyond their initially foreseeable impact. Indeed, in Figure 7–1, every cycle through the energy capacity variable corresponds to a positive feedback loop. This observation makes precise an observation made imprecisely by many environmentalists, and suggests why initial increases in energy capacity lead to more and more such increases. The cycle in Figure 7–1 from energy use to quality of the environment to population to energy use corresponds to a negative feedback loop. An initial increase in energy use leads to a decrease in environmental quality, which leads people to move out, which in turn leads to a decrease in energy use. The initial deviation was counteracted, and we say there was negative feedback through the system. Negative feedback loops often lead to stability, although they can lead to larger and larger oscillations, also another unstable situation. It is easy to identify negative and positive feedback loops: a cycle corresponds to a positive feedback loop if and only if it has an even number of minus signs, that is, if and only if it is balanced. In sum, identification of positive and negative feedback loops is one step in pinpointing the factors underlying the rapidly growing demand for energy. As has been pointed out in earlier chapters, many decision makers seem to disregard feedback: their cognitive maps have no cycles.

One can also use the signed digraph to identify new strategies for dealing with the energy demand system. Specifically, one can define a *strategy* as any change in the system. A typical change might be to change the sign of one of the arrows. The arrow between energy use and energy price in the signed digraph of Figure 7–1 is a case in point. At present, the more energy you use, the less you pay, which is why the arrow in question has a minus sign. It has been suggested that large users should pay more rather than less—this is the strategy of inverting the rate structure, and it corresponds to changing the sign of this arrow from minus to plus. Now, having seen that a change of sign on an arrow in a signed digraph corresponds to a potential "strategy," one can go about systematically identifying strategies for modifying the energy demand system by looking at all arrows of the energy demand signed digraph. Not all of these are interesting, have real-world interpretations, or are politically or economically feasible, but often we can uncover potentially useful strategies simply by systematically enumerating possibilities.

Many other things can be done with signed digraphs if one imagines that each variable reaches a certain level or value at each time, and these levels change depending on previous changes in other variables. The simplest assumption about how changes of value are propagated through the system amounts to the following. If variable x goes up by μ units at a given time, and there is an arrow from variable x to variable y and a plus sign, then as a result, one time period later variable y will go up by μ units. If variable x goes up by μ units at a given time, and there is an arrow from variable x to variable y with a minus sign, then as a result, one time period later variable y will go down by μ units. These assumptions can be formalized to define a so-called *pulse process*. For the details of this formalization, see Roberts (1971 or forthcoming a, Chapter 4).

If we assume that values change as in a pulse process, then we can consider the effect of new technologies or outside events on the energy demand system. These changes can be thought of as changes in value or level at certain variables, and we can trace out or "forecast" the resulting effect on the system, specifically, the long-term trends in values of other variables. For example, a sudden immigration would correspond to an increase in population level in Figure 7–1, and we would like to forecast the impact on energy use of this increase.

The results from trend forecasting are different from those in the identification of feedback loops. The specific numbers in a trend forecast are not regarded as important. What is important is the geometric nature of the forecast: is it rapid "exponential" growth, is it increasing oscillations, or what? Ideally, a structural analysis will relate the trend forecasts to the structural properties of the signed digraph. These forecasts should be regarded as suggestive, but should be verified by further study and analysis using alternative signed digraphs or other analysis techniques. Let me try to explain why I feel this way. The signed digraph should be regarded as a model of a complex system. As such, it is a simplified model. Conclusions from the signed digraph analysis may thus not be precisely correct, due to the simplifications in the model. What are some of these simplifications? First, signs of effects may change over time, depending on the levels of the variables involved. Second, some effects may be stronger than others. Third, some effects may take longer than others, that is, there are time lags. Fourth, values are assumed to change under the oversimplified rules that make up a pulse process; and so on. Unfortunately, it is virtually impossible, in dealing with complex systems such as the energy demand system, to get precise information as to strength of effects, time lags, and so on. Thus, we must use a simplified model, recognizing only that the conclusions drawn from the model should be subject to further test.

Some of the simplifications mentioned above can be avoided. Information about how effects change over time, if it is available, can be brought into some of the analyses, at least in computer-generated forecasts of trends. The strength of an effect can be represented by introducing a number (a weight) on each arrow of a signed digraph, obtaining a *weighted digraph*. (This weight represents a strength of effect, not a probability.) Similarly, numbers (or weights) representing time lags can be introduced, giving rise to complicated mathematical problems. See Roberts (forthcoming a) or Roberts and Brown (1974) for a discussion of the analysis of weighted digraphs, and Roberts (forthcoming b) for an example of construction and analysis of weighted and *double-weighted digraphs*. Finally, besides the pulse process rule, other change of value rules can be used. See Kane (1972) for one example. Although any change of value rule will be simplified, if the analysis is done with several alternative rules, and the geometric nature of the conclusions is unchanged, the results should give rise to more confidence.

If we study the trends forecast under various external changes in the system, we might be particularly concerned with the growth of certain variables—energy use, for example. Let us say that a given variable x is *stable* subject to an external change in variable y if the forecast trend in variable x indicates that x does not get larger and larger in value in the situation where an external change is introduced at variable y. This stability might be affected by introducing further external changes, to amplify or counteract the effect of the change in y. But we shall be mostly interested in tracing the unimpeded effect of simple external changes. We shall call the system stable if every variable is stable subject to external changes in any of the other variables.[2] In Brown, Roberts, and Spencer (1972) and Roberts and Brown (1974), techniques are developed for identifying stable signed digraphs. Some of these techniques relate the *geometric* conclusion of stability to the existence of certain *structural* properties of the signed digraphs. These are the theorems of structural analysis.[3]

---

[2] In my articles, a second notion of stability is discussed. The notion used here is then called value stability.

[3] Briefly, there are two procedures available for determining stability. The first involves calculating the *signed adjacency matrix,* a matrix A whose (i,j) entry is $+1$ if there is a positive arrow from variable i to variable j, -1 if there is a negative arrow from variable i to variable j, and 0 otherwise. Given the matrix A, one can calculate certain numbers corresponding to A, called the *eigenvalues* of A. An eigenvalue is a complex number $a + bi$, and its *magnitude* is $\sqrt{a^2 + b^2}$. If every eigenvalue has magnitude less than or equal to 1, if no two nonzero eigenvaleus are the same, and if 1

We shall take it as an important property of a system that it be stable. For us, the prediction of instability will amount to a prediction that the structure of the system will change. It seems that many naturally occurring systems cannot abide with ever-increasing levels at any variable; they eventually undergo a complete change in structure. Prediction of stability is not quite so meaningful as prediction of instability, for a system can stabilize at unacceptably high levels.

Prediction of stability or instability, like prediction of forecast trends in general, should be regarded as suggestive, but again should be verified by further study and analysis. For it, too, is based on the simplifying assumptions inherent in using signed digraphs and pulse processes on signed digraphs.

CONSTRUCTING A SIGNED DIGRAPH

In applying a signed digraph to problems of energy demand, and indeed to many similar problems of society, there are essentially two tasks: the analysis of a signed digraph once it is defined, and the construction of the signed digraph for analysis. Here, I will illustrate how both tasks are handled, by reporting on a specific signed digraph I built and analyzed that had to do with energy demand in transportation.

This signed digraph was built with the help of the subjective judgments of a panel of experts. I am interested in constructing the signed digraph that is based on the best available data, rather

---

is not an eigenvalue, then the signed digraph is stable. The second procedure for determination of stability applies to certain types of signed digraphs (called *advanced rosettes*). For these signed digraphs, it is neecssary to calculate the number a_i given by the number of positive cycles of length i minus the number of negative cycles of length i. If s is the highest number such that $a_s \neq 0$, then stability implies that

(a) $a_s = \pm 1$

(b) $a_i = -a_s(a_{s-i})$ for every $i = 1, 2, \ldots, s - 1$

and (c) $a_1 + a_2 + \ldots + a_s \neq 1$.

Each of the conditions (a), (b), and (c) is a structural condition about cycles in the signed digraph. To illustrate this idea, consider the signed digraph of Figure 7-1 (this is an advanced rosette). Here, $a_1 = 0$, $a_2 = +1$, $a_3 = +1$, $a_4 = 0$, and $a_5 = +1$. (Note that $a_3 = +1$ since there are three cycles of length 3, two positive and one negative.) Since s = 5, condition (b) is violated for $i = 2$, since $a_2 = 1 \neq -1 = -a_5(a_3)$. We conclude that the signed digraph is unstable. The reader is again warned that these structural results apply only to certain kinds of signed digraphs.

150

than one that best reflects the views of any single person. There-fore, I chose to experiment with the use of subjective judgments of a panel of experts. In many problems of a social or environmental nature, the best available data are the opinions of so-called experts. (Moreover, there is already a considerable literature on expert panels, especially with regard to transportation, using the Delphi method.[4]) For my purpose, the main advantage of using a panel of experts is that it allows me to build a signed digraph that is likely to be more accurate than a cognitive map based on the views of any one person.

The fact that I have limited my attention to the use of subjective judgments of groups of experts in building an energy demand signed digraph should not be taken to mean that, for all stages of the construction, this is the best available method. Rather, this method should be regarded as one possibility out of several, and the aim of my study was to discover some of its strong and weak points. In the next section, however, I discuss some general guidelines on when the use of expert judgments is appropriate, and how to select groups of experts.

It should be added that it is not reasonable to try to specify one procedure for constructing a signed digraph that provides a cognitive map for decision making. The procedure will vary with the problem being mapped and the use to be made of the map. Even the procedure I do describe has many variations, and each step has choices, possible modifications, and so on. The construc-tion procedure itself teaches the user much about the complex system he is trying to map. Alternative procedures just give more insight into the system. Indeed, trying to build cognitive maps under different sets of assumptions is a useful exercise. The reader should once again distinguish the goal of building a cognitive map to describe a system from the goal of building a cognitive map to describe a particular person's assertions or beliefs.

The problem of building a signed digraph of a system can be divided into three obvious stages: choosing the points or concept variables, choosing the arrows, and choosing the signs.

I look at concept variable definition as a twofold problem. First, one should try to identify as many potentially relevant variables as possible, allowing the imagination to run free. Second, one should attempt to limit the list of variables to a reasonable

[4] Brown, et al. (1969a, 1969b, 1970); Dalkey (1969); Dalkey, et al. (1970); Dalkey and Rourke (1971); Dalkey, et al. (forthcoming).

size by limiting the scope of the problem, by selecting a subset of variables that is most representative or most important. At least for the first problem, the use of subjective judgments of experts seems like the most reasonable procedure, if the term "expert" is used in a very broad sense to include lay people who are knowledgeable or well-read about the problems being considered. For the second problem, it became clear that, if one uses a group of experts, they should, whenever possible, truly be experts in the specific discipline in which they are casting judgment.[5]

A simple way to treat the problems of choosing arrows and signs is to lump them together, and again use expert judgments. The chosen variables are presented as ordered pairs (x, y), and for each such pair each expert judges whether x has a significant effect on y and, if so, what is the sign of this effect. Using expert judgments is, of course, not the only procedure that could be used here, but it is quite a reasonable one if choice of variables is also made by a panel of experts.

To test a potential methodology, I recruited a panel of experts from among the Rand NSF Energy Project team, and sent out three questionnaires. The first two were aimed at choosing the variables of an energy demand signed digraph: the first to identify relevant variables, and the second to limit the list of variables to a reasonable size. I limited the problem initially to energy demand in transportation, and later to energy demand in intraurban commuter transportation. Using the results of the second questionnaire, I sent out a third aimed at determining arrows and signs. The judgments of a number of different experts as to arrows and signs can be combined in various ways to form an energy demand signed digraph, and I chose one such way for illustrative purposes. I analyzed the resulting signed digraph, in particular identifying its feedback loops, determining both its stability and the stability resulting from various strategies corresponding to changing the sign of an arrow.

In what follows, I describe this whole procedure and discuss it critically. It should be emphasized that the main goal at this stage

[5] Methods developed for selecting a set of variables to use in studying energy demand have wider applicability than in choosing points for a signed digraph. Once a set of variables has been systematically selected, it can be used in various other ways—for example, to define scenarios for plausible futures that can be used to study future energy demand patterns. The scenarios could be defined by postulating certain changes in the level of (or relations between) one or more of these variables.

has been to try out a methodology and learn its strengths and weaknesses, rather than to obtain substantive results. However, the procedure, as well as the results, have interesting implications for policymaking.

GUIDELINES ON THE USE OF EXPERT JUDGMENTS

A word is in order about when the use of subjective judgments of experts is an appropriate method. In Dalkey (1969), three kinds of information that commonly play a role in decision making are distinguished. These are called speculation, opinion, and knowledge. To quote Dalkey:

> On the one hand, there are assertions that are highly confirmed—assertions for which there is a great deal of evidence backing them up. This kind of information can be called "knowledge." At the other end of the scale is material that has little or no evidential backing. Such material is usually called "speculation." In between is a broad area of material for which there is some basis for belief but that is not sufficiently confirmed to warrant being called knowledge. There is no good name for this middling area. Here it is called "opinion." The dividing lines between these three are very fuzzy, and the gross trichotomy smears over the large differences that exist within types.

Roughly speaking, the use of subjective judgments of experts has proved useful for dealing with questions falling in the middle area. There is, unfortunately, no really good criterion for deciding to which of the three areas of information a given question belongs. But it is certainly correct to say that choice of the variables for an energy demand signed digraph falls at least in part in the realm of opinion.

The next question that arises is: if we do decide to use expert opinions, which experts do we pick, and should we use a single expert or a group? In general, if a question falls within the realm of a well-defined discipline, such as the design of automobiles, we should use experts from that discipline. Even here, however, experts do tend to disagree on matters of opinion, so it is often wise to use a group of experts. The Delphi studies at the Rand Corporation (Dalkey, 1969) demonstrates that, under controlled interaction procedures with limited feedback of information, the

153

old adage of "two heads are better than one" seems to be upheld in areas of opinion. Although the specific Delphi procedures were not used in the study described here, this and other Delphi results were a justification for using groups of experts, and for letting them make choices without the usual group interaction. Each expert was asked to state his opinion without knowing the opinion of the others.

In the Delphi studies, larger groups have tended to be more accurate and more reliable on matters of opinion.[6] Moreover, the Delphi studies have shown that the controlled interaction leads to more accurate responses than the traditional face-to-face discussion technique of group decision making. A group of experts reaching a judgment in this traditional way has tended to do worse than another group working independently.[7] Groups under controlled interaction have tended to answer even more accurately if the individual judgments are repeated after giving some partial information.[8]

If a question does not fall in the realm of a particular discipline, use of subjective judgments of experts is still quite a reasonable procedure. Here, one should select experts representing all the disciplines that are particularly relevant to the question at hand when forming a group. It is worth noting that recent experiments have demonstrated that a group, each of whose members is expert only in one aspect of a problem, tends to do as well as a group, each of whose members is an expert in all aspects of the problem (Dalkey, et al., forthcoming). In these experiments, members of a group of "synthetic laymen" are each armed with a particular "synthetic fact" relevant to a particular question. Members of a group of "synthetic experts" are each armed with all the synthetic facts. The former group tends to do as well as the latter group, provided the former group, taken as a whole, has all the facts. Thus, it is not necessary that each judge be an expert in every

---

[6] The questions asked were almanac-type questions, with known answers. These were considered to fall in the realm of opinion for the "experts," because they did not know the exact answer, but had some relevant information with which to make a considered judgment. The group response was taken to be the median of the individual responses. Reliability was measured by taking a correlation between median responses of two randomly selected groups of equal size on a set of twenty questions.

[7] The median of individual responses is usually used as the group's response.

[8] Such as the first round median.

154

relevant discipline, but only that all relevant disciplines be represented. Finally, a group of experts from different disciplines should, in broad matters such as those of energy use and environment, be supplemented with at least several "lay" experts, knowledgeable or well-read or concerned people who are not necessarily experts in any relevant technical discipline.

ROUND ONE: IDENTIFYING POTENTIAL RELEVANT VARIABLES

I turn now to a description of the identification-of-potential-variables round of the variable choice procedure. To make the later task of limiting variables somewhat simpler, I decided at the very beginning to limit the problem of identification of variables to the transportation sector. This sector was chosen over other sectors of energy use for various reasons, one of which was that a similar study specifically using the Delphi technique and attempting to identify factors relating to quality of life was performed and applied to alternative transportation systems earlier (Dalkey, et al., 1970; Dalkey and Rourke, 1971).

A questionnaire, circulated to the team of experts, asked them to list as many variables as they could think of that might be relevant to (constrain, influence, cause, be affected by, etc.) the growing demand for energy in the transportation sector.

A follow-up questionnaire is, undoubtedly, a very good idea. This would present a summary of first-round responses and a request for additions. I did perform a sort of second round myself, by adding variables suggested by the respondents' variables. In response to the first questionnaire the team of experts succeeded in listing (counting my additions) more than five-hundred variables relevant to energy use in the transportation sector. That seems to me a good indication of the complexity of the energy-use problems with which we are dealing.

There was no hope of organizing this many variables by using techniques of clustering, such as those applied in the quality of life study (Dalkey, et al., 1970). Assuming there were five-hundred variables, this would have called for 125,000 similarity judgments! Instead, I began trying to classify the variables by grouping them. My questionnaire presented examples of relevant variables with the instructions, and these relevant variables were organized into seven categories. Whether because of this means of giving instructions, or because these categories were rather inclusive, almost all the variables listed by the respondents did fit into one of these seven categories. The remainder fitted into one additional category, number 8, below. Next time the questionnaire should be worded so that the examples given are not listed in distinct categories, to avoid the possibility of limiting the responses to these categories.

The eight categories into which all the variables fit are the following:

1. *descriptive variables:* variables describing the transportation system;

2. *design variables:* variables describing the design of the various carriers (car, rail, bus, etc.);

3. *demographic variables:* variables describing life-style, population trends, etc.;

4. *economic variables;*

5. *pollutant variables:* variables describing the different pollutants emitted by transportation modes;

6. *environmental and aesthetic impact variables:* variables describing the impact of transportation on the environment, aesthetics, and the like;

7. *quality-of-life variables;*

8. *energy system variables.*

I found that the variables could also be classified under a rather simple hierarchical classification. This began by characterizing the mode of transportation to which the variable applied: car, rail, bus, truck, plane, water, or pipe.[9] (Some, perhaps less important, modes were also mentioned by respondents: dirigible, motorcycle, hovercraft, bicycle, "feet.") For each mode, the variables relevant to it could be further classified according to the following scheme:

I. Freight transportation
   a. short distance (intraregional)
   b. long distance (interregional)
II. Passenger transportation
   a. commuting
      1. short distance
      2. long distance
   b. business
      1. short distance
      2. long distance

[9] Some variables apply to all modes.

156

    c. pleasure
      1. short distance
      2. long distance
    d. shopping and the like

Not all of the modes had both a freight and a passenger branch, so that this considerably cut down the number of classes. But new variables corresponding to subcategories in this systematic classification were added to the list. In general, such a classification could be sent to experts for comments to see if it suggested additional variables to them.

The first step in limiting the number of variables to be considered was to limit the problem further. I decided to concentrate on just the variables fitting into one subcategory of this classification scheme, and I chose the subcategory of short-distance commuter transportation (for passengers). For simplicity, I chose to deal with only the three most important modes: car, bus, and rail. (The others are not yet as important for intraregional commuter transportation.) Using the eight categories of variables and the three modes given above, I thus was able to organize the remaining variables into twenty-four new subcategories, each corresponding to a given category and mode. Typical subcategories were: descriptive variables—bus; economic variables—car; pollutant variables—car, etc. Table 7–1 shows all the variables in one sample category. Other variables may be found in Roberts (1972a).

It should be remarked that the procedure described so far for organizing variables once they have been defined is not as precise as such techniques as clustering. Much is left to the ingenuity and discretion of the individual analyzing the results. This might be unavoidable, given the large number of variables with which we are dealing. Similar comments apply to the other steps in the procedure for choosing variables. The procedure is defined by a combination of precise rules and ad hoc, subjective ones.

ROUND TWO: LIMITING THE NUMBER OF VARIABLES BY RATING THEIR IMPORTANCE

The technique used to limit further the number of variables was to have the experts rate the importance of these variables. This was done in two ways, for purposes of comparison. Experts were asked for an "overall importance" rating and a "relative importance" rating. The overall importance rating was given on a seven-

TABLE 7–1

QUALITY-OF-LIFE VARIABLES FOR THE RAIL MODE (Category 20)[a]

	Variables	Median overall importance (1 to 7)	Geometric mean relative importance (1 to 100)
20.1	Comfort of train	4	68.7
20.2	Number of conveniences, lounges, dining rooms, bars, etc.)	3	36.2
20.3	Probability of delay	5	82.3
20.4	Noise level (inside)	4	50.5
20.5	Ride quality	2	28.1
20.6	Degree of concentration required to ride	1	13.2
20.7	Tolerance to high passenger densities	4	58.3
20.8	Crowding (number of passengers per square foot)	4	68.9
20.9	Number of passengers per train	3	42.7
20.10	Number of seats abreast	3	59.3
20.11	Aesthetic impression of travel route	3	27.0
20.12	Convenience of schedule (frequency)	6	85.6
20.13	Number of trains daily	5	80.4

[a] Kendall's τ for this subcategory is 0.83, which is significant at 0.001.

point scale, with 1 meaning "unimportant," 4 meaning "moderately important," and 7 mean "extremely important." The relative importance of a variable was obtained on a scale of 1 to 100, using the magnitude estimation procedure. Experts were asked to rate the given variable relative to other variables in the same subcategory. The most important variable in the subcategory was chosen and given a rating of 100. The other variables were rated in terms of the most important one, so that a variable receiving a rating of 50 was considered "half as important" as one receiving a rating of 100, and so on. Use of the two specific rating schemes chosen was modeled after the procedure used in obtaining importance ratings in Dalkey and Rourke (1917).

In all, seven respondents returned their completed questionnaires for Round 2. I computed the median overall importance rating over responses for each variable, and the geometric mean of relative importance ratings over responses for each variable. These statistics are shown for a sample subcategory in Table 7–1. (The reader is referred to Roberts, 1973, for a discussion of why I chose these statistics.)

I also computed Kendall's τ, a coefficient of rank correlation, between median overall ratings and geometric mean relative ratings for each subcategory. As expected, there was a great deal of agreement between the two ranking procedures. (See Roberts, 1972a, for detailed data.)

The ratings raised some rather interesting points. No environmental or aesthetic variable received even a "moderately important" rating in the rail and bus subcategories, and only the variables "accidents" and "land use impact" received ratings as high as 5 among all the environmental and aesthetic variables. Was this because it was the consensus of the experts that environmental and aesthetic variables are not as important for the study of energy demand as are some of the other variables? Or was it because the first round did not produce environmental variables that are considered important?

For the economic variables, the consensus of the experts was that the cost of reducing emissions to acceptable levels was relatively unimportant. Among the variables related to cost of emission reduction, the highest median overall importance rating was 3. But one expert did add a note on his questionnaire, saying that he would rate them higher if the variables were stated as "cost of reducing . . . emissions (if this cost > x percent of the cost of the car)," and x was large enough.

There were several important issues raised by the ratings in the three subcategories dealing with pollutant variables. The method of measuring emissions that received the highest importance rating was, in general, "emissions per passenger mile," rather than "total emissions," "average emissions per day," or "total emissions on maximum day." Some participants, however, felt that there was no a priori way to decide which means of measurement is better or leads to a "more important" variable. In general, carbon dioxide emissions, particulate emissions, and noise emissions received lowest median overall importance ratings, while carbon monoxide, nitrogen oxide, and hydrocarbon emissions received highest ratings. Some respondents felt that they were not well enough informed to make intelligent ratings of importance in these subcategories. These were singled out, more than any others, as ones where ratings would best be done by experts in the particular subcategory.

CHOICE OF VARIABLES

There are a number of alternative procedures for choosing variables as points for a signed digraph, given results such as those from Round 2. It is probably best first to choose a preliminary list of variables, and then further to limit the list. For each of these steps, there are again a number of alternative methods. It is probably not a good idea to try to limit oneself to one method for choosing variables as best in all circumstances. Rather, different methods might be more appropriate for different sets of data. When several methods seem appropriate, it might be worthwhile to build several lists of chosen variables, using different methods. These lists can be used to build several signed digraphs, each of which could be useful. (Again, just the process of construction and analysis of several signed digraphs can help the experts understand the complete processes they are modeling.) If there is a good reason for wanting one final signed digraph, the choice among the final signed digraphs can be left to the experts.[10]

For choosing the preliminary list of variables, the following methods suggest themselves: [11]

Method 1. Choose one or two variables from each subcategory on the basis of overall or relative importance.

Method 2. Choose one or two variables from each subcategory

[10] If a more systematic procedure for choosing a consensus among alternative signed digraphs is desired, a promising technique is that used for choosing a consensus among alternative partial orders in Bogart (1971). It has been pointed out by Bogart (personal communication) that the procedure generalizes in a straightforward way to the case of signed digraphs.

[11] There are a number of variants of these methods, using more sophisticated statistical techniques. The problem of choosing one variable (or one ranking) out of a subcategory, when presented with differing rankings by a group of experts, has been studied in some detail in the literature. Statistical procedures are described in Kendall (1962) and Friedman (1937). One particularly interesting procedure, somewhat different and not well known, is that used by Kemeny and Snell (1973, chapter 2). They describe how to calculate the distance between two rankings, and then pick a consensus ranking as one centrally located among the alternative rankings, as far as the distance measure is concerned. (Bogart's procedure, referred to in the previous footnote, is a generalization of this one.)

160

that has at least one variable with overall importance rating of, say, 6 or more. The problem here is that not every major category will necessarily be represented.

Method 3. Choose all variables, regardless of subcategory, that have overall importance ratings of, say, 6 or more. Again, not every major category will necessarily be represented.

Method 4. Choose one or two variables from each collection of subcategories belonging to a given category.

After a preliminary list of variables has been chosen, it can be further limited by applying one of several methods, possibly with a number of iterations. Some possible methods are:

Method A. Obtain relative importance ratings among the variables on the preliminary list, and choose the most important ones.

Method B. Use a clustering procedure.

Method C. Choose only those variables on the preliminary list that have overall importance ratings of, say, 5 or greater.

For illustrative purposes, I decided to use Method 1 on the data, with the choice based on the median overall ranking, and a geometric mean relative ranking used in case of ties. Then I limited the list with Method B, and refined the list further with Method C.

By using Method 1, a preliminary list of twenty-four variables was chosen. These preliminary variables clustered into well-defined groups; that is, variables in subcategories of the same category tended to be closely related, and could usually be lumped together. Without performing a sophisticated clustering analysis, as in Dalkey, et al. (1970), I chose ten variables to replace the initial twenty-four. These variables were different from those in the initial subcategories—they were, of course, the lumped variables. For example, one lumped variable was "probability of delay," which was obtained by lumping probability of delay (car), probability of delay (bus), and convenience of schedule (rail). In general, it might be necessary to perform a more sophisticated clustering analysis, though the present clustering was deemed satisfactory for illustrative purposes. A second iteration to limit the list of variables further was performed using Method C. Here, one variable was eliminated, since its overall importance rating was only 3. This left nine variables in all, the ones shown in Table 7–2.

161

TABLE 7–2

Variables Chosen in Rounds 1 and 2

	Variable	Abbreviation	Category
1	Number of passenger miles (annually, over all commuter modes)	Passenger miles	Descriptive
2	Fuel economy (miles per BTU, average over all commuter modes)	Fuel economy	Design
3	Population size	Population size	Demographic
4	Cost of car	Cost of car	Economic
5	Price of commuter ticket (average over all modes)	Price of commuter ticket	Economic
6	Tons of emissions per passenger mile (averaged over all modes, and including carbon monoxide, nitrogen oxides, and hydrocarbons, but not carbon dioxide, particulates, or noise)	Emissions	Pollutant
7	Accidents	Accidents	Environmental and aesthetic impact
8	Probability of delay	Probability of delay	Quality of life
9	Total fuel consumption (over all modes)	Fuel consumption	Energy system

CHOICE OF ARROWS AND SIGNS: THE ROUND THREE PROCEDURE

With the nine variables chosen as a result of Round 2 (see Table 7–2), a questionnaire was prepared and sent asking the panel of experts to indicate for each ordered pair of distinct variables (x,y) whether, all other things being equal, a change in variable x has a significant effect on variable y, and if so, whether the change in x is reflected or reversed in y. This led to assignment of a sign + or −, or assignment of a 0 (corresponding to a negligible effect), to each ordered pair (x,y), with x ≠ y. (With his instructions each expert was given a pack of seventy-two cards, one for each ordered pair of variables (x,y) with x ≠ y. The cards were shuffled before being distributed to attempt to minimize the effect of extraneous order-of-presentation factors. Each respondent received a deck in a different order. Perhaps in the future a more sophisticated randomization technique than mere shuffling of cards could be used, but here, as in Rounds 1 and 2, the outlines of the methodology were considered more important than the details.)[12]

The procedure described is sometimes called *cross-impact analysis*. Asking for interaction data in a systematic way for each ordered pair of variables seems to avoid many problems. Cognitive maps described in this book often have few or no feedback loops, and otherwise omit important effects. The simple act of systematically considering all pairwise impact should significantly diminish the possibility that important effects and feedback loops will be omitted. The reader will notice later that there are a fair number of feedback loops in the signed digraph presented below.

Choice of arrows and signs, just as choice of variables, can be very "context-sensitive." It has been pointed out to me by J. Baird (personal communication) that it might be reasonable to spell out for the experts the context in which they are making their judgments before gathering their responses. Thus, they might be given a scenario describing various social, technological, or economic changes that have been made from the present, and be asked to make their judgments relative to such a scenario. Different signed digraphs would be built under each scenario. Exactly this procedure is carried out in Roberts (forthcoming b), where the impact of energy use on clean air in San Diego transportation is studied in two different scenarios, one a "business as usual" nominal case, in which transportation is almost completely by private automobile, and the other a radical all-bus case, in which automobiles are banned from San Diego and a wide-ranging bus system is introduced. Once again, the reason we can consider alternative signed digraphs rather than one cognitive map is that we are not trying to describe an individual's cognitive map. Rather, we are trying to build a map as an aid in decision making. In different contexts, different maps are called for.

To give an example of how sensitive judgments of sign can be to the scenario, suppose we consider in intraurban commuter transportation the sign of the arrow from the probability of delay to emissions. The sign of this arrow will depend upon the pattern

---

[12] It should be remarked that it is relatively straightforward to extend the methodology to obtain numbers (weights) representing the relative strength of the effect of a change in x or y, and the time lag before the effect takes place. See Roberts (forthcoming b).

of commuting in the area. If a high fraction of commuting is accomplished by automobile (as in Los Angeles, for example), then the increased stop-and-go driving caused by delay will increase the amount of pollutants. If, on the other hand, a large fraction of commuting is by electric subway or train (as in New York, for example), then delays will not have great influence on pollutants (since no power is being used in "idling"), and might even somewhat decrease the effluents from electric power stations.[13]

BUILDING THE SIGNED DIGRAPH

There were seven respondents in Round 3. The data from these respondents are summarized in Table 7–3. One respondent put

TABLE 7–3

ROUND 3 DATA

Variable pair x,y	Respondents							Totals [a]			
	1	2	3	4	5	6	7	0	+	−	?
1,2	+	0	0	0	0	+	+	4	3	0	
1,3	0	0	0	0	0	0	0	7	0	0	
1,4	0	0	−	0	+	−	0	4	1	2	
1,5	−	−	+	−	+	+	−	0	3	4	
1,6	+	+	0	+	+	+	0	2	5	0	
1,7	+	+	+	+	+	+	+	0	7	0	
1,8	0	+	+	+	+	+	+	1	6	0	
1,9	+	+	+	+	+	0	+	1	6	0	
2,1	−	0	0	+	+	0	+	3	3	1	
2,3	0	0	0	0	0	0	0	7	0	0	
2,4	−	(−)	−	0	0	−	0	4	0	3	
2,5	−	−	0	−	−	−	−	1	0	6	
2,6	−	−	−	−	−	−	−	0	0	7	
2,7	0	0	0	0	−	+	0	5	1	1	
2,8	0	0	0	0	0	−	0	6	0	1	
2,9	−	−	−	−	−	+	−	0	1	6	
3,1	+	+	+	+	+	+	+	0	7	0	
3,2	0	0	0	0	0	0	0	7	0	0	
3,4	0	−	0	−	0	0	0	5	0	2	
3,5	0	(−)	0	−	+	0	0	5	1	1	
3,6	+	+	+	+	0	+	+	1	6	0	
3,7	+	+	0	+	+	+	0	2	5	0	
3,8	+	+	+	+	+	+	+	0	7	0	
3,9	+	+	+	+	+	+	+	0	7	0	
4,1	0	0	0	0	−	0	0	6	0	1	
4,2	−	(+)	0	0	−	−	+	3	1	3	

[13] The author thanks J. Bigelow and J. DeHaven for making this observation.

TABLE 7–3 (Continued)

Variable pair x,y	Respondents							Totals [a]			
	1	2	3	4	5	6	7	0	+	−	?
4,3	0	0	0	0	0	0	0	7	0	0	
4,5	+	−	0	−	+	+	0	2	3	2	
4,6	+	−	0	0	0	−	0	4	1	2	
4,7	−	(−)	0	0	0	−	−	4	0	3	
4,8	0	0	0	0	0	0	0	7	0	0	
4,9	+	+	0	0	+	−	0	3	3	1	
5,1	+	−	−	−	−	−	−	0	1	6	
5,2	0	+	−	0	0	0	0	5	1	1	
5,3	0	0	0	0	0	0	0	7	0	0	
5,4	+	0	0	−	+	+	0	3	3	1	
5,6	0	−	0	+	0	+	+	3	3	1	
5,7	0	−	0	+	0	+	0	4	2	1	
5,8	0	−	0	+	0	−	−	3	1	3	
5,9	0	0	0	+	−	+	+	3	3	1	
6,1	+	0	0	0	−	−	−	3	1	3	
6,2	−	+	0	0	+	−	−	2	2	3	
6,3	0	0	0	0	−	−	−	4	0	3	
6,4	−	+	0	0	−	−	0	3	1	3	
6,5	0	−	0	0	0	+	0	5	1	1	
6,7	+	+	+	0	0	+	+	2	5	0	
6,8	0	0	0	0	0	+	0	6	1	0	
6,9	+	−	0	0	+	−	−	2	2	3	
7,1	0	0	0	−	+	−	−	3	1	3	
7,2	0	(−)	0	−	0	0	0	6	0	1	
7,3	−	(−)	0	−	0	−	−	3	0	4	
7,4	0	+	0	−	0	0	0	5	1	1	
7,5	0	+	?	0	0	+	0	4	2	0	1
7,6	0	(+)	0	+	0	−	0	5	1	1	
7,8	+	+	+	+	+	+	+	0	7	0	
7,9	0	0	0	+	0	0	0	6	1	0	
8,1	0	−	−	−	−	−	−	1	0	6	
8,2	0	−	0	0	−	−	−	3	0	4	
8,3	−	0	0	?	0	0	0	5	0	1	1
8,4	0	0	0	0	+	0	0	6	1	0	
8,5	0	+	0	0	?	+	0	4	2	0	1
8,6	0	+	+	0	+	+	+	2	5	0	
8,7	−	0	0	0	+	+	−	3	2	2	
8,9	−	+	+	0	0	−	+	2	3	2	
9,1	−	−	−	−	0	−	0	2	0	5	
9,3	0	0	0	0	0	0	0	7	0	0	
9,4	+	0	0	0	0	+	0	5	2	0	
9,5	+	+	0	−	0	−	0	3	2	2	
9,6	+	+	+	+	+	−	+	0	6	1	
9,7	+	0	0	0	0	0	0	6	1	0	
9,8	0	0	0	0	+	−	0	5	1	1	

[a] Counting (+) and (−) as 0. (+) and (−) mean "weakly."

some of his plus and minus responses in parentheses, indicating this meant "weakly." In the analysis these "weak" effects were counted as no effects, though a similar analysis could be used if they were counted as strong effects. There were three cases of missing data. For purposes of the analysis below, these three cases turned out to be unimportant, since they were all cases in which a majority of the respondents listed the effect as negligible.

There are a number of plausible techniques for combining the data of Table 7–3 to form a signed digraph, though there does not seem, *a priori,* to be a good way to distinguish among these various procedures. Indeed, digraphs built under different procedures could again be usefully compared and contrasted. Perhaps it clarifies the selection procedure if construction is based on two separate decisions:

(1) Is there an arrow (x,y)?

(2) If so, what is the sign of this arrow?

If we use this two-step decision procedure, the following method seems reasonable. If at least six of the seven respondents said there was a significant effect on y if there is a change in x, then include (x,y) as an arrow. Moreover, give (x,y) that sign agreed to by 60 percent of the respondents, if there is this much agreement. If this procedure is used on the data of Table 7–3, there is only one undecided sign, that on the arrow from passenger miles (variable 1) to price of commuter ticket (variable 5). Here all seven experts felt there is a significant effect, but three felt the effect is plus, while four felt it is minus. We can summarize the data in the signed digraph G of Figure 7–2, putting a question mark (?) on the arrow (1,5). In our analysis below, we consider the various possible choices of sign on this arrow (including sign 0, which is interpreted as not having the arrow).

There are, of course, other plausible procedures for building a signed digraph from the data of Table 7–3. We could vary the number of experts who have to agree on the existence of a significant effect. We could vary the number of experts who have to agree on a sign before we definitely choose that sign. A quite different procedure would be the following: if any two experts who say there is an arrow disagree on the sign of the arrow, then let there be no arrow. If all who say there is an arrow agree on the sign, then let there be an arrow only if there is a large enough number of experts who think there is one, and if so, give the arrow the sign chosen by all experts believing in arrows. Still a different

FIGURE 7–2.

Signed Digraph G Constructed from Expert Data
of Table 7–3

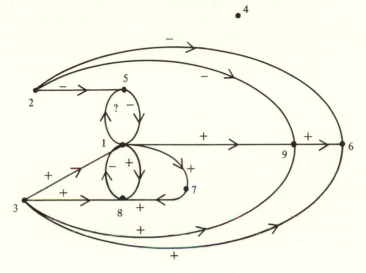

Key to Figure 7–2

1	Passenger miles	6	Emissions
2	Fuel economy	7	Accidents
3	Population size	8	Probability of delay
4	Cost of car	9	Fuel consumption
5	Price of commuter ticket		

procedure is the following: let x be the number of experts who say there is a positive arrow minus the number of experts who say there is a negative arrow. If x is sufficiently large and positive, introduce an arrow and make it positive. If x is sufficiently large and negative, introduce an arrow and make it negative. As we mentioned before, there seems to be no a priori reason for choosing one of these alternative procedures (or other equally plausible ones) over another.

ANALYZING THE SIGNED DIGRAPH

Having constructed a signed digraph such as G by the method described in the previous section, we can apply the methodology developed in Brown, Roberts, and Spencer (1972) and Roberts

167

and Brown (1974) to analyze the signed digraph. In particular, we shall illustrate this application by discussing the stability of the energy demand system described by the signed digraph G (Figure 7–2). We shall also consider the effect of various strategies for modifying the energy demand system, and see which of these is stabilizing. We shall do the same with various outside events, determining which of these lead to stability and which to instability. Throughout, we shall consider the policy implications of the conclusions.

A detailed analysis of the stability properties of the signed digraph G may be found in Appendix B of Roberts (1972b), though the more up-to-date techniques of Roberts and Brown (1974) can be used to make an even simpler analysis. To summarize the results, we recall that the system is called *stable* if the value of no variable gets larger and larger in any situation in which some external change is introduced at some other variable. The stability of signed digraph G will depend, of course, on the sign of the arrow (1,5) from passenger miles to price of commuter ticket. Line 1 of Tables 7–4, 7–5, and 7–6, respectively, shows

TABLE 7–4

EFFECT OF VARIOUS STRATEGIES ON SIGNED DIGRAPH G
WITH ARROW (1,5) TAKEN AS +

Strategy: change sign of edge	Evaluation	Stable starting variables (in new signed digraph)	Unstable starting variables
none	unstable	[4, 6, 9]	[1, 2, 3, 5, 7, 8]
18, 51	stable	all	none
all others	unstable	[4, 6, 9]	[1, 2, 3, 5, 7, 8]

TABLE 7–5

EFFECT OF VARIOUS STRATEGIES ON SIGNED DIGRAPH G
WITH ARROW (1,5) TAKEN AS −

Strategy: change sign of edge	Evaluation	Stable starting variables (in new signed digraph)	Unstable starting variables
none	stable	all	none
17, 78	unstable	[3, 4, 6, 9]	[1, 2, 5, 7, 8]
18, 51, 81	unstable	[4, 6, 9]	[1, 2, 3, 5, 7, 8]
all others	stable	all	none

168

TABLE 7–6

EFFECT OF VARIOUS STRATEGIES ON SIGNED DIGRAPH G
WITH ARROW (1,5) TAKEN AS 0

Strategy: change sign of edge	Evaluation	Stable starting variables (in new signed digraph)	Unstable starting variables
none	unstable	[4, 6, 9]	[1, 2, 3, 5, 7, 8]
all others	unstable	[4, 6, 9]	[1, 2, 3, 5, 7, 8]

stability in each of the three cases: the signed digraph is stable if arrow (1,5) is minus, and not stable otherwise. We shall discuss the significance of this conclusion in the next section.

The first lines of Table 7–4, 7–5, and 7–6 also give us some information about the effect of certain outside events on the energy demand system, those outside events that correspond to a change in some variable x. We shall call variable x a *stable starting variable* if, whenever a sudden increase is introduced at variable x, the resulting changes in the system lead to stability at each other variable. That is, x is a stable starting variable if a sudden increase in x does not lead to ever-larger values somewhere in the system. Thus, we see from Table 7–4 that if the arrow (1,5) is plus, the variables cost of car (4), emissions (6), and fuel consumption (9) are stable starting variables, and the rest of the variables are not. That is to say, a sudden increase in fuel consumption will not lead to indefinite growth in other variables in the system, while a sudden increase in price of a commuter ticket (5) will. We shall discuss the meaning of these predictions in detail below. In the same way, we note from line 1 of Table 7–5 that if the arrow (1,5) is taken to be minus, then every variable is a stable starting variable. The system is so stable that sudden external changes imposed at any of its variables do not lead to arbitrarily large values anywhere.

One important remark must be made about stable starting variables. The reader will recall that we analyze stability given an initial increase in a variable x under the assumption that further external influences are not introduced into the system. The instability comes from the propagation of changes *within* the system itself. Thus, if a given variable is known to be an unstable starting variable, the unstabilizing tendencies could be counteracted by introducing further external changes in the system at other variables.

Table 7–7 gives more detailed descriptions of stability properties of the signed digraph G. Specifically, we see that fuel consumption (9) will grow unboundedly large in the situation where arrow (1,5) is plus and an external increase is introduced at one of the

TABLE 7–7

STABILITY OF VARIABLES IN G UNDER STRATEGIES
GIVEN IN TABLES 7–4, 7–5, and 7–6

Variable	Stability behavior
1, 6, 7, 8, 9	Unbounded in value from external changes at any of the unstable starting variables
2, 3, 4	Bounded regardless of starting variables
5	Unbounded from external changes at unstable starting variable if and only if arrow (1, 5) exists

unstable starting variables, such as price of commuter ticket (5). However, population size (3) will remain bounded in value regardless of the sign of arrow (1,5), and regardless of where an external change is introduced. (We shall discuss this prediction below.) Once again, these predictions are made under the assumption that no external changes outside of an initial one are introduced.

One of the advantages of the signed digraph technique is that it allows us to evaluate the effect of various strategies, that is, deliberate changes in the energy demand system. Specifically, we are interested in strategies that correspond to changing the sign of a given arrow, and in discovering which of these strategies lead to stability. Tables 7–4, 7–5, and 7–6 show the stability of any signed digraph resulting from changing the sign of any given arrow in signed digraph G. Also indicated are the stable and unstable starting variables corresponding to each new signed digraph. We see, for example, from line 2 of Table 7–4 that if the arrow (1,5) is plus, and we change the sign of arrow (1,8), this strategy is stabilizing. However, if we change the sign of arrow (2,5) this strategy is not stabilizing. Again, we shall interpret the results in the next section. It is easy to discover what strategies will be stabilizing by studying the structural properties of the digraph.

Those strategies that make a certain cycle positive turn out to be the stabilizing ones. We shall see this below.

CONCLUSIONS AND DISCUSSION

In this section, we shall try to translate the graph-theoretical conclusions of the previous section into statements about the demand for energy, about policies for changing demand, and so on. We shall assume that the signed digraph G is an accurate model of the energy demand system, and the pulse process assumption of propagation of values is accurate enough. Then we shall discuss the various predictions attainable from the signed digraph. It should be understood that many of these predictions, especially those on stability, are to be regarded as tentative and suggestive, and should be tested by other means.

Specifically, we shall deal with the following issues, taking them as illustrative of the kinds of analyses possible with a signed digraph. First, should the price of commuter tickets be set as a function of passenger miles, and if so, should the price go up when passenger miles go up, or should it go down? Second, what strategies for changing the energy demand system in transportation are stabilizing? Third, of the various strategies considered, which are really feasible, that is, which can be implemented in practice? Finally, what feedback loops contribute to the instability of the situation?

Stability

Studying the results in Tables 7–4, 7–5, and 7–6, we note first that if the arrow (1,5) is 0, that is, if a change in number of passenger miles has an insignificant effect on the price of a commuter ticket, then the situation is unstable, and no strategy from the simple ones we have considered can change the situation. If the arrow (1,5) is plus, the situation is also unstable. Changing the sign of the arrows (5,1) or (1,8) makes it stable. If arrow (1,5) is minus, the situation is stable. Any strategy changing the sign of an arrow joining any pair of variables among 1, 5, 7, and 8 will destabilize the situation.

These conclusions can be interpreted as follows. It is suggested that if prices of commuter tickets are set as a function of total passenger miles, with prices decreasing as total passenger miles increase, then the energy demand system (in intraurban commuter transportation) will be stable. That is to say, under any external change in any of the relevant variables, no other variable will grow arbitrarily large. (This is not predicted if continuing changes are introduced at any variable.) If the pricing of commuter tickets is not critically dependent on passenger miles, or if the price is increased when passenger miles increase, then the situation will be unstable. That is to say, external changes in certain variables can lead to arbitrarily large values at other variables. For example, as we shall see below, it is predicted that emissions and fuel consumption will grow arbitrarily large if population is given an external increase. In the case in which the price of a commuter ticket increases when passenger miles increase, there are possible stabilizing strategies of a simple nature: arranging that passenger miles decrease as price of commuter tickets increases, or arranging that the probability of delay goes down as passenger miles increase. The question of whether these strategies are feasible, that is, whether they can be implemented, becomes a crucial one. We return to it below. If we think stability is important to attain, and instability is to be avoided, even using the limited notion of stability we are dealing with, the policy implications are quite clear. However, even if stability is attained, it is important to emphasize again that things might stabilize at unacceptably high levels, so further "forecasts" of future levels should probably be made.

The results on stability are conveniently stated by cases that are defined in terms of the sign of the arrow (1,5). This should not be taken to mean that arrow (1,5) is more important than any of the other arrows. It was, however, an arrow about which there was considerable disagreement. Analysis of why there was disagreement can be very useful. In this case, it might be due to the extreme sensitivity of the effect to context. That is, under certain scenarios, it might be reasonable to assume that an increase in passenger miles has no effect on the price of commuter tickets. This might be true if it has been decided as a matter of policy to make commuter tickets free. On the other hand, under other scenarios, it might be reasonable to charge more per commuter ticket if passenger miles went up. This might be the case if there were a very limited capacity, and it was hoped that the number of passenger miles could be limited.

Tables 7–4, 7–5, and 7–6 also list stable and unstable starting variables under the various sign change strategies. This allows us to evaluate the effect of introducing changes in certain variables under these sign change strategies. For example, we see that if arrow (1,5) is minus, then the introduction of a sudden increase in population size (3) leads to instabilities only if one of the arrows (1,8), (5,1), or (8,1) is changed in sign. Similarly, if arrow (1,5) is plus, then any increase in price of commuter tickets (5) leads to instability.

We have already observed that Table 7–7 gives more detailed information on the stability behavior at various variables. For example, expanding on the instabilities brought on by an increase in commuter ticket prices (5) if arrow (1,5) is plus, we see that this leads to large values in such important variables as tons of emissions (6) and fuel consumption (9). Another potentially interesting conclusion from Table 7–7 is that population size (3) is bounded regardless of starting variable. Such a conclusion can be interpreted in a number of ways. It is not necessarily surprising, in the sense that population can become rather large without being unbounded; all the conclusion asserts is that the population size variable has a bound beyond which it does not grow. Further, the conclusion does not assert that population will remain bounded if repeated outside changes are introduced. But it does imply that population will remain bounded by the operation of feedback in the system so long as no repeated external changes are made. The analysis predicts that this will not be the case for such other variables as emissions or fuel consumption. Thus, the prediction is that these variables will grow large much faster than population; or alternatively, that the structure of the system will change before that happens.

Strategies

One of the useful applications of the signed digraph technique is in the systematic generation of potentially useful strategies, which then can be evaluated by other methods. These strategies can be generated without introducing precise models of the kind that would be needed to be sure of the conclusions about stability.

The signed digraph G generated by the experts gives rise to a large number of strategies relevant to energy demand in the intra-urban commuter transportation sector. In particular, all strategies corresponding to changing the sign of an arrow are of potential interest. The analysis we have made, that is, one based on stability, suggests that the most promising strategies to consider further correspond to changing arrow (1,5) to minus, or, if (1,5) is determined to be plus, then to changing arrow (5,1) or (1,8). Relatively little attention has heretofore been given to these particular strategies in the way they relate to energy demand, in particular to the strategy of changing the sign of the arrow (1,8). (We shall further discuss this strategy below.) In addition to these strategies, the analysis has defined many other strategies that might be worth assessing, using other techniques. Thus, although the signed digraph analysis has indicated that change of the sign of arrow (2,5) (to choose an arrow from G at random) will not change stability, at least it has identified this as a potential strategy that perhaps should be evaluated by other methods. Perhaps analyzing this effect, that of change in fuel economy on price of a commuter ticket, will be interesting.

It is one thing to try to analyze strategies once they are given, and another thing to try to pinpoint ahead of time which strategies are likely to be effective. The structure of the signed digraph can be used to pinpoint such strategies. Indeed, the conclusion that if (1,5) is plus, then changing the sign of arrow (5,1) or arrow (1,8) is stabilizing, was first suggested by structural analysis of the cycles of the signed digraph.

It should be remarked that there are other strategies than changing the sign of an arrow. Some involve changing the sign of several arrows. For example, we might want to try to change the sign of both arrows (5,1) and (1,8) at the same time, thus changing the effect of an increase in price of commuter ticket on passenger miles *and* the effect of an increase in passenger miles on the probability of delay. (Incidentally, a stability analysis indicates that if (1,5) is plus, then making both these changes simultaneously leaves the unstable situation that prevailed before the simultaneous changes.) Another type of strategy could eliminate or add arrows. For example, variable 4 (cost of car) is now isolated, and it might be considered important to give this variable a role by introducing an arrow with a minus sign from it to passenger miles. Conversely, if (1,5) is 0, that is, if the price of a commuter ticket does not depend on passenger miles, then a stabilizing strategy is to eliminate the arrow (1,8), that is, to eliminate the effect of passenger miles on probability of delay. Similarly, a strategy might correspond to the addition of new variables. One such variable might be public expenditure on pollution control. This variable might have a negative arrow leading to emissions, and a positive arrow leading from emissions. Finally, one could define various strategies that correspond to inducing certain external changes in various variables, independent of the operation of the system itself. A typical strategy might be to add 10 percent to the cost-of-car variable every time period, say every two years. We have analyzed only the strategies that correspond to changing the sign of a single arrow. These other strategies can and should be analyzed similarly. But the kinds of conclusions attainable are in principle quite similar, namely, whether a given strategy is stabilizing, what future trends will follow from different strategies, which variables are stable under different strategies, which variables will reach unboundedly large values, and so on.

Feasibility [14]

Let us consider briefly the feasibility of the strategies corresponding to changing the signs of the arrow (1,5), (5,1), and (1,8). Questions of feasibility are, of course, not signed digraph questions. We are asking whether these strategies could be implemented, and if so, how.

It might be feasible to change the sign of the effect of an increase in the price of a commuter ticket on passenger miles, the sign of arrow (5,1). This could be through a system of "time-pricing," as discussed in Vickrey (1968). The idea is that ticket prices do not remain uniform, but are raised during peak demand periods (to reflect their contribution to fixed costs), and are lowered during off hours to attract riders. By using this procedure carefully to set ticket prices, it is possible to arrange increases in the average price of a commuter ticket so that they bring about an increase in total passenger miles.

As for the strategy of changing the effect of a change in passenger miles on the price of a commuter ticket, the sign of arrow (1,5), this is certainly feasible: it is simply a matter of deciding to set ticket prices on the basis of passenger miles.

The strategy of changing the effect of a change in passenger miles on the probability of delay, the sign of arrow (1,8), to minus might also be feasible. For example, if work schedules are shifted so that peak demand is lessened, then total passenger miles might

---

[14] The discussion in this section is based largely on the observations of J. Bigelow and J. DeHaven, and the author gratefully acknowledges their ideas.

be increased, while probability of a delay goes down. Thus, even if increased passenger miles lead to increased commuter ticket prices, the shifting of work schedules could be stabilizing.

Strictly speaking, however, the shift in work schedules or the addition of a new commuter mode are changes in the scenario under which the signs of arrows are defined rather than changes in the signs of the arrows themselves. Alternatively, one might say that they correspond to the introduction of an external *decrease* in the probability of delay variable (8) rather than a change in the sign of arrow (1,8).

Other strategies whose feasibility should be considered are those corresponding to the introduction of an external change at a particular variable. It seems at first glance that the most feasible or "manipulable" variables are fuel economy (2), cost of car (4), and price of commuter ticket (5). However, using the signed digraph G, we see that cost of car is relatively unimportant, because in the signed digraph it has no arrows connecting it to any other variable. Thus, although the strategy of introducing an external change at the cost-of-car variable is feasible, the analysis suggests it will be ineffective. It was pointed out earlier that this situation is altered by replacing variable 4 by a variable "cost of car." The strategy of introducing an external change in this new variable is again feasible, and might very well be effective. To decide, one would have to build a new signed digraph with this as a variable in place of the old variable cost of car.

Feedback loops

Another potentially useful application of the signed digraph is the identification of feedback loops using a constructed signed digraph. It is these loops that contribute so greatly to stability or instability, and knowing these loops can help us to understand the major forces for change present *within* the system. The identification of a feedback loop can be accomplished without knowing the strengths of effects, time lags, or how changes are propagated through the system. Similarly, its character as positive and deviation-amplifying, or as negative and deviation-counteracting, is easy to ascertain without knowing all these things. It is a good rule of thumb that if there are many positive feedback loops, this will lead to increasing deviations and instability. Also, if there are many negative feedback loops, these can lead to increasing oscillations, which is also an unstable situation. If there is a mixture of feedback loops, some positive and some negative, it is not easy to determine what the total effect will be. Indeed, that is one of the problems with analysis of a complex system: there are many interacting processes going on simultaneously. Specification of a rule by which changes are propagated through a system—for example, specification of a pulse process—allows one to analyze the interacting feedback loops. This sort of analysis shows that a positive feedback loop is not always destabilizing. Indeed, if there is already one negative loop, and a second loop has an undecided sign, it might be more stabilizing to make the second one positive than to make it negative. We shall see this in the signed digraph G.

In the case of G, there are three simple feedback loops if arrow (1,5) exists, namely, the cycle from passenger miles to price of a commuter ticket to passenger miles (1,5,1); the cycle from passenger miles to probability of delay to passenger miles (1,8,1); and the cycle from passenger miles to accidents to probability of delay to passenger miles (1,7,8,1). Thus, if this signed digraph accurately reflects the qualitative relations underlying the energy demand system in intraurban commuter transportation, then we have homed in on the basic feedback processes that contribute to instability or can be exploited to attain stability. The cycle 1,7,8,1 is negative; the cycle 1,8,1 is also negative; and the cycle 1,5,1 has undecided sign. It is interesting to note that the sign on arrow (1,5), which stabilizes the situation, is that sign ($-$) which makes this cycle positive, not negative. We thus have a graphic illustration of the fact that a positive cycle is sometimes stabilizing. Here, it plays the role of counteracting the negative cycle 1,8,1. Indeed, if the undecided sign of (1,5) is taken to be plus, then the undecided cycle 1,5,1 becomes negative, and the situation is not stable unless the sign of arrow (5,1) is changed to make the undecided cycle 1,5,1 positive again, or the sign of arrow (1,8) is changed to make the other cycle (1,8,1) positive.

In any case, identification of the feedback loops is a crucial step in determining the behavior of the system. It can suggest numerous policy alternatives, and aid in identifying stabilizing strategies.

SUMMARY

To summarize, use of a panel of experts to construct a signed digraph to study energy demand or other societal problems is a

177

promising methodology. (It is fairly easy to modify the procedure to obtain estimates of strengths of effects and of time lags, as well.) It is probably not desirable to construct just one signed digraph for the energy demand system or any societal system being studied. Rather, a number of signed digraphs should be built, using different parameters, different methods, or under different scenarios. Conclusions obtained from one signed digraph should be compared and contrasted to those derivable from another signed digraph or, indeed, to conclusions derivable by other methods. Techniques are needed for obtaining consensus signed digraphs from among the various alternatives. However, often it is more interesting to have a class of digraphs to compare than it is to have just one "correct" signed digraph. Indeed, to have faith in the conclusions from analysis of signed digraphs, it is often necessary to see that these conclusions are derivable under various situations or under various methods of analysis.

Once a signed digraph is constructed, it should be returned to the experts for discussion and modifications. Disagreements should be identified and analyzed.

Conclusions from the analysis of the constructed signed digraphs are usually not very interesting for their specific numerical predictions. Rather, they are interesting for their prediction of general geometric trends. Specifically, these are conclusions about stability or instability of the system, and about the type of growth it will exhibit (exponential, oscillatory), and so on. Such conclusions should be regarded as tentative and suggestive, and should be explored using other techniques. These conclusions might become less tentative as more information is added to the digraphs, information such as strengths of effects, time lags, and so on.

Structural analysis of the constructed signed digraph pinpoints possible strategies for modifying the energy demand system and feedback loops that contribute to instability or stability. The enumeration of the possible strategies and of the feedback loops can be done without knowing too much about the complex system being studied—indeed, simply by knowing the arrows and signs joining members of the class of variables. Preliminary analysis of the effects of these strategies and feedback loops can also be made by using just the signed digraphs, without assumptions about how changes are propagated through the system. If such additional assumptions are made, then it can be interesting to perform tests of which strategies are stabilizing, and what combination of signs on feedback loops leads to stability. Again, conclusions about stability are subject to verification by other techniques. But these conclusions can be of considerable value in aiding us to understand the potential impacts of both public policies and changes in technology or society. In short, the signed digraph can be a useful tool for the policy maker.

CHAPTER EIGHT

Comparative Cognition: Politics of International Control of the Oceans
—Jeffrey Hart

This empirical study begins to explore the relationships between the cognitive maps of different actors, in contrast to the previous studies, all of which analyzed one cognitive map at a time. The relevant political actors in this study are, moreover, highly complex groups of people, including nations, groups of nations, and the international oil industry. Comparative data on the perceived causal linkages of these actors is generated by using the questionnaire technique with a panel of experts who are familiar with a large body of source material on the relevant actors.

The particular problems that this study begins to answer are important for virtually all policy domains:

(1) How does the objective situation of an actor affect its perception (or nonperception) of causal linkages in its policy environment?

(2) How does the internal complexity of an actor affect the consistency between its stated assertions and its policy positions?

(3) Do actors who agree on policy positions also tend to agree on the causal linkages supporting these positions?*

The subject of this chapter is international cooperation in the exploitation and conservation of ocean resources. In 1969, a United Nations resolution called for the establishment of an international regime to regulate and control the oceans. The objective of this chapter is to consider the feasibility of analyzing the cognitive maps of the principal actors involved in this issue and to obtain in this manner information about the probable outcome of the debate. The actors to be examined include individual nations, groups of nations with common views on the issue, and the world petroleum industry. In this trial study the derivation of

* For acknowledgements, see p. 217.

180

cognitive maps for a variety of actors is based on the conclusions of a panel of judges. These judges estimated the cognitive maps of the principal actors on the basis of a wide variety of documentary materials. Unlike Roberts' study in Chapter 7 of this book, in the present study the judges estimated others' beliefs, rather than simply their own.

Two types of propositions will be used to analyze the estimated cognitive maps: propositions about the nature of each actor's cognitive map taken as a single, and relatively coherent, entity; and propositions about the differences between pairs of cognitive maps. In addition, the chapter focuses on the subgraphs (called goal structures) of individual cognitive maps formed by the goal variables (variables whose values directly impinge upon the actor's utility). From this analysis, several educated guesses about the final outcome of the 1974–1975 Law of the Sea Conference will emerge.

HISTORY OF THE OCEAN REGIME PROPOSAL

A regime for the control of ocean space was first proposed by the Maltese ambassador to the United Nations, Arvid Pardo, in the General Assembly on August 18, 1967.[1] Pardo's visions of wealth from the oceans, along with his designs for using that wealth to finance a more effective international organization and to redistribute the world's wealth, took most of the members of the United Nations by surprise. The less developed nations were delighted with the idea of benefiting from the exploitation of ocean resources and supported the proposal strongly. The developed nations were not delighted. Vital interests such as military capabilities, energy supplies, and mineral resources were at stake. They wanted more time to think. Nevertheless, in December of 1969, a resolution was passed in the General Assembly reserving the seabed and its resources beyond the limit of national jurisdiction exclusively for peaceful purposes and in the interest of mankind.[2] In 1970, a resolution calling for a new conference on the law of the sea was passed.[3] After several delays, the first session of this conference began in Caracas in June of 1974. Well over a

[1] United Nations, Document A/6840 Add. 2 and A/6695.
[2] This resolution, No. 2574 (XXIV), was passed by a vote of 62 in favor, 28 against, and 28 abstaining.
[3] This was Resolution No. 2749 (XXV) of December 17, 1970.

181

dozen different proposals were put forth and discussed. Although some progress was made in Caracas toward the narrowing of debate, no agreement was reached, and it is not likely that an agreement will emerge until the next session, scheduled to take place in March 1975, in Vienna. Since the estimation of cognitive maps used in this study was completed prior to the Caracas meeting, it will be possible to examine the results of the analysis in the light of that debate, while still allowing speculation about the final outcome.

GOAL STRUCTURES IN COGNITIVE MAPS

A cognitive map is an actor's belief about the causal relations between pairs of variables in his conceptual inventory. We assume that there are three types of concept variables: (1) policy variables, (2) goal variables, and (3) utility. Goal variables are variables that impinge directly and positively upon the actor's utility variable. We then define a *goal structure* of an actor as the subgraph of that actor's cognitive map which consists of all of his goals and the causal relationships between them. These definitions are illustrated in Figure 8–1. A hypothetical cognitive map is given in the first part of the figure, and the goal structure of this map is given in the second part.

It will sometimes be convenient to represent cognitive maps and their derived goal structures in the form of adjacency matrices (see Bonham and Shapiro in Chapter 6). For illustrative purposes, this is done in the third part of Figure 8–1, where the adjacency matrix of the goal structure is indicated by dotted lines within the larger adjacency matrix of the hypothetical cognitive map.

The fact that different actors may have different cognitive maps with respect to the same set of variables suggests that differences in cognitive maps, and especially differences in goal structures, can be used to explain differences in positions taken on policy and goal variables. The basic idea is the notion of "distance" between the goal structures of two actors. Distance will be defined here in terms of an entry-by-entry comparison of the goal adjacency matrices of the two actors. For example, if two goal structures differ in only one entry in their adjacency matrices, their distance from each other is very small. Admittedly, the changing of a single causal link may have a very strong effect on the actor's position,

FIGURE 8–1.

Cognitive Maps and Goal Structures

A Hypothetical Cognitive Map
The Goal Structure of the Hypothetical Cognitive Map
Adjacency Matrix for the Cognitive Map with the Adjacency Matrix
for the Goal Structure Shown in Dotted Lines

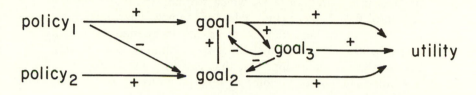

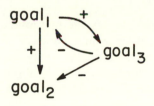

	p_1	p_2	g_1	g_2	g_3	u
policy$_1$/	o	o	+	−	o	o
policy$_2$	o	o	o	+	o	o
goal$_1$	o	o	o	+	+	+
goal$_2$	o	o	o	o	o	+
goal$_3$	o	o	−	−	o	+
utility	o	o	o	o	o	o

and, thus, another way of explaining positions would be to investigate the consequences of slight differences in goal structures.

The point is that if actors take different positions on political issues because their cognitions are different, rather than because of some fundamental differences that are independent of cognitive factors, then it may be possible to get actors to agree on some mutually beneficial policy by altering their cognitions. This may be done in a variety of ways, which will be explored in the final section of this chapter. One could, for example, change an actor's cognitions by making him aware of the temptation to simplify causal beliefs. Thus, the analysis of cognitive maps is an abstract, but relatively simple, approach that can help us to understand how international actors come to take positions on international issues, such as the international ocean regime, while also suggesting novel ways of influencing this process.

HYPOTHESES

In order to help clarify the presentation of the data, it is helpful to present the three main hypotheses of this study. As we shall see, these three hypotheses are partly supported and partly refuted by the data. Fortunately, in situations such as these we are able to learn at least as much from our surprises as from our successes.

Hypothesis 1. The developed nations will have denser goal structures than the developing nations.

This is a hypothesis about how the nature of an actor affects its perception of the linkages. It is based on the expectation that the greater research capabilities and wider interests of the developed nations will lead them to perceive more causal linkages than the developing nations perceive with respect to the complex issues of an ocean regime. The formal measure of density of a goal structure is the proportion of all possible linkages that are actually perceived.[4]

Hypothesis 2. The positions taken by the actors will be consistent with their goal structures.

This hypothesis states that even complex actors, such as nations and the oil industry, are consistent, at least on a specialized policy domain such as ocean regime issues. The formal test is that inconsistency can be observed whenever an actor has

[4] The formula for density is $m/n(n-1)$, where m is the number of arrows and n is the number of points in the graph.

184

a balanced goal structures but does not take positions in accordance with that structure.

Hypothesis 3. Actors with similar positions will have similar beliefs.

This hypothesis states that it is rare for two actors to support the same positions but have widely divergent images of the causal linkages that lead them to their positions. If true, it would mean that alignments of convenience (based on similarity of positions) would also tend to be alignments of perception (based on similarity of beliefs).

In order to test these hypotheses, a methodology was developed to generate data on the goal structures of the relevant actors. After explaining this methodology in the next section, the data will be presented and analyzed. Then implications will be drawn for the potential alignments of the actors and the future of an ocean regime.

METHODS

In order to show how one might gain knowledge about the way the cognitions of international actors affect their positions on political issues, a group of judges was used to estimate the cognitive maps of a small set of actors on a specific issue, the establishment of an international ocean regime. The group consisted of three individuals in the Technology and International Systems Project at the Institute of International Studies in Berkeley, California.[5] All of these individuals are citizens of the United States. They are widely read on the subject of the international ocean regime and international politics in general. They had a self-consciously favorable view toward the regime and Pardo's plan.

The Actors

Two preliminary tasks were the selection of actors and the selection of goal variables. For the actors, there were two criteria. The first was that the actor must be essential to the success of an international ocean regime. The second was that the elements of compound actors share a large number of beliefs about the causal links between variables. Six actors were chosen for this

---

[5] The individuals are Professor Ernst B. Haas, Peter Cowhey, and Janet Schmidt.

exercise: (1) the United States, (2) the Soviet Union, (3) the other developed nations (the OECD nations minus the United States),[6] (4) the oil-exporting developing nations,[7] (5) the non-oil-exporting developing nations (called the Other LDCs), and (6) the world oil industry.

The Goal Variables

Fourteen variables were chosen by the expert group to be the basis for comparing the cognitive maps of the six actors (see Table 8–1). These variables were selected on the basis that at least one of the actors considered the variable to be a goal.

TABLE 8–1

GOALS PERTAINING TO THE ESTABLISHMENT
OF AN OCEAN REGIME

1 Obtaining a high level of petroleum exploitation of the sea bed
2 Obtaining a high level of hard mineral (manganese nodule) exploitation of the sea bed
3 Obtaining the maximum sustainable yield from ocean fisheries
4 Conserving mineral resources (nodules) in the ocean
5 Scheduling the development of land and ocean reserves of petroleum to meet future demand
6 Conservation of ocean fisheries
7 Alleviation of world protein deficiencies
8 Reduction of the potential for conflict over matters pertaining to the ocean
9 Establishment of machinery for resolving conflicts pertaining to the ocean
10 Reduction of military use of the sea bed and deep ocean (emplacement of installations on the sea bed and/or free passage of submarines)
11 Preventing expansion of national jurisdiction into the sea
12 Maintaining the right of innocent passage through territorial waters
13 Preserving the nonliving environment of the ocean
14 Establishing an international regime for ocean space

[6] The states referred to as the OECD states are France, Britain, West Germany, Belgium, the Netherlands, Ireland, Denmark, Spain, Italy, Norway, Sweden, Greece, Portugal, Iceland, Japan, Canada, Australia, and New Zealand.

[7] The major oil-exporting nations are Abu Dhabi, Algeria, Indonesia, Iran, Iraq, Kuwait, Libya, Nigeria, Qatar, and Venezuela. All are members of OPEC. Ecuador, Gabon, and Trinidad/Tobago are members of OPEC, or have applied for membership, but have not yet become major exporters.

A distinction was made between exploitation of petroleum (goal 1) and hard minerals (2) for a number of reasons: several actors make the distinction; the technology for the two types of exploitation will be very different; and petroleum exploitation is most likely to occur within the territorial waters of nations, while hard minerals are mainly to be found in the deep ocean. A maximum sustainable yield (abbreviated as MSY) for ocean fisheries (3) is obtained when fishing is limited to levels that can be supported by the fisheries without decreasing the stock or future catches. Exploitation of hard minerals, in the form of manganese nodules, can be accompanied by a management system that maintains the exploitation at levels that permit the natural replenishment of the resources. Thus, the conservation of mineral resources (4) was included as a goal variable.

Scheduling the development of land and ocean reserves of petroleum (5) means maintaining a balance between the exploitation of these two forms of petroleum deposits. The United States, for example, wants to develop offshore reserves as an alternative to imported oil, even though offshore oil is much more expensive than oil from land reserves. In addition, the United States maintains land reserves in case of war or emergency, since offshore reserves would be more vulnerable. The goal of conserving fisheries (6) is taken here to include management techniques such as stocking and mariculture, as well as the more limited techniques of setting quotas, issuing licences, and inspecting fishing grounds. A separate goal of preserving the nonliving environment (13) was included, since many of the actors do not consider fishery conservation to involve management of the nonliving environment. For example, a fishery management regime would be expected to react to an oil spill, but not to prevent it. Alleviating world protein deficiencies (7) is a straightforward goal that could be achieved through the use of fish meal for animal feed, through the direct consumption of fish, or possibly from the synthesis of protein from petrochemical by-products.

The goals concerning conflict or potential conflict are: reducing potential conflict over matters pertaining to the ocean (8), the establishment of machinery for resolving conflicts pertaining to the ocean (9), and the reduction of military uses of the ocean (10). It was assumed that conflict reduction could take place on an *ad hoc* basis without extensive machinery—that is, without formal organizations designed to perform such conflict-resolving tasks as mediation, arbitration, inspection, or peace keeping.

There are two goals concerning national control over adjacent waters. Preventing expansion of national jurisdiction into the sea (11) does not have to affect navigation. It may be limited to jurisdiction over mineral or living resources. Another goal (12) is innocent passage, involving the rights of ocean vessels to pass through territorial waters of other nations without interference.

Finally, there is the variable of establishing an international regime for ocean space (14). It was assumed that this regime would have the following minimal properties: (1) the regime would include standing machinery, that is, a formal organization with a staff and a budget; (2) this organization would have jurisdiction over more than one of the general domains of mineral resources, living resources, conflict resolution, and control over national waters; and (3) some area of the ocean would be specified as res communis, to be explored, if at all, for the benefit of all mankind. Not all of the current proposals for an international regime meet these criteria, but the group of judges had the Pardo proposal uppermost in their minds.

Estimating the Goal Structures

After selecting the actors and the variables, the group of judges was asked to fill out a goal adjacency matrix, similar to the one in Figure 8–1, for each of the actors. Members of the group consulted an extensive set of fifty-one documentary sources (a list of which may be obtained from the author on request). These documents included position papers, transcripts of debates, and commentaries on the evolution of the law of the sea by legal scholars and social scientists. In an initial trial run, good intercoder agreement was obtained.[8] Because of limitations of time, expertise, and mental capacity, it was impossible for each member of the group to fill out a matrix for each actor. Therefore, the group subsequently arrived at a group consensus by discussion. This was very time-consuming, but the payoff in accuracy was judged to be more important than a more complete test of intercoder reliability.

The end result of this process is displayed in Tables 8–2 through 8–9. The symbols +, −, a, and cd in Tables 8–3 through

[8] In the initial run, goal structures for the two superpowers were estimated. Over 80 percent of the entries of the goal adjacency matrices were in agreement for each pair of coders. Most discrepancies were the result of a zero entry in one matrix and a non-zero entry in the other.

TABLE 8-2

POSITIONS TAKEN ON THE OCEAN GOALS AND THE
RELATIVE SALIENCE OF GOALS FOR EACH ACTOR

Goals	U.S. P[a]	U.S. S[b]	USSR P	USSR S	OECD P	OECD S	Oil exporters P	Oil exporters S	Other LDCs P	Other LDCs S	Oil industry P	Oil industry S
Oil exploitation	+	m	o	l	+	h	+	h	−	m	+	h
Nodule exploitation	+	m	+	m	+	m	o	l	+	m	o	l
MSY (sustainable yield)	−	m	+	h	+	m	o	l	+	h	o	l
Nodule conservation	−	l	−	l	−	l	o	l	+	m	−	m
Scheduled development	+	l	+	l	−	h	+	h	o	l	−	m
Fishery conservation	+	m	−	m	+	m	o	l	−	h	o	l
World protein	+	l	−	l	+	l	o	l	+	h	o	l
Conflict reduction	+	m	+	m	+	h	o	l	+	h	+	h
Conflict machinery	+	l	−	h	a[c]	m	−	h	?		−	l
Reduction of military	−	h	−	h	+	m	+	h	+	m	o	l
Prevention of expansion	+	m	+	h	+	h	−	h	−	h	−	h
Innocent passage	+	h	+	h	+	h	−	h	−	h	+	h
Nonliving environment	+	h	o	l	+	m	−	l	+	m	−	l
International regime	+	m	−	l	a[d]	m	o	l	+	h	−	h

[a] P stands for "position," and + = favor or support, − = oppose, o = no position or neutral, and a = ambiguous (some support and some oppose).

[b] S stands for "salience," and l = low, m = medium, and h = high.

[c] Britain and France are opposed to reduction of military use of the oceans, since they have substantial naval forces and some submarines. Australia and New Zealand would also oppose reduced military use, since they depend on American naval forces to deter Chinese or Russian aggression in that part of the world. The other OECD members generally favor demilitarization in world politics.

[d] Some OECD nations, such as Canada, are in favor of limited international regimes, while others are opposed.

TABLE 8–3

GOAL ADJACENCY MATRIX FOR THE UNITED STATES

	1	2	3	4	5	6	7	8	9	10	11	12	13	14
1 Oil exploitation	o	+	–	–	cd	–	a	–	+	+	–	–	–	–
2 Nodule exploitation	+	o	o	–	o	o	o	–	+	a	–	–	–	–
3 MSY (sustainable yield)	o	o	o	+	o	–	+	–	+	o	–	+	o	cd
4 Nodule conservation	–	–	o	o	a	o	o	–	+	o	o	+	+	+
5 Scheduled development	+	o	o	o	o	o	o	–	+	o	–	–	+	+
6 Fishery conservation	–	–	cd	o	o	o	+	–	+	o	–	+	+	+
7 World protein	+	o	+	+	+	+	o	cd	o	+	cd	o	o	o
8 Conflict reduction	+	+	o	+	+	o	o	o	–	–	+	+	o	cd
9 Conflict machinery	+	+	o	+	o	+	o	+	o	o	+	+	o	o
10 Reduction of military use	o	–	o	o	o	o	o	–	o	+	o	o	+	o
11 Prevention of expansion	–	–	a	o	–	o	o	–	+	–	o	–	o	–
12 Innocent passage	+	+	–	+	+	+	+	–	+	–	o	o	o	+
13 Nonliving environment	–	–	o	+	–	+	o	–	+	+	o	–	o	+
14 International regime	+	+	+	+	+	+	+	+	+	–	–	+	+	o

TABLE 8-4
GOAL ADJACENCY MATRIX FOR THE SOVIET UNION

	1	2	3	4	5	6	7	8	9	10	11	12	13	14
1. Oil exploitation	o	+	−	−	cd	−	a	−	+	+	−	−	−	o
2. Nodule exploitation	+	o	−	−	o	o	o	−	+	a	−	−	−	−
3. MSY (sustainable yield)	o	o	o	+	o	−	+	−	+	o	+	+	o	cd
4. Nodule conservation	o	−	o	o	o	o	o	−	+	o	o	−	+	+
5. Scheduled development	o	o	o	o	o	o	o	−	+	o	−	o	o	+
6. Fishery conservation	o	o	cd	o	o	o	+	−	+	o	−	+	+	+
7. World protein	+	+	+	+	+	o	o	cd	o	o	cd	+	o	o
8. Conflict reduction	+	+	o	o	+	o	o	o	−	+	+	+	o	cd
9. Conflict machinery	o	o	o	o	o	o	o	o	o	o	+	+	o	o
10. Reduction of military use	o	−	o	o	o	o	o	o	o	o	o	o	o	o
11. Prevention of expansion	−	−	a	o	−	o	o	−	+	−	o	−	+	−
12. Innocent passage	+	+	+	o	+	o	+	o	+	−	o	o	o	+
13. Nonliving environment	−	−	o	+	−	+	o	−	+	+	o	o	o	+
14. International regime	+	+	+	+	+	+	+	+	o	−	−	+	+	o

TABLE 8-5

GOAL ADJACENCY MATRIX FOR THE OECD STATES
(MINUS THE U.S.)

	1	2	3	4	5	6	7	8	9	10	11	12	13	14
Oil exploitation	o	+	-	-	-	-	cd	+	-	+	-	+	-	-
Nodule exploitation	+	o	-	-	-	-	o	+	-	+	-	-	-	-
MSY (sustainable yield)	-	-	o	+	-	+	+	o	+	+	o	o	o	o
Nodule conservation	o	-	+	o	o	o	o	o	+	+	+	o	+	+
Scheduled development	+	o	o	o	o	o	o	o	o	o	-	+	-	+
Fishery conservation	o	o	o	o	o	o	+	o	+	+	o	o	o	cd
World protein	+	+	+	+	o	+	o	o	o	o	+	+	o	+
Conflict reduction	+	+	+	o	o	o	o	o	+	+	+	+	o	cd
Conflict machinery	+	+	+	+	o	+	o	+	o	+	+	+	o	cd
Reduction of military use	+	+	+	+	o	+	o	+	+	o	+	+	o	+
Prevention of expansion	-	o	+	o	-	o	o	+	o	o	o	+	+	+
Innocent passage	+	+	+	+	+	o	a	+	-	-	+	o	-	cd
Nonliving environment	-	-	+	o	-	+	+	+	+	+	-	-	o	+
International regime	o	-	+	+	o	+	+	+	+	o	-	+	o	o

TABLE 8-6
GOAL ADJACENCY MATRIX FOR THE OIL EXPORTERS

	1	2	3	4	5	6	7	8	9	10	11	12	13	14
1 Oil exploitation	o	+	−	o	+	o	+	+	o	+	−	−	o	cd
2 Nodule exploitation	+	o	o	−	+	o	o	−	o	o	−	−	−	−
3 MSY (sustainable yield)	o	o	o	o	o	o	o	o	o	o	o	o	o	o
4 Nodule conservation	o	o	o	o	o	o	o	+	+	+	+	+	+	cd
5 Scheduled development	+	o	o	o	o	o	+	+	o	+	−	−	+	o
6 Fishery conservation	o	o	o	o	o	o	o	o	o	o	o	o	o	o
7 World protein	+	o	o	o	+	o	o	o	o	o	o	o	o	o
8 Conflict reduction	+	o	o	o	+	o	o	o	o	o	o	o	o	o
9 Conflict machinery	+	o	o	o	+	o	o	o	o	o	o	o	o	o
10 Reduction of military use	+	+	o	o	+	o	o	o	o	o	+	+	o	+
11 Prevention of expansion	+	+	o	+	−	o	o	−	−	−	o	o	o	−
12 Innocent passage	+	o	o	+	−	o	o	−	−	−	o	o	o	o
13 Nonliving environment	−	o	o	+	−	o	o	−	o	+	o	o	o	+
14 International regime	o	−	o	cd	o	o	o	+	+	+	o	o	+	o

TABLE 8-7

GOAL ADJACENCY MATRIX FOR THE OTHER LDCs

	1	2	3	4	5	6	7	8	9	10	11	12	13	14
1 Oil exploitation	o	+	–	–	–	–	o	–	–	–	–	–	–	–
2 Nodule exploitation	+	o	–	–	o	–	–	–	–	–	–	–	–	–
3 MSY (sustainable yield)	–	–	o	o	o	+	+	–	+	+	o	–	+	cd
4 Nodule conservation	o	–	o	o	+	o	o	+	+	+	+	+	+	+
5 Scheduled development	+	o	o	o	o	o	o	o	o	o	–	o	o	cd
6 Fishery conservation	o	–	+	+	o	o	+	–	+	+	o	o	+	+
7 World protein	o	–	+	o	o	o	o	+	o	o	o	+	+	+
8 Conflict reduction	o	o	+	+	+	+	o	o	+	+	o	o	o	+
9 Conflict machinery	o	o	+	+	+	+	o	+	o	+	o	o	o	+
10 Reduction of military use	o	o	+	+	+	+	o	+	+	o	o	o	o	cd
11 Prevention of expansion	+	+	–	–	–	o	–	–	–	–	o	–	–	+
12 Innocent passage	+	–	–	–	–	–	o	–	–	–	o	o	–	cd
13 Nonliving environment	–	–	+	+	o	+	o	o	+	+	o	–	o	+
14 International regime	+	–	+	+	+	+	+	o	o	+	+	–	+	o

TABLE 8-8

GOAL ADJACENCY MATRIX FOR THE OIL INDUSTRY

	1	2	3	4	5	6	7	8	9	10	11	12	13	14
1 Oil exploitation	o	+	o	o	+	o	+	+	−	o	−	+	−	−
2 Nodule exploitation	+	o	o	−	+	o	o	+	−	o	−	+	−	−
3 MSY (sustainable yield)	o	−	o	o	−	o	+	o	o	o	o	−	o	o
4 Nodule conservation	o	−	o	o	−	o	o	o	o	o	o	o	o	o
5 Scheduled development	cd	+	o	o	o	o	o	+	−	o	−	o	o	o
6 Fishery conservation	−	−	o	o	o	o	o	o	o	o	o	+	o	o
7 World protein	o	o	o	o	o	o	o	o	o	o	o	+	o	o
8 Conflict reduction	+	+	o	o	+	o	o	o	o	o	−	+	−	−
9 Conflict machinery	o	o	o	o	o	o	o	o	o	o	−	o	o	−
10 Reduction of military use	o	o	o	o	o	o	o	o	o	o	o	−	o	o
11 Prevention of expansion	−	−	o	o	−	o	o	−	o	o	o	o	o	o
12 Innocent passage	+	+	o	o	+	o	+	+	+	−	o	o	o	o
13 Nonliving environment	−	−	o	o	−	o	o	−	−	o	−	−	o	+
14 International regime	−	−	o	o	−	o	o	−	−	o	−	−	+	o

TABLE 8-9

GOAL ADJACENCY MATRIX FOR THE GROUP OF JUDGES

	1	2	3	4	5	6	7	8	9	10	11	12	13	14
1 Oil exploitation	o	+	−	o	cd	−	a	−	+	a	−	−	−	+
2 Nodule exploitation	+	o	a	−	+	−	o	−	+	+	−	−	−	+
3 MSY (sustainable yield)	−	−	o	+	o	+	+	−	+	−	+	+	o	cd
4 Nodule conservation	o	cd	+	o	o	o	o	−	+	o	+	+	+	+
5 Scheduled development	+	+	+	o	o	o	o	−	+	o	−	o	+	o
6 Fishery conservation	−	−	+	+	o	o	+	−	+	o	+	+	+	+
7 World protein	o	o	+	o	o	+	o	+	o	+	o	o	o	o
8 Conflict reduction	+	+	+	+	+	+	o	o	cd	+	+	+	+	cd
9 Conflict machinery	+	+	o	+	o	+	o	+	o	+	+	o	o	+
10 Reduction of military	+	+	+	o	o	+	o	+	+	o	+	+	+	+
11 Prevention of expansion	−	−	o	o	o	a	o	+	o	a	o	+	a	+
12 Innocent passage	+	+	+	+	−	+	o	−	+	−	+	o	−	+
13 Nonliving environment	−	−	+	+	+	+	o	−	+	+	−	−	o	o
14 International regime	+	−	+	+	+	+	+	o	+	o	+	+	+	o

8–9 stand for positive, negative, ambiguous, and curvilinear downward causal relations between variables. A curvilinear downward relation between goals x and y means that the realization of goal x facilitates that of goal y only if partial success is obtained in goal x; otherwise, goal y is blocked or impeded. This means that intermediate values of x result in high values of y, and extreme values of x (either high or low) result in low values of y. The curvilinear downward relation was included in this study because the group of judges consistently expressed a need for a curvilinear relation to supplement the monotonic positive and negative relations. After the curvilinear downward relation was explained to the group, they seemed satisfied that it would solve most of the problems they were having in estimating the causal beliefs of the actors. The fact that the group saw no need for using the curvilinear upward relation is interesting in itself, and could bear further study.

The group of judges was then asked to estimate the positions taken on each of the goal variables and the salience of the variable. The results, given in Table 8–2, correspond to the last column of the causal adjacency matrix of the cognitive map in Figure 8–1. The sequence of estimation—goal structure first and positions second—was thought to have a significant impact on the results. Considerable knowledge about the positions of the actors was gained in the process of estimating their goal structures.

At no time were the members of the group of judges informed of the three central hypotheses of this study. None of the members of the group had any previous exposure to graph theory or the analysis of cognitive maps. Nevertheless, the group knew that one of the purposes of the exercise was to use differences in cognitions to explain why certain actors favored an international ocean regime and others did not. Since the data here is purely judgmental, the separation of hypothesis and estimation was considered important. To allow for a test of the possibility that the group's estimates of perceived causal links were too clearly related to their personal estimates, the group was also asked to give their own ideas about the causal relations among variables (see Table 8–15 below).

The fact that the expert group's goal structure most closely resembled that of the United States may cast some doubt on the impartiality of the group. The fact that their goal structure more closely resembled the goal structure of the non-oil-exporting developing nations than those of the oil industry or the oil exporters, however, suggests that this resemblance was more a function of the comparative densities of the structures than of ethnocentricity or differences of opinion on the sign of specific causal links. That is, most differences between goal structures involved the expert group's estimating a causal link where an actor does not. Thus there are several possible explanations for the variance among distances from the expert group's goal structure: (1) bias on the part of the expert group; (2) the density of the actor's goal structure; and (3) lack of information on the part of the expert group about the causal beliefs of the actor.

Several things may be done to increase one's confidence in the estimated goal structures: (1) the use of experts from a number of different countries; (2) the use of a more context-free method of estimating goal structures (see Roberts in Chapter 7); and (3) more extensive checks on the reliability of individual estimates. Each of these would have involved more time and expense than this trial study allowed. Nevertheless, it is believed that the use of experts to estimate the beliefs of international actors is both feasible and desirable for many research purposes. Transcripts of governmental strategy sessions are not always available. The actors are not always accessible for interviews. The probable alternative to the procedures used here would be to increase the number and variety of experts estimating goal structures, or to simplify the task by limiting the number of goal variables so that the time required of the actors, or their representatives, would be minimized.

The analysis of all the estimated goal structures will now be undertaken from both a separate and a comparative basis. The maps will be separately analyzed in terms of complexity, density, imbalance, and inconsistencies relative to subgraphs of salient goals; the analysis will allow a test of the first two hypotheses. The comparative analysis focuses on the patterns of similarities and differences between actors with respect to both their causal beliefs and their policy positions; the comparative analysis will allow a test of the third hypothesis. Throughout both analyses it will be assumed that the judges were accurate in estimating the actors' beliefs. The importance of this assumption will be re-examined in the section on "Explanations of Cognitive Inconsistencies."

ANALYSIS OF THE GOAL STRUCTURES OF THE SEPARATE ACTORS

The most striking feature of the goal structures estimated by the expert group is their relatively high complexity. They are not balanced; they are not acyclic; and they have relatively high density. The structures are too complex to be readily comprehended when presented in pictorial form. Even the structure with the lowest density, the oil industry's goal structure, has 66 of a possible 182 linkages, or 36 percent (see Table 8–10).

The first hypothesis can now be evaluated. The developed nations do indeed have relatively dense goal structures, as shown in Table 8–10. The United States, the Soviet Union, and the

TABLE 8–10

DENSITY OF GOAL STRUCTURES
(percent)

U.S.	USSR	OECD	Oil exporters	Other LDCs	Oil industry	Expert group
68	60	80	37	69	36	76

OECD states perceive causal linkages between the 14 goal variables at levels of 68 percent, 60 percent, and 80 percent, respectively. The Oil Exporters, on the other hand, perceive that only 37 percent of the possible linkages exist. The only anomaly is that the Other LDCs perceive more linkages than the two superpowers.

With only one exception (the Other LDCs) the density of substructures of highly salient goal variables is greater than the density of the whole structure (see Table 8–11). The substruc-

TABLE 8–11

DENSITY OF SUBSTRUCTURES OF HIGHLY SALIENT GOALS
(percent)

U.S.	USSR	OECD	Oil exporters	Other LDCs	Oil industry
83	67	90	77	63	75

199

tures of the highly salient goal variables were, therefore, more dense than the substructures of less salient goals. Such a result suggests that the salience of goals is positively associated with the density of the goal structure. This conclusion may help to explain why the developing nations that do not export oil have goal structures with higher densities than was first expected. Even though they do not have great research capabilities, many of the goals included in this analysis were salient to them. A supplementary explanation would be that the Pardo proposal made them aware of more causal linkages.

Substructures of Salient Goals

In view of these findings of differences between the actors, as well as the initial investigation of the density of the goal structures, it is possible to proceed to test the second hypothesis about the tendency to hold positions that are consistent with beliefs. None of the goal structures in Tables 8–3 to 8–9 is perfectly balanced. This a rather unusual finding, for which explanations will be proposed. In any case, positions may be consistent only to a limited degree with goal structures that are not balanced. One kind of limited consistency will be explored by focusing on the substructures of highly salient goal variables (see Figure 8–2). These substructures are substantially more balanced than the entire structures, but there are still only two perfectly balanced substructures, those of the United States and the oil exporters.

Strangely enough, even though these two are balanced, the United States' substructure provides evidence that the positions taken on goal variables may be inconsistent with even *balanced* goal substructures. The United States should be either in favor of innocent passage and against both protection of the nonliving environment and reduced military use, or vice versa. Table 8–2 demonstrates, however, that the United States is for innocent passage and protection of the nonliving environment, while being against reduction of military use of the oceans. Possible explanations for this will be explored later.

The oil industry, on the other hand, has taken positions consistent with the substructure of its most salient goals: it favors oil exploitation, conflict reduction, and innocent passage, but opposes preventing the expansion of national jurisdictions. This opposition to limiting expansion, consistent with the perceived incompatibilities between preventing expansion and reducing conflict or increasing offshore exploitation, has led the oil industry to take the same position on expansion that most of the developing nations have chosen. Some observers have commented on a possible alliance between the developing nations and the oil companies. Judging from the full range of goals and from perceived linkages, such an alliance is extremely unlikely unless limited to this issue.

The developing nations (minus the oil exporters) favor a maximum sustainable yield for fisheries, conflict reduction, and alleviation of world protein deficiencies, while opposing fishery conservation (primarily the position of fishing LDCs), innocent passage, and limiting expansion. The last two goals were both opposed despite the fact that they were perceived to be mutually incompatible. This inconsistency is partially a result of nationalist domestic pressures, and partly an indication of an inclination to bargain with innocent passage in order to get concessions from major powers to expand their national jurisdictions.

Other actors also permitted the existence of imbalance within goal structures and inconsistencies between positions and structures. The Soviet Union wants to prevent the expansion of national jurisdictions for reasons concerned with fishing. At the same time, it is fully aware of the possibility that preventing expansion may result in decreased willingness to allow military or scientific vessels to operate in national waters. Even so, they do not view innocent passage to be incompatible with the limitation of expansion of national jurisdictions. In these inconsistent perceptions, they are in perfect agreement with the United States, although the issue of preventing expansion is much less salient for the United States. The crucial question for the establishment of an ocean regime is whether the superpowers will be willing to trade some expansion of jurisdictions for guarantees of innocent passage. Although the superpowers share perceptions of the linkages involved, they do not consider the goals to be equally salient. This difference may impede efforts to negotiate, since the United States may be more flexible on the question of expansion than the Soviet Union.

For the oil exporters, the goals of high oil exploitation, scheduled development, establishment of conflict machinery, and reduction of military use of the oceans are all compatible. It is surprising, therefore, that the expert group believed them to be opposed to conflict machinery, while in favor of the other three goals. There is a substantial amount of asymmetry and inconsistency in the substructure, however, which could affect the choice of posi-

FIGURE 8–2.

Goal Substructures of Highly Salient Goals for Each Actor

United States

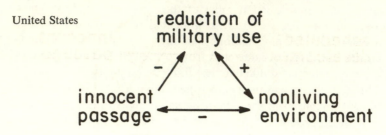

Soviet Union

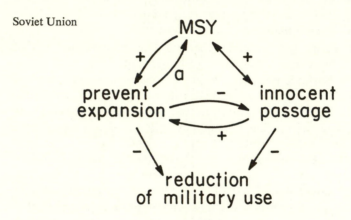

OECD States

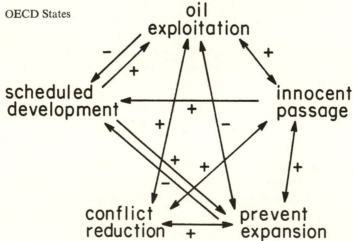

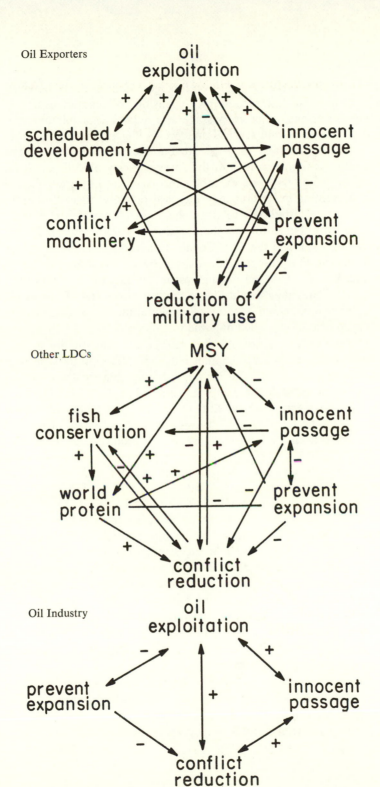

tions. Positive-negative pairs of linkages include those between oil exploitation and preventing expansion, oil exploitation and innocent passage, innocent passage and reduction of military use, and reduction of military use and preventing expansion. Several of these asymmetries may be attributable to conflicts between domestic economic goals and the foreign policy objectives of the Arab oil exporters. For example, the Arab oil exporters realize that preventing expansion may increase offshore oil exploitation. Even so, they preferred to deny the right of nations who sympathize with Israel to use their national waters, especially the Straits of Tiran and the Suez Canal. In addition, the oil exporters may believe that unregulated offshore oil exploitation will be of greater benefit to the oil companies or the major consumers than to them. Thus, they would like to convey to the rest of the world the idea that increased offshore oil exploitation can take place only in the context of expanded national jurisdictions.

For the OECD nations, a high degree of compatibility is perceived among the goals of conflict reduction, innocent passage, and preventing expansion. The incompatibilities that exist are due to the goals of scheduled development and oil exploitation. High oil exploitation means "scheduled development" for them, since their main domestic reserves are offshore, in the North Sea. They are opposed to what the United States and oil-producing states understand of scheduled development, which requires maintaining an approximately constant ratio between onshore and offshore reserves. Their opposition derived from the policy's implication of continued dependence on Middle East oil at levels that they would prefer not to maintain. They favor intensive offshore oil exploitation, not because it is compatible or incompatible with scheduled development, but because it reduces their dependence on oil imports. Although they believe that preventing expansion goes along with preserving innocent passage and reducing conflict in the oceans, they also believe, on the basis of North Sea experiences, that oil exploitation is inconsistent with limiting expansion. Yet, despite this perceived incompatibility, they take the position of favoring oil exploitation, preventing expansion, preserving innocent passage, and reducing conflict.

There is, generally, a tendency for actors to take positions consistent with the substructures of their most salient goals, but it is stronger for some actors than for others. In this study, the oil industry demonstrated the strongest tendency.

Explanations of Cognitive Inconsistencies

There is a number of possible explanations for imbalance and inconsistencies; yet reasons are generally found at two levels. First, there may be methodological errors in the research design. The most obvious is that the group of judges might not have accurately estimated the goal structures or the positions of the actors. They may have overestimated the complexity of causal beliefs of some actors, while underestimating the complexity of others. For example, the consistency of the oil industry's positions may be the result of the group's lack of information on the beliefs of the oil companies. They may have compensated for this lack of information by estimating what the oil industry's position *should* be, rather than what it is. This might bias their estimates in the direction of balance, which would increase the opportunity for inconsistencies between the goal structure and the position of a given actor. But notice, too, that lack of information about positions could also work to lessen observed inconsistencies if the judges let their estimates of an actor's beliefs affect their estimates of the actor's position, or vice versa.

Another possibility is that the actors consciously concealed their cognitions, making the accurate estimation of cognitive maps very difficult. It has been suggested above, however, that the attempt to convince others that a particular causal relation exists between two goals is an important part of the political process, especially in bargaining. Even if the actor does not really believe that the relation exists, he may be bound to behave as if it did.

Second, aside from measurement error or deception, and assuming the research design to be valid, explanations may be drawn from data based on other supporting evidence. The most convincing explanation of the inconsistencies uncovered is that nations simply do not feel strongly pressed to maintain positions that are consistent with their goal structures. On the contrary, they are often forced to take highly inconsistent positions for domestic political reasons, or to justify their positions by altering their causal beliefs, rather than vice versa. Alain Joxe (1966), in a pioneering article on the inconsistency of West German foreign policy objectives, was the first to suggest that a high level of inconsistency may result from domestic pressures. In a related work, Wolfram Hanrieder (1967, pp. 7–8) distinguished between "consensus," internal agreement on goals, and "compatibility," the logical consistency of a set of goals that is dependent on the conditions prevailing in the international system. He hypothesized that consensus may be positively associated with compatibility. In other words, professing incompatible goals may make it difficult to win agreement for a particular set of policies. Since the West Germans were forced to maintain incompatible goals during the Cold War (e.g., the reuniting of Germany and the maintenance of the alliance with the United States) due to the bipolarized nature of the international system, they were bound to experience a certain amount of domestic dissension. Their ability to pursue incompatible goals during this period testifies to the ability of national actors to tolerate inconsistency.

Analysis at the national level indicates that the sources of inconsistency are various. Several sources suggested above were: the desire on the part of an actor to impress upon others a threat that certain undesirable consequences will result from the pursuit of goals that are contrary to its interests; pressure from domestic groups of various sorts to take positions that are not considered to be consistent with links between goals that are perceived by central decision-makers; and conflicts between primarily internal goals, such as economic development, and primarily external ones, such as pursuing a hostile policy toward another sector.

On the individual, cognitive level, the sources of imbalance and inconsistency may be differential abilities to process complex information or to tolerate imbalance and ambiguity. It may also be a function of differential levels of access to technical information. People who have a low tolerance for ambiguity are likely to perceive balanced goal structures and take positions consistent with those structures. People with greater access to technical information are more likely to have goal structures that take into account the most recent technological factors. These structures may be more or less balanced than those of individuals with less access to information, depending upon the nature of that information. For example, scientists at Woods Hole Observatory are more likely to know about the recent technological aspects of ocean drilling than government officials in Burma. Knowledge of these details may have an important effect on perceptions of linkages between oil exploitation and other goals. Since the goal structures and positions estimated above were imputed to international actors (generalized aggregates composed of numerous individuals), and since the individuals within each actor may have different levels of access to information and differential abilities to tolerate ambiguity, the goal structure of the actor may be imbalanced because of the compromises that must be made among individuals in order to obtain an overall internal consensus.

Finally, it is possible that the nature of the situation contributes to the inconsistency between goal and positions. The oceans are used for a large number of purposes, many of which are in conflict with one another. Because of the increasing levels of usage and awareness that the oceans are part of a global ecosystem, ocean goals are becoming more interrelated. This high level of complexity and conflict among goals makes it harder for actors to decide on a consistent set of positions. The low salience of the ocean debate also contributes to the inconsistencies between goal structures and positions. Except during periods of crisis, such as the *Torrey Canyon* and Santa Barbara oil spills, the issues of ocean exploitation and preservation are not salient compared to domestic issues such as the health of the economy, the electoral process, or problems of succession. However, the low salience of the debate also creates opportunities for scientific and technical experts to affect policies by changing perceptions of links between goals. Scientifically informed perceptions may be less subject to over-simplification than perceptions based on the policy makers' experiences.

Comparative Analysis of the Goal Structures

The pattern of similarities and differences between actors will now be compared, first in terms of the beliefs that compose their goal structures. The resulting measure is called the "matrix distance" between two given actors because it is based on a comparison of the adjacency matrices of the goal structures of the actors. A second way to examine the pattern of similarities and differences between actors will be to analyze the positions they take for or against each of the goal variables. This will give a "position distance" measure for each pair of actors. The relationship of these two measures over the entire set of actors will allow a test of the third hypothesis, concerning whether alignments of convenience are likely to be alignments of perception as well.

Such comparative measures are important for three reasons. First, they augment comparisons of positions taken on the ocean regime. Second, they enable the analyst to estimate potential alignments. Third, they support predictions on outcomes in light of changing beliefs. Each of the two measures will be defined and the computations involved explained. Tables showing results for each pair of actors will be presented. Finally, a comparison among the methods for validity and usefulness will be made.

Measuring Differences in Goal Structures

The matrix distance between two actors is a measure of the difference between the goal structures of two actors. It takes into account not only the number of causal links on which the actors disagree, but also the magnitude of each disagreement.

For example, a comparison of the United States to the Soviet Union illustrated the matrix distance measure. Each of the entries of the goal structures (Tables 8–3 and 8–4) were compared, and the results are summarized in Table 8–12. The range of the set

TABLE 8–12

AGREEMENT OF ENTRIES IN GOAL STRUCTURES:
THE UNITED STATES AND THE SOVIET UNION

		United States					
		o	+	−	*cd*	*a*	*Total*
	o	57	8	6	0	1	72
	+	0	56	2	0	0	58
Soviet	−	1	0	42	0	0	43
Union	cd	0	0	0	6	0	6
	a	0	0	0	0	3	3
Total		58	64	50	6	4	182

of possible relationships is positive (+), negative (−), none (0), curvilinear downward (cd), and ambiguous (a). In two cases the Soviet Union perceived goals to be compatible that the United States considered incompatible. They were MSY (Maximum Sustainable Yield in fisheries) and preventing expansion; and innocent passage and MSY. In fifteen cases the United States perceived a linkage that the Soviet Union did not, and in one case the Soviet Union perceived a negative linkage not perceived by the United States. To determine the matrix distance between the goal structures of the two actors, the following weighting factors are used:

(1) 0=linkages are equal;

(2) ½=one linkage is curvilinear downward, and the other is positive or negative;

(3) 1=all unequal linkages, neither (2) nor (4);

(4) 2=one linkage is positive, the other is negative. The matrix distance is computed by first determining the weighting factor for each pair of goal variables of the two actors. Then a summation of the weighting factors is made. For example, the matrix distance of the United States and the Soviet Union is $1 \times (8+6+1+1) + 2 \times (2) = 20$.

The second measure, position distance, compares two actors by concentrating on the positions of the actors over the entire range of ocean goals. This measure takes into account the salience of the goal for each actor and the magnitude of the difference between the positions of the actors on the goal. Position distance for a pair of actors is computed in the following manner:

(1) Each actor is given a score of from 3 to -3 on each goal, depending on support or opposition and salience:

3 = support, high salience
2 = support, medium salience
1 = support, low salience
0 = no position
-1 = oppose, low salience
-2 = oppose, medium salience
-3 = oppose, high salience.

(2) Absolute differences between scores on the same goals for a given pair of actors were summed and divided by the maximum possible difference (in most cases, $6 \times 14 = 84$). For example, the absolute difference between the United States and the Soviet Union on oil exploitation is $|2 - 0| = 2$.

The results of the calculations for the two measures, matrix distance and position distance, are summarized in Tables 8–13 and 8–14. Using these results, it is possible to make a comparative

TABLE 8–13

MATRIX DISTANCE SCORES FOR EACH PAIR OF ACTORS

	U.S.	USSR	OECD	Oil exporters	Other LDCs	Oil industry
Soviet Union	20					
OECD	71	96				
Oil exporters	110	102	104			
Other LDCs	108	109	84	108		
Oil industry	112	106	107	74	140	
Group of judges	69	76	71	124	95	128

TABLE 8–14

POSITION DISTANCE SCORES (times 100)

	U.S.	USSR	OECD	Oil exporters	Other LDCs
Soviet Union	26				
OECD [a]	21	28			
Oil exporters	50	45	50		
Other LDCs [b]	60	47	54	40	
Oil industry	38	33	31	26	60

[a] Since the OECD states differed among themselves on the issues of reducing military use and the international ocean regime, a range of scores was calculated and the midpoint used. An error factor of around 10 percent may be involved.

[b] Since this actor's position on conflict machinery was not known, the total difference score was divided by $78 = (6 \times 13)$ instead of 84.

analysis between the goal structures of pairs of actors. Before undertaking the comparative analysis, the relationship between the measures will be explored.

Examination of the results of the matrix distance and position distance measures shows that the scores generated by these measures tend to be positively correlated. The rank order (gamma) correlation between matrix distance and position distance is .46. The positive correlation is clearly shown in Figure 8–3. This result

FIGURE 8–3.

Possible Structures of Cooperation-Conflict in the Ocean Debate

Matrix Distance [a]
Position Distance [b]

[a] Rules for drawing lines were:
    ▬ if matrix distance less than 75
    — if matrix distance greater than 75 but less than 100
[b] Rules for drawing lines were:
    ▬ if position distance less than 30
    — if position distance greater than 30 but less than 38

supports hypothesis three, that actors with similar positions will tend to have similar beliefs about linkages between goals.

Comparison among Actors and Potential Coalitions

Given these relationships between the two measures, a comparative analysis of the actors can be undertaken. The objective of the analysis is to locate *groupings of goals* that could result in *coalitions of actors* on the issue of establishment of an ocean regime. The three pairs of actors with the lowest matrix distances are the same as the three pairs of actors with the lowest position distances: oil exporting nations and the oil industry; the two superpowers; and the United States and the OECD. This finding coincides with the results from the other measures. The pair with the greatest matrix distance, Other LDCs and the oil industry, also has a large position distance.

The relationships demonstrated by the measures of goal variables suggest that coalitions between the following pairs of actors may arise: the United States and the Soviet Union; the United States and the OECD; the oil-exporting nations and the oil industry.

It is not clear, of course, that actors will form coalitions purely on the basis of shared perceptions of causal linkages between goals. For example, if two actors perceive the same negative linkage between two goals, they may take opposite positions on both goals because their underlying interests are opposed. Both oil companies and fishermen may see offshore oil exploitation as incompatible with fishing, but the oil companies will favor exploitation over fishing, and the fishermen will oppose oil exploitation. Thus shared perceptions may actually enhance the likelihood of conflict if a real conflict of interests exists.

One fact that can be derived from Table 8–2 is that the ocean debate is not unidimensional. There are several goals, for which actors tend to divide into opposing groups in different ways. For example, on the issue of innocent passage, it is the oil exporters and the Other LDCs versus all others. On the other hand, on oil exploitation the oil exporters join with the developed nations in favor of offshore oil, with only the Other LDCs opposed. On fishery conservation, the Other LDCs share the Soviet Union's view that conservation is undesirable. There are, therefore, opportunities for the creation of issue-specific alliances between developed and developing nations. The total pattern of alignments could be cross-cutting and nonpolarized.

211

Possible Determinants of Support for an Ocean Regime

Analysis of the data and definitions for comparative measures of the separate actors' goal structures provide the preface for a more detailed analysis of the primary concern, establishment of an international ocean regime. In that regard, the present considerations will include a presentation of separate actors' views toward the establishment of an ocean regime. Table 8–15 presents: the position of each actor on the establishment of such a regime; the salience of this goal for each actor; the distance of the goal structure of each actor from that of the judges; and the structural influence of the regime.

TABLE 8–15

RELATION BETWEEN POSITION TOWARD INTERNATIONAL OCEAN
REGIME AND OTHER STRUCTURAL MEASURES FOR
EACH ACTOR

	U.S.	USSR	OECD	Oil ex- porters	Other LCDs	Oil in- dustry
Position [a]	+	−	a	o	+	−
Salience [a]	med	low	med	low	high	high
Distance from judges [b]	69	76	71	124	95	128
Symmetry [c]	.95	.72	1.06	.44	1.06	.86
Structural influence [d]	.01	.03	−.02	−.01	.01	.05

[a] See Table 8–2.
[b] Distance of goal structure from the estimates of the group of judges: see Table 8–13.
[c] The number of positive and negative linkages between pairs of goals divided by the number of positive-nil and negative-nil asymmetric linkages.
[d] In computing this measure for the ocean regime goal, I considered all non-nil linkages to be the same. Thus, all signs were ignored. See text for an explanation of the structural influence measure.

As Table 8–15 illustrates, the United States supported the goal of establishing an ocean regime with a moderate saliency, while the other LDCs were supportive of the issue, which had high saliency for them. The OECD states demonstrated ambiguous feelings and moderate salience, while oil exporters had no opinion. The major opponents to a regime are the oil industry, the Soviet Union, and some OECD states. Can opposition or indifference to an international ocean regime be explained in terms of other characteristics of the goal structure than its density or balance?

Table 8–15 shows that opposition to an international ocean regime is associated with the perception of asymmetric linkages, distance from the judges' goal structure, and a high estimate of the causal independence of the ocean regime. The two actors with the greatest distance from the judges' goal structure, the oil exporters and the oil industry, actively oppose or do not favor the regime. The three lowest scores on a symmetry index correspond to the three actors who least favor an international regime. The two main opponents of the regime, the oil industry and the Soviet Union, are also the actors that give the regime the highest scores in terms of "structural influence." The measure of structural influence is an indicator of the ability of a specific goal variable, in this case the international ocean regime, to affect other goal variables, both directly and indirectly, without being affected by them (Taylor 1969). Thus, even though the ocean regime affects many of the other goal variables for the United States, the structural influence of the regime is low because it is affected by a large number of the other variables.

Having completed this detailed analysis of the cognitive maps, I would now like to describe what took place at the Caracas Conference on the Law of the Sea. This description will aid in evaluating of the cognitive map technique as a way of understanding the ocean debates.

WHAT HAPPENED IN CARACAS?

More than 5,000 delegates and observers from 148 nations attended the Caracas Conference.[9] Although there was some dispute over the failure to invite the Vietcong and Taiwanese representatives, the delegates soon got down to the business at hand. The range of issues discussed closely resembled those listed in Table 8–1, with a few important exceptions. Limiting the expansion of national jurisdictions was divided into two subissues: (1) setting a limit on the width of the "territorial sea"; and (2) setting a limit

---

[9] This description of the Caracas Conference is based on journalistic accounts in the following sources: *New York Times,* June 21, 1974, p. 12; July 2, 1974, p. 8. *The Times* (London), August 19, 1974, p. 5; August 20, 1974, p. 4; August 25, 1974, p. 3. *The Economist,* June 22, 1974, pp. 28–30; July 20, 1974, pp. 39–40.

213

on the width of a wider "economic zone." Most versions of this compromise called for national control over fishing and mineral exploitation in the economic zone and over navigation and scientific research in the territorial sea. However, Canada, Iceland and most of the developing nations favored extending national control over pollution and scientific research to the economic zone. Most nations came to the conference willing to settle for a 12-mile territorial sea and a 200-mile economic zone, with the notable exceptions of Japan and the Soviet Union. This created new difficulties, since the wider territorial sea meant that certain straits, including the Straits of Gibraltar and Malacca, which had previously been open to all navigation, could theoretically be closed by coastal states. The United States, Britain, and the Soviet Union therefore called for "unimpeded passage through straits." Unlike innocent passage, unimpeded passage does not require submarines to navigate on the surface and to show their flag when passing through another nation's territorial sea. This surfacing procedure would make it impossible for the superpowers to conceal the movement of their submarine fleets.

The nature of the regime (or regimes) that would be responsible for the regulation or exploitation of the international part of the oceans (the area beyond the economic zones) was a matter of considerable disagreement, both before and after the conference. A number of developing nations, including the People's Republic of China, favored a strong authority which, by entering into joint ventures, would itself develop ocean resources for the benefit of all nations. The United States and the European Community nations wanted the authority to be limited to the licensing of private or public enterprises, with the licensing revenues to be distributed to all nations.

Formation of coalitions was not as marked as one might have expected from the analysis above. Although there was clearly a split between major powers and developing nations on the issue of national control over the economic zone and passage through straits, that debate and the debate over the international regime saw divisions within both groups. For example, the British and the Soviets were opposed to even a limited licensing authority, while the developing nations with onshore mineral resources were opposed to a strong regime because of the expected effect on world prices. Canada and Iceland took strong stands in favor of the control of pollution in the economic zone. Lobbying by commercial interests was extensive both before and during the conference. Nevertheless, the oil industry and the oil-exporting nations played a much smaller role than expected in the debate because of the initial consensus on the expansion of national jurisdictions. A strong division between the landlocked countries and others did not materialise. The thirty-one landlocked nations tied their hopes to the proposal for a strong international regime, effectively allying themselves with the developing nations.

The next session of the conference will probably focus on a compromise in which a stronger international regime is traded for guarantees of free passage through straits and outside the territorial sea. The number of alternatives on other issues was considerably decreased in the Caracas meeting, so the agenda will be less filled with items for discussion.

Also, the Caracas meeting agreed on a voting formula by which the required majority will be two-thirds of those voting yes or no, so long as those voting yes include at least half of the participants. So the outlook for the successful conclusion of an agreement on a new law of the sea is good, as long as there is a chance of resolving the issues of: (1) the distinction between the territorial sea and the economic zone; (2) unimpeded passage through straits; and (3) the nature of the regime for the exploitation of the international part of the oceans.

SUMMARY OF RESULTS AND EVALUATION OF
THE COGNITIVE MAP TECHNIQUES

Given the events in Caracas as described above, it becomes possible to say something about the utility of the technique. Some vital elements of the debate were reflected in the estimation of cognitive maps. Actors did tend to rationalize their positions on the basis of connections between issues. A good example is the issue of economic zones that include national control over pollution and scientific research. Nations favored such control, not because of their irrational nationalistic tendencies, but primarily because they believed such control necessary for the management of coastal fisheries or the regulation of offshore oil exploitation. Nations that opposed this control were concerned that strict pollution control might limit the access of merchant and military fleets to the economic zones.

Several rather important shortcomings of the analysis were evi-

215

dent, however. First, and probably most important, the study did not take into account the variety of *types* of regimes that would be under discussion. The group of judges looked at a regime that resembled the most ambitious proposal put before the Caracas Conference. A separate analysis for each type of regime proposed would have been desirable, and certainly would have improved the descriptive and explanatory value of the exercise. Second, the issues changed over time in ways that were not foreseen. For example, the research group did not foresee the division of national jurisdictions into territorial seas and economic zones. They did not foresee the development of the idea of unimpeded passage as an alternative to innocent passage. Third, some issues, like the alleviation of world protein deficiences, did not obtain the prominence that was expected.

In the absence of a detailed description of the Caracas Conference in terms of cognitive maps, it is impossible to evaluate systematically the technique's descriptive accuracy. Nevertheless, it clearly failed to take into account changes in the issues, and perhaps the beliefs of the participants. However, it did yield several hypotheses or conjectures about cognition that may be of general interest: (1) positions of actors may be inconsistent with causal beliefs about linkages between goals when the actor is a nation-state, because of domestic pressures, bargaining behavior, compromises within the government, and the differential ability of individuals to tolerate ambiguity; (2) actors with similar positions tend to have similar beliefs; (3) actors tend to perceive more linkages between highly salient goals than between less salient ones; and (4) in a situation of high complexity and ambiguity, actors may favor a policy that they perceive to have low causal independence more than one that promises to have a direct effect on several issues without being subject to feedbacks.

These hypotheses, if backed by further empirical study, could help to improve the utility of the technique as an explanatory and predictive, as well as descriptive, device. That is, one could begin to explain *why* nations take the positions they do or *why* they choose specific coalition partners in terms of cognitive maps. This would make it possible to suggest ways in which positions or alignments may be changed by the judicious mustering of facts and evidence about the linkages between goals. If, for example, it is true that actors with highly connected maps prefer policies with low causal independence, and if one would like to see a particular policy implemented, then one would presumably want to encourage the view that the policy will be subject to a lot of feedbacks. Similarly, if one is merely interested in obtaining agreement or consensus among a group of actors, one should encourage the actors to harmonize their beliefs about causal linkages. Finally, one could change the position of some actors by manipulating the salience of issues. These are procedures that would probably not occur to anyone without exposure to the use of cognitive maps. It is precisely this potential for generating accurate descriptions, rational explanations, and new (and even counterintuitive) propositions about persuasion and consensus-building in situations with actors of highly divergent political perspectives that recommends the cognitive mapping technique for further study.

I would like to thank Ernst Haas, Robert Axelrod, Arthur Stinchcombe, John Ruggie, William Wrightson, Margaret Wrightson, Hayward Alker, Peter Cowhey, and Janet Schmidt for their comments and criticisms of earlier drafts of this work.

PART THREE

Conclusions

CHAPTER NINE

Results
—Robert Axelrod

This chapter integrates the findings of the separate empirical studies in order to extend our knowledge about decision making. It discusses the different ways in which cognitive maps can be used in decision making, what can be inferred about individual decision making, and how belief systems of collectivities differ from those of individuals.

One finding is particularly curious. In the three studies of spontaneous cognitive maps that were derived from policy discussion, no recognition of feedback was observed. By contrast, in the two studies using the forced-response questionnaire method, feedback was found frequently. After a series of alternative explanations are examined, the conclusion is drawn that this pattern is due to decision makers' having more relevant beliefs than they can handle. The chapter ends with a discussion of what can be done to enlarge the ability of decision makers to make fuller use of their own beliefs.

The central question of this concluding chapter is, From the five separate studies of cognitive maps in specific contexts, what can be learned about decision making in general?

An epilogue is offered after this concluding chapter to answer two supplementary questions: What are the limitations of the cognitive mapping approach? And what would be a promising project for someone who wanted to have fun doing research with cognitive maps and wanted his or her work to be meaningful as part of a larger whole?

The main task of this chapter, then, is to compare and contrast the five empirical studies, drawing from them inferences about cognitive maps and their role in decision making. First, there is the prior question: why bother?

For their helpful criticisms, I would like to thank Stan Bernstein, Matthew Bonham, Michael Cohen, Jeffrey Hart, Heikki Heiskanen, Arnold Kanter, Stuart Ross, and Paul Sniderman.

221

A. THE VALUE OF COGNITIVE MAPS

What difference does it make which cognitive map a person has on a policy issue? Why would we want to know about a person's cognitive map?

There are two broad answers to these questions. The first is that we want to know about cognitive maps so that we can better *understand* the decision-making process. The second is that we want to know about cognitive maps so that we can *improve* the decision-making process.

This, in turn, raises the question of why we should expect that knowing about cognitive maps can help us to understand and to improve decision making. The broad answer is that people have bounded rationality, and thus their belief systems are a major factor intervening between the objective conditions of the external world and how they choose to act. Cognitive mapping is one specific approach to belief systems. It focuses on causal beliefs and values and their structural relationships. Cognitive mapping is, therefore especially suitable to the study of the means-ends arguments people use when they try to evaluate the policy alternatives that they perceive are available to them.

Putting it another way, people have to simplify their view of the world in order to cope with the complexities of their policy environment. Therefore, if the analyses of cognitive maps could help us understand more about how they do simplify their view of their policy environment, we could better understand how they make decisions.

But why should we suppose that if we understood better how people make decisions we could understand better how to help them make better decisions? There are, actually, two quite distinct reasons. First, we could help them understand how *others* make decisions, and second, we could help them make more sophisticated decisions *themselves.*

First is the point that understanding how some people make decisions should help us predict the decisions of others. The Bonham and Shapiro study in Chapter 6 is the most directly relevant to this point, because it demonstrates that the goal of prediction is not impossible and that some progress has already been made in this direction with the cognitive mapping approach. The significance of being better able to predict the choices of decision makers is tremendous.

222

Take international relations, for example. International relations is full of examples of disasters and near disasters caused by national leaders failing to predict accurately the decisions of other leaders. The Americans failed to predict Japan's attack on Pearl Harbor, the Japanese failed to predict the perseverance of the American response to Pearl Harbor, the Russians failed to predict the American response to their putting nuclear missiles in Cuba in 1962, and the Israelis failed to predict the Egyptian and Syrian attacks in 1973.

It seems that nations are far from perfect at understanding each other. The study of cognitive maps will not make a huge difference in this regard. It will not usher in an age of predictive perfection. But even a little hard-won progress would be worthwhile.

Nevertheless, one may ask if it is reasonable to expect even a little progress in our ability to predict the actions of leaders of other nations through the analysis of cognitive maps? After all, the source material from which to derive the cognitive maps of the leaders of potentially adversary nations is not readily available in the form of undeniably sincere causal assertions. While this is true, one should also consider the present state of the art. Each nation is able to collect a great deal of material about the assertions of the leaders of other nations, including potential adversaries—as well as of friends, whose behavior also needs prediction. The problem has been not only a lack of suitable material from which to draw inferences, but also an inadequate supply of theoretical ideas and empirical tools with which to assess this (however limited) material. Again, the point is not that we should expect great progress from cognitive mapping, but rather that any real progress we can achieve will be valuable.

What cognitive mapping offers is a systematic way to proceed in our search for understanding how others will act. Its real strength (especially as compared to other formal approaches to decision making) is that it is able to employ the concepts of the decision maker who is being predicted, rather than the concepts of the person who is doing the predicting.

Not only can understanding of cognitive maps potentially help to make better decisions by allowing better predictions of others, but it can also allow better use of previously existing beliefs. For one thing, the cognitive mapping techniques can be used to generate more accurate descriptions of a policy environment than can be generated by any one person acting without formal tools.

223

Roberts' work in Chapter 7 and Appendix 2 suggests how this task of combining beliefs of different people can be undertaken. Another method is to teach decision makers actually to use the cognitive mapping techniques themselves with their own beliefs. My chapter on the Eastern Committee (Chapter 4) and Ross's chapter on the Constitutional Convention (Chapter 5) are especially relevant in supporting the idea that decision makers have "more beliefs than they know what to do with" (to put loosely an idea that will be discussed in sections C and D below). Since decision makers have more beliefs than they can handle, knowing how to combine and draw appropriate inferences from their beliefs could help decision makers become more sophisticated than they are now.

One could ask whether it is really a good thing to help high-level decision makers become more sophisticated. At first this seems like a silly question, but it is not. If your beliefs and/or values are sufficiently different from those of major decision makers, then making them more sophisticated may only serve to make them more efficient at accomplishing things that you are against. A special consideration is that there is typically a class of things which can, in retrospect, be regarded as blunders that hurt virtually everyone, regardless of policy preferences. In international relations, an important example is a nuclear holocaust. National leaders of whatever persuasion would try to avoid that, and it would be useful to help them be more sophisticated so that they can succeed. Even this example is complicated by the fact that a more sophisticated decision maker might feel justified in taking greater risks for immediate goals, and therefore make just such a war more likely (Schelling, 1963). Nevertheless, it is clear that what should be avoided is a pseudosophistication in which the decision maker has a false confidence in his own ability to understand and control his policy environment.

Just such a pseudosophistication is probably one of the things that went wrong with the American involvement in Vietnam. Some of the top decision makers had an unwarranted belief in the value of such tools as body counts and pacification figures. To a considerable extent the problem was one of misleading concreteness; decision makers believed in the validity of questionable numbers provided by others in the bureaucracy.

This is exactly where cognitive mapping is more promising. First, cognitive mapping can use the concepts that the decision maker himself wants to use, rather than the concepts of others. Second, he himself can estimate the magnitudes, when necessary, of the causal links, and is thus not likely to forget that his own subjective estimates are just that, subjective. In essence, cognitive mapping has the potential of helping decision makers help themselves, rather than having to rely too much on unsuitable quantitative or technical procedures that they cannot properly understand or evaluate.

Greater sophistication is itself a value, and thus the cognitive mapping approach is definitely value laden. This approach might, for example, help the elites at the expense of the masses, since the elites are more likely to take advantage of any such new mode of analysis. Alternatively, elites might use their greater sophistication on behalf of the masses. It is hard to say. Nevertheless, the world does have many real problems, not only in international relations, but also in ecology, population, and mundane things, such as which kind of garbage truck a town should buy. To a very large extent, politics within nations is a matter of problem solving rather than competition.[1] To the extent that political or other forms of decision making involve problem solving rather than competition, sophistication promotes the solution of shared problems.

When all is said and done, the scholar does not know exactly how his techniques will be applied. Nevertheless, he has to take some responsibility for the assumption that in the long run his work is likely to do more good than harm.

The long-run promise of the cognitive mapping approach for the understanding and the improvement of the decision-making process can best be evaluated at this time by seeing how much can be learned from the studies that have already been conducted with the cognitive mapping approach. It is to this task of integrating previous empirical work that we now turn.

B. THE RELIABILITY OF COGNITIVE MAPS

One of the most important results of this volume is that cognitive maps based on documents can be measured reliably. After more than three years of work, the coding procedures have reached a state of precision such that intercoder reliability is fully compatible with the accepted standards of good quantitative work in the social

[1] For a good exposition of this point see Putnam (1973).

sciences.[2] This was, actually, a surprising result. A natural language, such as English, is so rich in meaning, and the political discourse of elites is so complex, that the ability to get two coders to agree on the details of something as intricate as a cognitive map came as a very pleasant surprise.

This achievement of intercoder reliability is an important result, because it provides the foundation for scientific validity. Only if repeated measurements of the same phenomena give similar answers can there be any confidence in the validity of the inferences drawn from the data. More specifically, reliability of the coding of cognitive maps provides a foundation for other empirical work, including:

(1) the exploration of how people simplify their images of their policy environment, as was done for the Eastern Committee in Chapter 4;

(2) the analysis of the structure of specific people's assertions, as was done for Morris on the presidency in Chapter 5;

(3) the testing of a simulation model for the prediction of how a person will respond to unexpected events, as was done for the Middle East game in Chapter 6;

(4) the comparison of cognitive maps derived from spontaneous discussions to cognitive maps derived from closed-ended questionnaires, as will be done later in this chapter; and

(5) the specification of many projects that could be undertaken with the use of cognitive maps, as will be done in Chapter 11.

The attainment of reliability of the coding rules is not only the foundation for other work; it is an important result in its own right. The fact that such reliability is possible reflects an important aspect of elite decision making, namely, that causal imagery (including values and derived values) is not too far below the surface of what happens at a policy meeting. Of course, if the coding rules were a simple process, such as word counts from a previously determined list, then intercoder reliability would be an almost trivial result. But instead, the coding rules require many subjective judgments about the meaning of a document in order to capture the causal assertions themselves, and especially their structural relationships. The fact that this can be done in such a way that two coders can reach a high level of agreement on what is being said in a meeting says something about the documents themselves, namely, that they are susceptible to causal analysis.

[2] See Chapter 4 for details.

This is a subtle point: the susceptibility of the documents to reliable causal analysis suggests that the structure perceived in the speaker's argument is probably not too far from the structure intended by the speaker and understood by the listener. After all, if the conceptual framework being used in the coding process were too greatly at variance with the communication processes, it would be difficult to translate the document into the formal language of causal assertions with reliability, and at the same time allow the coders plenty of room to use their own natural language skills in the understanding of each passage based on the context.

To be specific, consider the reliability of coding decisions to equate concept variables that appear in different assertions. An example would be the decision of whether or not "British power" and "British strength" are the same concept in two different contexts. The coders agreed on 88 percent of such merging decisions. The fact that they can agree despite the lack of highly precise coding rules on this point means that these decisions were not arbitrary. This, in turn, means that the distinctions must have been fairly large between two phrases that represented the same concept and two that did not. This, in turn, tells us something about the document itself, namely, that it is usually clear whether two terms are the same concept or not. And this, in turn, supports the validity of the idea of a concept variable which, along with the idea of a causal link, provides the heart of the cognitive mapping approach.

Similarly, the fact that agreement on location of cause and effect occurs 96 percent of the time demonstrates that there was no problem with these aspects of the cognitive mapping approach either. Moreover, the 97-percent agreement on the sign of a relationship shows that this was an especially easy coding decision, suggesting that this, too, must be a distinction easily drawn from the document.

There was a less overwhelming (although still acceptable) level of agreement about whether a statement was causal or not. This demonstrates that there are probably many fine distinctions about the type of relationship in a given assertion. There are probably some assertions that are similar to pure causal assertions, but are not unambiguously either causal or not causal.

The overall result that the coding of cognitive maps can be made reliable with rules that allow the coders considerable discretion indicates that the distinctions used in cognitive mapping are, on the whole, fairly natural ones. The distinctions are probably meaningful not only to the coders, but also to the audience in the meeting itself, and even to the speaker. That is to say, the distinctions on which cognitive maps are based are in the message itself. So the reliability of coding not only provides the foundation for scientific validity of inferences about cognitive maps, but also tells us that high-level policy discussions can naturally be thought of in the same terms as are used in the construction of cognitive maps.

C. THE SIMPLICITY OF SPONTANEOUS COGNITIVE MAPS

Using the reliability of the cognitive maps derived from policy discussions as a foundation, we can compare and contrast the results of the three separate studies of such spontaneous cognitive maps. Fortunately, we have at our disposal three studies that are different enough in setting so that when they yield similar results we can have some confidence in the generality of the findings. Naturally, three studies cannot decisively prove any generalization, but since each study is based on dozens of assertions, the cumulative impact of their results is substantial.

In each of these three studies, the cognitive maps were based on the spontaneously generated words of elite decision makers in the process of a group discussion of significant policy. In each case, the cognitive maps were derived from people speaking in policy settings on issues within their own personal domain of competence. My own study in Chapter 4 was of the British Eastern Committee in 1918, in which cabinet-level decision makers were deciding what British postwar policy in Persia should be, and especially whether and in what form Britain should continue her intervention there. Ross's study in Chapter 6 was of the assertions made by Gouverneur Morris, one of the delegates to the Constitutional Convention in 1787, with respect to the arrangements to be made for the presidency. The study by Bonham and Shapiro in Chapter 7 was of a Middle East expert in the course of a gaming exercise in which the expert was part of a three-man team in the role of advisors to the President.

A useful way to compare the results of these three studies of spontaneous cognitive maps is to regard the Eastern Committee study as a pilot study, and to see which of its conclusions apply to other settings and which do not.

1. Many concepts are used. This result is confirmed for both of the other studies as well as for the Eastern Committee. In Morris's map there are 53 points, and in the Middle East expert's map there are 73 points. Thus, Marling's map from the Eastern Committee, with 31 points, is far from an upper limit of the number of concept variables a decision maker can employ.

2. Many causal assertions are made. Cognitive maps are also large in the sense of the number of causal assertions that are employed, as well as the number of concept variables. The Marling map had 43 assertions, the Morris map 84 assertions, and the Middle East expert's map 116 assertions. The significance of this is that people do not seem simply to repeat a few assertions. Instead, they employ rather large structures in presenting their images of their policy environment.[3]

3. The conclusions people draw are consistent with their large cognitive maps. The direct way to have tested this proposition would have been to see if the policy preferences that a speaker articulates are consistent with the inferences that could be derived from his cognitive map. Such a test, however, would not be very powerful, since the coders of the cognitive map tend to *assume* consistency in determining which causal linkages were not made explicit. The confirmation of consistency is, then, indirect. It is based on the observation that a speaker is rarely challenged about his own consistency, even though his opponents have a major interest in doing so whenever they spot a case in which the arguments used actually contradict the policy preference that is expressed.

4. Some previously suggested forms of bounded rationality do not explain how people can employ such large cognitive structures. Selective attention to goals, lexicographic decision rules, and satisficing within the cognitive map were not used by Morris, just as they were not used by the members of the Eastern Committee.

In the pilot study of the British Eastern Committee, these four results led to a puzzle. How could people have such large and interconnected cognitive maps, with which they were apparently able to operate consistently, and yet not use the shortcuts discussed in the literature on bounded rationality in complex decision making? The significance of this puzzle is now highlighted by the new

---

[3] The precise size of a spontaneous cognitive map depended in part, of course, on the length of the document. But causal assertions are so frequent that even short documents generate large maps.

cases just reviewed, which suggest that it may be applicable to a wide range of policy domains.

A partial explanation for the ability of a decision maker to employ such a large cognitive map would be that he does not develop his cognitive map from scratch for each new situation that arises. The next finding supports this partial explanation.

5. *Causal paths within a person's cognitive map may be stable over long periods.* When asked to explain an unexpected event, the Middle East expert did so in terms that bore some striking parallels to the predictions made on the basis of his cognitive map of three years earlier. This suggests that at least important segments of a cognitive map can remain stable over relatively long periods of time.

This result is quite exciting, because it suggests that cognitive mapping based on one context might be usable to predict actual decisions in some other and even later context. The value of such an accomplishment would be great. It would help Kremlinologists, China watchers, Washington pundits, and other soothsayers. Unfortunately, the evidence indicates that the state of the art of cognitive mapping is still unable to make such predictions with any confidence. For example, the predictions about what the Middle East specialist would want to do about the Jordanian civil war of 1970 were only partly successful. The policy option that was predicted by Bonham and Shapiro's simulation turned out to be the expert's fall-back position in case his own plan did not work.

While predictions of *policy choices* are still very difficult, predictions of *explanations of events* may be feasible. Bonham and Shapiro had considerable success in predicting how the Middle East expert would explain the unanticipated events of the Jordanian civil war, including what were seen to be the antecedents of the events, as well as their consequences. This is no small accomplishment for a simulation based on three-year-old source material of a person playing a game. It certainly indicates the promise of cognitive mapping in understanding more about how actual elites interpret the causes and effects of actual events.

The ability of decision makers to employ large cognitive maps is undoubtedly helped by the stability of many of the causal paths in their maps. In the pilot study, the explanation was suggested that while the cognitive maps were large and interconnected, they were also structurally simple in two distinct ways: they tended to be balanced, and they lacked cycles. Now further evidence on these suggestions is available.

6. *In decision-making groups, cognitive maps tend to be balanced, but this tendency is not always complete.* A completely balanced cognitive map would imply that the decision maker never gave arguments on both sides of policy proposal, but only spoke on one side of any policy issue.[4] Such a style would certainly help the decision maker keep track of large sets of assertions. Marling's map from the Eastern Committee was completely balanced, and so was the cognitive map of the Middle East expert. Morris' map, derived from the multiple sessions of the Constitutional Convention, has a tendency toward balance, but was far from being a completely balanced cognitive map. Morris was deliberately chosen for his complex style, which according to Madison was "fickle and inconstant, never pursuing one train of thinking, nor ever regular." The implication is that in extreme cases, at least, decision makers need not use the simplifying technique of keeping their cognitive maps completely balanced, even when they have large and highly interconnected maps, as Morris did.

So far the analysis of the three studies of spontaneous cognitive maps has shown that elite decision makers in policy making groups employ large cognitive maps, that they may take advantage of stability of segments of their own maps, but that they do not necessarily keep to one side of each argument. Since within the meetings they do not usually focus on only one goal at a time or opt for the first satisfactory policy alternative that is presented (as we have seen in Chapters 4 and 5), the puzzle remains as to how people with limited cognitive capabilities can employ such large and highly interconnected cognitive maps. How do these elites simplify their cognitive task? A large part of the answer is provided by the next finding, which is one of the most important results of the comparative study of cognitive maps.

7. *In decision-making groups, cognitive maps rarely have cycles.* Marling's map had no cycles. Morris's map had no cycles. The Middle East expert's map had no cycles.

That is, none of these men made assertions of the form "A causes B, B causes C, and C causes A." Such a set of assertions

---

[4] See Chapter 3 for the basic definitions in analyzing terms used in cognitive maps. For more on the implications of balance in cognitive maps, see Chapter 10, section E.

231

is a cycle, since it traces a closed loop of causation from a concept variable back to itself. A cycle can be of any length, so long as it consists of a sequence of arrows that comes back to where it starts. Cycles represent feedback loops. As was explained in Chapter 3, a cycle may be a positive feedback loop, which is deviation-amplifying, or a negative feedback loop, which is deviation-counteracting. But the point is that neither positive nor negative feedback loops, and neither long nor short loops are present in any of the three spontaneous cognitive maps that have been investigated in detail.

This is curious. The absence of cycles in these maps seems to indicate that the images of the policy environment which these decision makers present to each other in their meetings are devoid of feedback. It is curious precisely because we know that feedback is a vital aspect of the dynamics of almost any complex environment, especially social environments.[5]

How can the absence of cycles in spontaneous cognitive maps be explained? This question is worth a section of its own.

D. THE CASE OF THE MISSING CYCLES

1. Is the absence of cycles due to an unusually low level of sophistication among these particular decision makers?

This could hardly be the explanation. The British Eastern Committee was a cabinet-level group, and Marling was an expert on the subject at hand. The Middle East expert was speaking to other policy specialists, and had sufficient time in the gaming exercise to develop his arguments in some detail. But most convincing is Gouverneur Morris in the Constitutional Convention who, over the course of many sessions, developed a highly complex set of arguments about such matters as the potential dangers of giving the President too much power over the legislature and of giving the legislature too much power over the President. Each of these men was discussing issues which he knew and cared about. They were talking to intelligent colleagues of similar background and interest. They had little fear that their words would be soon repeated to the public. Thus, we have men of above-average sophistication trying to persuade other sophisticated men about complex issues of substantial importance.

[5] This point has been persuasively argued for policy-relevant environments by Easton (1965), Deutsch (1966), and Steinbruner (1974), among others.

2. Can the lack of cycles be due to the unusual nature of the policy problems that have been selected for analysis? In particular, could it be due to the fact that two of the settings deal with strong nations deciding policies toward weaker nations?

The British policy with respect to Persia and the American policy with respect to Syria are both cases of the strong dealing with the weak, situations in which the strong might not have to pay much attention to feedback. The force of this argument is severely limited, however, by several considerations. The Middle East expert did explicitly consider the reactions of another strong nation, the Soviet Union, to be an important factor in the policy environment; he used concepts such as "arms supplied by the Soviet Union" and "Soviet penetration in the Middle East." Even more decisive is that the Constitutional Convention did not deal with such an asymmetric power relationship, but Morris' map also showed a lack of cycles. If there was a dominant tension between actors in Morris' cognitive map, it was between the future executive and the future legislature, both of which were to be of comparable strength. Thus, absence of feedback loops in the Middle East expert's map and in Morris' cognitive map cannot be attributed to their perception of a policy environment in which the strong would dominate the weak without concern for the responses of others.

3. Can the lack of cycles be due to the speakers' having thought out their arguments in advance and eliminated any feedback loops ahead of time after careful deliberation?

The Eastern Committee and the Constitutional Convention would have allowed the participants time to work out their arguments with care had the participants chosen to do so. On the other hand, the Middle East simulation would not have. The Middle East expert was given a scenario involving the Russians putting nuclear missiles in Syria, and he was almost immediately asked to start discussing it with his colleagues. Naturally, any policy maker had a large repertory of thoughts on the subject area of his competence. So the Middle East expert was hardly starting from scratch when he confronted this new problem. Indeed, the concepts he used to analyze the problem (such as "Arab perception of threat," "intraregional feuds," "militant pan-Arabism," and "access to oil") turned out to be quite useful in predicting his reactions to the Syrian civil war three years later. No one ever comes to a policy issue with a completely clear slate, and especially not an elite analyst dealing with his subject of competence. Nevertheless, the lack of cycles cannot be explained by any process of having thought through the arguments on the case at hand and in advance and deliberately eliminating any feedback loops ahead of time. The Middle East expert was given no such opportunity in the game-playing situation in which he found himself.

If cycles are not eliminated by careful deliberation, can their absence be explained in part by the difficulty of getting any set of concept variables to be connected in a cycle? This idea is captured in the next question.

4. Can the lack of cycles be explained by chance?

The answer is, simply, "no." The lack of cycles can hardly be due to simple chance, and is therefore not a spurious result. This can be demonstrated precisely. Suppose we take a map with a given set of points and a given set of arrows between the points, but we do not assume that the direction of the arrows is known. Now suppose that each arrow is *given* a direction at random (for example, by flipping a coin to determine if an arrow between P and Q will go from P to Q or from Q to P). Then the question is whether cognitive maps with the same points and arrows as the ones we have seen would tend to have any cycles if the direction of the links were drawn at random. The answer is that such randomly drawn cognitive maps would be virtually certain to contain cycles.

As an illustration, notice that for a triangle of points connected by three arrows there is a ¼ chance that the arrows will form a cycle.[6] Likewise for a set of four points joined in a quadrangle, there is a ⅛ chance. If there are more than ten triangles, as there are in both Morris's and the Middle East expert's maps, there is less than a 5 percent probability that there would be no cycles purely by chance.[7] The odds that, given their overall structure, none of the three maps would have a cycle of length three is less than one in five hundred. The odds are even less that none of the three maps has a cycle of any length. Given that the maps are as

[6] Let P, Q, and R be the points. Without loss of generality, assume that the PQ link goes from P to Q. Then there is a cycle if and only if two independent events occur, each of which has a ½ chance of occurring. These two events are that the QR link will go from Q to R and the PR link will go from R to P.

[7] For example, the chance that a map with eleven triangles would have no cycle is $1 - (1 - .25)^{11} = .042$.

large and as interconnected as they are, there is virtually no chance that if the links were given random directions, no cycle would result. So the lack of cycles can hardly be attributable to chance.

5. Is the lack of cycles due to the speakers' dealing only with short-range effects and therefore not considering feedback mechanisms that would take longer and would be less certain than immediate effects?

Marling does have a fairly short-term point of view, being largely concerned with concepts such as "the amount of blackmail on the trade caravans" and "the lack of quality of the kind of Shah at present." On the other hand, the Middle East expert has a broader perspective and is concerned about such long-range concepts as possible "virtual satellization of Arab states" and "the pattern of [nuclear] proliferation in the world." Even more striking is Morris' discussion of the powers of the presidency, with a truly long-term point of view. He is concerned about both "the event of a despot in America" and "usurpations of the legislature on the executive." The drafters of the Constitution saw themselves as planning for the ages, and Morris was no exception. So, while some decision makers may not be concerned with the long run, both the Middle East expert and Morris did have long-run factors entering explicitly into their cognitive maps. Thus their lack of cycles could not be explained by a short time perspective.

6. Is the lack of cycles due to an artifact in the coding process itself?

The coding rules explicitly allow two phrases to be regarded as the same concept variable even if they are worded differently.[8] This would tend to make for more rather than fewer feedback cycles in the cognitive map. For example, if a person says that A causes B, B causes C, and C causes A', and if A is regarded as equivalent to A', then a cycle will result. Thus, by allowing two different phrases to represent the same concept variable, the coding rules actually increase the chance of a cycle occurring.

Errors in the coding of points to be connected to each other, or in the direction of a connection between two given points, would also tend to increase rather than decrease the potential for cycles in a map. This is so because randomly directed arrows tend to form cycles just by chance, as we have already seen. If anything, the coding process is skewed to make cycles appear rather than disappear.

[8] See Appendix 1, section U on merging rules.

If the lack of cycles is not due to an unusually low level of sophistication, unusually one-sided policy settings, careful elimination of cycles before the discussion, chance, the consideration of only short range effects, or an artifact of the coding process, what is left as an explanation?

7. Can the lack of cycles be due to decision makers' not being able to recognize the existence of each of the causal links separately that go into the formation of any given cycle?

Here is where it is extremely helpful to have more than one method of deriving cognitive maps. Recall that the documentary method generates spontaneous cognitive maps based on what people say when describing their policy environment in a policy meeting. The questionnaire method, on the other hand, forces the respondents to consider *every* ordered pair of concept variables to decide whether or not there is a causal connection from (say) A to B, and also from B to A. Roberts' study of transportation policy (Chapter 7) used judges from a variety of related fields to determine first what the relevant concepts were, and then to determine the causal linkages between them. The result was a cognitive map that contained three different cycles. These three cycles occurred even though the map was much smaller than the cognitive maps derived from the documentary method. Specifically, the collective map derived from asking about each possible link had only 9 points and 15 arrows, compared to 73 points and 115 arrows for the Middle East expert's spontaneous map. Yet the smaller map still had cycles. Just as interesting is that six of the seven judges used by Roberts saw each of the links in each of these three cycles, and the seventh also saw causal linkages that formed several cycles.

The conclusion from this study based on questionnaires is that people can have beliefs about a policy environment which, when combined, do form cycles. But if the kind of people Roberts used as judges see the separate links of cycles, is it that elite policy makers in high positions are somehow less perceptive? This is the next question.

8. Can the lack of cycles in spontaneous cognitive maps be due to actual policy makers not having the separate beliefs that would form a cycle?

Fortunately there is another study of cognitive maps that allows us to eliminate this possibility as well. Hart's study of ocean regime policy (Chapter 8) analyzed a wide variety of source material from national and transnational actors by having a set of judges read the material and then engage in the questionnaire method to derive the cognitive maps of the actors. The result was that the cognitive maps of the actors (nations, groups of nations, and the transnational oil industry) did display separate linkages which, taken together, composed cycles. This was true, even looking at the subgraph of goal structures within the overall cognitive map, and even within the sub-subgraph of the salient goals. So we know that actual policy makers who are responsible for the official documents do assert the separate links that form cycles.

What does this lack of cycles in *spontaneous* cognitive maps mean? Why do decision makers not have cycles in their cognitive maps when they spontaneously talk about their policy environment, whereas when judges are forced to consider every ordered pair of concepts they do express beliefs that form cycles?

An explanation that may partly account for this result is the next one.

9. In advocacy contexts do people avoid cycles because cycles would interfere with the thrust of their arguments?

This might well be a partial explanation, but it seems incomplete. For one thing, we have seen that some participants in high-level meetings are willing to use very complex arguments, and even make arguments on both sides of a given issue. Morris was an example of such a man. Yet even Morris did not have any cycles in his cognitive map.

Even more to the point is that cycles can often help arguments. Let me illustrate. Suppose that one person at a policy meeting says that their country should buy more arms to keep ahead of their potential enemy, while another policy maker opposes the purchase of more arms because of their expense. The opponent of further armament would have a natural opportunity to strengthen his own policy preferences through the use of an argument that employed a feedback cycle: if we buy arms, then we may get ahead, but then the other side is behind, so they would buy more arms, which would put us behind, so we would buy more arms, and thus our purchasing arms does not get us the advantages it seems to. This is clearly a cyclic argument, and would be coded as such. Now why should a person who opposes further arms purchases not make such an argument? Clearly it is not simply because the feedback argument is so complicated that it would interfere with the thrust of the case against armaments on other grounds.

What all of this leads to is simply a cognitive explanation for the lack of cycles.

10. Even sophisticated decision makers operating in the field of their competence have a very strong tendency to conceptualize causation in a way that prevents them from spontaneously recognizing feedback in their policy environments.

People have no trouble accepting the separate beliefs that make up a feedback cycle when each link is given explicit attention (as shown by the evidence from cognitive maps derived with questionnaires). But when they spontaneously describe their environment, they do not include even implicit feedback cycles. Thus the explanation seems to be in the way people conceptualize causation: they seem to see it as flowing outwards, and not turning back to affect some other concept variable that is regarded as causally prior.

This explanation in terms of the difficulty of recognizing feedback cycles in a policy environment seems at first glance to be inconsistent with the plain fact that people can understand and even spontaneously employ some types of arguments that are clearly feedback arguments. The example of the arms race cited earlier is certainly the type of argument that is not too difficult for even a moderately sophisticated decision maker to use. How can feedback arguments be so difficult to employ in general, and yet relatively easy to use in particular instances?

To resolve this apparent contradiction, we need to recall that even the simple arms race feedback mechanism has been widely comprehended only in the twentieth century, and become commonplace only since World War II. Here we are beyond our data, but it seems reasonable to suppose that the learning of one feedback mechanism does not necessarily make it much easier to recognize other types of feedback. When a person learns to recognize and even spontaneously use the feedback inherent in an arms race application, that same person does not necessarily transfer this learning to become more sensitive to the recognition of other types of feedback mechanisms in entirely different substantive areas of policy. For example, despite the widespread understanding of the arms race feedback mechanism, a major educational effort had to be made by those who wanted to emphasize the presence of feedback in the relationship between people and their physical environment.[9] So not only is feedback hard to recognize spontaneously, but it is apparently difficult to learn as an abstract principle that can be readily generalized from one instance to another. The lack of cycles in the cognitive maps of even sophisticated decision makers is an interesting finding. But to understand its full significance, it would be helpful to study individual decision making in the context of collectivities that are larger than individuals.

E. THE COGNITIVE MAPS OF COLLECTIVITIES

In the modern world, important matters of public policy are usually determined by collectivities, rather than by individuals acting alone. Therefore, the understanding of how the beliefs and assertions of individual decision makers aggregate in decision-making groups is vital to a more complete understanding of how policy is formed.

One way to study a collectivity is to analyze its cognitive map. The reader's first reaction to the idea of a collectivity having a "cognitive map" might be incredulity. Clearly collectivities do not think and have internal cognitive processes as individuals do. Nevertheless, there are two meaningful senses in which collectivities can be said to have cognitive maps.

First, there is the sense in which a collectivity can be regarded as an artificial aggregate of its members, with "beliefs" that are then simply aggregated from the known beliefs of its members. This type of aggregation was used by Roberts in Chapter 7 to build a single cognitive map about causal linkages in commuter transportation, which would represent the aggregate of the cognitive maps of the separate judges he used. The aggregation in his case was mechanical, in the sense that the collectivity was said to hold a certain belief if six of the seven judges thought there was a significant relationship and a majority agreed on what the sign of the relationship was. The whole point of aggregating the beliefs of judges in this mechanical way is that earlier research on subjective estimation has demonstrated that mechanically aggregated collectivities are more accurate than either individuals or even the consensus of group discussions.[10] There is good reason,

[9] Most successful in this enterprise were those who gave an apocalyptic vision of the world, such as Meadows, et al. (1972).

[10] See the references cited in footnote 2 of Chapter 7.

therefore, to expect that the cognitive map assigned mechanically to a group of judges will be a more accurate reflection of the actual causal laws operating in the policy environment than the cognitive map of the typical judge. The aggregated cognitive map of the judges is likely to be a better guide to policy than the cognitive map of one of the judges.

Of course, to combine the cognitive maps of a group of judges mechanically requires that the judges all use the same set of concept variables. The methodology for using the judges themselves to develop this list of common concept variables and the methodology for combining the separate cognitive maps into a single map is the principal contribution of Roberts' study of transportation policy.[11] This methodology can now be readily applied to other policy domains in which one desires a more accurate causal picture than any single judge is likely to be able to offer.[12]

While the mechanical combination of beliefs is one way to derive cognitive maps of a collectivity, another way is to let the collectivity speak for itself. Collectivities, such as committees or nations, frequently issue documents that make assertions about causal relationships, state preferences, and announce decisions. Such documents can then be used directly to attribute cognitive maps to the collectivity that issues them. This is the approach used by Hart in Chapter 8 to study ocean regime policy.

Hart's comparative analysis provides some interesting results about the cognitive maps of collectivities based on assertions expressed in the documents of the collectivities themselves.[13] Hart concentrated on the part of the cognitive map that relates goals to each other, and this allowed him to compare the goal structures of different actors. The actors he chose to examine were the ones most relevant to ocean regime policy: the United States, the Soviet Union, the other developed states, the oil exporters, the other less developed states, and the oil industry itself. Here are some comments on the highlights of his empirical results on these collectivities:

[11] For details see Appendix 2 as well as Chapter 7.

[12] Roberts' other major contribution is in the mathematical exploration of pulse processes and their implications for the stability of causal structures.

[13] Hart used the questionnaire method on a panel of judges who had read the documents, because the volume of the documents made the documentary coding method impractical.

240

1. *Less developed nations recognize at least as many causal relationships as developed nations, despite their lower research capacity and their smaller bureaucracies.* This is a fascinating result, because it suggests that the amount of "organizational perception" does not necessarily increase with organizational size and complexity, as might be supposed. The reason for this counterintuitive result is probably provided by the next finding.

2. *There are proportionally more relationships seen between salient goals than there are between all goals.* Put in other terms, salient substructures are more dense than overall structures. This seems quite reasonable. Actors recognize more relationships between concepts that are salient to them. When put together with the finding that underdeveloped nations have more salient goals concerning the ocean than do developed nations, the greater density of linkages between salient goals helps to explain why the underdeveloped nations perceive at least as many relationships between the goals as do the developed nations.

3. *National actors sometimes take inconsistent positions in the sense of asserting that two goals are positively related and at the same time taking different policy stands toward them, or asserting that two goals are negatively related while taking similar policy stands toward them.* This finding of inconsistencies at the national level is especially interesting in contrast to the earlier finding that individual decision makers can handle their own large and highly interconnected cognitive maps. Among the possible explanations for this finding, the most intriguing one is that domestic pressures lead nations to be inconsistent in this specific sense. This explanation is supported by the finding that the oil industry itself shows less inconsistency than any of the nations or groups of nations on these ocean-related issues.[14]

4. *Actors with similar issue positions tend to have similar perceptions of causal linkages.* The evidence is that among the fifteen possible pairs of actors studied by Hart, there was a correlation (gamma) of .46 between their matrix distances and their position distances. This is an important result because of its implication for the way actors interact over time. It suggests that the coalitions between actors that are based on similarity of

[14] Because Hart did not develop the entire cognitive map of the collectivities, but only the goal structure portion of the map, it is not possible to compare directly the type of inconsistency exhibited in the collective cognitive maps with the imbalance exhibited in Morris' cognitive map.

241

positions would also tend to bring together actors that recognize fairly similar sets of causal linkages. In other words, this is evidence that politics need not make strange bedfellows. It suggests that coalitions can be like-minded on the underlying beliefs about causal linkages, and need not be restricted to opportunistic alliances of actors with similar policy preferences but quite different beliefs about the underlying causal mechanisms that lead to these preferences.

A completely different orientation to collectivities is the analysis of theoretical possibilities rather than empirical actualities. In particular, one can ask about the relationship of individual cognitive maps to the cognitive maps of a collectivity composed of those individuals. Suppose a group uses a simple decision rule, such as majority vote, to determine the group's linkages. Then the fascinating result emerges that a group can be more sophisticated than any of its members.

Consider the situation illustrated in Figure 9–1. Here the first member believes that A promotes B and B promotes C. The second member believes that B promotes C and C promotes A. The

FIGURE 9–1.

The Cognitive Maps of the Members of a Hypothetical Group, and the Cognitive Map Derived by Majority Vote

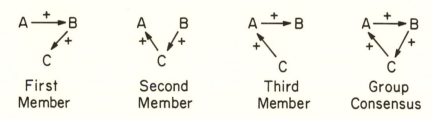

| First Member | Second Member | Third Member | Group Consensus |

third member believes that C promotes A and A promotes B. Thus each member in this hypothetical group perceives two of the three sides of a positive feedback cycle. If the group's cognitive map were decided by majority vote, there would be a 2 to 1 majority in favor of each of the three linkages. For example, the first two members would agree that B promotes C.

The point of this illustration is that it is possible for none of the members of the group to see a feedback cycle, but the group as a whole to recognize a cycle. In such a situation the group could be said to be more sophisticated than its members.[15] Indeed, it is not too hard to find examples of this phenomenon. One such example would arise if Roberts' judges 4, 6, and 7 considered the effect of passenger miles on emissions (positive), the effect of emissions on fuel economy (negative), and the effect of fuel economy on passenger miles (positive). Each of these causal linkages was seen by two of the three judges, but the entire cycle was seen by none of them.

Unfortunately, groups cannot always be relied upon to be more sophisticated than their members. Different individuals might see different cycles and the consensus of the group might not recognize any of them. In fact, using Roberts' method of aggregating, each of Roberts' judges saw *more* cycles than the group as a whole did. An even more powerful reason for not relying too heavily on the collective view of a group is that if all of their individual members misperceive a linkage, the group is bound to get it wrong as well.

F. POLICY IMPLICATIONS

If groups cannot always be relied upon to be more sophisticated than their members, this leads us back to consider what can be done to help individuals become more sophisticated. Our fundamental result from the empirical analysis of individual cognitive maps was that while people do employ large cognitive maps, they tend to simplify them by not spontaneously recognizing feedback cycles. Yet we also have seen that when asked in a questionnaire format about all possible linkages, people do recognize the separate links that form cycles. This led to the conclusion that can be stated informally as "people have more beliefs than they can handle."

What happens is that people use images of the policy environment that are large, but structurally very simple. In this sense, even sophisticated decision makers use unsophisticated cognitive maps. Within the limits of these simplified images, the policy makers do operate rationally. They can make inferences consistent with their assertions, and choose the best alternative or

---

[15] This result is closely analogous to the paradox of voting discussed by Arrow (1951) in which the graphs represent preference functions and the meaning of a cycle is an intransitive preference function. For more on the formal theory of collectivities, see project 7 in Chapter 11.

alternatives in terms of these simplified images. *The picture of a decision maker that emerges from the analysis of cognitive maps is of one who has more beliefs than he can handle, who employs a simplified image of the policy environment that is structurally easy to operate with, and who then acts rationally within the context of his simplified image.*

The implication is that the cognitive maps of elite decision makers are less accurate than they might be. Accuracy refers to the degree to which a cognitive map correctly reflects the causal mechanisms operating in the environment. The accuracy of a cognitive map is evaluated in terms of the extent to which its inherent predictions are correct. Accuracy in one's image of the policy environment is obviously important in the making of good policy.

Let us take a closer look at the meaning of "good policy." From the decision maker's point of view, good policy is policy that maximizes his utility.[16] If a decision maker knows what his nearly ultimate goals are, then the arrows that go directly to utility are accurate by definition (assuming the cognitive map is based on sincere assertions and that we do not worry about "false consciousness"). The arrows that are not directly connected to utility, however, are likely to be more or less dependent upon factual matters. If those linkages are incomplete or incorrect, then the total effect of a given policy alternative upon utility is likely to be incorrect. Thus, to make good policy, a person needs a cognitive map that makes accurate predictions, especially about the impact of the policy alternatives upon utility. By his not recognizing or acknowledging cycles, a decision maker's cognitive maps tend to be incomplete and potentially inaccurate.

What can be done? At present the primary use of cognitive mapping is in research. Perhaps in the long run, however, the cognitive mapping approach can not only help identify problems in decision making but can also help overcome them. In other words, cognitive maps may have potential not only as a research tool, but also as a policy aid.

It must be stressed that a long-run perspective is intended. I do not claim that I am ready to advise State Department experts or anyone else on how to make better policy. The cognitive

---

[16] For some purposes, there is an important distinction between a decision maker's conception of his private utility and his conception of the utility of his organization or nation. Which type of utility should be used depends on the purpose of the analysis.

mapping approach is still far from that. But it would ultimately be helpful if we could advise decision makers on how to become more sophisticated. With this in mind, here are some long-run possibilities.

1. *Use of one's own enlarged cognitive map.* The most exciting possibility is that a decision maker can be more sophisticated if he can externalize his implicit cognitive map. This principle is based on the finding that people have more beliefs than they typically use in a policy context. With a written cognitive map there are formal ways of handling beliefs, that is, rational ways of combining them and drawing inferences from them. Why not, then, teach a person to externalize his beliefs and do the calculations on paper? The decision maker could provide his own beliefs, and he could do the calculations for himself. The calculations described in Chapter 3 are simple and could probably be taught in a day or two.[17]

As we have seen, decision makers are able to employ large cognitive maps by keeping them structurally simple through a tendency to avoid imbalance and through a lack of feedback cycles. Once a person learned how to write his own cognitive map, how to expand it to include beliefs previously left out of consideration, and how to draw inferences from such an expanded map, he would be able to handle maps of greater structural complexity. This would make him a more sophisticated decision maker than he was before. This is what was meant by the analogy in Chapter 1 that in the world of Roman numeral users, the person trained in the use of Arabic numerals would be a prodigy.

The advantages of training decision makers to be able to write out, expand, and draw inferences from their own cognitive maps derive largely from the fact that the user of such a procedure would not have to rely on others any more than he wanted to. This is a tremendous help and a substantial advantage over many of the more esoteric approaches to decision making, such as linear programming or computer simulations, which require an outside expert to give advice that might look like magic to the decision maker himself.[18] Compared to more complex policy tools, such

[17] For a description of a research project to evaluate the feasibility of training for externalization, see project 11 in Chapter 11.

[18] This is one of the most powerful criticisms of the MIT approach to world forecasting. See Cole, et al. (1973), and especially Freeman (1973) in their attacks on Meadows, et al. (1972).

as these, the advantages of the cognitive mapping approach as a "do it yourself" method are the following:

a. The decision maker can be honest with himself in stating his separate beliefs, since no one else needs to see the private cognitive map which they compose.

b. The decision maker can use his own concepts. This makes the cognitive map relatively easy to use despite its potentially large size. Any method that required the decision maker to use predetermined categories would not only be difficult to learn but woud also be very difficult to employ when the number of things to be taken into account grows very large.

c. With a "do it yourself" technique of drawing one's own cognitive map, the decision maker does not have to worry about outside values slipping in on him unawares. For one thing, a cognitive map allows the decision maker to represent his own values as concept variables that are directly tied to utility. For another thing, the simplicity inherent in the use of points and arrows in a cognitive map lets the decision maker avoid relying on an outside expert who might be tempted (even unwittingly) to let his own preferences affect the result.

d. A final advantage of the cognitive mapping approach as a help to a decision maker is that the decision maker will not become overconfident in the methodology, since he can see how simple it is and how directly the inferences are based on his own beliefs and values. There is no lure of the magical, since everything is explicit and easy to understand. To the extent that the beliefs are oversimplified so that they can be represented in the format of a cognitive map, the decision maker himself is in a position to evaluate the nature of the oversimplifications, since he made them himself.

The use of one's own externalized and enlarged cognitive map is one way in which the cognitive mapping approach might be developed to help decision makers. Here are three more ideas on the long-range policy relevance of the cognitive mapping approach:

2. *Reform of Institutions.* It might be possible to reform the institutional setting in which decision makers interact in such a way as to promote more sophisticated decisions. The most typical formal methods of interaction are through the writing of memos and the holding of committee meetings, which are inherently advocacy sessions. Perhaps the level of communication and argumentation could be improved if the participants had a

common way to express more complex images of the environment than they typically employ. For example, it might help if people presented their arguments explicitly in terms of points and arrows, so that the others could more readily see the whole structure of the argument. This might help raise the level of the written or spoken discussion by making it easier for people to understand and respond to each other's cognitive maps.

3. *Use of experts in a systematic manner.* From the point of view of the decision maker, "experts should be kept on tap and not on top." The problem arises as to how best to keep them on tap. From the expert's point of view, the problem is how his specialized knowledge can be effectively brought to bear on the actual decision-making process. The cognitive mapping approach suggests a method by which an expert or group of experts can present views in a systematic manner that distinguishes beliefs about causation from beliefs about goals. Thus an expert or a whole panel of experts could be used by a decision maker to provide subjective opinions about what the most relevant concept variables are in a policy domain, and what the causal linkages are between their concept variables. Or the decision maker himself could list the concept variables he was concerned about and ask experts to estimate the linkages between them.

There are several specific suggestions on the use of experts inherent in the empirical studies on cognitive maps:

a. Roberts, in Chapter 7, suggested that specially chosen judges (or experts) could contribute more to the decision-making process if their beliefs could be aggregated in a systematic way. In particular, the systematic aggregation of cognitive maps derived from the questionnaire method holds out the prospect of being more accurate than the causal beliefs of a single person.

b. Hart, in Chapter 8, showed how judges could be used to estimate the beliefs represented in a set of documents, and thereby distill previous knowledge into a more useable form.

c. Bonham and Shapiro, in Chapter 6, looked forward to the time when machine-aided policy recommendations could be made that would be congruent with the way decision makers use concepts and justify choices.

4. *Prediction of others' decisions.* The last way decision makers might benefit from cognitive mapping procedures would be if the procedures could be used to help them predict what other decision makers will do. This is obviously difficult, but even a little help

247

would be valuable. The suggestion is that decision makers could study the cognitive maps derived from the assertions of other actors who are important in the policy environment. Naturally, such cognitive maps would have to be used with care, since the assertions a person makes are not necessarily sincere.[19] But decision makers already use the statements of others as important sources of information, and any technique that would allow the systematic representation of such data holds promise of being helpful in such analysis.[20] As a start, an analysis of someone else's cognitive map would help one understand the way concepts are being used, the overall structure of the argument, and the way particular arguments change over time.

The central theme of this last section can be expressed as a series of propositions:

1. Decision makers want to be rational.

2. Decision makers have limitations in their cognitive capacity.

3. Because of these cognitive limitations they simplify their view of their policy environment.

4. The particular ways in which they simplify their images of the policy environment include the failure to recognize feedback mechanisms.

5. Such simplifications are costly in terms of yielding less accurate images, less sophisticated policy choices, and ultimately less satisfactory outcomes than are necessary, even given a decision maker's own concepts, beliefs, and values.

6. Decision makers can therefore become more sophisticated through the use of cognitive mapping techniques applied by them to their own cognitive maps and to the cognitive maps of others.

[19] For a discussion of the question of sincerity, see Chapter 10, section A.

[20] For a discussion of descriptive use of cognitive maps, see project 15 in Chapter 11.

PART FOUR

Epilogue

CHAPTER TEN

Limitations
—Robert Axelrod

This chapter will explore the limitations of the cognitive mapping approach. Among the problems considered are the potential for insincerity in policy discussions, the slowness of the documentary coding method, the absence of any types of relationships in cognitive maps other than causal or value relationships, and the lack of quantification in the relationships that are represented. For each problem, the origin of the problem is explained, the nature of the limitation is assessed, and suggestions are made as to how to alleviate its effects.

It pays to be explicit about the limitations of the cognitive mapping approach for two different reasons. The first is to avoid misuse (or overuse) of the approach. From the research point of view, the misuse of an approach is costly, because it wastes time in an attempt to do something that is not feasible and may inhibit later work that would be feasible. From the applied point of view, the misuse of an approach is costly because invalid implications for policy are themselves costly if followed. To avoid these costs, it is important to be explicit about the limitations of any new approach.

Being explicit about limitations also has a positive side. By focusing on what these limitations are, we can get a clearer understanding of how these limitations may eventually be eliminated, or at least alleviated. We can also get a clearer understanding of how the relevance of each specific limitation is determined by the object of the inquiry.

One more point before going into the details. The categorization of limitations presented here is somewhat arbitrary, because there is so much interaction between the effects of the various kinds of limitations. For example, if the measurement techniques for

For their helpful criticisms I would like to thank Stan Bernstein, Matthew Bonham, Michael Cohen, Jeffrey Hart, Heikki Heiskanen, Arnold Kanter, Stuart Ross, and Paul Sniderman.

cognitive maps improve, then the quality of the available source materials becomes less of a limitation.

A. LIMITATIONS IN INTERPRETING A COGNITIVE MAP

The term "cognitive map" might mislead some people to think that the approach is trying to make some direct inferences about what a person's "true" beliefs are. The cognitive mapping approach is, of course, in no better (or worse) position in this regard than any other procedure that relies on a person's conscious and monitored linguistic behavior to make inferences about his or her beliefs.[1]

One way to conceptualize the problem of using verbal or written assertions for the drawing of inferences about beliefs was suggested by Holsti in Chapter 2, where he drew the distinction between the representational and the instrumental views of communication. As he puts it, the representational view assumes that assertions are valid indicators of the person's beliefs, whereas the instrumental view presumes that words are chosen to have an impact on the target of the communication.

The point is that we need to be careful about what types of inferences we wish to draw from a cognitive map, and then make sure that the assumptions needed for those inferences are met. For example, in the study of the Eastern Committee (Chapter 4), the initial goal was to study the structure of the images that decision makers present to one another. For such a goal, the instrumental view is sufficient. But then I wanted to go further in Chapter 9, section D, and interpret the lack of cycles as being inherent in the way decision makers themselves view their policy environment— that is, I wanted to take the representational view. For this purpose I had to pay considerable attention to the alternative interpretations of the results to see if any of them would explain the results more parsimoniously. This type of argument is lengthy and

[1] There are some research techniques that attempt to avoid the reliance on conscious monitoring of behavior. These include projective techniques (such as the famous Rorschach test), and physiological measurements (such as galvanic skin response and pupil dilation). In the present state of the art, these techniques have their own severe limitations for the study of elite decision making, but it would take us too far afield to consider them here. See, for example, Murstein (1965) on projective techniques and Shapiro and Crider (1969) on psychophysiological approaches.

can never be completely decisive, although under certain circumstances its plausibility can be supported.

The reason why this is a major issue is that we sometimes want to draw inferences about how a decision maker (or group) comes to a decision. For that reason, we want to know whether we can take assertions of beliefs at face value or not. More specifically, we would then be concerned with whether the person was sincere in making the assertions, that is, whether his assertions matched his beliefs.

A good method to evaluate the sincerity of an assertion is to investigate the incentives the speaker has to be insincere. These incentives certainly depend on the context of the assertion, especially the relationship between the speaker and the audience. Typically, we assume for a politician that his statements to the general public are not as sincere as his private statements to his colleagues, and that private statements to his colleagues are not as sincere as statements to an academic interviewer who credibly promises anonymity.

A second way to evaluate sincerity is based on the fact that a speaker typically desires to act in a manner consistent with his assertion, since otherwise he will *appear* to be insincere. The appearance of insincerity is very costly for an elite decision maker. For this reason, it can usually be assumed that a decision maker tends to be sincere when he knows that his assertions can be checked against his actions. Indeed, this is a major reason why elites are more sincere with colleagues inside an organization than they are with the public outside the organization.

Now this is precisely where the question of sincerity gets interesting. If a decision maker is heavily constrained to keep his assertions and actions consistent with each other, then he may not only monitor his assertions (to keep them sincere), but he may also monitor his actions (to keep them consistent with his assertions). To the extent that actions are monitored to keep them consistent with the assertions, the assertions themselves constrain action. Because in certain contexts actions and assertions can be mutually constraining, the use of suitable documentary material from which to derive a cognitive map promises to be fruitful in understanding not only the assertions themselves but also the actual choices of the decision maker.

This is not to say that there cannot be elaborate hoaxes in which the decision maker deliberately misleads part or all of his audience.

253

There can be hoaxes, of course. But the incentives to carry out a hoax and the chances for its success depend in large measure on the nature of the on-going relationship between the audience and the speaker. The general principle in evaluating the sincerity of a cognitive map is to evaluate the communication on which it is based for the presence or absence of the conditions that promote sincerity.

With the documentary method of deriving cognitive maps, there are special problems that arise from the fact that not all beliefs and values are explicitly stated in any given communication. A belief may be left unstated because it is irrelevant to the subject at hand. Because of this, the researcher must be careful when making inferences about the speaker's beliefs in situations different from the one discussed in the original document. The work of Bonham and Shapiro (in Chapter 6) shows, however, that some types of generalizations can be made. In their case the cognitive map derived from a discussion about missiles in Syria proved to be useful in making predictions about how the speaker would explain the antecedents and consequences of the Jordanian civil war.

Some beliefs that *are* relevant to the subject at hand are also left unstated. Sometimes this is because they are so obvious to the speaker and the audience that they need not be made explicit. Fortunately, this is not always a problem. The reason is that the speaker was trying to communicate to the original audience, and the coder can often be placed in roughly the same state of knowledge as the original audience. Thus, if a British speaker says that a certain policy will lead to the sinking of the British fleet, he need not also add "and that would be a disaster for us." The speaker knows it, the audience knows it, and more to the point, the well-prepared coder knows it. So the coder can add an assumed (and negative) linkage from "sinking of the British fleet" to "British utility." Two coders can agree with each other quite closely on the consequences of these assumed relationships. An indication of this (as mentioned in Chapter 3) is that there is a 91 percent agreement on the direct relationship to utility of a given variable in a given assertion.

Thus beliefs that are too obvious to be stated are not a major coding problem. But there is another type of unstated belief that does limit the usability of cognitive maps derived from documents. This is the belief that is unstated because it works against the speaker's actual preferences. This type of unstated belief is prob-

254

ably what accounts for much of the tendency for documentary cognitive maps to be balanced. In decision-making contexts, the speakers often know what they want to achieve, and are presumably reluctant to admit the validity of arguments that go against their preferred policy alternative. Documents from such policy contexts cannot, therefore, be used directly to draw inferences about the full range of "true" or "inner" beliefs of the speaker. This is definitely a limitation in the cognitive mapping approach. What can be done about it is our next question.

In the first place, one can refrain from asking about "true" or "inner" beliefs of a speaker, and instead concentrate on more directly answerable questions, such as questions about the *images* of the policy environment that one decision maker presents to the others. Or one could be careful to try to eliminate other alternatives before inferring that a property of a cognitive map reflected anything about the cognitive style of the speaker. Both alternatives have been used in this volume. Still other possibilities will be discussed in the next chapter as potential projects. Included among the ways of getting closer to a person's "true" beliefs are the use of source material that is less likely to be argumentative (such as private interviews), and a systematic comparison of what a person says in different contexts.

Even if a person is sincere in the sense that he does not say anything that he does not believe (although he may not say everything he does believe), there is still another problem. A person may not know the basis of his own decisions. The arguments may be rationalizations of a decision reached on other grounds altogether. One cannot tell from the arguments of a general in favor of sending more troops to Vietnam whether the "underlying" reason for his position was a desire to be promoted, to serve his country, to aid the military-industrial complex, or to please his wife. Even he may not have been fully aware of how these factors affect his judgments. To study this type of issue one needs a different methodology altogether, or at least a more comparative orientation to see if images differ between a general who plans to retire from the military and join an aerospace company and a general who plans to retire and go fishing.

For some purposes, another important limitation of cognitive maps is that, whatever they reveal about the speaker, they are not necessarily accurate images of the environment. This simply means that a cognitive map may not correctly reflect the environmental contingencies that actually exist. Although a map may include a positive linkage from A to B, it remains an open question whether an increase in A will actually result in an increase in B. Indeed, we have already seen in Chapter 9 that spontaneous cognitive maps tend to contain systematic inaccuracies—namely, the lack of feedback cycles. Since cognitive maps are not necessarily accurate, one must be careful about inferring features of the environment from features of the map.

While cognitive maps may not be accurate, there is often no other way to generate a reliably accurate image of the policy environment, either. Moreover, to make any policy decision on an analytic basis requires a more or less explicit model of the environment.[2] The model used must ultimately rest on the subjective beliefs of individuals. So we might as well be systematic about how these subjective views are gathered and aggregated. This is one of the ways the questionnaire method of cognitive mapping can be useful. For, as Roberts argues in Chapter 7, the questionnaire method can be helpful in systematically soliciting individual beliefs from a panel and in aggregating these individuals beliefs into a relatively accurate image of a particular policy environment.

B. LIMITATIONS DUE TO COSTS

The cognitive mapping approach is costly in terms of the time required to derive the maps. This naturally limits the applicability of the approach to cases in which the necessary resources are available.

Each of the two different methods of deriving cognitive maps has different factors that determine the amount of time required. For the documentary method, the principal determinant is the length of the document to be coded. Unlike content analysis based on simple word counts, there seems no way to automate the coding of cognitive maps. The subtle types of interpretations that are required of the coder are far beyond the present state of the art of automatic language-processing programs. Working by hand, typical coding rates are in the range of two to four hours per thousand words of text, depending on the proficiency of the coder and the density of causal assertions in the text. Another hour or two per thousand words is needed for related tasks, such as

[2] See Steinbruner (1974) for a discussion of the analytic paradigm as well as the alternative cybernetic paradigm of decision making.

256

checking reliability between coders and constructing the actual map. This means that a trained coder working half time could process a 20,000-word document in three to six weeks.

The best way to hold down the cost of coding documents is to limit the length of the material to be coded. One method of doing this is to specify in advance the subject matter and/or the participants considered to be relevant to the research. Another method is to use minutes of discussions rather than verbatim transcripts. A third method is to code only a selected sample of the relevant documents, every fifth meeting, for example. Which of these methods are suitable depends on the specific research goals of the project.

For the questionnaire method, it is the respondents' time that is a major factor. The number of questions about possible causal links that they must answer goes up nearly as the square of the number of variables to be considered. The careful screening of potentially interesting variables is therefore especially important to hold down the time required of the judges. When the questionnaire method is used to derive maps based on the judges' interpretation of a large set of documents, another major factor will be the time it takes the judges to absorb the source material. This time can be reduced by using judges who are already familiar with the selected subject area.

C. LIMITATIONS IN SOURCE MATERIALS

Limitations in the use of cognitive maps for research and prediction arise from the limited availability of source materials on which the maps can be based. Once again, there is a substantial difference in the mix of advantages and disadvantages of the documentary and questionnaire methods. The questionnaire method typically requires questionnaire response specially generated for that purpose. It therefore suffers from a lack of source material to the extent that suitable respondents are hard to get. But the documentary method suffers in another way, because it typically uses material that was generated for other purposes altogether. Suitable documentary materials may therefore not exist for a given setting, because the discussions were too unimportant to make records of or, conversely, too sensitive to keep records of. It sometimes also happens that perfectly fine records were kept, but remain unavailable for analysis.[3]

[3] For more on this point see Holsti's discussion of source material in Chapter 2.

The availability of suitable documentary material seems at first to be a major limitation of the cognitive mapping approach. For this reason, I have done a good deal of searching for interesting materials, and I present the results of my searching in Appendix 5. For now it suffices to say that the surprising thing is that there are many more suitable documents than one would at first imagine, even if one wants actual transcripts rather than just detailed summaries of meetings. The transcripts of former President Nixon's White House tapes are just one recent set of wonderful materials that are available.

Even if a document is available, it is not necessarily suitable. Here are five requirements that should be borne in mind in determining the suitability of a document for analysis with the cognitive mapping approach:

1. The most important point is that the document must reflect the features that are to be studied. For example, if the purpose of a particular analysis is to determine what a person is thinking, it would be inappropriate to use the arguments of his lawyers at his trial. Conversely, if the purpose of the analysis is to study courtroom tactics, these same arguments might provide perfectly suitable documentary material.

2. In order to be suitable for cognitive mapping, a document should contain enough causal assertions to provide material for analysis. Of course, the types of causal assertions which are analyzable with the cognitive mapping approach include value statements, statements of policy preferences, and in general any assertion that can be represented in the format "the more A, the more B" or the format "the more A, the less B." The studies based on documentary materials that are presented in this volume are based on policy discussions, but this is by no means a requirement of the method. The document need not be about policy, and need not be from a discussion. But it must have some assertions that can be regarded as causal.

3. Another requirement is that there be enough background information about the context of the document so that the coder can understand the meaning of the words. For example, in an American foreign policy document, the statements "Moscow wants to avoid war" and "the Soviet Union wants to avoid war" have the same meaning. Any well-informed coder of an American foreign policy document should know this, so there would be no problem. The problem arises when the speaker and the audience share

information that is needed for an understanding of the meaning of the assertions, but the coder does not share this information. This can cause problems when the participants have built up a substantial body of shared knowledge in the early meetings whose records are now unavailable. In most other situations, however, the necessary background information is available to the coder, either from the records of previous meetings or from outside information about the issue under discussion.

4. In order to be suitable for cognitive mapping, a document should be complete in terms of the scope of the investigation. The material that is coded should be complete in the sense that it is reasonable to assume that the speaker was able to express himself fully. The assumption is needed so that any relationship that is not explicitly said or obviously implied can be assumed to be either irrelevant or of negligible magnitude.

5. Finally, a document should also be a reliable representation of the speaker's (or author's) message. Thus, if the document is a transcript, it should be an accurate one. If the document is someone's notes of the speaker's words, the notes must not introduce any distortions that are important for the particular analytic purpose at hand. Naturally, the coder who relies on documentary material will not have as much information to go on as the coder who also has a tape recording or videotape of the discussion. But for most purposes, the loss of gestures and even tone of voice is not a serious problem in understanding the meaning of a causal assertion, so long as enough of the context of the discussion is available to resolve ambiguities.

D. LIMITATIONS IN THE FLEXIBILITY OF COGNITIVE MAPS

Representing a person's assertions in terms of a cognitive map is a quite flexible procedure in some ways, and quite limited in others. Specifically, a cognitive map can represent the cause-effect structure of an argument no matter how many concepts and relationships there are in the argument. It can deal with policy proposals, utility, and intermediate concepts. It can deal with both beliefs and values, as well as with derived values based on other values and beliefs.

On the other hand, there are many important modes of thought that do not involve means-ends or causal imagery—even in the

259

broad sense used to define assertions for a cognitive map. There were three advantages in limiting cognitive mapping to such causal imagery: reliability, inferability, and comparability. Inter-coder reliability of documentary cognitive maps is fostered by keeping the foundations of the mapping simple. The more types of images, arguments, and assertions that are allowed into the map, the less chance that the map can be coded the same way by two different coders. Inferability refers to the extent to which conclusions can be derived from a set of assertions. Thus, from "A promotes B" and "B retards C," one can infer that (other things being equal) "A retards C." With other types of relation-ships, the equivalent forms of inference are much harder.[4] Com-parability between cognitive maps derived from documents and cognitive maps derived from questionnaires has proven highly useful in understanding the origins of the differences in structures that are typical of these two types of cognitive maps. Thus, at the cost of considering only causal imagery, the cognitive mapping approach has achieved valuable levels of reliability, inferability, and comparability.

Even within the rubric of causation, the cognitive mapping approach has been limited to only the most straightforward inter-pretation of the causal relationship. To be specific, there are three aspects of causation that could conceivably be added to the cognitive mapping approach, provided that due concern is paid to maintaining reliability, inferability, and comparability.

1. Conditional or interactive causation. Sometimes the causal impact of two or more different variables interact in determining the result of the effect variable. For example, "if A is high, B promotes C, but if A is low, B retards C." An example of this would be "If the President has a long term of office then impeach-ability is needed (that is, promotes utility), but if the President has a short term, then impeachability would be bad (that is, would lower utility)." [5]

---

[4] An important example is inclusion, which describes the relationship between a part and the whole, or between an example and the general principle. The problem is that inferences with such relationships are often difficult to predict because they involve inductive inference. For some ex-perimental evidence on how people do draw inferences from assertions of inductive evidence, see Gilson and Abelson (1965) and Abelson and Kanouse (1966). For some helpful ideas relevant to coding noncausal assertions, see Heiskanen (1974b).

[5] The lack of conditional or interactive relationships is not as serious a limitation as it might seem. There are three reasons. First, two of the most

2. Nonreversible causation. Nonreversible causation occurs when "an increase in A causes an increase in B, but a decrease in A does not cause a decrease in B." For example, the normal interpretation of "lighting matches causes forest fires" involves nonreversible causation because putting out matches does not put out forest fires. In cognitive maps only reversible causation is allowed, because "A promotes B" is taken to mean *both* that an increase in A causes an increase in B *and* that a decrease in A causes a decrease in B (see Chapter 3). Fortunately, nonreversible causation can often be converted to reversible causation without much distortion of the meaning. In the forest fire example, the sentence might be coded as "carelessness with matches causes forest fires." This is reversible because more carelessness will cause more forest fires, and less carelessness will cause fewer forest fires.

3. Nonmonotonic causation. The basic type of causal relationship assumes that a change in the cause variable in a given direction causes a change in the effect variable in a determinable direction. For a positive relationship, the change in the effect variable will be in the same direction as the change in the cause variable, while for a negative relationship, the change in the effect variable will be in the opposite direction from the change in the cause variable. In a nonmonotonic relationship, this does not hold. Instead, for some values of the cause variable an increase will yield an increase in the effect variable, while for other values of the cause variable an increase will yield a decrease in the effect variable. For example, during a limited war one is likely to hear an assertion of a nonmonotonic relationship between the number of troops and national utility, as in "we should either send enough troops to really win or we should send none at all. Anything in between is a bad policy." Nonmonotonic relationships were intro-

---

common forms of apparently interactive relationships can actually be treated as a simple causal relationship. When different causal variables always covary in the relevant context, then these causal variables can be merged into a single concept variable. When all but one of the causal variables are essentially constant in the relevant context, they can be assumed to have their constant values and the relationship is equivalent to a simple one, a principle which is already built into the coding of conditional ideas (see Appendix 1, section N). Second, genuinely interactive relationships are relatively rare, even for complex speakers such as Morris. Third, when all else fails, one can use the mathematical techniques offered by Roberts in Chapter 7; namely, the use of alternative maps to represent the alternative possible values of a relationship and the explicit use of time lags to study the propagation of effects through the system.

duced by Hart when he found that his judges asked for them while filling out their questionnaires. Nonmonotonic relationships have not been used in coding rules for deriving cognitive maps from documents because of problems of inferability.

These are limitations in the type of causal relationships that may be coded. But a much more troublesome limitation is that even for simple causal relationships there is no way at present to measure the relationship's magnitude. The next section is devoted to this problem and its implications.

E. LIMITATIONS IN QUANTITATIVE MEASUREMENT

When decision makers discuss policy in high-level meetings they rarely speak of causation in quantitative terms. Few decision makers are likely to say something like, "if our fleet were 12 percent stronger, our chance of winning the war would be 17 percent greater." This lack of quantification is a limitation in the cognitive mapping approach, but it is also an empirical finding of major importance and a significant opportunity for the improvement of decision making.

The lack of quantification is, first of all, a limitation in the cognitive mapping approach. The reason is that without knowing the magnitudes of the linkages, there is no guarantee that one can infer even the sign of the total effect of one point on another. This is so because if there are alternative paths carrying the effect from the first point to the second, and if some of these paths are positive and others negative, then the total effect of them taken together cannot be unambiguously determined.[6] This is especially relevant if the first point to be considered is a policy variable and the other point is the utility variable. Then one could not, in general, determine from a cognitive map whether a given policy should be favored (as having a positive total effect on utility), or whether it should be opposed (as having a negative total effect on utility). This is a substantial limitation on the value of cognitive maps. It means that, in general, the decision-making problem cannot be solved using a cognitive map with only positive and negative signs.

For the questionnaire approach, this limitation could be lifted

[6] See Chapter 3 for an explanation of the basic principles, and see Appendix 3 for the more formal mathematics.

without too much difficulty. All that would be required would be to ask the judges to give their subjective estimates of the magnitude of each causal relationship, rather than just the sign of the relationship. The judges may find the task difficult, of course, but they might be able to make some progress toward deriving meaningful quantitative estimates of causal relationships within the sphere of their competence. And, after all, decision making is always based on subjective estimates in the end, so the systematic gathering and aggregating of the estimates might help the decision maker, especially if the estimates were made in a format that allowed separate pieces of information to be integrated into a single interdependent system. And this is exactly what the questionnaire approach to cognitive mapping does allow.

For the documentary approach to cognitive mapping, quantification could also be attempted. For documentary materials (as opposed to interviews), one must work with what one has. There may be clues about magnitudes of some of the relationships, as when someone spontaneously says that "a relatively small increase in A will cause a pretty big drop in B." This statement clearly implies not only that the causal linkage from A to B is negative, but also that it is of considerable magnitude. The difficulty is that only a few assertions carry any significant information at all about magnitudes, and even these do not usually carry very precise information. To solve the decision-making problem, what would be needed would be a comparison of the sums of the strengths of all the positive paths (which are products of the magnitudes of their component linkages) with the sums of the strengths of the negative paths (which are also products of the magnitudes of component linkages). And this formulation does not even take into account paths that are only known to be "nonpositive," "nonnegative," or "ambiguous."

This leads to a wholly different interpretation of the lack of quantification in documentary cognitive maps. Not only is the difficulty of quantifying a spontaneous cognitive map a limitation in the method, it is also an empirical result of major importance. After all, if the researcher cannot solve the decision-making problem because the linkages are not quantified, how could the original audience listening to the same communication solve the same problem to determine what the separate assertions of the speaker added up to? If a speaker gives some arguments in favor of a proposal and some against, he usually has to be quite explicit about the conclusion (or at least the relative strengths of whole argument), because the separate assertions rarely carry enough precision to allow the audience to combine them and determine even the sign of the total effect for themselves.

This says something important about policy discussions, and perhaps even about thought processes. It says that the images of the policy environment that top-level decision makers provide each other are in general not sufficient for the audience to evaluate in terms of their separate parts. The way the parts add up simply has to be specified separately. This may be only a statement about the simplicity of what is said in meetings, but it may also be relevant to how elite decision makers think about a problem on their own.

But there is an out. This is indicated by the repeated use of the phrase "in general" in the preceding discussion of the difficulty of drawing policy inferences from the set of separate assertions made by a speaker. The "out" is that there is a strong tendency for cognitive maps not to have just any structure, but to be balanced. Recall from Chapter 3 that a balanced cognitive map is one in which none of the paths between two given points, A and B, has an indirect effect opposite to any other path. With such a cognitive map, the total effect of a policy variable on utility is never ambiguous. That is to say, with a balanced map all the inferences can be drawn and the decision-making problem solved in terms of the separate assertions in the map.

With balanced cognitive maps, the limitations imposed by the lack of quantification simply disappear. With balanced maps, every inference can be readily drawn without any estimates of the magnitudes of the separate linkages, because different paths between the same two points always have consistent signs. Balance is a convenient way out of the ambiguity of inference—and decision makers frequently use it.

This tendency for spontaneous cognitive maps to be balanced is strong, but it is not irresistible. As we have seen, Marling's map was completely balanced, and so was the map of the Middle East expert. But the map of Morris speaking in the Constitutional Convention on the powers of the presidency was not completely balanced, despite a tendency in that direction.[7]

Balance may be convenient, but it is not very enlightening for the audience. This is because a balanced map provides arguments

---

[7] See Chapter 9, section C for a discussion of these findings.

264

on only one side of each issue. In an advocacy context, the audience may be able to hear opposite sides of each argument from different speakers, so that even if all the maps they are presented with are balanced, the audience may be in a position to pick and choose. But then the lack of quantification becomes a problem all over again, since paths with opposite signs must still be combined according to their relative magnitudes. This suggests the third interpretation of lack of quantification in the assertions of decision makers.

At first, the lack of quantification in cognitive maps was viewed as a limitation in the cognitive mapping approach. The fact that people typically do not speak in ways that allow their separate assertions to be quantified suggested the second interpretation, namely, that the lack of quantification can be regarded as a significant empirical result. The fact is that some elite decision makers overcome the limitations of quantification by the use of completely balanced cognitive maps. This use of balanced maps suggests a third interpretation of the lack of quantification: the opportunity for the improvement of the decision-making process.

An opportunity for improving decision making is through the externalization of one's own cognitive map. If a decision maker could be trained to write out his or her own set of causal beliefs about a policy domain, then the limitations in quantification could be ameliorated. The decision maker could learn to identify and avoid the use of completely balanced maps by learning how to write down more separate beliefs than might be manageable without some external aid. In Chapter 9, section F, we have already seen how this type of training for externalization can help a decision maker to handle maps of greater structural complexity (including cycles as well as imbalance).[8] Here the point is that by externalizing a cognitive map a decision maker will be able to identify which specific relationships need to be quantified in order to draw which specific inferences. Thus the lack of quantification, which looked like a limitation in cognitive mapping, is also an opportunity for improved decision making through the use of cognitive mapping.

[8] For a suggestion on training decision makers in the art of externalization, see Chapter 11, project 11.

CHAPTER ELEVEN

Projects
—Robert Axelrod

This final chapter offers fifteen suggestions for research projects using the cognitive mapping approach to decision making. These projects are built upon the findings and the state of the art represented by previous chapters. They are motivated by the desire to learn more about the decision-making process and the desire to improve that process. The suggestions for projects are grouped into these subject areas: cognitive process of individuals, functioning of groups, improvement of decision making, advance of methodology, and description of specific policy settings.

A. THE CONCEPT OF RIPENESS IN SCIENCE

A scientific subfield is ripe for substantial progress when three factors are present: a set of key empirical results that demonstrate the potential value of future discoveries, a theoretical orientation that suggests a more or less elaborate research program, and a methodological capacity that provides the means to carry out the research program. An examination of cognitive mapping in terms of these three factors shows that the approach is indeed ripe as a domain for substantial further progress.

A set of key empirical results already exists that demonstrates the potential value of the cognitive mapping approach. The most important of these in terms of their value as a foundation for future work are that *cognitive maps are used, consistent, simplified, and quasi-stable.* Cognitive maps are *used* by decision makers in the sense that the causal imagery captured by a cognitive map is a

For their helpful criticisms I would like to thank Stan Bernstein, Matthew Bonham, Michael Cohen, Jeffrey Hart, Heikki Herskanen, Arnold Kanter, Stuart Ross, and Paul Sniderman. I would also like to thank the students who have tried their hand at one of the cognitive mapping projects described here, or who have invented their own: Shai Feldman, Kristen Grim, Evelyn Deborah Jay, Steven J. Rosenstone, Mine Sabuncuoglu, and Ben Schiff.

large part of what decision makers talk about when they are in meetings to decide upon policy. Cognitive maps are *consistent* in the sense that decision makers tend to make choices that are consistent with their own cognitive maps. Cognitive maps are *simplified* in the sense that they tend to leave out certain important structural features of the actual policy environment. Cognitive maps are *quasi-stable* in the sense that some segments of a person's cognitive map remain quite recognizable over periods ranging up to several years.[1] These empirical results show that it would be very useful to know how people come to form their cognitive maps, and how their cognitive maps can be made more sophisticated.

A theoretical orientation exists in the form of an image of the decision making as a person of bounded rationality who tries to do his best, but has limited cognitive capacity. The limited cognitive capacity leads to large, but structurally simplified, images of the policy environment. The attempt to do one's best leads to the potential for improved decision making through the development of procedures by which the decision maker could examine and improve his own cognitive map, and thereby make his own decisions more sophisticated.

A methodological capacity exists to study cognitive maps in a comparative format. Cognitive maps can be derived from documents for the study of spontaneous discussion, and they can be derived from questionnaires or interviews for the more controlled study of beliefs. Especially important for the study of decision making in its full institutional context is the methodological capacity to derive a cognitive map *reliably* from a natural language text. This guarantees that the formal representation of the image presented by the speaker is not overly sensitive to the subjective judgments of a particular coder.

The research program that follows is suggested by the theoretical orientation, is made possible by the methodological capacity, and is motivated by the existing empirical results. The program itself is presented as a list of fifteen research projects. Some of these projects are fairly straightforward, and can be done in a few months. Such projects are suitable for graduate students in a research seminar. Other projects are much larger, and would probably require one or two years of work. Most of them are flexible, in that both the data base and the depth of the analysis

---

[1] For a more complete review and synthesis of the empirical results, see Chapter 9.

can be contracted or expanded to fit the interests and resources of the researcher.

These projects are genuine research projects, not classroom exercises. The descriptions of the projects suggest questions that might be asked, procedures that might be used, and even source material that might be employed, but the project description cannot provide more than this. Research is characterized by the property that the answers to the questions are not known in advance. So the project description cannot specify how to proceed once the project is well under way and the results begin to indicate that interesting surprises are just over the horizon. These project descriptions are suggestions that might help someone get under way, or might simply be used to inspire the development of other projects altogether. The extended rigors of research and the full joys of discovery reside with the one who does the work.

Taken as a whole, the suggested projects form a substantial research program. One set of questions involves how specific variables affect cognition and decision making. This first set of projects is designed to study the effects on individual cognitive maps of culture, roles, individual background, substantive issues, new information, and audiences. The second set of projects is designed to study not just individuals, but the interaction of individuals in groups. The major issues here involve the aggregation of individual beliefs, the effects of group structure, the mechanisms of persuasion, and the nature of mass belief systems. Questions in the third set are directly relevant to public policy. One such question is whether decision makers can learn to be more sophisticated with the help of cognitive mapping ideas. Another question directly relevant to public policy is, Which factors tend to make for accurate cognitive maps, that is, what conditions make it easier for decision makers to understand correctly their policy environment? A fourth set of questions is aimed at improving the methodological capacity of the cognitive mapping approach. These questions involve the improvement of the techniques for measuring cognitive maps and for representing causal imagery. The final set of questions aims at achieving a better understanding of specific situations, such as the Watergate cover-up plans, as discussed in former President Nixon's White House tapes.

Again, it must be stressed that these project descriptions do not provide the answers; they only suggest some questions and some ways in which the answers might be sought. As a further aid to

268

the prospective researcher, a guide to source material that might prove helpful in generating data for projects such as these is provided in Appendix 5.

B. FACTORS AFFECTING INDIVIDUAL COGNITIVE PROCESSES

This first set of questions deals with the effect of specific variables on the cognitive processes of individuals. The principal reason for asking these questions is that knowledge about the determinants of people's cognitive maps will help us to understand the decision-making process, and will, perhaps, allow us to improve that process. The factors that might affect a person's cognitive processes are regarded as independent variables whose effect is to be studied. The properties of the person's cognitive map are the dependent variables. The research strategy in these projects is comparative analysis. Situations with different values of the independent variables are observed, and inferences are drawn based on the observed differences in the dependent variables.[2]

Project 1. The Effects of Culture

A fascinating question concerns the extent to which cognitive maps of individuals from other cultures are similar to cognitive maps of individuals of our own culture. For example, is the lack of cycles in the spontaneous cognitive maps of American and British elites a feature only of these societies, or do people from completely different cultural backgrounds also tend to avoid the recognition of feedback when discussing policy problems?

A research design to find out is quite straightforward. The documentary method can be used to code and analyze cognitive maps of policy discussions that take place in other cultures. The use of the coding rules given in Appendix 1 will help assure comparable results. An example of documentary source material available for such a project are the minutes of the Japanese decision in 1941 to attack the United States and Britain rather than the Soviet

---

[2] There are many books on research design that might be suggested. For the type of quasi-experimental designs that are most helpful in these projects, I recommend Campbell and Stanley (1963). A central problem in such quasi-experimental projects is the potential for spurious correlations, and the consequent need to formulate and test alternative explanations.

269

Union. These records are available in translation by Ike (1967).[3] Another interesting example comes from Africa. This is the verbatim records of the Aburi Conference in 1965, which brought together the leading military figures of Nigeria in an unsuccessful effort to reach an understanding that would head off the impending civil war (Nigeria, 1967). These and other documents are described in more detail in the annotated guide to source material provided in Appendix 5.

The value of understanding the cognitve maps of members of other cultures is obvious. By understanding others we can better predict how they will act in an interdependent world and, perhaps equally important, we can attain a better perspective on how we ourselves operate.

Project 2. The Effects of Role

Once enough individuals have been analyzed, one could readily investigate the effect of roles. For example, does the formal leader of a group present a more complex image of the policy environment than do the others? Do military leaders have different kinds of images than do civilian leaders? Do members who are in the minority on a particular issue try tactics in making their assertions in policy meetings different from those of members who are in the majority? To study these and similar questions, it is necessary to have information on a suitable range of people whose different roles can each be identified. The large sociological literature on role theory can be used to suggest specific hypotheses (see especially the references on small-group research cited in note 10 below), but to a considerable extent the cognitive mapping approach itself can be used to suggest questions about such factors as the structure of arguments, the density of causal (versus noncausal) assertions, and the statements of near ultimate (versus immediate) values.

Project 3. The Effects of an Individual's Background and Personality

Do people with different backgrounds operate differently in policy environments? For example, in Chapter 9 it was suggested that

[3] Whether documents in other languages should be studied in English translation, or whether the coding rules themselves should be adapted to the source language, is an open question. Considerations of convenience and comparability point to the former technique, while considerations of potential distortion point to the latter.

people with a background in economics may see more cycles than others because they have learned many models that include feed-back processes. Is this actually so? I do not know of any source materials that would allow a direct test of this question. The differences between business leaders and trade union leaders would allow an indirect test, and there are available transcripts of a whole set of meetings in a labor/management bargaining process (Douglas, 1962).

Another approach would be to code transcripts of open-ended interviews with people of different backgrounds. An example of a fine set of material would be the raw interviews by Robert Putnam of the University of Michigan with almost two hundred British and Italian members of parliament.[4] These interviews include open-ended discussions on a variety of policy problems, including both their causes and what can be done about them. Since background information is available on each respondent, and since there are almost two hundred respondents, a great deal of comparative analysis could be done to determine the effects of differences in individual background on cognitive processes.

The effects of personality could be studied in a similar manner. Questions from standard personality measures could be asked of the respondents, along with the questions needed to derive their cognitive maps on a given subject. Especially interesting to explore would be whether certain personality factors or cognitive styles are systematically associated with various measures of complexity and sophistication in cognitive maps. Knowing more about the effects of background and personality might be useful in the training and selection of decision makers.

Project 4. The Effects of Issue Domain

Are structural properties of cognitive maps independent of the issue domain being considered, or do different domains elicit different types of images? For example, how do images of a scientific domain differ from issues of a policy domain? One could use a published review of the scientific literature of a field to develop a cognitive map of the state of the art in that field. An especially suitable field would be experimental or social psychology, because dominant statistical procedures yield results that are easy to represent in the form of causal assertions such as "the more A, the more B." A documentary example that is distinguished by its scope,

---

[4] For a description of these interviews, see Putnam (1973).

271

authoritativeness, and clarity is a survey of the attitude and attitude change literature by McGuire (1969).

Project 5. The Effects of New Information

How does a person update his cognitive map over time with the
reception of new information and argument? This is an important
question, because it relates directly to the accuracy of the image
as a reflection of the actual environmental contingencies in the
policy domain. One way to study the effects of new information
would be to take some arena in which the information input
received by the person is known, and for which his cognitive map
over a period of time could be determined. The changes in the
cognitive map could then be associated with the reception of new
information or arguments.[5] The weeks preceding the outbreak of
World War I might be a fruitful period for investigation because
the available documentary materials are especially rich.[6] For
greater control of the situation, one could study the same questions
using laboratory experiments with set tasks.[7] This project could
explore which aspects of a cognitive map change over time, and
which are relatively stable. For example, under what conditions
does a person add a new concept variable and causal beliefs about
it, and under what conditions does a person simply change his
preexisting beliefs? These questions are relevant not only to individual cognition, but also to interactions between individuals when
the object of the interaction is persuasion—a topic considered
below, in project 9.

Project 6. The Effects of the Audience

Different audiences elicit different communications. In Chapter 10
it was argued that the sincerity of a communication is dependent
in large measure on the nature of the audience. A small audience
composed of people who can check the veracity of the communication and who will be important to the speaker in the future is
likely to elicit a more sincere expression of the speaker's beliefs
than is a large audience with members who cannot check the

---

[5] For a guide to the cognitive psychology literature on this question, and
an information-processing model of cognition, see Axelrod (1973).

[6] See, for example, Zinnes (1963) and Holsti (1972).

[7] See, for example, Burnstein and Vinokur (1973).

speaker's veracity.[8] What people say to their colleagues in private is not always the same as what they say to a large audience in public. The more we know about the systematic differences in these communications, the better we would be at making inferences from generally available public statements to sincere beliefs of the speaker. This is an extremely difficult problem of inference, but its importance to voters and diplomats (to name two groups) is so great that any significant improvement would be quite valuable.

To study such a question would require documents about private assertions that are likely to be sincere, and corresponding public assertions that can be systematically compared to the private assertions. Two very large and very momentous collections of private assertions (which can readily be compared to corresponding public assertions over the same period of time) are the Pentagon Papers and former President Nixon's White House transcripts. The former consist of score of secret memos on American policy in Vietnam, and the latter consist of the tape recordings of a president's most sensitive conversations. What more could a political voyeur ask for?

C. THE FUNCTIONING OF GROUPS

The preceding set of projects dealt with individuals in groups, as, indeed, has most of this volume. Ideally, people should not be studied only one at a time; due consideration should also be given to the way they interact with each other.

One result, which has already been discussed (in Chapter 8 and 9), is Hart's finding that nations sometimes take inconsistent positions in the sense of asserting that two goals are positively related to each other, and at the same time taking different policy stands toward them. One explanation is that domestic pressures keep nations from being consistent in international discussions. In any case, the finding emphasizes that the movement from individual to group decisions is not trivial and must be carefully studied.

[8] A related methodological point is that communications with large audiences are easier to code. This is because with large audiences the speaker cannot assume as much shared knowledge as he can when speaking to one or two intimate associates.

Project 7. The Formal Theory of Group Belief

One way of studying groups is to regard them as aggregates of the individuals of which they are composed. Some interesting results of this formal approach have already been discussed in Chapter 9. One result is that even when no member of a group has beliefs that compose cycles, the group as a whole may, by majority vote, accept the separate beliefs that do compose a cycle. In this sense, a group may be more sophisticated than any of its members. In close analogy with the formal theory of collective choice, there can be a formal theory of collective beliefs.[9] The questions that could be addressed by such a formal theory include: what are the implications of using one aggregation rule rather than another on what the group will accept? What rules (if any) for aggregating beliefs satisfy a given set of conditions that are thought to be desirable? And what difference does it make in which order the separate possible linkages are considered by the group?

The mathematical results of the theory of collective choice have strikingly different interpretations when thought of in terms of cognitive maps. The basic isomorphism is from alternatives to concept variables that are shared by all members, and from preferences to causal impact. Thus the transformation of "alternative A is preferred to alternative B" is that "concept variable A is believed to have a direct or indirect impact on concept variable B." Arrow (1951) has shown that under almost any reasonable decision rule, individuals who are not irrational (that is, who have no cycles in their preferences) can compose a group that *is* irrational (that is, it does have a cycle in its social welfare function). The isomorphic result is that under almost any reasonable rule for aggregating beliefs, individuals who are unsophisticated (that is, who have no cycles in their cognitive maps) can compose a group that *is* sophisticated (that is, it does have a cycle in its group cognitive map).

Project 8. The Effects of Group Structure

There is more to a group than the static aggregation of its members. What lies beyond the formal theory of group belief is the study of how beliefs and decisions emerge from the actual functioning of a group. There are several ways to study group processes, and one of the most popular is the study of the effects of

[9] For an excellent introduction to the formal theory of collective choice, see Sen (1970). I would like to thank John Chamberlin for helping me to formulate the questions for this project.

group structure. The reason this approach has been so popular, especially in sociology, is threefold: group structure can readily be examined (and even controlled) in the laboratory, the effects of group structure are substantial, and, because of the first two factors, group structure promises to be relevant to the improvement of actual decision-making groups.[10]

In experimental groups it is often possible to assess group performance by measuring the length of time it takes to solve a problem of known difficulty or by measuring the quality of the group's decision. These two methods are of little help, however, in assessing groups dealing with problems of policy that cannot be precisely specified in advance. What cognitive mapping has to offer is an indirect way to assess performance when straightforward measures of group performance are not available.

Many policy-making bodies not only announce their decisions, but also issue statements of justification for their decisions. Committees, courts, and governments frequently justify their decisions with more or less extensive arguments proclaimed to the outside world. Documentary coding procedures could be applied to such statements to represent them as cognitive maps. Then the sophistication of the derived map could be assessed in terms of its structural properties, such as whether cycles were recognized. The difficulty with this method is that the sophistication of a group's statement might be more a function of the audience it addresses than of the group itself.

An alternative method of assessing a group's performance is to assess the sophistication of the discussion that preceded its decision. The sophistication of the discussion can be assessed through the sophistication of the causal images presented by the participants in the discussion. When records of the group's discussion are available, they provide an alternative way of assessing the performance of the group. It is certainly not as valid a measure of the quality of group performance as direct measures of the quality of the decisions would be, but when the quality of the decision cannot be accurately assessed, the sophistication of the participants' cognitive maps might provide a useful indirect measure. The assumption is, of course, that the more sophisticated the dis-

[10] The literature of small-group research is huge. Four useful and overlapping reviews of the literature are, in chronological order, Bales, Hare, and Borgatta (1957), Hare (1962), Kelley and Thibaut (1969), and Hare (1972).

cussion, the better the final decision. With this assumption and with internal records of various policy groups, we can learn more about how group structure affects group performance.

Project 9. Persuasion

Another approach to the study of group processes is the analysis of the dynamics rather than the structure of a group. One of the most elementary questions about group dynamics is: what happens in groups? An important part of the answer is that in policy discussions the participants try to persuade each other. Who persuades whom goes a long way toward determining what decision the group as a whole will reach. These group documents can be analyzed with the documentary coding method to yield the cognitive map of the group's output. Such group reports are probably substantially different from the cognitive maps of their members, even though they need not be quite as simple as the "greatest common denominator" of the beliefs shared by the majority. But just how do group justifications differ from the assertions of their separate members? Do small groups tend to issue justifications of greater sophistication than do large groups? Do groups with highly decentralized communications issue justifications of greater sophistication than do groups with highly centralized communications? Dealing with such questions in a systematic manner would probably require the formation of a series of experimental groups whose structure could be controlled and whose interactions could be monitored.

The persuasive efforts of the participants can be studied by viewing the assertions they make as attempts to change the cognitive maps of others. It is, of course, unnecessary for one person to try to get another to accept completely his own cognitive map. It suffices to get another person to draw the same policy inferences —even if the other person's reasoning is different. This may require changing several of the other person's beliefs. But which set of beliefs will be attacked? An answer based on efficiency considerations is that the mode of attack will be the one that requires least effort to succeed, where effort is measured in terms of the sum of degrees of firmness with which each of the attacked beliefs is held.

This line of reasoning leads me to the formulation of two hypotheses about persuasion. The first is about what is persuasive. It says that the less total change is required in a person's cognitive

276

map by a given persuasive attack, the more likely it is that the person will be persuaded by that attack.

The second hypothesis deals with which persuasive attack will be tried. It says that the persuasive attack chosen by a person will be selected from among those which, if they did work, would make the target person(s) support the speaker's preferred policy alternative(s). It goes on to say that among all such persuasive attacks, the speaker will tend to select those that have the greatest possible chance of working. The chance of a persuasive attack working increases as the amount of total change it requires decreases.

An estimate of the amount of effort required to get a particular belief to change can be based on indications of the firmness with which the belief was held by the target person. Indications of firmness of a belief might include: the emphasis with which the belief was originally stated, repetition, illustration, presence in relatively short paths (as Bonham and Shapiro hypothesize in Chapter 6), centrality (which is another principle of Bonham and Shapiro's simulation), and closeness in the map to ultimate utility (which may make the belief less subject to attack with evidence).

To test these hypotheses about persuasion, documents of meetings can be used by interpreting the early assertions as indications of the participants' cognitive maps, and the later assertions as indications of the persuasive attack used by the participants. Then the task would be to try to predict what happened in the later parts of the meetings from what happened in the earlier parts of the meetings.

In case the reader has not already guessed, this is the project that I want to try.

Project 10. Belief Systems of Mass Publics

The belief systems of the mass public are quite different from those of elites. Besides being less complex, the belief systems of members of the mass public are also less constrained, in the sense that knowledge of some of their beliefs is not much help in predicting knowledge of other beliefs (Converse, 1964). In contrast to the belief system of a mass public, the cognitive map of a high-level decision maker dealing with the area of his competence tends to be highly constrained. If he asserts that "A promotes B" and "B promotes C," then (assuming no other indirect causal paths from A to B) he will almost certainly agree that "A promotes C." More to the point, this type of constraint on elite consistency holds for rather large and highly interconnected maps, as we have seen in Chapter 9.

Here are three suggestions for the study of the belief systems of mass publics: The first is to supplement the survey approach with the techniques available from cognitive mapping. The second is to examine the assertions of groups that mediate between the mass public and the elites. The third is to take an historical orientation to the study of the development of belief systems in large groups.

The survey approach has been the dominant method of investigating belief systems of mass publics. Some of the principal questions in the field deal with the structure of the pattern of relationships between issues, the role of mass belief systems in determining a person's vote, and the causes of stability and change in such belief systems.[11] What cognitive mapping has to add to the survey approach are two ways of deriving new information about the structural patterns of beliefs in a manner that could reveal more about the structure of the perceived causal relationships between the concepts than could a correlational analysis of responses to attitude questions. One way would be to use the questionnaire method of deriving cognitive maps through a series of closed-ended questions on a given domain. The second method would be to let the respondents express in their own words their views about a given domain, and then use the documentary approach to code their responses. The former method would allow a direct comparison between the maps of different people, and the latter would allow an analysis of properties of the spontaneous assertions made by members of the mass public on the given domain.

An important issue that has not yet received enough systematic attention is the belief systems of groups that mediate between the mass public and the governing elites. Groups such as political parties, journalists, citizen lobbying groups, church groups, and labor unions all mediate between the mass public and the elites. And in this process they issue document after document that provide expressions of their belief systems. The cognitive maps that could be derived from such documents might reveal a great deal about the way in which these mediating groups form a bridge between the mass public and the governing elites. For example,

---

[11] Some of the trail-blazing works in this field are Lipset (1960), Campbell, et al. (1960), McClosky (1964), and Converse (1964). For an additional blaze, see Axelrod (1967).

one could test the hypothesis that such groups tend to use specific concepts and causal linkages that are similar to those used by members of the mass public, but at the same time they put them together in the relatively complex and constrained manner typical of high-level policy makers.

An historical orientation could also be taken to the study of belief systems in large groups. For example, there seems to be a tendency for certain arguments to go with certain other arguments on any given topic. To study the intellectual history of a given topic, one could compare the cognitive maps derived from a sequence of historical documents on the topic. Besides the interest inherent in a coherent description of the intellectual development of common opinions on a given subject, there are some fascinating hypotheses that could be evaluated. Is it actually true that people come to like (or dislike) something that has positive (or negative) effects, and retain that attitude long after the effects cease, or long after the effects are valued? If so, the phenomena would appear as the development of a *direct* link to utility from any concept that has long had only an *indirect* impact on utility. Such an effect would be consistent with the "evaluative transfer" process formulated by Abelson (1968b, pp. 121ff). More to the point, it would go far toward explaining cultural lag in terms of the retention of an attitude long after the attitude was functional.

D. IMPROVING DECISION MAKING

Many of the proposed projects have indirect relevance to the improvement of decision making, but there are two projects that have this as their primary purpose. These are projects aimed primarily at helping decision makers rather than studying them.

Project 11. A Learning Demonstration

The application of cognitive mapping techniques is still a long way from the point where it should be used to guide decision makers. What are needed are steps to get to that desired state. One set of steps is through continued research on the characteristics of actual maps as expressed in documents or through questionnaires. Many of the previous projects are aimed in this direction. Another, more directly applied direction, is toward the evaluation of whether the cognitive mapping tools can help decision makers to help themselves.

279

Projects at various levels of difficulty can be invented along these lines. For example, one could try teaching the mapping procedures to decision makers, so that they could map their own beliefs and be able to externalize the calculations needed to make inferences from them. In Chapter 9 it was argued that such an externalization might allow decision makers to be more sophisticated, because it now appears that decision makers typically have more beliefs than they can handle.

A more modest design would probably be a better place to begin, however. Instead of trying to make decision makers more sophisticated in terms of their own sets of beliefs, one might try to make them more sophisticated in terms of specific postulated sets of beliefs. To test the success of such an enterprise, an experiment could be undertaken to see if a relatively short training session could increase the ability of decision makers to handle problems involving more or less complex causal structures.

The first step would be the construction of a graduated set of abstract causal structures with a set of questions about them. The simplest one would be of the form "If A promotes B, and A increases, what happens to B?" A somewhat more complicated question would be "Suppose A retards B which helps C which hurts D. A also helps E which hurts F which hurts G which helps D. What happens to D if A goes down?" [12] These abstract problems would then be made concrete by translating into simple prose, using plausible examples from the domain of competence of the decision makers themselves.

My conjecture is that there is a significant set of such problems that could not be answered reliably before any special training, but that could easily be answered after only a day or so of instruction. What would be taught are the basic ideas presented in Chapter 3, namely, how to represent on paper a set of causal ideas as a directed graph of points and arrows, and how to make inferences from such a graph.

If my conjecture is correct, the learning experiment would demonstrate that significant improvements are possible in handling moderately complex sets of causal arguments with only a day or so of training. Of course, the ultimate benefits of such training would only come if the decision makers applied their new skills to their everyday analytic tasks. An informal evaluation of whether this

[12] The answer is that D goes down because A goes down, and both paths from A to D are positive. If you did not get this, go back to Chapter 3.

was done could be attained from a follow-up interview or questionnaire asking whether the participants found specific occasions to use their new skills.

To determine whether the trained decision makers make better decisions would require a much more ambitious design. But a relatively simple project design is sufficient to determine whether decision makers can easily become more skilled at causal reasoning by learning how to draw cognitive maps.

Project 12. Accuracy of Causal Images

For a decision maker to be able to draw correct inferences from his own set of beliefs is desirable, but only if the beliefs themselves bear some constructive relationship to reality. So the improvement of the accuracy of a decision maker's cognitive map is just as important as the improvement of his ability to manipulate that map.

To clarify what is meant by accuracy, it is helpful to review the distinctions between some of the different properties a cognitive map may have. A given representation of a person's cognitive map is a *valid* representation if it correctly measures what it purports to measure, namely, the structure of the assertions made by that person. The cognitive map itself is *sincere* if the assertions on which it is based are actually believed by the speaker to be true.

The third property is accuracy. Accuracy is different from validity or sincerity in that accuracy depends not only on the speaker but also on the environment. A cognitive map is *accurate* if the predictions derivable from the map are correct. For example, if a map predicts that an increase in A will cause an increase in G, then the map is accurate in this prediction if G actually does go up when A goes up. Put another way, a map is accurate if it correctly reflects environmental contingencies. Accuracy, like validity and sincerity, is a matter of degree.

Validity has already been discussed in Chapters 4, 9, and 10, especially in terms of the reliability of the documentary method of deriving cognitive maps. Sincerity has also been discussed. The problems caused by questionable sincerity and how these may be dealt with were considered in Chapter 10. The question of accuracy has received attention in two places. Roberts, in Chapter 7, regarded the attainment of greater accuracy as the principal reason why beliefs of several judges should be aggregated, and why the questionnaire method was developed to provide a systematic way of doing this. In my own study of the Eastern Committee (Chapter 4), I noted that the expectations of the members were actually quite inaccurate. They had a complex view of their policy domain and made decisions accordingly, but within a few years events proved them quite wrong. Unfortunately, such inaccuracies are hardly rare in major domains of policy. Therefore, a better understanding of when people are inaccurate and why, and what might be done about it could be a valuable aid to those who have to make decisions in such major domains of policy.

The difficulty with studying accuracy is simply that the researcher is often in no better position to evaluate the accuracy of a set of assertions than is the decision maker himself. For example, while an assertion about the direct impact of a concept variable on utility can be disputed, it may not be subject to empirical testing. Even for empirically testable causal assertions, the researcher may not be better placed than the decision maker to make such a test. After all, the decision maker may be an expert in the policy domain in question, whereas the researcher is probably not.

There are two ways to deal with these problems of evaluating accuracy. One is to take a situation in which the subject matter is controlled by the researcher so that at least some of the environmental contingencies are known, and then watch how inferences about the causal relationships are drawn. This has been the main method used by experimentally oriented psychologists in their cognitive studies, although the experiments typically involve relationships other than causation, such as liking relationships.[13] One limitation of experimental studies, however, is that estimation procedures of a decision maker that are not very good in the laboratory may be quite good in policy situations because the environmental contingencies in policy situations cannot be fully duplicated in the laboratory.

Another method of studying accuracy is to take a situation in which the experimenter has a great deal more information about environmental contingencies than does the decision maker.[14] One

[13] See, for example, the material reviewed in Slovic and Lichtenstein (1971) and Axelrod (1973).

[14] The psychological field called attribution theory does this, although it is more concerned with the type of conclusions the subjects draw than with the accuracy of their conclusions. Attribution theory is principally about how a person comes to have the existence of a specific belief, whereas cognitive mapping is about the structure formed by the entire set of beliefs in a given domain. Thus, attribution theory can be thought of as dealing with the

282

way to do this is to analyze the cognitive map wth twenty-twenty hindsight. This is what was done for the Eastern Committee. This approach has the limitation, of course, that the researcher still does not know what would have happened if another policy option had been undertaken. Nevertheless, by using previous rather than current problems the researcher may be able to evaluate the accuracy of a cognitive map better than the original participants could.

Using either method, the basic idea is be in a position to compare the (presumably more accurate) cognitive map of the researcher with the cognitive map of the decision maker in order to see where the decision maker was wrong. Some of the questions that would be most worth asking are: What types of factually based beliefs are most likely to be in error? What types of inferences from the map are most likely to be in error? Which types of evidence are systematically underused or misused? And what types of people are likely to be relatively accurate? With further knowledge about these questions we could eventually be in a better position to advise decision makers on how to be more accurate.

E. IMPROVING RESEARCH CAPABILITIES

This set of projects involves the furtherance of the cognitive mapping approach itself. These projects seek to improve the measurement of cognitive maps and to extend the mathematical analysis of beliefs. The basic idea is to alleviate some of the limitations in the cognitive mapping approach that were discussed in Chapter 10. Progress in these methodological areas will be helpful to virtually all of the other projects.

Project 13. Measurement

Expanding the range of what is measured is an important and feasible direction to move in. With the questionnaire method it would be relatively easy to expand the range of relationships by simply expanding the instructions to the judges. This is what Hart did in Chapter 8, when he added the "concave downward" relationship as a choice for the judges to handle some types of non-monotonic relationships. Adding a request for quantitative

---

origin of the pieces of a cognitive map, a topic that has not been addressed at all in this volume. Unfortunately, the field has concentrated on perceiving the causes of other people's behavior, to the exclusion of other causal possibilities. See Jones (1971) and, especially, Kelley (1971).

estimates of causal linkages would also be feasible with the questionnaire method.

With the documentary method the problem is more difficult, since whatever new coding instructions are written would have to pass a test of intercoder reliability. Among the limitations in measurement that might be lifted are those discussed in Chapter 10, namely, the absence of provisions in the current coding rules for interactive causation (in which two or more variables interact in affecting some other variable), nonreversible causation (in which "an increase in A causes an increase in B," but "a decrease in A does not cause a decrease in B"), and nonmonotonic causation (in which for some values of the cause variable the linkage is positive, but for other values the linkage is negative).

Equally useful would be ways to code any indications of the magnitude of a causal relationship (such as, "a little increase in A causes a big increase in B"), and important forms of noncausal relationships (such as, "A is included in B" or "A and B usually occur together"). For a given relationship there are also properties that might be coded, including confidence (such as, "I am very certain that A increases B") and emphasis (such as, "it is important that A promotes B"). The ability to take these factors into account would improve the ability of a cognitive map to reflect more of the full richness of a person's assertions.

Project 14. Mathematics

Just as the measurement techniques could be expanded, so too could the mathematical techniques used to analyze a given cognitive map. In fact, for some purposes the measurement and the mathematics go hand in hand. The reason is that the measurement of a new type of relationship is of little value in offering advice unless the mathematics has also been developed to determine what inferences a person should make with a map that contains that specific type of relationship. In fact, the mathematics of eight-valued logic and pulse processes were specifically developed by myself (in Chapter 4 and Appendix 3) and Roberts (in Chapter 7), respectively, for the purpose of making just such inferences from cognitive maps. So for each of the new things that might be measured, there is the corresponding mathematical problem of deducing what would be a maximally consistent set of inferences from a given map that contained that type of relationship, as well as all other allowable relationships.

284

F. DESCRIPTIVE PROJECTS

The final category of projects aims at a better understanding of specific situations rather than decision making in general. In fact, three of the five empirical studies in this volume gain added interest because of their descriptions of important policy areas: the powers of the President (Chapter 5 by Ross), commuter transportation (Chapter 7 by Roberts), and the international ocean regime (Chapter 8 by Hart). The other two studies selected topics that were more convenient for other research purposes, if less valuable from a purely descriptive point of view: British intervention in Persia in 1918 (Chapter 4 by Axelrod), and a hypothetical scenario dealing with the Middle East (Chapter 6 by Bonham and Shapiro).

The value of a descriptive project lies in the ability to understand the specific situation better through the use of techniques that have been used in a variety of situations. Used in this way, cognitive mapping can be regarded as an extention of content analysis.[15] For while content analysis is in principle capable of being used to derive generalizations, it is more commonly used in a descriptive mode. Moreover, while content analysis is in principle capable of very flexible types of measurement, in practice it usually deals with word counting. What cognitive mapping techniques have to offer to content analysis is a way of studying the overall *structure* of a communication, and not simply a way to aggregate its separate elements. To be more concrete, an example follows.

Project 15. Former President Nixon's White House Tapes

An analysis of Nixon's White House tapes would be useful for many of the projects already discussed, including the ones on the effects of new information (project 5), the effect of different audiences (project 6), and persuasion (project 9). But the cognitive maps derived from the transcripts of the tapes could also be used to study some of the questions that people have asked about Watergate itself, such as what the participants were trying to do at each stage. It must be emphasized that cognitive mapping is

---

[15] Some of the most helpful works on content analysis are: North et al. (1963), Stone et al. (1966), Gerbner et al. (1969), and Holsti (1969). Interactions between people are coded by Bales (1950), and the evaluative linkages between concepts are coded by Osgood, Saporta, and Nunnally (1956).

285

still experimental, and that for most purposes it could not be regarded as substantially more valid than less formal modes of interpretation. In particular, its representation of specific relationships is quite simple. Cognitive maps are, however, quite good at representing the structure of a causal argument, despite all the limitations discussed in Chapter 10.

A better knowledge of the overall structure of an argument can be very helpful in understanding the context in which a specific utterance was made. And this is precisely the problem with rigorous modes of analysis that rely on the selection of short passages to support or refute a given interpretation. It is difficult for different people to agree on an understanding of the full context, since each can readily cite other passages in isolation to support his own interpretation. Cognitive mapping, on the other hand, provides a way to see readily where each given assertion fits into the whole collection of a person's assertions.

Cognitive mapping has another advantage in the interpretation of controversial documents. Its coding rules have been worked out in advance and applied to a variety of documents. Because of this, its representation of a specific person's map is less subject to the biases of the interpreter than are less systematic modes of interpretation. There is still the need for subjective judgments in coding a document, of course. While the intercoder reliability of these judgments is high, it is certainly not perfect (see Chapter 4 for details). Therefore, one would not want to rely on inferences that were sensitive to one or two coding decisions. Nevertheless, an entire cognitive map could give a clear picture of the structure of each person's assertions, and this could be of considerable assistance in seeing "the forest instead of the trees." One could also analyze the overall structure of each cognitive map to determine such things as which concepts were most central, when specific lines of discussion emerged, and what concepts were treated as most directly related to their own utility.

These projects with cognitive maps may seem to reflect what Kaplan (1964) calls the law of the instrument: Give a small boy a hammer, and he will find that everything he encounters needs pounding. I plead guilty. Pounding away at problems of how decisions are made and how they can be improved is a lot of fun, especially when the pounding is done with a new tool.

Now the question is whether the new tool is sufficiently powerful and versatile to be added to the tool kit of the master craftsman. Considering that cognitive mapping can do some things that no other technique can do, the case is strong. In particular, cognitive mapping provides a systematic, reliable way to measure and analyze the structure of an argument and not just its separate parts. Moreover, it provides the capacity to represent and make inferences from both causal assertions and statements of value, the very foundations of analytic decision making.

Someday the cognitive mapping approach might be used directly by decision makers themselves. Research with cognitive mapping has already led to the conclusion that high-level decision makers probably have more beliefs than they can handle, and that the way they simplify their images of the policy environment introduces systematic distortions. Perhaps the externalization of their own beliefs and values can help them to be more sophisticated in achieving their own goals, given their own beliefs about the causal linkages present in the world. It will still be up to the rest of us to be sure that those who make important decisions do so for our benefit rather than at our expense.

APPENDICES

The Documentary Coding Method
—*Margaret Tucker Wrightson*

The rules for the derivation of cognitive maps from documentary material are set forth in this manual for coders. These are the rules used in the three empirical studies by Axelrod, Ross, and Bonham and Shapiro. The high level of intercoder reliability achieved by these coding rules is discussed in Chapter 4.

This coding manual is useful not only for explaining what has already been done, but also for showing future researchers exactly how cognitive maps can be derived from documentary sources. Many such projects are suggested in Chapter 10, and a variety of suitable source material is cited in Appendix 5.

The coder's job is one of encoding.[1] The coder must scrutinize an assigned primary resource text in an effort to record all cause-effect relationships within the text into a more formal body of relationships. To accomplish this, the coder must be provided with a comprehensive set of decision rules appropriate for the solution to any problems that might arise. Before presenting these decision rules it might be helpful to set the coder's job in its total context. Coding is the first step in the process of building a cognitive map. The cognitive map is used to analyze the assertions of

---

[1] These coding rules are the direct descendants of the original rules developed by Robert Axelrod and the more extensive coding instructions written under his supervision by Jeffrey Hart. I learned those rules as a coder for the Eastern Committee Project (Chapter 4), and wrote a second version while serving as Matthew Bonham's research assistant. The present revised edition I wrote during the period I was research assistant to Robert Axelrod. This final set of rules differs principally by the addition of some directions for special cases and by providing what, I hope, are more easily understood explanations based on new examples. I would like to thank Professor Bonham for his editorial help and to acknowledge Professor Robert Axelrod, Stan Bernstein, and especially Stuart Ross for their invaluable criticism and advice on this latest effort.

All new material is marked for identification.

a given decision maker. The end product of the analysis is a cognitive map. This map is a graphic representation of the decision maker's views on a given subject (or subjects) about which he has expressed verbal or written opinions. Its most basic building block is the "relationship," which is one statement having a subject, or cause concept, related positively or negatively to an object, or effect concept. Because each different relationship is connected to others by matching common cause or effect variables until all relationships are depicted graphically, the coder's accurate account is important for a correct representation of the speaker's viewpoint.

The presentation and resolution of all possible relationship variations that the coder might face is best approached in terms of sample problem case studies.[2] Even so, a general explanation of the nature of the coder's job and the way in which he should approach the text is important.

The most successful coder is the one who has internalized a dual outlook. That is, he is at once perceiving the text structurally and by content. As stated, the sentences, phrases, or paragraphs that are of interest to the coder are those that assert a causal relationship. In other words, a given subject "A" affects, either positively or negatively, a given object "B." In English grammar, the simple sentence structure paralleling this relationship is Subject/Verb/Object. In coder terminology the most basic structure is: "Cause Concept/Linkage/Effect Concept." The most simple sentence type, for example, would be, "Nuclear escalation harms world peace." It is asserted that the cause concept, "nuclear escalation," has a negative linkage to, or "harms," "world peace," the effect concept. In this case the structure of the sentence itself serves as the guide to the coder's transcription of the relationship. As this example illustrates, the coder must keep the basic structure, "Cause Concept/Linkage/Effect Concept," in mind at all times when examining a text in order not to miss a single relationship. This is important, for the validity of the project rests upon a successful account of *all* relationships. Of course, not all sentences or relationships are this straightforward, but all sentences that contain some relationships are variations of the simplest type.

The basic form of a relationship is, as stated, "Cause Concept/ Linkage/Effect Concept." The cause concept and the effect con-

---

[2] No sample sentences are taken from documentary material. Neither are they paraphrased from the materials used in any of the studies in *Structure of Decision*.

cept must be represented as variables, which have the potential to take on different values. For example, "the amount of British strength" is a valid cause or effect concept, since such strength can be great or small. An entity such as "Britain" is not a valid concept, since it can take on no other values.

In coding concepts as variables, the alternative values of the variables (for example, "great" and "small") need not be specified if they are clearly understood. When the other values of a concept variable are not clearly implied by its formulation, they must be explicitly included in the description of the variable, as in "buying food" (rather than buying luxuries).

In a few cases no structural analysis will insure a correct coding of the relationship. Some relationships are implicit in the phrase, sentence, or group of sentences. These cases are those in which the phrase, sentence, or sentences do not constitute relationships in a grammatical, structural sense. These situations present the most difficult types of coding problems. They are best approached by content analysis. In content analysis the critical question to ask is, "Does the thrust of the phrase, sentence, or sentence group imply a relationship?" A simple example is, "The most dangerous thought by the Ukrainian people is revanchism." There is no structural relationship; nevertheless, the implication is that "revanchism" is bad for the Ukraine. Thus, a relationship must be coded.

A coder must attempt to maintain the original language as faithfully as possible. At times, this effort may involve rather extended writing of concepts; nevertheless, it is important that the coder list the entire concept, complete with adjectival or adverbial clauses, so that its meaning may not be distorted later.

The importance of maintaining the original language is equaled by the need to reflect the speaker's statements in kind and number. Thus, if the speaker states a relationship two or more times, the coder should also. If a document includes contradictory statements, they must each be recorded. Moreover, refutations of relationships are not recorded as relationships. If the speaker, for example, states a relationship and then terms it spurious, the relationship is from his view invalid and not, therefore, codable. If, however, after such a refutation the speaker then asserts the correct view of the relationship as he perceives it, this should be recorded. A good rule to follow in these cases would be, "Denotation rather than interpretation."

If a speaker agrees with an assertion made by someone else, a judgment must be made by the coder. If the coder believes that the assent indicates the speaker takes on the assertion as his own, it is coded as an assertion of the speaker. "Yes, I think so too," would be so coded. A passive "uh-huh" or "O.K." may simply indicate acknowledgement. These ambiguous passive assents must not be coded unless they are in response to a question requesting or demanding explicit agreement with the assertion, such as "You agree this is true, don't you?"

With regard to structural assertions, the language of the original sentence is almost always easily preserved. For example, "The existence of a peaceful, strong, and unanimously supported Swiss foreign policy is of great benefit to the current Swiss position in world affairs." The structure of the sentence itself is such that the coder has no trouble denoting both cause and effect concepts exactly as they have been stated by the writer. The cause concept is, "The existence of a peaceful, strong, and unanimously supported Swiss foreign policy." The effect variable is, "the current Swiss position in world affairs."

Some assertions may require coders to paraphrase the original words in order to achieve the form, "Cause Concept/Linkage/ Effect Concept." A simple example of this sentence type would be, "We know the decisive importance of mutual trust in international affairs." The sentence, once again, structurally establishes no direct cause-effect relationship; yet, from a contextual viewpoint we see that "mutual trust" carries a decisive importance for international affairs. Thus, the relationship is: "mutual trust/ decisive importance for/international affairs." Such paraphrasing, maintaining as much of the original language as possible, presents no necessary inaccuracy between coders because the relationship has been denoted. Moreover, the process by which these initial concepts are ultimately merged into broader categories of variables guards against comparative inaccuracy. This process will later be explained.

The chief danger of content analysis is that a coder may, in his search for assertions, impute his own assumptions into coding to create assertions. The danger of overzealously creating relationships that have no basis in the text is twofold. First, it immediately introduces coder bias and text distortion. Second, it opens the door to comparative coder incongruence. This problem becomes increasingly dangerous when the coder becomes familiar with the speakers' viewpoint. When this is the case, the coder may see a relationship where there is none, simply because he is familiar with the cause-effect relationship that he has seen a number of times previously. In this instance, he must be careful not to code spurious implications. Once again, the rule, "Denotation rather than interpretation" applied. Moreover, because of the dangers involved in searching for the elusive assertion, a rule of thumb in content analysis is never to paraphrase an assertion that must be drawn from more than a few sentences. Do not, certainly, look for assertions by linking paragraphs.

When a coder wishes to analyze a large text, one of several pages or more, he should set up his clerical techniques in detail and in advance. Without a system of abbreviations and clear, well constructed coding sheets, he will soon be lost in his notes. Good preparation saves later backtracking.

There are eight types of structural relationships, as well as numerous special cases of relationship problems. In the following pages, abstract and concrete examples will be presented, followed by a step-by-step resolution.

Before examining the eight types and special cases, a word about linkages is useful. Thus far, we have presented only two types of linkages, "plus" and "minus." Nevertheless, there are five other symbols that may be of use to more rigorous coders, for all linkages do not fit comfortably into a simple plus-or-minus world. They are:

$\oplus$ will not hurt, does not prevent, is not harmful to
$\ominus$ will not help, does not promote, is of no benefit to
a   may or may not be related to, affects indeterminately
m   effects in some non-zero way
0   does not matter for, has no effect on, has no relation to.

Occasionally, a speaker will not actively promote or discourage a policy. When he speaks in this passive manner he asserts that a given policy is "not bad" without saying "it is good," and vice versa. The general linkages of "$\oplus$" and "$\ominus$" are useful in these cases. When the relationship exists, but has an indefinite linkage, the symbol "a" is applicable. Finally, when the cause and effect are unrelated, according to the speaker, the symbol "0" is useful. Sample sentences might be as follows:

"The Mayor's labor policy would not hurt his political support."

| the Mayor's labor policy | $/\oplus/$ | Mayor's political support |

"Violent picketing would not be beneficial to the negotiations."

violent picketing $\qquad$ /⊖/ $\qquad$ negotiations

"The Mideast War will affect trade negotiations in ways not yet forseen."

Mideast War $\qquad$ /a/ $\qquad$ trade negotiations

"We can be sure that adoption of the new rules will affect the outcome of the meeting; whether it is good or bad is not known."

adoption of new rules $\qquad$ /m/ $\qquad$ outcome of the meeting

"These new tariff laws will have no effect on the American economy."

new tariff laws $\qquad$ /0/ $\qquad$ American economy

Each of these additional symbols allows the coding of a greater variety of phrasings; each may occur in any of the simple or complex linkage structures outlined in this text.

SIXTEEN CASE STUDIES

A. SIMPLE CAUSE CONCEPT/SIMPLE LINKAGE/ SIMPLE EFFECT CONCEPT

Sample sentence: "Our present topic is the militarism of Germany, which is maintaining a state of tension in the Baltic Area."

1. The first step is the realization of the relationship. Does a subject affect an object?

2. Having recognized that it does, the isolation of the cause and effect concepts is the second step. As the sentence structure indicates, "the militarism of Germany" is the causal concept, because it is the initiator of the action, while the direct object clause, "a state of tension in the Baltic area," constitutes that which is somehow influenced, the effect concept.

3. The linkage, which indicates the nature of the relationship, must be established. If the relationship is one that negatively influences the effect concept, the relationship receives the linkage indication, "minus." If, on the other hand, it is positive, the linkage is denoted by the sign, "plus." In this case, the linkage words, "is

maintaining," indicate a positive relationship, "plus." Thus the final relationship is coded as follows:

| the militarism of Germany | / + / | maintaining a state of tension in the Baltic area |

B. SIMPLE CAUSE CONCEPT/SIMPLE LINKAGE/ COMPLEX EFFECT CONCEPT

Sample sentence: "The development of international cooperation in all fields across ideological frontiers will gradually remove the hostility and fear that poison international relations."

1. This example is illustrative of a double object, single subject relationship. In such situations, the object must always be coded separately; that is, the list of coded concepts must contain no double effect relationships.

2. The causal concept is "The development of international cooperation in all fields across ideological frontiers," because it is the initiator of the relationships.

3. The effect concepts seem to be "hostility" and "fear." However, as has previously been mentioned and should now be recalled, all concepts must be rigorously denoted, including all adjectival and adverbial clauses. In this case, the adjectival clause modifying both fear and hostility is, "that poison international relations." Because the clause adds greater information to the total concept's meaning, it must be included as a clause of both "fear" and "hostility" concepts. Thus, the two effect concepts are "fear that poisons international relations" and "hostility that poisons international relations." With regard to adverbial and adjectival clauses modifying concepts, it is a good practice for the coder to include all such clauses regardless of his personal opinion of their relevance. By this method, all concepts will be more likely to retain their original, full meaning.

4. The linkage is, as the verb structure indicates, "will gradually remove." Because "remove" indicates taking away something over time, the linkage is a negative one and is indicated by "minus."

5. Thus, finally, there are two distinct relationships to be coded in this case. They are as follows:

| the development of international coopera- | / − / | hostility that poisons international relations |

tion in all fields across
ideological frontiers

the development of   / — /   fear that poisons
international coopera-   international relations
tion in all fields across
ideological frontiers

6. It should be noted that, as has been done above, the cause
concept should be rewritten for each relationship as part of good
clerical practice.

C. COMPLEX CAUSE CONCEPT/COMPLEX LINKAGE/SIMPLE EFFECT CONCEPT

Sample sentence: "We note the success we have achieved in our
endeavors to safeguard Finland's security, not by the dangerous
expedient of relying on military means, but by gaining the confidence of the great power which is our neighbor, by maintaining
friendly relations with all countries near and far, by dissociating
ourselves from the conflicts of interests and tensions between
others and by adhering faithfully to all obligations undertaken."

1. The first aspect the reader notices is that a contrast is being
set up through the sentence structure. In such cases there will
always be two linkages, one positive, the other negative. The
words, "not by relying on" and "but by" set up this contrast in the
sample sentence and their linkages are therefore, "minus" and
"plus," respectively.

2. How many subjects, cause concepts, are there? To what
linkages are they connected? "Relying on military means" is linked
by "not by," and thus it carires a negative value. The other cause
concepts are "gaining the confidence of a great power which is our
neighbor," "maintaining friendly relations with all countries near
and far," "dissociating ourselves from the conflicts of interest and
tensions between others," and "adhering faithfully to all obligations undertaken." Each of these concepts is linked structurally
to "but by" and their linkage is, thus "plus."

It should be noted that "by" and other such words precede cause
concepts rather than effect concepts. "By," "from," "because of,"
and other words and phrases of this type create structural reversals
in sentence structure. The diagrammed sentence will always carry
the noun clause which follows these words as the subject of the

sentence, the initiator of the action. The coded phrase also carries these noun phrases as the cause concepts as well. In grammar, as in coding, this is done in order to maintain the logic of the relationship in the sentence.

3. There is only one effect concept among these multiple cause concepts, which is, "the success we have achieved in our endeavors to safeguard Finland's security."

4. Because none of the cause concepts is meaningfully or structurally dependent upon another for maintenance of the stated relationship, the relationships are all coded separately. Thus, the final coding is as follows:

military means	/ − /	the success we have achieved in our endeavors to safeguard Finland's security
gaining the confidence of the great power which is our neighbor	/ + /	the success we have achieved in our endeavors to safeguard Finland's security
maintaining friendly relations with all countries near and far	/ + /	the success we have achieved in our endeavors to safeguard Finland's security
dissociating ourselves from the conflicts of interests and tensions of others	/ + /	the success we have achieved in our endeavors to safeguard Finland's security
adhering faithfully to all obligations undertaken	/ + /	the success we have achieved in our endeavors to safeguard Finland's security

D. EITHER/OR RELATIONSHIPS

Sample sentence: "Either the Soviet Union pursues the policy of detente with the United States or it must obtain guarantees for its security by a continuation of the Cold War."

1. Either/or assertions automatically indicate two relationships. Thus, the coder must look for several concepts. It is not always necessary for the coder to look for the cause concepts first, the

linkages second, and the effect concepts last. He or she may look for each in whatever order seems most appropriate. In this sample sentence, for example, let us look for the effect concepts first.

2. What is the object or effect concept? In cases that are not clear-cut, such as this one, the question to ask is, "What is receiving the action?" In this sentence it is "guarantees for its security." As will be explained, no pronouns are to appear in concepts; thus, the correctly coded effect concept is, "guarantees for the Soviet Union's security." We already know that because this is an "either/or" type of sentence that two relationships exist. Is there then a second effect concept? Because none is readily apparent, the coder may leave the search for the present and later, having isolated the cause concepts, see if other effect concepts are necessary for recording the coded relationships.

3. The subject concepts are not immediately clear, either. In this situation, the question to ask is, "What is affecting 'guarantees for the Soviet Union's security?' " In this case we realize that there are two optional alternatives in the phrases, "either the Soviet Union pursues the policy of detente with the United States" and "or by a continuation of the Cold War." Although, in a crude sense, these may be construed to be concepts as they are written, they do not constitute properly phrased concepts in the ideal sense. In this case, as in all cases involving unsatisfactory concepts, a paraphrasing or revision of the original structure to achieve the more easily recognized cause concept form is necessary. Thus, "either the Soviet Union pursues the policy of detente with the United States" is changed to form the more appropriate cause concept, "Soviet Union's pursuit of detente with the United States." Likewise, "or by a continuation of the Cold War" is changed to "Soviet Union's continuation of the Cold War."

4. The linkages in the original sentence, "it must obtain" and "by continuing," are both positive in meaning. Thus they constitute "plus" relationships. They are positive because they indicate that the implementation of either cause concept will have a positive effect on "guarantees for Soviet security."

5. All "either/or" relationships present a situation of exclusiveness between the relationships; the relationships are therefore independent of one another for their individual meanings. That is, for the linkage relationship to maintain, it is not necessary that both cause concepts act on the effect concept jointly. Examples of other interdependent cause concepts will be presented later; never-

theless, a simple example, at this point, may help to explain the differences between independent and interdependent cause concepts. Interdependent cause concepts are those for which a joint application is a prerequisite to affect the stated relationship on the coder's sheet. This statement means that together "A" and "B" will affect in a given way "C," but separately applied, neither will insure that same effect on "C." A sample sentence will illustrate. "Together, our neutral policy as well as other nations' confidence in it will maintain India's independence." Separately, the cause concepts do not necessarily insure maintenance of Indian independence. The coder must therefore be careful to code such examples jointly.

Independent "either/or" relationships, on the other hand, imply that the relationships are definitely distinct and must be coded as two separate relationships. Thus, the final coding of the sentence is as follows:

Soviet Union's pursuit of detente with the United States	/ + /	guarantees for the Soviet Union's security
Soviet Union's continuation of the Cold War	/ + /	guarantees for the Soviet Union's security

E. PROBABILITY RELATIONSHIPS

Probability relationships may occur in any sentence type; they differ only in that they indicate a probable positive or probable negative relationship. Key words to look for in probability relationships lie in the linkages that directly precede the cause or effect concepts. Some examples of words that indicate probability are: "likelihood," "little likelihood," "unlikely," "apt to," "liable to," "chance of," "chance that," "chance for," "probability that," "will probably," "might," "may," "could," as well as variations of these types. The coder should note, however, that words such as "should," "must," and "will have to" are not probability indicators, because they only express a desire that the relationship will maintain, not the probability that it will.

Sample sentence: "Russian shipment of arms to Portugal is apt to increase the chance of war on the Iberian peninsula."

1. The cause variable is "Russian shipment of arms to Portu-

gal." It is related to the effect variable, "the chance of war on the Iberian peninsula."

2. There is a single linkage between these concepts. It is indicated by the word "increase." The direction of the relationship is positive. The relationship is qualified by the probability indicator, "apt to." This qualification does not alter the direction but only the likelihood of the relation. The coding system allows the coding of direction. Probability modifiers do not affect the coding of the direction of the relationship when they indicate only increasing or decreasing possibility of application of the relationship. Such variation is not captured in the coding of assertions. The final coding is as follows:

Russian shipment of   / + /   chance of war on the
arms to Portugal   Iberian peninsula

Sample sentence: "Neutrality in the present stage of arms technique offers small states in an unfavorable geographical position a better chance of survival in a general war, than does an alliance with one of the nuclear, great powers, which offers less."

1. What are the effect variable and linkage? That is, what is being influenced in this sentence and how? Clearly, "offers" indicates a positive relationship to "survival in a general war," the effect concept. However, the coder should ask himself whether or not there is a phrase or word in the sentence that modifies the concept and in so doing adds meaning. In this case, "small states in an unfavorable geographical position" further defines the effect concept and, therefore, should be added. The final effect concept then is, "survival, in general war, of small states in an unfavorable geographical position."

2. There are two cause concepts offered for comparison in the sentence. Comparisons generally contain two relationships, one positive, the other negative, because they attempt to contrast two relationships. In this sentence, the two cause concepts are "neutrality in the present stage of arms technique" and "an alliance with one of the nuclear, great powers." The modifier mentioned above, "small states in an unfavorable geographic position," could also be added to these cause concepts because they further clarify and define the policies of neutrality and alliance as well as help maintain the speaker's logic.

3. The linkages "offers a better chance," and "than does, which offers less" connote the comparison of two probability relation-

ships. In these cases the second concept to be compared is often obscured by the absence of a more obvious linkage, such as in the case of the first concept. This is often the case in English sentence structure. Phrases such as "than does" imply that the second concept included in the sentence is affected by the same linkage as the first but in a lesser sense. These sentence types in English are called complex/compound sentences. Having established the linkages, the coder must then ask himself, "Are the relationships positive or negative?" "Seems to offer a better chance" is unquestionably positive. Why, though, is "than does, offers less" negative? The comparison being made in this sentence implies that "neutrality, in the present stage of arms technique" offers a *better* chance. Consequently, "an alliance with one of the nuclear, great powers" offers *less* chance, indicated by the comparison, "than does." A hypothetical sentence indicating this comparison might read, "An alliance with one of the nuclear, great powers offers less chance for survival in a general war." Thus, the relationship indicated by *less* is negative. The final coding is as follows:

neutrality of small states in the present stage of arms technique	/+/	small states in a favorable geographical position survival in a general war
an alliance of small states with one of the nuclear great powers	/−/	small states in a favorable geographical position survival in a general war

F. PRONOUN CAUSE OR EFFECT CONCEPTS

The pronoun cause or effect concepts are those sentence groups in which the cause or effect concepts referred to are pronouns such as "this," "it," "that," "which," "he," "she," "they," or "we." Such pronouns refer to concepts that have been mentioned previously in the text. In these cases the coder must look to the text for the concept that the pronoun is replacing. This may or may not be closely connected to the sentence containing the relationship. Nevertheless, the concept referred to should be located and substituted for the pronoun in the denotation as coded.

Sample sentence: "It is reasonable, therefore, to revert once more to the proposal concerning an anti-ballistic missile system in the hope that it may be taken as a step toward building up United States' security and reducing the risk of nuclear war."

1. The relationship in this sentence may be isolated in the phrase, "it may be taken as a step towards building up United States' security and reducing the risk of nuclear war." In the sentence the cause concept would seem to be "it." "It," however, is not meaningful or correct as it stands. Because "it" refers to the proposal concerning "an anti-ballistic missile system," the correct concept is "proposition of an anti-ballistic missile system."

2. There are two effect concepts, "United States' security" and "the risk of nuclear war." For the coder there can be no question of interdependence between the two concepts; the effect concepts must always be coded separately.

3. The linkages are "reducing" and "building up," "minus" and "plus," respectively. The coder should be careful not to confuse the relative "goodness" or "badness" of the concepts and the positiveness or negativeness of the linkage. That is, although the "risk of nuclear war" is universally accepted to be a bad thing, if its linkage is, for example, something that enhances the "risk of nuclear war," the relationship is still positive, "plus." If the linkage is negative, it is negative; the concept in no way affects the linkage.

4. The sample sentence contains one other pronoun, namely, the "it" at the beginning of the sentence. "It" is an example of an expletive, an idiomatic usage in which "it" stands as the subject of a sentence or phrase but carries no definitive meaning. Such idiomatic expressions are not relationships, and do not concern the coder. Thus, the final coding appears as follows:

| the proposal concerning an anti-ballistic missile system | / + / | international security |
| the proposal concerning an anti-ballistic missile system | / − / | risk of nuclear war |

G. CONTENT ANALYSIS

As has been mentioned, some sentence groups carry assertions that cannot be coded on the basis of their structure alone. For example, consider the following case:

Sample sentence: "The foreign minister's behavior has been entirely erratic. It is difficult . . . No, I would go even further. This department is now unable to plan rationally."

1. It is clear that there is a causal relationship; but what is it, and how should it be coded? Content analysis cases, once resolved, are coded in the same manner as all other problems. The coder should not attempt to handle these types of problems as casually and quickly as he or she would simpler structures.

2. That there is not a structural relationship between the two sentences is clear. As in most content analysis cases, in this example, the relationship between the behavior of the foreign minister and rational planning is not structurally linked (that is, there is no overt, structural causal linkage). The linkage is, however, implied by the logical content of the statement.

3. The relationship should be coded by including the implied linkage. In this case the linkage is a negative one because it is implied that the foreign minister's erratic behavior hurts rational planning in this department. The final coding is as follows:

| the foreign minister's erratic behavior | / − / | this department's ability to plan rationally |

H. INVERTED CAUSE/EFFECT RELATIONSHIPS

Some sentences contain relationships in reverse order. They may even carry transitive verb linkages that seem to indicate that they themselves are causing some action. However, a closer analysis often indicates that the verb linkages are actually not causal and transitive, but intransitive indicators of an effect relationship. Often, these verbs will indicate permission or some negation of permission. Other types are constructed, such as need or lack of need. Some of these constructions are such that the transitive verb clause is followed with "by," "from," "without," or "unless," for example.

Sample sentence: "Bulgaria's national interests do not permit ties, nor the pursuit of alignment with a pro-Western policy."

The cause concept would appear to be Bulgaria's national interests but, if this were the case, there is not an effect concept to form a sensible relationship. Bulgaria's national interests do not affect anything directly. The real causal variables are "ties with a pro-Western policy" and "pursuit of an alignment with a pro-Western policy." They affect Bulgaria's national interests in a negative sense. The negative quality is denoted by negation of permission.

More abstractedly, this sentence is of the form, "anticipated consequences prevent policy adoption." Sentences stating relationships between the anticipated consequences of policies and the adoption of those policies should be coded "(adoption of) policy/relationship/consequence of policy."

ties with a pro-Western policy	/ − /	utility of Bulgaria
pursuit of an alignment with a pro-Western policy	/ − /	utility of Bulgaria

Sample sentence: "America cannot secure a permanent peace without the Russians' help."

This is an example of a transitive verb clause followed by "without." America's securing permanent peace again affects nothing. On the other hand, "the Russians' help" has an effect on America. Thus, the correct relationship is as follows:

Russians' help	/ + /	America's securing a permanent peace

I. UTILITY RELATIONSHIPS

Utility relationships are those in which some cause concept has an effect on something or someone's well being or general utility. By utility we refer to those effect concepts that refer to the unspecified best interests of a person, institution, country, and so on. The utility concept must only be used when the benefit or best interest is unspecified. Almost all utility variables include a noun or noun clause and most refer to a proper noun. Such examples are France, the Democratic party, Indiana's well-being, British interests, and so on. They are preceded by modifiers indicating a positive or negative utility relationship. In utility relationships and situations these modifiers are actually indications of the nature of the linkage. Unlike other modifiers, they do not shed light on the concept itself, but on the relationship. Thus, for example, "cost of foreign policy" is a regular concept, while "peril of Finland" expresses a negative relationship of some cause concept to Finnish best interests. To use coder language, Finnish best interests are recorded as "Finnish utility." Likewise, "economic prosperity of Finland," because it sheds light on a particular type of benefit, is not a utility variable, while "Finnish interests" may be translated into Finnish utility because the interests are general.

The coder should not begin immediately to associate terms such as "bad," "good," "advantageous," or "disadvantageous" with utility, although in special cases to be mentioned they may be. As has been stated, these types of words should appear as structural modifiers of a noun or noun clause, to qualify as utility linkages. Thus, whereas "his is a dangerous plan" is a utility statement, "in regard to Plan B, Plan A is dangerous" is not. It is the basic type of simple causal relation, with a negative linkage.

Understanding that noun modifiers shed light on utility, and that they indicate the positiveness or negativeness of a relation, will help the coder understand the following two types of utility relations:

In some specific contexts even less explicit statements may be interpreted as utility assertions. If an entire article or speech is about England, then such statements as "the policy is dangerous," or "the proposal ought not to be adopted," given without further specification, may legitimately be interpreted as having a negative linkage to "English utility."

Obviously "loaded" terms such as "tyranny" or "collapse of the army" may with safety be given a linkage to utility. The linkage, though not explicit, is implied in the choice of terms. The coder should take care to make such assumptions only in obvious cases, and to note "assumed" under the linkage on the coding sheets. One way to make this determination would be as follows:

If we look at nouns and noun clauses it is clear that in some cases a value is being placed on each noun. If a value can be divided into either the "plus" or "minus" category, and if it does not significantly further define the nouns it modifies, then it is likely the modifier qualifies as an assumed utility linkage.

The coder should take care not to code a case unless the modifier in *isolation* can be clearly classed as positive or negative. In this way he or she will be careful not to impute the speaker's expressed value preference to the variable, unless it is present in the variable itself. Imputing a "plus" or "minus" to a descriptive modifier constitutes distortion.

A coder translates any positively or negatively valued modifier into a utility assertion by his assumption that the value is related to unspecified best interests. This type is an "assumed utility relation," because we make an assumption that when, for example, we say "unwise choice" we are really stating that the choice is unwise for someone or something's utility. Whenever the coder encounters these types of modifiers, he codes them as the positive or negative linkage from the noun or noun clause to utility. If, on the other hand, the adjective is not clearly positive or negative, it is classified as descriptive and is included as part of the variable to which it is structurally attached.

One difficult aspect of locating "assumed utility relations" is that they often lie in the middle of other structural relations. These sentences may contain two or more assertions. Only by internalizing the dual outlook of content and structure can they both be ascertained.

The final type of utility relation is the simple statement of utility, which supports or derides a choice, plan, policy, person, or group; for example, "Infantry are impractical in this modern age" is a clear statement of utility. In isolation, these types are clear, while in context they are at times more complex. A speaker may make a series of comparative statements. But comparisons are not relations. For example, he might say, "We need more aircraft, not more infantry, infantry is useless." Aircraft are not causally related to infantry. Rather, they are both independent and related to utility, the first positively, the latter negatively. Let us examine four sample sentences a coder might encounter.

Sample sentence: "The repercussions of international tensions bode ill for France."

"France" is the object of "repercussions of international tensions," while "bode ill for" indicates a negative link. In the case where a proper noun, such as France, is receiving some action for or against its best interests, the relationship is one of utility; thus, the final coding is as follows:

repercussions of $\quad\quad\quad$ / − / $\quad\quad$ utility of France
international tensions

Sample sentence: "National interests demand that America returns her relations with Latin America to the same basis of trust which existed, for example, at the signing of the Monroe Doctrine."

1. "National interests" is the utility variable here, because "national" and "interests" in no way specify special interests different from the general best interests of America.

2. "Demand" is linkage of the type specified earlier, indicating need. Thus, the linkage is positive.

3. The cause variable is, "America returns in her relations with Latin America to the same basis as at the time of the signing of the Monroe Doctrine." The final coding is as follows:

America's return in   / + /   American utility
her relations with
Latin America to the
same basis as at the
time of the signing of
the Monroe Doctrine

Sample sentence: "Adoption of the policy of impeachment will cause tyranny in the United States Legislature."

Examination of the sentence reveals an assertion of the most basic type first described in this test. But within the sentence, the effect variable, "tyranny in the United States Legislature," carries an implicit negative descriptive modifier, "tyranny in." Since tyranny in a democratic society is antithetical ito its goals, we may say an assumption of negative utility exists. The final coding is as follows:

adoption of the policy   / + /   tyranny in the United
of impeachment   States Legislature

tyranny in the United   / − /   United States utility
States Legislature

Sample sentence: "If the Governor of California cuts the budget he will be making a mistake."

Structurally, the sentence is an "If . . . then" type of assertion. As has previously been explained, these are treated as if the event were a fact and not a future possibility. Because the sentence simply states that the policy is a "mistake" for an unspecified best interest, it is coded as a negative utility relation.

California's Governor   / − /   California utility
cutting the budget

J. COMPLEX SUBJECT/SIMPLE LINKAGE/ SIMPLE OBJECT

Sample sentence: "It was not in Poland's interests that she should be an ally of France, standing watch along the Russian border, and the first to be overrun, without the political significance to influence the decisions of war and peace."

1. What is being affected? "Poland's interests" is the object. Thus, because the concept expresses general best interests, the concept is "utility of Poland."

2. "Cannot be" indicates a negative effect on "utility of Poland"; thus, the linkage is "minus."

3. Because there is only one "minus" linkage, it is clear that cause concepts are only those that are negatively linked to "utility of Poland." They appear in this sentence, as in most sentences of this type, as a series of connected subject clauses. Thus, the cause concepts are: "she (Poland), an ally of France"; "Poland, standing watch along the Russian border"; "Poland, the first to be overrun"; "Poland, without the political significance to influence decisions of war and peace." It should be noted that "Poland" has been added to all these cause concepts in order to specify the identity intended by the meaning of the sentences. If, however, there are cases where no specific identity is intended, the general nature of the concept should be preserved.

4. The last question to ask when multiple causes occur is whether or not they are dependent upon each other to maintain the relationship to the effect concept. That is, are both Cause A and Cause B necessary to cause a negative relationship to Effect C, or will each separately still be capable of carrying the same negative charge? In this case, Polish utility is negatively affected by any of the cause concepts, regardless of the existence of the other concepts, according to the speaker. Thus, the coding should include four separate relationships. The coder must not search for interdependence; it should be obvious. For example, the sentence might read, "both A and B cause C," or "without A, B will not cause C." If the interdependence is not explicitly stated, the concepts should be coded as independent. The final coding of the sample sentence is as follows:

Poland as an ally of   / — /   Polish utility
great power

Poland's standing watch along the border	/ − /	Polish utility
Poland's being the first to be overrun	/ − /	Polish utility
Poland's being without the political significance to influence the decisions	/ − /	Polish utility

K. COMPLEX SUBJECT/SIMPLE LINKAGE/ COMPLEX OBJECT

Complex subjects, like complex objects, must be coded separately. When subjects are independent of one another, this is not difficult. The coder's task is more complex when he is faced with "interdependent cause concepts." The structure of such patterns follows the basic model, "If B is high, then A helps C." The nature of the relationship between A and C is dependent on the value of B; B determines whether A "helps" or "hurts" C. Other than this, B has no function.

There is a special convention created to solve such dilemmas. The first step is to determine whether the concept that is not a direct cause is a "fact" or a "preference." If it is a fact, the relationship between A and C is coded as stated, in view of the fact. A sentence modeled after relationships dependent on facts would be, "Because the fact B is true, A hurts C." The relationship is coded simply as A / − / C. The same basic model stated in the negative would be, "If the fact B were not true, A would help C." In all cases the coder derives the true positiveness or negativeness of the fact. Here we assume that because B is true, A still hurts C. The coding for the negative model is the same as for the positive.

If B is not a "fact" but a "preference," we must assign a value to that preference according to the speaker's viewpoint. Often, the value will be evident from the statement itself. If not, the coder is called upon to find the stated value of the preference in his coding sheets as it has been recorded, and to assign the stated value to the relationship at hand. The sentence, "If B is high then A helps C" is coded as "A / + / C," assuming that the speaker

311

prefers that B is high. In all cases the final linkage value would be found by multiplying the value of the preference by the stated dependent value of the relation to find the resultant, recorded value.

Sample sentence: "If there is unanimous domestic support for it, adoption of a peace-oriented neutral policy is the best basis for maintaining Finnish security and independence."

1. In this case, there are two interdependent cause concepts. Their interdependence is indicated by the connector "if there is," which precludes by definition an independent application of cause concepts to achieve the stated relationship. On the contrary, "if there is" demands a joint application for achieving the expected effect. This interdependence is further supported by the use of the singular term, "basis," in the sentence, which indicates a joint platform for action. When looking for interdependent cause concepts, nouns such as "basis," for example, which combine preceding noun concepts in a single grammatical statement, are excellent indications of interdependence.

Of the two variables, it is clear that "unanimous domestic support" is a condition placed upon "it," "adoption of a peace oriented neutral policy." Placement in a subjunctive phrase is the best indication of a concept's role. It is safe to assume that "unanimous domestic support" was meant to restrict the nature of the stated relationship. Thus, assuming that the speaker prefers "unanimous domestic support," it is given a positive value.

2. The phrase "Finnish security and independence" is not a single effect concept because it does not carry one single concept. Rather, it is a set of concepts, "Finnish security" and "Finnish independence."

3. The linkage is indicated by the phrase "is the best basis for maintaining." The stated relationship is, of course, "plus." Because the conditional value is "plus," and since a positive times a positive is a positive, the resultant linkage is positive.

The final coding is as follows:

the adoption of a peace-oriented neutral policy	/ + /	Finnish security
the adoption of a peace-oriented neutral policy	/ + /	Finnish independence

312

L. SIMPLE SUBJECT/COMPLEX LINKAGE/ COMPLEX OBJECT

Sample sentence: "Acceptance of the proposed arms limitation agreement will weaken the power of American military planners, strengthen the power of American proponents of general disarmament, but not affect the short-range military spending of either the U.S. or the USSR."

1. "Acceptance of the arms limitation agreement" is the cause concept, and there are multiple effect concepts with different relations to it. The effect concepts are "the power of American military planners," "the power of American proponents of general disarmament," "short-range U.S. military spending," and "short-range USSR military spending."

2. There are four linkages: the first is "plus," the second "minus," and the remaining are "0." The entire sentence is a simple subject with a complex linkage relationship to four separate effect variables. The final coding is as follows:

acceptance of the arms limitation agreement	/ − /	power of American military planners
acceptance of the arms limitation agreement	/ + /	power of American proponents of general disarmament
acceptance of the arms limitation agreement	/0/	short-range U.S. miiltary spending
acceptance of the arms limitation agreement	/0/	short-range USSR military spending

M. COMPLEX SUBJECT/COMPLEX LINKAGE/ COMPLEX OBJECT

Sample sentence: "Honest recognition of the superior force of the Soviet Union will be the condition and touchstone of our national existence, for to harbor revanchist thoughts or indulge in open or secret scheming to regain lost territory means the destruction of the Ukrainian people."

1. First breakdown: In cases of this complexity the coder may

313

find it easier to separate concepts by putting quotes around each and underlining seeming linkages, as follows: "Honest recognition of the superior force of the Soviet Union" *will be the condition and touchstone of* "our national existence," for to "harbor revanchist thoughts" or to "indulge in open or secret scheming to regain lost territory" *means* the "destruction of the Ukrainian people."

2. The above is an example of a sentence carrying multiple cause and effect concepts, as well as both negative and positive linkages.

3. The "honest recognition of the superior force of the Soviet Union" is the first cause concept. "Will be the condition and touchstone" indicates a supportive role, hence a "plus" relationship to "our (Ukrainian) national existence" is established. "Ukrainian national existence" is the effect concept.

4. Second, two negative relationships are stated. "Harboring revanchist thoughts" must be adjusted to indicate that it refers to the Ukraine. Thus, the concept should read, "Ukraine's harboring of revanchist thoughts." "Open or secret scheming to regain lost territory" should, for clarity, be regarded as two concepts, because it indicates that either may be applied separately and the stated relationship will still maintain. Thus, the seeming concept is split to form two, as follows: "open scheming to regain lost territory" and "secret scheming to regain lost territory." It should be noted that the Ukraine will ultimately be included as an identification for these concepts. "Destruction of the Ukrainian people" is the effect concept, while "means" indicates a "plus" relationship even though, in an absolute sense, the result is not a good one. The whole relationship, though negative, is positive in its linkage.

The final coding is as follows:

the honest recognition of the superior forces of the Soviet Union by the Ukraine	/+/	Ukrainian national existence
harboring revanchist thoughts by the Ukraine	/+/	destruction of the Ukrainian people
open scheming by the Ukraine to regain lost territory	/+/	destruction of the Ukrainian people

secret scheming by	/+/	destruction of the
the Ukraine to regain		Ukrainian people
lost territory		

N. DOUBLE ROLES FOR CONCEPTS WITHIN RELATIONSHIPS

A graphic example of double roles looks like Figure A1–1.

FIGURE A1–1.

An Example of Double Roles for Concepts

Cause A ⟶ (Effect A / Cause B) ⟶ (Effect B / Cause C) ⟶ Effect C

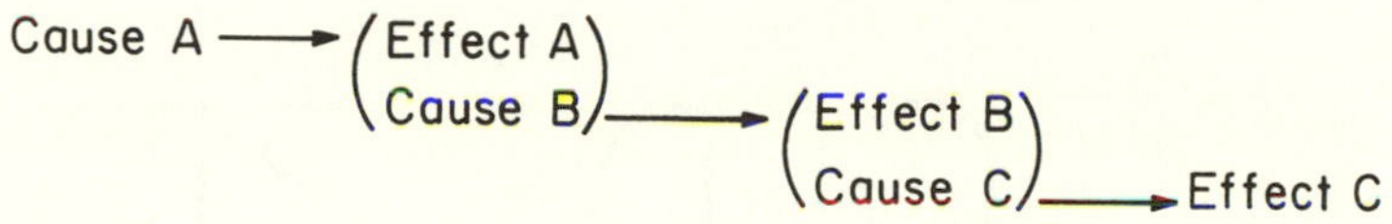

Sample sentence: "I believe that Italy's alliance with Germany would make the country a sleeping partner in an alliance that would impose on her overwhelming burdens which could not be borne in the long term."

1. Concepts may at one point be cause concepts and yet may at other times even within the same sentence, be effect concepts. The example of the above sentence is illustrative.

2. The initial question in these cases is, "What are all the possible concepts?" They are: "Italy's alliance with Germany"; "Italy as a sleeping partner in an alliance"; "overwhelming burdens."

3. What are the relationships? Italy's alliance with Germany has a positive relationship indicated by "would make [Italy] a sleeping partner in an alliance."

4. Then, "Italy, a sleeping partner in an alliance" carries a positive relationship indicated by "would impose . . . overwhelming burdens."

5. Finally "which" replaced with "overwhelming burdens," as outlined in the procedure for pronoun substitutions, negatively affects some unspecified object. The linkage is negative due to the use of the words, "could not be borne." Moreover, "borne"

315

must take an indirect object that is inferred but unstated. That object must be Italy, since Italy is the lesser partner in the alliance.

6. The coder must be careful to note where effect concepts or cause concepts are implied, for the implied relationship must be coded like any other relationship. The final coding of all relationships is as follows:

Italy's alliance with Germany	/ + /	Italy as a sleeping partner in an alliance with Germany
Italy as a sleeping partner in an alliance with Germany	/ + /	creation of overwhelming burdens for Italy
creation of overwhelming burdens for Italy	/ − /	Italian utility

7. The coder should note that in such cases as that of the unspecified and implied object, a utility variable is used.

O. CODING CHAIN-OF-EVENTS ASSERTIONS[3]

When a double role is not obvious but implied, relationships may be deduced from the principle of a chain of interdependent events. Coding a chain of events requires careful attention to the logic of the speaker's statement. There are several different types of chains, which require different codings. The first type is the most straightforward. This type can be considered to be one statement with an initial cause setting off a chain of events, where the first effect becomes the second cause and the second effect becomes the third cause, and so on. The line of cause and effect is a direct line without branches. Graphically, the statement looks like Figure A1–2.

FIGURE A1–2.

Simple Chain of Events

---

[3] New material.

Sample sentence: "Adopting the policy of ineligibility would cause the President not to relinquish his office when the term is over: he will take over the military force: a civil war will ensue and when it is over, the victorious side will put a despot in power."

1. The initial step the coder must take is to locate the precipitating cause, the one which initiates the chain. In this case it is the first clause in the sentence, "adopting the policy of ineligibility." Often the first part of the sentence or first sentence in a series is the most likely first cause.

2. Once the first cause is located, the first relationship is as easily established as any "simple cause/simple linkage/simple effect" relationship. It is coded as follows:

adopting the policy of ineligibility	$/+/$	President not relinquishing his office at the end of term
President not relinquishing his office	$/+/$	President taking over the military force
President taking over military force	$/+/$	a civil war ensuing
a civil war ensuing	$/+/$	victorious side putting despot in power

The loaded term "despot" is used to indicate that the outcome is harmful to the general American utility. Therefore we add the following:

victorious side putting a despot in power	$/-/$	American utility

3. There are other types of chains of events, of course. In the English language there are as many combinations of the above two types as is graphically possible to create. Even so, they are all combinations of the basic two patterns, "simple cause/multiple effect" and "simple cause/simple effect chain." Let us look at one example of a more complex possibility. Graphically, it would appear as in Figure A1–3. A sample group of sentences for such a graph might be as follows: "The policy of impeachment would have three immediate effects. One, it would bring about a check on the President's power. Two, it would make more feasible the provision of a four-year term. And finally, it would place impeachment power with the legislature. Of the three, this is the

317

FIGURE A1–3.

Chain with Simple Cause and Multiple Effects

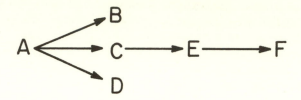

only unacceptable one. It will bring about the President's dependence on Congress and will lead to tyranny in the legislature."

The statements would be coded as follows:

policy of impeach-ment	/ + /	check on Presidential power
policy of impeach-ment	/ + /	policy of four-year term
policy of impeach-ment	/ + /	President's dependence on Congress
president's depend-ence on Congress	/ + /	tyranny in the legislature
tyranny in the legis-lature	/ – /	U.S. utility

P. THE PROBLEM OF IRRELEVANT RELATIONS[4]

The coder will be called upon to exercise discretion in deciding to omit some relationships not relevant for the purposes of his analysis. Determination of such cases is a difficult matter, at best; there are, however, certain types of statements that often call for exclusion.

Examples

In general, the rule the coder should follow is not to code examples of previously asserted relationships. Examples fall into three general categories: 1) exemplary specifications of the general causal relationship; 2) historical analogies supporting the

[4] New material.

relationship; 3) general "Universal Truth Claims" supporting the relationship.

The logic behind the elimination of examples is clear. If we think in terms of the cognitive map, we can imagine that examples would have no place in the speaker's overall logical picture. Neither would refutation of examples. They would appear as isolated assertions on the cognitive map, without links to the relationships they support. Because, for coding purposes, they are essentially considered repetitious of previously coded relationships, their elimination is justified.

Although each of the three types of examples is somewhat different, the determining factors and the points common to all examples are that examples can add nothing new to the general case relationship, nor are they related, either by cause or effect, to any other variable in the coder's list. If such a relationship exists, the statement is not an "example" as defined in this text, and should be coded as a relationship. In addition, an example could have a double role, in which the second role may qualify as a cause or effect concept.

Sample sentence: "Any growing economy requires foreign markets; Japan's does."

Assuming that Japan is *not* the subject of the document being coded, it is clear that "Japan's does" has a supportive role in the sentence. The relationship asserted is that, in general, growing economies need foreign markets. The Japan example is a specific, isolated case of the stated relationship and, as such, is not coded. The final coding would be as follows:

existence of foreign markets	/ + /	health in economy

Sample sentence: "During the Cuban missile crisis it was a wise choice of Kennedy's to establish a trusted, representative policy-making group. This was not done in the Bay of Pigs invasion and the results were disastrous."

Let us assume that the subject matter of the document is a case study of the Cuban missile crisis. It is, then, clear that the first statement is codable. On the other hand, the second sentence, if coded in its own terms and carried into the cognitive map, would stand unconnected to any other part of the map, making no apparent contribution. Although both sentences have common points, the Bay of Pigs invasion does not fall within the direct parameters of the subject, the Cuban missile crisis. It is considered an historical example. The sentences are coded as follows:

Kennedy's establishment of a trusted, representative policy-making body during the Cuban missile crisis	/ + /	United States utility

Sample sentence: "We must not choose the policy of an election by the Senate. The people at large should choose the President. History shows that elections decided by a few in closed conclave are never better than those decided by many in the open."

The first two sentences in the sample are "utility statements" coded under the rules described for such cases. How should the coder treat the third sentence, "History shows that elections decided by a few in closed conclave are never better than those decided by many in the open"?

Initially, the coder notes that it falls directly after two coded statements and is logically supportive of them. Second, it adds no new information to those statements; rather, it is a general repetition of them. Most general statements of this type include such phrases as "history shows" and "everyone knows that." For this reason, they are termed "Universal Truth Claims." When used as merely supportive examples, they are not coded as separate assertions. The final list of relationships should be as follows:

policy of election of President by Senate	/ − /	United States utility
policy of election of the President by the people at large	/ + /	United States utility

IRRELEVANT SUBJECT MATTER

All analyses should have parameters set according to the researcher's concerns. Relationships falling outside those parameters are safely excluded. If a windy speech in the British parliament is being coded only for its comments on foreign policy, comments on agricultural policy may, of course, be excluded. Establishing a clear definition, preferably prior to coding, will be important to the nature of the cognitive map that results.

NONCAUSAL ASSERTIONS

There are some statements that may have the appearance of a causal assertion but do not actually reflect a cause-effect belief. Consider the sentence, "Since World War I arms limitations agreements have failed."

This sentence could have a causal or merely a temporal interpretation. The former is equivalent to the assertion:

World War I   / − /   success of arms
                                            limitation agreements

The latter interpretation is that World War I is a reference point in time and not the causal agent. Sentences of this type should not be coded as causal assertions unless the context unambiguously indicates the speaker is making a causal assertion.

Definitions sometimes take on the appearance of a causal assertion. Consider the following sentence:

"The security of a nation's borders is its ability to defend its frontiers. When one increases, so does the other."

While an apparent cause-effect relation is stated in the second sentence, the first indicates that the relation is true by definition. Statements of definitions are important considerations in the merging process described below, but are not to be taken as causal assertions.

If a speaker introduces two concepts with a cause-effect relation and later indicates that the relation is definitional, the coded assertions are invalidated and should be crossed out. For example, if the two sentences of our example (with pronoun modifications) were reversed or separated by other text, the initial cause-effect assertion would be invalidated by the established definitional equivalence.

THE PROBLEM OF SIMILAR CONCEPTS

Once all the causal assertions in a text have been found and coded, an important problem arises. Realizing that the list of relationships over a given text, once recorded, will become the cognitive map, it is clear that duplicate concepts are misleading

321

redundancies and should be eliminated. The coder must decide which, if any, of the similar concepts can be treated as one for the purposes of mapping. The question is a crucial one, for it may make a significant difference to the form and properties of the cognitive map itself.

Many of these duplicates can easily be identified; some, however, are more difficult. Before presenting a method for eliminating duplicates, a few words about prerequisite clerical techniques that will greatly simplify this and other coder tasks seem helpful.

CLERICAL TECHNIQUES

As the coder records the relationships in the text it is necessary to devise a method for assigning identifying symbols to each unique concept. One successful method is to assign all concepts a symbol derived from the page in the text where they first appear. If three new concepts are encountered on page 12 of a document, the first concept would be "12A," the second, "12B," and the third, "12C." If the identical concept appears later in the text it is denoted not only by its paraphrase, but by the assigned symbol as well. "Page/letter" symbols greatly simplify construction of the speaker's cognitive map. By using this system, most clearly identical concepts will have been located during the course of coding by their duplicate page/letter symbols. By good clerical practices the coder has eliminated the great majority of merging problems.

THE MERGING PROCESS

Although most concepts are not candidates for merging and need not be scrutinized, some are superfluous. Merging is the retrospective analysis of some possibly repetitive concepts generated in coding to eliminate unnecessary ones by merging them into their more likely counterpart concept also found in the text.

This process should not be attempted (with the possible exception of clear opposites, discussed below) until the text has been completely coded. The following instructions indicate the nature of merging by substituting common symbols to be used for the merged concept for all appearances of the concepts. Thus, concepts that initially have been given different page/letter symbols are, during this process, assigned one symbol and, consequently, one identity in the speaker's map.

In making merging decisions, the coder will have to keep close track of the speaker's meaning in each instance of the concept's use which is now under scrutiny, for discretion must be used at key points. There is no single best way to merge concepts because the process necessarily involves judgments by the individual. One successful method has been to group concepts to be scrutinized by their content, in isolation first, and then to submit them to contextual tests to determine whether or not a merger is appropriate. The basic categories of merging decisions are explained below. The coder is encouraged to be conservative in applying these tests. All concepts should be treated as separate and distinct until it is demonstrated that they are the same. This is particularly true when considering whether different speakers are using the same concept, a problem discussed below.

There are, generally, two approaches to merging that the coder should use, and they are applied simultaneously. One includes some general considerations that may apply to any case of merging; the other is a structural view of the problem that involves separating the individual cases into a range of concept types such as nouns, noun clauses, and modifiers.

General Considerations for Merging

One initial determination the coder must make involves the general text. If a document is broad in scope, it follows that mergers of concepts are more likely to be appropriate than if the text is highly specific. The general nature of concepts should vary more or less proportionally with the generality of the text. For example, if a short document concerns the broad aspects of domestic policy, "amount of agriculture" and "amount of horticulture" may safely be merged, since the speaker probably does not mean to distinguish between them. If, however, the document were concerned with agriculture, the nuance is probably significant and should be maintained.

If a coder finds a group of similar concepts, he must also satisfy other key criteria before merging one or more. The coder should locate any predominant concepts. These are concepts that are used often by the speaker. In general, when a speaker refers to a concept numerous times he has attached a specific identity to it. When selecting among concepts to be merged, such concepts are maintained. The other, less frequently used, concepts may be merged in these predominant types.

323

One excellent general question to ask about concepts under consideration is whether or not the variable appears again in the text. If it does not, the chance is that the nuance need not be maintained. If the speaker at all times refers to "British military strength," for example, and breaks this habit once to say "British air and sea power," it is likely to be a safe merger. If, on the other hand, the speaker makes an express distinction between the two concepts, they should not be merged. Distinctions are made by comparing the two concepts in some fashion. For example, if it is the speaker's contention that British military strength is partly measured by air and sea power, but also partly measured by land forces, the speaker has made a distinction that should be maintained. Such comparisons may be direct or indirect. In this respect, one good way to tell that one variable is distinct from another is that there is an express relationship between them, which at some point has been recorded by the coder. Another clue that two variables cannot be merged is that they have different causes or effects.

Structural distinctions are made when the speaker links the less predominant concept to other concepts not connected to the more predominant concept. If this occurs several times, the merger is questionable. In respect to structural distinctions, two considerations are: whether the concept is connected by cause or effect to other concepts, and whether it is used generally in conjunction with another concept. Many times, if the concept under consideration has been referred to only in conjunction with a more general variable, it may safely be considered part of that variable. If, on the other hand, it is linked to other variables with which the more general concept is not associated, it may well have a value of its own in the speaker's logic.

One final general question the coder must ask himself is the following: would the speaker feel that a substantive part of his logic had been distorted if the merger were made? This question is evaluative; nevertheless, it must be asked and answered by the coder on each merger. Even if a probable merger has satisfied all the previous stipulations and yet seems tangibly different by the coder's evaluation, a discretionary judgment is required. But by using all the provided rules, this remnant of art in coding is not often encountered.

Having explained the general rules that are applicable to all merging cases, it is possible to break merging problems down into more specific categories for further analysis.

Ordinary Meanings of Singular Nouns and Noun Opposites

Sample sentences:

"Neutrality is in our best interests."
"Nonalignment should always be our policy."

1. The sample sentences present the simplest merging case. Assuming the coder is also approaching the example in view of the general merging guidelines, what can be said about the specific case? It is plausible that, in isolation, and for most purposes, "nonalignment" and "neutrality" are two versions of the same policy. If this supposition is supported by inspection of their patterns of use, the validity of this merger is insured. Thus, the relationships should appear identical by assigning one symbol to the two concepts, called hypothetically 1A. The relationship to appear in the coder's sheets will be altered to appear as follows:

(1A)		(1B)
neutrality	/ + /	utility

(1A)		(1B)
nonalignment	/ + /	utility

2. By this method of reassignment the relationship will appear only once in the cognitive map.

Like synonymous nouns, antonyms (concepts that are opposite in meaning) may be merged. For concepts to be opposites in coding, they must have juxtaposed positive and negative values without possible gradations of value. That is, if the absence of one invariably and necessarily means the presence of the other, the concepts are true opposites. If this criterion is met, one of the two values may be selected and used in the map. Whenever the opposite value of the concept appears in the text it is assigned a negative value and multiplied by the linkage value to achieve a resultant value for the relationship to be mapped.

Sample sentences:

"Having the quality of perseverance helped the pilgrims."
"The lack of it (perseverance) would have hurt them."

1. It is clear that the "lack of perseverance" is the opposite case of "having the quality of perseverance." By the speaker's meaning, either one has perseverance or not; a case of positiveness and negativeness in values has been assigned to one concept. For this reason, maintaining two concepts would be misleading; it would

325

not show the contrast in the sentence that was meant by the speaker. One concept with two opposite values is not treated like two concepts when constructing the cognitive map. Assuming the coder selects "having the quality of perseverance" (which will be called 1A, to appear on the map), how is the opposite case, "lack of perseverance," treated? It is always assigned a negative value, "minus," to be multiplied by the value of the stated linkage in each sentence in which it occurs. In the sample sentence the linkage value is "minus." Multiplying the two values in the example nets a positive value, "plus," for the resultant relationship. The final coding would then be as follows:

$$\begin{array}{ccc}
\text{(1A)} & & \text{(1B)} \\
\text{having the quality of} & /+/ & \text{pilgrims' utility} \\
\text{perseverance} & &
\end{array}$$

$$\begin{array}{ccc}
\text{(−1A)} & & \text{(1B)} \\
\text{the lack of perseverance} & /-/ & \text{pilgrims' utility}
\end{array}$$

2. In these two cases of noun synonyms and noun antonyms, the coder may find it helpful to consult a standard reference work on synonyms and antonyms, such as *Roget's Thesaurus*.

Ordinary Meanings of Phrases

The logic applicable to the case of synonymous and antonymous nouns is also applicable to noun phrases. The case of noun phrases is more complex, however, because it may still be possible to merge phrases that contain no clear synonym or antonym. The key to deciding whether or not phrases may be merged is that the coder must be convinced that they are equivalent. For example, if one phrase can be true when the other is not, then the phrases are not equivalent.

Antonymous phrases are a somewhat special case, and pose one possible qualification to this rule. Thus, before the equivalency test can be applied to such pairs of concepts, any opposite values in concepts to be compared must be resolved. When the opposite, negative, juxtaposed value of the concept ($-A_1$) is encountered, it is considered as if it were the positive case of the concept ($+A_1$) for the purpose of testing the rule against the merging case. By making both values comparable, the equivalency test is universally applicable to all pairs. One other test to determine if phrases are in fact opposites is that the phrases could never be simultaneously true; the truth of either one must always imply the falsity of the other.

Sample sentence pairs:

"The executive should be removable for flagrant offenses."
"The executive should serve during good behavior."

"We must avoid having the city manager completely dependent on the city council."
"If we have the city manager appointed by the council, he will be a mere creature of the council."

"Finland will be strengthened if it adheres faithfully to all of its obligations."
"Finland would be strengthened if it were to maintain friendly relations with all countries near and far."

1. In the first two pairs of sentences, the similar phrases should be merged as one concept; in the third pair they should not. An executive who serves "during good behavior" is removable, or else the qualifying phrase would have no meaning at all, and an executive "removable for flagrant offenses" is presumably not removable as long as he behaves well. A city manager who is a "mere creature" of the city council is certainly dependent on it, and a "completely dependent" manager may rightly be said to be the mere creature of the council. However, Finland could maintain friendly relations while breaking minor obligations right and left, and keeping to certain kinds of treaty obligations could lead to war.

2. If the variables are assigned hypothetical page/letter symbols such as 1A, 2A, and so forth, the coding will be as follows:

(1A)		(1B)
removal of executive for flagrant offenses	$/+/$	utility

(1A)		(1B)
executive serving during good behavior	$/+/$	utility

(2A)		(2B)
complete dependence of city manager on city council	$/-/$	utility

(2A)		(2B)
city manager as a mere creature of the city council	/ − /	utility

(3A)		(3B)
Finland adhering faithfully to all obligations	/ + /	strengthening Finland

(3C)		(3B)
Finland maintaining friendly relations with all nations near and far	/ + /	strengthening Finland

Modifiers

Noun concepts often have modifiers attached to them. Differences in modifiers usually signal that the concepts are distinct in the speaker's logic. In almost all cases, for example, "British foreign policy" and "Finnish foreign policy" would be mapped separately. "Nuclear weapons policy" and "conventional weapons policy" are also separate. As a third example, "tyranny by the executive" would be distinct from "tyranny by the legislature." Not all cases are so simple, for reasons to be examined.

Initially, there may be similarity or opposition among modifiers, as among concepts. The speaker may for stylistic variation refer to "complete honesty" at one point and to "thoroughgoing honesty" at another. These would usually be treated as the same concept, unless the speaker had made a distinction, somewhere in the text, between them.

In addition, modifiers used together in one place may be used separately elsewhere. If reference is made in one place to "an explicit and permanent neutrality policy" and in another to "an explicit neutrality policy," it is nevertheless likely that more than stylistic variation is occurring; the speaker seems to be drawing an important distinction. Two concepts, two identities on the cognitive map, are necessary.

There may on occasion be modifiers that do not readily change the noun concept. In an essay on planning, for example, the author may refer to "planning" and to "planning for the future." Unless the author clearly intends a difference between the two ideas, the coder should feel secure in his common-sense notion that since all planning is for the future, the two concepts are really the same.

Finally, differences in modifiers may appear in the presentation by the speaker. In such cases, the coder's instruction to ignore exemplary relationships should take precedence over the impulse to record the concepts separately. Consider the most complex case of the modifier, for example.

Sample sentences: "Military might is the key to our successful defense. Our military strength is needed to dissuade the enemy from aggressive actions. Our conventional troop strength stopped his aggressions in Belgium, and our strength in nuclear missiles stalled his aggressive plans for Brazil."

Clearly, there are not four relationships here, even though different modifiers are applied to "strength," "aggression," and to "might." There are, rather, two general points exemplified by two specific ones. In accordance with the rules on examples and merging, only the general points should be coded. The final relationships appear as follows:

(14A)		(14B)
military might	/+/	(our) defense

(14A)		(14C)
military strength	/+/	Dissuading enemy from aggressive actions

Specified Meanings

Whatever a dictionary may say or the coder may think about various words, the policymaker will occasionally assert his own definitions of concepts and how they are related to one another. In these cases the policymaker's interpretations must be followed.

Sample sentence: "Intrigue is to be expected in politics and may at times help the political process, but with cabal comes palpable danger to the state."

Although the two concepts "intrigue" and "cabal" seem mergeable in isolation, by the logic of the sentence the final coding would be as follows:

(1A)		(1B)
intrigue in politics	/+/	quality of the political process

(1C)		(ID)
cabal	/ − /	state's utility

The coder should be sensitive to the fact that meanings can be specified by context as well as by explicit statements. Assume, for example, that a general is discussing relations between Egypt and Israel, and that all of his remarks pertain to military matters. If the general uses the apparently distinguishable concepts "strength" and "military strength," but never draws or implies a distinction between them, the coder may safely combine the two as one concept, based on the context. For, although it could be argued that "military strength" is different from overall "strength," and is therefore separable, nonetheless in this speaker's mind the two concepts are as one, and that view should be respected by the coder.

In addition, there may arise a case in which the policymaker is inconsistent in his specification of definitions.

Sample sentences:

"Planning is advising; if you do one you are doing the other."

"Planning, based as it is on known technical procedures, can guarantee success."

"Advising, which is really an art rather than a science, is a favorite activity of politicians."

Here there are contradictory indications of whether the speaker considers the concepts "planning" and "advising" to be the same concept. The rule here is rather simple: if the speaker makes a clear statement that the two concepts are the same, as he has here, then they should be coded as one, and resultant inconsistencies in argument can then be observed in the map. If there is no such clear statement, and no obvious connection between the two by ordinary meaning, they should be left separate. The final coding would be as follows:

(1A)		(1B)
planning, based as it is on known technical procedures	/ + /	success

(1A)		(1C)
activity of advising, which is really an art rather than a science	/ + /	politicians' utility

The task of merging concepts that are similar is difficult but essential. If no such combinations were made, a normally coherent and understandable document might appear fragmented and disconnected; consequently it would not present an accurate representation of the speaker's logical thought. For this reason, the coder is advised to approach merging problems cautiously, using all of the guidelines outlined. Content and context are critical to merging. When, however, from all the rules on merging similar concepts it still does not seem possible to make a clear decision, it is best to leave the concepts separate.

Merging concepts used by different speakers poses an even more difficult judgmental process. As in the case of merging one individual's concepts over different assertions, there are critical context tests that must be applied before deciding that two or more people are using the same concept.

Any special definitions of a concept mentioned, and any serious disagreements about the kinds of other concepts used in relation to a concept, serve to question the propriety of a cross-individual merger. Agreement of use, explicit mention of agreement, and identical operations suggested for measuring a concept all serve to validate a proposed merger. When in doubt, again, do not merge across individuals.

On occasion clarifying questions are asked by participants to discover if they, in fact, mean the same thing by a particular concept. If they decide that they do mean the same thing then a cross-individual merge is justified beyond doubt. There is only one caution to be considered here. Sometimes clarifying questions will lead a speaker to redefine a concept, to change his usage. If a speaker so changes his mind, mentions of the concept before the questioning may not merge properly with mentions after the revision. The coder must decide: 1) Is the concept the same before and after clarification? 2) Is the concept now shared by other participants? 3) Was the concept used before clarification shared with the concept used by other participants?

The general principle is that if two speakers use the same concept in the same way, then there must be a merger between them. For example, if one speaker uses the phrase "British strength" to refer to what another speaker calls "British power," then these two concepts must be merged. Unlike the merging of concepts used by a single person, cross-individual merging does not require that the merged concepts have the same causes and the same effects.

CONCLUSION

The fact that the English language is as varied as those who use it makes the coder's task complex and difficult. No set of rules will completely solve the problems he or she might encounter. These rules, however, provide the coder with guidelines which, if conscientiously followed, will result in outcomes meeting social scientific standards of comparative validity and reliability.

The Questionnaire Method
—Fred S. Roberts

As a do-it-yourself guide for future researchers, some pro-
cedures for derivation of cognitive maps from questionnaires are
set forth in this section. These are the procedures used in the
empirical study by Roberts, and are similar to the procedures
used in Hart's empirical study. They can be readily adapted to a
variety of research designs of greater or lesser complexity.

The questionnaire method for deriving cognitive maps or signed
digraphs was briefly described in the empirical study of energy
demand (Chapter 7). Here, I shall describe the steps involved in
this method, and discuss the issues involved in this type of
procedure.

Many of the judgments needed to build a cognitive map with the
questionnaire method are subjective, even though experts form the
panel. To see that many opinions are included, groups of experts
are used. The basic problems involved are how best to solicit the
judgments of each expert, and how to combine the judgments of
the different experts to obtain one cognitive map.

The procedure I describe first identifies variables, then arrows
and signs. We concentrate on the identification of variables, for this
is the part of the procedure that is sloughed over by most authors
who have solicited subjective judgments from panels of experts.
It is also the part of the procedure that might be most crucial.

I look at variable identification as a two-step procedure. First,
I identify all potentially relevant variables, and then I select from
these a set of most representative or most important variables.

Parts of this appendix appeared earlier under the title "Building and Analyzing an Energy Demand Signed Digraph," in *Environment and Planning,* 3 (1973), pp. 199–221. The author gratefully acknowledges the permission of Pion Press, Ltd., the publishers of *Environment and Planning,* to
include this material here.

I also wish to repeat the other acknowledgement list at the end of
Chapter 7.

The procedure I shall outline is far from being the only possible procedure, and it will not be applicable in many situations, even though it has many choices and variants. No one procedure will be appropriate for every problem being mapped. Use of several alternative construction procedures can only lead to further insights into the decision problems being considered, and so is encouraged.

In the procedure I have found useful, the first step (Round 1) is a free response round. This could be done in a group session of the traditional sort—everyone sits around a table and volunteers potential variables. However, it could also be done on an individual basis, by questionnaire, with each person responding freely on his own, and not subject to any restrictions that might be imposed on him in a group situation. He is asked to list as many variables as he can think of that might be relevant to (constrain, influence, cause, be affected by, and so on) the problem at hand. There seems to be no substitute for the use of subjective judgments of experts in this step. But the experts here should be chosen from a wide variety of disciplines, and should include "lay" experts who are knowledgeable, well-read, or concerned about the problem being considered, but who do not necessarily represent a specific technical discipline.

The second step is a feedback of Round 1 results. This is especially important if the Round 1 results were obtained by combining individual free responses. The group list should be compiled and sent back to all the experts, requesting additions. Alternatively, this could be done by the person building the cognitive map.

If the size of the total list of variables is not too great, the experts may be used to limit the number of variables by a clustering procedure, as in Dalkey, et al. (1970). Again, for this step, the experts need not be specialists. If the size of the total list of variables is large, clustering is not feasible, and some other procedure must be employed.

If clustering is not appropriate, or perhaps even if it is, it is useful to try to classify the variables obtained in Round 1 (with iteration) into well-defined categories, subcategories, and so on. A hierarchical classification procedure such as that described in Raiffa (1969) might be appropriate. This classification procedure most likely would be carried out by the person doing the construction of the cognitive map, as it was in the energy demand situation described in Chapter 7. In the process of making this systematic classification, the categories and subcategories might very well suggest variables not previously listed.

To be completely faithful to the use of experts at each step, one would send out the classification scheme to the experts to get their comments, and to get them to add variables suggested by it. However, this is a fine point to the gathering of variables that might not always be necessary.

If the number of variables is too large, this number can be limited to some extent by using the classification scheme. In the energy demand study, only the variables listed in one of the possible subcategories (energy demand in intraurban commuter transportation) were used for further analysis. Other subcategories could also be used. This limitation, while making the remaining steps in construction easier, does limit the scope of the final variable set.

Having a collection of variables and a new scope for the problem, one tries to limit the set of variables further. Perhaps clustering would be appropriate here, if it has not been used before.

The method I chose to limit the variable set is the use of importance ratings. In this method the experts are asked to rate the importance of the variables in each subcategory in a number of ways. In particular, it is usually useful to obtain ratings of overall importance (judged independently of subcategory) and relative importance (judged in relation to subcategory).[1] It is suggested that different subcategories be handled by different groups of experts, and, whenever possible, that the ratings be done by people expert in the specific discipline related to the subcategory. Not all raters must be expert in each of the disciplines relevant to the subcategory, so long as all important relevant disciplines are represented. It is also suggested that overall importance and relative importance ratings be done by different experts, though this is not essential. The importance ratings can be obtained by asking the experts to sit around in a group, in the usual decision-making situation. Or they can be obtained by having the experts fill out individual questionnaires, without cooperation. The latter technique is recommended in many situations to minimize the effects of extraneous personality factors present in group discussion.[2]

---

[1] Specific procedures for obtaining overall and relative importance ratings are outlined in Chapter 7.

[2] For further arguments in favor of individualized questionnaires, see the section on the use of expert judgments in Chapter 7.

The initial importance ratings can be presented to the experts for iteration, if that is desired. This could be done in a group session. Alternatively, it could be a Delphi-type iteration, with limited interaction. Here, the experts are given some information about the results—for example, median overall importance rating and geometric mean relative importance rating for each item. With this information as input, the experts are asked to reestimate their importance ratings. The advantages of this limited-interaction iteration are, again, the basic advantages of the Delphi procedure: elimination of extraneous personality factors, role-playing, and so on, from the group's decision making.[3]

Rating importance can be a difficult task. In the importance-rating exercise discussed in Chapter 7, the experts found the work tedious because it was so long. Some felt that they could not give a meaningful answer in the short time allotted to each judgment. These problems could be avoided by using different sets of experts for different subcategories. One respondent said he felt that all his numbers were "totally meaningless." The data of such a respondent could be eliminated by having experts estimate their confidence, as was done in Dalkey and Rourke (1971) and Roberts (forthcoming b).

Perhaps more significantly, in this exercise the experts felt that the issue at hand was not well enough defined. Several asked for a clarification of the meaning of "important": "important for what?" "important in what context?" and so on. The instructions were, indeed, vague on this point. They called for rating the "importance of a variable for the problems we are concerned with." When asked for clarification, I usually said "important for (impact on) energy use and related environmental factors." I clarified this further for the persistent questioners, explaining that they could think of this rating of relative importance as an "indicator" of the subcategory or the subcategory's impact. This seemed to satisfy them somewhat. But it should be pointed out that there is a subtle distinction between having an impact on energy use and the environment, as opposed to being an indicator of such impact, with a further distinction between being an indicator of a subcategory and being an indicator of a subcategory's impact. These differences are probably not important enough to invalidate the results. However, it must be emphasized that in-

[3] Further discussion of Delphi can be found in Chapter 7 and in the paper by Dalkey (1969).

structions in connection with questionnaires should be precise and detailed. Specifically, the term "importance" should be carefully defined for the respondents.

One of the respondents felt that it was impossible to rate the variables because they were all interrelated, hence all equally important. I do not think this is true, but it raises a significant point. To illustrate this, consider two of the variables, fuel economy of a car and quantity of safety equipment. Fuel economy is certainly related to quantity of safety equipment. But I doubt whether anyone will argue that these two variables are equally important as far as the growing demand for energy is concerned. On the other hand, there are some serious difficulties in comparing the relative importance of two variables that are closely related. It might, indeed, be reasonable to expect that two closely related variables would have equal importance ratings.

One expert remarked on his questionnaire that the ratings depended on the order of magnitude of the phenomena. He gave the example of safety: "As it is presently, this problem is not sensed very strongly by people for commuting, because there are few accidents. If cars were really made unsafe, say 100 times more than now, the ratings would have been very different." This comment points up the fact that, unless specified otherwise, a questionnaire deals with levels of the variable at present or in the immediately foreseeable future. Presumably the questionnaire would have markedly different responses if the variables were interpreted at levels in the distant future, or under various scenarios different from the present. Thus, responses to questionnaires should be made in context. If the situation is interesting under various different contexts, separate cognitive maps (signed digraphs) should be built under each context. Thus, along with the instructions, a specification of the scenario or context under which the answers are solicited should be provided.

There was one additional comment about the importance questionnaire, which was repeated several times and is important to mention. Some respondents felt that they were not competent to make such importance ratings, or rather that an expert on, say, pollution, would be the better one to make the ratings in the subcategory relating to his expertise. That point is well taken. Probably every effort should be made to have importance ratings within a subcategory. However, as mentioned in Chapter 7, it is not necessary that each judge be an expert in *all* of the disciplines

337

relevant to the subcategory, so long as all the important disciplines are represented.

Unfortunately, as we also remarked in Chapter 7, for the problems with which we are dealing it is often not easy to define (or obtain) the type of expertise that is needed. And even if that can be done, experts frequently disagree. Thus, whenever possible, judgments in a subcategory should be made by more than one expert. The group judgment technique has been developed because experts do disagree.

Let us pass now to the stage where importance ratings have been made, either in one step or in two. Now we come to the question of how to use these ratings to choose a particular set of variables. There is, once again, no a priori way to choose a good method. Indeed, it is probably a good idea to use a number of methods of iteration. In the exercise described in Chapter 7, I used three methods in iteration. I chose a preliminary list of twenty-four variables by choosing from each of the twenty-four subcategories of variables that variable with highest median overall importance ranking. In case of ties, I chose the variable with the highest geometric mean relative importance ranking.[4] This preliminary list could have been chosen in numerous other ways—for example, choosing one or two variables from each subcategory that has at least one variable with median overall importance rating of, say, six or more on a seven-point scale. The problem with this method is that not every major category will necessarily be represented. The preliminary list could be obtained by choosing all variables, regardless of subcategory, that have median overall importance ratings of, say, six or more on a seven-point scale. Again, not every major category will necessarily be represented. Alternatively, this preliminary list could have been obtained by choosing one or two variables from each collection of subcategories belonging to a given category. There are no firm rules for choosing one of these procedures over any other.

Once the preliminary list was chosen, I performed a clustering analysis to pick out ten variables in all. Finally, I iterated again, choosing from among the ten variables in question only those that had median overall importance ratings of five or greater in a seven-point scale. These two iterative steps could, of course, have been done in reverse order. Alternatively, one of the steps could

---

[4] The reason for using median overall importance and geometric mean relative importance is discussed in Roberts (1973).

have been the gathering of relative importance ratings on the preliminary list, and using these ratings to choose variables.

The message from all this is that there is not one specific technique for gathering variables to use in a signed digraph or cognitive map. Rather, there is a "bag of tricks" that is available for use, and only by experience does one learn which tricks are most appropriate to a given situation.

Indeed, since there are so many ways of building a list of variables, it is perhaps better to build several such lists, and then use them to build several contrasting cognitive maps. As a final test of the "correctness" of the variable list(s), experts could again be asked to give comments.

Actually, any list developed by the questionnaire method is always open to the question: how do you know you have an accurate or representative set of variables? This same question can be directed at the final cognitive map, as well. We return to this issue below.

Let us assume now that we have obtained a list of variables for use in a cognitive map. The next question is how to determine the arrows and signs.

To me, the most important advantage of the questionnaire method is that it allows for the systematic consideration of all ordered pairs of variables. Too often, policy makers do not use a systematic approach, and the result is that important causal relationships are omitted. Indeed, as has been pointed out by Axelrod in Chapter 4 and emphasized in Chapter 9, there is great danger of omitting feedback from consideration when people spontaneously describe a policy domain without being forced to consider all ordered pairs of variables systematically.

It is usually a good idea to randomize the presentation of variable pairs. If there are nine variables, there are seventy-two ordered pairs (without repetitions), and this calls for many judgments. Clearly, early judgments will affect later judgments. In some situations, it might be advantageous to allow those making judgments to return and change earlier judgments on the basis of later ones. And to minimize the effect of order of presentation, it is worthwhile to present each expert who makes the judgments with a list of ordered pairs of variables in a different order.

When an expert is presented with an ordered pair of variables (x,y), it is usually a simple matter for him to decide if a change in x has a significant effect on y, and if so, whether the effect

339

is positive or negative. Experts do not complain as much about the difficulty of this task as they do about the difficulty of, say, importance ratings. Indeed, I have found that it is even possible to ask experts to estimate the relative strength of the effect of a change in x on y, and the time lag involved before the effect takes place. The questions must be asked very carefully, however. Indeed, one must be careful to specify, if possible, what one means by significant; more important, one must be careful to specify, if one is interested in causation, that the effect you are interested in is not an indirect effect, but a direct causal effect. If the instructions are not clear, they can lead to difficulties. For example, in the exercise described in Chapter 7, the instructions were not entirely clear on this point. The result was that the experts agreed on a negative arrow from fuel economy to emissions. Now an increase in fuel economy does not directly cause a decrease in emissions, although it does so indirectly by leading to a decrease in fuel consumption. But the experts confused direct causation with this indirect causal path, which also appears in the final cognitive map or signed digraph of Figure 7–2. It is a good idea to check systematically for inclusion of indirect effects by considering all triples x,y,z for which there are arrows from x to y, y to z, and also x to z. Is x to z truly a direct effect?

After getting judgments of arrows and signs, there is no further work to be done if there is only one expert involved, except that it might be a good idea to let him see the final cognitive map and give him a chance to reconsider some of his decisions.

If several experts have identified arrows and signs, there is the problem of reaching some consensus. Where there is disagreement, perhaps this should not be hidden, and several cognitive maps drawn, with alternative arrows and signs. Alternatively, one can think of many procedures for reaching consensus. Some of these are described in Chapter 7. The method I used was to say that there was an arrow from x to y if at least a certain proportion of the experts (6 of 7) said there was an arrow. Then, I chose for the arrow that sign which a sufficiently large number of the experts (60 percent) agreed on. If there wasn't that much agreement, I let the sign of the arrow be undecided, and considered a number of alternative signed digraphs with different signs on the arrow. Again, there is no a priori way of deciding what is a good method for combining experts' judgments of arrows and signs. But this method seems as reasonable as any other, and it is easy to use.

340

Before closing, we should discuss a question that is critical to the success of any construction technique: once you have built a cognitive map, how do you know you have an accurate description of the system?

The answer is, you never know for sure. All mathematical models, including cognitive maps, rest on the supposition that you have included all the relevant information in your assumptions. Obviously, such models can be checked by simply feeding them back to experts. In the case of the cognitive maps constructed by the questionnaire method, these should be given back to the panel of experts for comment and possible modification, or to an independent expert for evaluation. This is one kind of feedback. A second kind of feedback comes from the conclusions attainable, rather than from the structure of the model itself. The method of mathematical models works by means of a continuing feedback loop such as that in Figure A2–1.[5]

FIGURE A2–1.

Continuing Feedback Loop

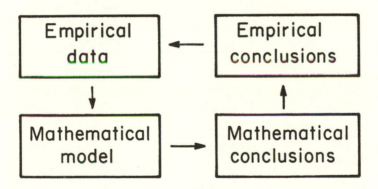

The mathematical conclusions obtained from the model must be translated into empirical conclusions, and these must be checked against empirical data. In the case of the cognitive maps, these empirical conclusions can be presented to the panel of experts. On the basis of their knowledge of the empirical data, they can in turn modify the mathematical model, that is, the cognitive map.

[5] This diagram is motivated by the discussion in Kemeny and Snell (1973, chapter 1).

By these means, an initial cognitive map might be modified a number of times before the experts are satisfied. It should always, as are all mathematical models, be regarded as tentative and subject to the constant review of the feedback loop shown above.

In addition to regarding a cognitive map as tentative, one should probably not expect that a single cognitive map will accurately represent the system being studied. Alternative cognitive maps could be built using other methods or new scenarios, resulting in different, context-senstive judgments on arrows and signs. Each of these cognitive maps will yield information, and it should be very useful for the policymakers to compare and contrast the conclusions.

The Mathematics of Cognitive Maps
—Robert Axelrod

This appendix establishes the mathematical basis for the manipulation of cognitive maps. Using the theory of directed graphs, it introduces an eight-valued system of relationships that includes values such as "nonnegative" and "ambivalent" as well as "positive" and "negative."

The mathematical system is used to derive a cognitive map from a set of assertions, to determine the total effect of any concept variable on any other concept variable, and to offer advice on how policy choices can be derived from a cognitive map.

INTRODUCTION

This appendix describes the basic mathematical operations needed for a full understanding of the derivation and manipulation of cognitive maps. It assumes a knowledge of basic set theory and matrix multiplication. It also assumes a knowledge of the terms introduced in Chapter 3 for the analysis of cognitive maps.

This appendix will show how assertions made by a person about the same causal relationship can be combined, how the indirect effect of arrows in a single path can be calculated, how the total effect of different paths can be determined, and how advice about policy choices can be derived from a cognitive map.

THE VALUES THAT A RELATIONSHIP MAY TAKE

Relationships from one concept variable to another are regarded as causal.[1] These causal relationships can take on different values.

---

[1] In this appendix, as elsewhere in this volume, the terms "concept variable" and "point" are used to refer to the nodes of a directed graph, while the terms "relationship," "link," and "arrow" are used to refer to the arcs of a directed graph. The "cognitive map" is the entire directed graph with values attached to the arrows.

The most basic values are positive and negative. These values are described in Chapter 3. Chapters 6 and 7 and Appendices 2 and 4 employ only these two values. An expanded set of eight values is used in Chapters 4 and 5 and Appendix 1. The operations are the same in either case, but for completeness the expanded set is presented here.[2] The collection of eight values is simply all of the logical combinations of positive, negative, and zero:

+ positive
− negative
0 zero
⊕ nonnegative, i.e., $\{0,+\}$
⊖ nonpositive, i.e., $\{0,-\}$
m nonzero, i.e., $\{+,-\}$
u universal, i.e., $\{+,-,0\}$
a ambivalent, i.e., the empty set.[3]

COMBINING ASSERTIONS TO FORM RELATIONSHIPS

To build a cognitive map from a set of assertions it is necessary to combine into one relationship all assertions that have the same cause variable and the same effect variable. When each member of a panel of judges makes an assertion about each relationship (as in the questionnaire method), a method analogous to voting is used. Details are given by Roberts in Chapter 7 and Appendix 2. When a single person may make several assertions about the same relationship (as in a document), the assertions are combined by taking the intersection of their values. This latter procedure is quite simple.

All the assertions a person makes about the effect of A on B are combined into a single causal relationship by taking the intersection of their values. For example, the intersection of ⊕ (i.e., the set consisting of 0 and +) and + is simply +. Thus if a person says "A can't hurt B" and also says that "A helps B" the relation-

---

[2] For a formal treatment of alternative sets of values see the Mathematical Appendix in Axelrod (1972b). Incidentally, Hart introduces yet another value, "concave downward," which he explains in his Chapter 8.

[3] The ambivalent value can not be coded from a single assertion. It arises only when two or more assertions are combined, as indicated in the next section.

ship is entered into the cognitive map as "A helps B." As another example, the intersection of + and − is the empty set that is represented by the ambivalent value, a. Thus, if a person says "C helps D" and also says "C hurts D" this is represented in the cognitive map as an ambivalent relationship from C to D.[4] Such a relationship can be seen in Morris' cognitive map in Chapter 5, where Morris made two inconsistent statements about the relationship from P6 to R, that is, about the effect of a particular way of choosing the President and Vice President on "the existence of excessive Senate power." If a person makes no explicit or implicit assertion about the effect of one concept variable on another, that particular relationship is assumed to be zero.[5]

CALCULATING THE INDIRECT EFFECT OF A SINGLE PATH

Once the relationships between all of the variables are determined, the cognitive map can be drawn. Relationships that are in sequence form paths, and paths transmit indirect effects. For example, suppose there is a positive arrow (that is, causal relationship) from A to B and another positive arrow from B to C, then there is a path from A to C through B, and this path carries an indirect positive effect. The positive value of the arrow from A to B is combined with the positive value of the arrow from B to C to yield the positive value of the path from A to C through B. The operation of combining direct effects of relationships that are in sequence into indirect effects of a path is called multiplication. If the exact numerical values of the arrows were known, regular multiplication could be used, but when only the signs of the values are known, the rules of multiplication give these results:

1. Positive times anything is that thing.
2. Zero times anything is zero.
3. Ambivalent times anything (except zero) is ambivalent.
4. Negative times negative is positive.
5. Multiplication distributes over union. For example,
   $$(-)(\ominus) = (-)(- \cup 0) = ((-)(-)) \cup ((-)(0)) = (+) \cup (0) = \oplus.$$

[4] This assumes that both statements are about the *direct* effect of C on D.
[5] This is why it is important to have a document that is complete in terms of the scope of the investigation.

345

6. Multiplication is symmetric. For example, $(\ominus)(-) = (-)(\ominus)$.

DETERMINING THE TOTAL EFFECTS OF DIFFERENT PATHS

When two or more paths start with the same point and end with the same point, their effects can be added into a total effect of the first point on the second. The operation is called addition. The rules governing addition of effects of paths from A to B are the following:

1. Zero plus anything is that thing.
2. Ambivalent plus anything is ambivalent.
3. Positive or negative plus itself is itself.
4. Positive plus negative is universal.
5. Addition distributes over union.
6. Addition is symmetric.

SOLVING THE DECISION-MAKING PROBLEM

The decision-making problem, as stated in Chapter 3, is the following: given a cognitive map with one or more policy variables and a utility variable, which policies should be chosen and which should be rejected? The solution to the problem is given by calculating the total effect of each policy on the utility variable. Policies that have a positive total effect on utility should be chosen, and policies that have a negative total effect should be rejected. Policies with a nonnegative total effect should not be rejected, policies with a nonpositive total effect should not be accepted. Policies with a zero total effect on utility do not matter. No advice can be given about policies with a universal total effect, a non-zero total effect, or an ambivalent total effect on utility.

With a little practice, the operations of multiplication and addition can be done in one's head while tracing out the paths of a moderate-sized cognitive map that is displayed as a graph. For large scale work, however, it is useful to have a more systematic way of performing the calculations. Matrix algebra provides a convenient means to this end, especially since matrix operations are easy to implement on a computer.

The matrix of direct effects is called the valency matrix, V. It has as its ij[th] entry the value of the (direct) causal relationship from concept variable i to concept variable j. When this matrix is multiplied by itself, the ij[th] entry of the new matrix is the indirect effect of concept variable i on concept variable j through all the paths of length exactly equal to two. This is because matrix multiplication is defined by

$$(AB)_{ij} = \sum_k A_{ik} B_{kj}$$

For $A = V$ and $B = V$, this gives

$$V^2_{ij} = \sum_k V_{ik} V_{kj}$$

Each of the terms of the form $V_{ik} V_{kj}$ expresses the indirect effect of a path from i to some k and from that k to j. Summing the effects of all such paths (through each possible concept variable k) gives the indirect effect of all paths of length two from i to j. Likewise, raising the valency matrix to the third power gives the indirect effect of all paths of length three from i to j. Likewise, raising the valency effects matrix to the qth power gives the indirect effect of all paths of length q from i to j.[6] In an acyclic cognitive map of n concept variables, there is no path longer than $n - 1$. Therefore, the valency matrix which has as its ij[th] entry the total effect of i on j for an acyclic cognitive map can be calculated from the direct effects matrix with the operations of addition and multiplication defined above as follows:

$$T = \sum_{q=1}^{n-1} V^q$$

This total effects matrix, T, can be used for generating advice based on the total effect of each policy variable on the utility variable. It can also be used to study the structure of a cognitive map. A cognitive map is acyclic if and only if all of the main diagonal entries of its total effects matrix, T, are zero (that is, no concept variable has an effect on itself). A cognitive map is balanced if and only if there is no universal, non-zero, or ambivalent entry in its total effects matrix (that is, if the total effect of

---

[6] This idea is adapted from Harary, Norman, and Cartwright (1965).

every concept variable on every other concept variable is not indeterminate).[7]

Further applications of matrix operations on cognitive maps, including some with different types of addition and multiplication, are given in the next appendix by Nozicka, Bonham, and Shapiro. For more on the mathematics of cognitive maps that have cycles, see Roberts, Chapter 7.

[7] This extends the common definition of semipath balance to cover the eight-valued case of cognitive maps discussed here.

Simulation Techniques
—*George J. Nozicka, G. Matthew Bonham,* and *Michael J. Shapiro*

Cognitive maps can be used in the simulation of individual belief systems. One such simulation, of a Middle East expert, was employed in Chapter 6 by Bonham and Shapiro. This appendix describes the techniques used in that simulation. Among the operations performed by the simulation on a given cognitive map are the formulation of alternative explanations of an unanticipated event, the selection of the preferred explanation, the development of expected consequences of the event, the search for relevant policy options, and the ranking of the relevant policy options.

The computer simulation used in Chapter 6 was developed in the course of our investigations of foreign policy decision-making behavior (Shapiro and Bonham, 1973). The simulation uses digraph theory as its mathematical base. Digraph theory, or the theory of directed graphs, provides convenient matrix techniques for the representation and manipulation of structural relationships (Harary, Norman, and Cartwright, 1965), and this enables the computer processing of decision makers' belief systems.

The cognitive map that represents the subset of a decision maker's belief system relevant to the foreign policy situation being analyzed is converted to the form of a *valency matrix*. The valency matrix A is a square matrix of size $n \times n$, where n is the total number of concepts in the corresponding cognitive map. For the purposes of our simulation, A is a signed binary matrix. Each element v_{ij} can take on the values $+1$, 0, or -1; $v_{ij} = 1$ if a positive relationship from i to j is present in the cognitive map, -1 if a negative relationship from i to j is present in the cognitive map, and 0 otherwise. The diagonal elements a_{ij} are considered to be 0.

This research was supported by grants from the Institute of International Studies, University of California, Berkeley, and the National Science Foundation (Grant GS–36558).

349

The transformation of a cognitive map into its corresponding valency matrix is illustrated in figures A4–1 and A4–2. Figure

FIGURE A4–1.

Illustrative Cognitive Map

Concepts 1 and 2 are policy concepts.
Concepts 3 through 9 are cognitive concepts.
Concepts 10 and 11 are affective (value) concepts.

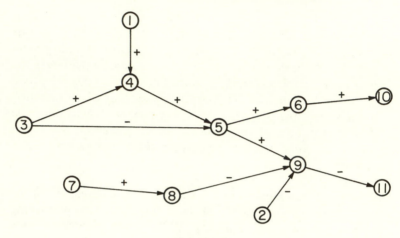

FIGURE A4–2.

Valency Matrix and Associated Row and Column Sums for the
Cognitive Map in Figure A4–1

	1	2	3	4	5	6	7	8	9	10	11	Row abs. sums
1	0	0	0	1	0	0	0	0	0	0	0	1
2	0	0	0	0	0	0	0	0	−1	0	0	1
3	0	0	0	1	−1	0	0	0	0	0	0	2
4	0	0	0	0	1	0	0	0	0	0	0	1
5	0	0	0	0	0	1	0	0	1	0	0	2
6	0	0	0	0	0	0	0	0	0	1	0	1
7	0	0	0	0	0	0	0	1	0	0	0	1
8	0	0	0	0	0	0	0	0	−1	0	0	1
9	0	0	0	0	0	0	0	0	0	0	−1	1
10	0	0	0	0	0	0	0	0	0	0	0	0
11	0	0	0	0	0	0	0	0	0	0	0	0
Column abs. sums	0	0	0	2	2	1	0	1	3	1	1	11

A4–1 shows a small cognitive map involving eleven concepts and the causal relationships that are perceived to exist among them. Figure A4–2 then shows the valency matrix that results when the above-stated transformation rules are applied to this illustrative cognitive map.

The valency matrix has a number of useful properties.[1] The row sum of the absolute values of the elements of row i gives the *outdegree* (od) of concept i, that is, the number of concepts perceived to be affected directly by concept i. Similarly, the column sum of the absolute values of the elements of column i gives the *indegree* (id) of concept i, the number of concepts perceived to affect concept i directly. The sum of the indegree and outdegree for concept i gives the *total degree* (td) of concept i, a useful operational measure of that concept's *cognitive centrality* in the decision maker's belief structure. Mathematically, these relationships can be expressed as

$$id(i) = \sum_{j=1}^{n} v_{ij}$$

$$od(i) = \sum_{j=1}^{n} v_{ji}$$

$$td(i) = id(i) + od(i)$$

Applying the total degree criterion for measuring cognitive centrality to the valency matrix in Figure A4–2, concepts 5 and 9 are found to have the highest total degree (4; $2+2$ and $1+3$, respectively). Examination of the cognitive map in Figure A4–1 confirms that these two concepts are, indeed, the most central.

Operationally, however, cognitive centrality is not determined on the basis of total degree alone. Some of the perceived relationships in a decision maker's cognitive map are based on analogies from past events. In such cases, the relational paths between historical events and the affected concepts are also added to the cognitive centrality index. Moreover, since many of our cognitive maps are based on the perceptions of several decision makers, the possibility of multiple relations between a pair of concepts exists, and such multiple paths are also considered in the computation of cognitive centrality.

The most useful property of the valency matrix is that it readily permits the computation of the *reachability matrix* R. The reach-

[1] See Harary, Norman, and Cartwright (1965), pp. 17–18.

ability matrix [2] raised to the second power is a square matrix also of size $n \times n$, each of whose elements r_{ij} is 1 if concept j is reachable from concept i, and 0 otherwise. Whereas the valency matrix A indicates only direct relationships between concepts, that is, concept linkage paths of length 1, the reachability matrix reflects the existence of indirect or deductive relationships as well. Indirect paths, that is, concept linkage paths of length greater than 1, can be located by raising the adjacency matrix to successive powers. If element v^2_{ij} of matrix V^2 is non-zero, a path of length 2 exists between concepts i and j; if $a^2_{ij} = 0$, such a path does not exist.

Figure A4–3 shows this property of the valency matrix; there, the illustrative valency matrix is squared to test the existence of paths of length 2. Element a^2_{15}, for example, is non-zero; this reflects the existence of a path of length 2 between concepts 1 and 5. Such a path exists, indeed, in the cognitive map via concept 4.

FIGURE A4–3.

Valency Matrix in Figure A4–2 Squared (A^2), Showing the Existence of Paths of Length 2

	1	2	3	4	5	6	7	8	9	10	11
1	0	0	0	0	1	0	0	0	0	0	0
2	0	0	0	0	0	0	0	0	0	0	1
3	0	0	0	0	1	−1	0	0	−1	0	0
4	0	0	0	0	0	1	0	0	1	0	0
5	0	0	0	0	0	0	0	0	0	1	−1
6	0	0	0	0	0	0	0	0	0	0	0
7	0	0	0	0	0	0	0	0	−1	0	0
8	0	0	0	0	0	0	0	0	0	0	1
9	0	0	0	0	0	0	0	0	0	0	0
10	0	0	0	0	0	0	0	0	0	0	0
11	0	0	0	0	0	0	0	0	0	0	0

Similar relationships exist between the matrix V^3 and paths of length 3, the matrix V^4 and paths of length 4, etc. By using boolean operations, the reachability matrix can thus be computed as $R = V + V^2 + V^3 + \ldots V^{n-1}$ since the longest possible path in a cognitive map with n concepts is of length $n-1$. In computation, it is rarely necessary to raise A to the $(n-1)^{th}$ power, since such long paths rarely exist; it is only required to raise A to a power k such that $A^k = 0$. Once this point is attained, no additional non-zero reachability matrix elements will be located. The full reachability matrix for the illustrative cognitive map is shown in Figure A4–4.

[2] See Harary, Norman, and Cartwright (1965), pp. 117–122.

FIGURE A4–4.

Reachability Matrix and Associated Row and Column Sums
for the Cognitive Map in Figure A4–1

	1	2	3	4	5	6	7	8	9	10	11	Row sums
1	0	0	0	1	1	1	0	0	1	1	1	6
2	0	0	0	0	0	0	0	0	1	0	1	2
3	0	0	0	1	1	1	0	0	1	1	1	6
4	0	0	0	0	1	1	0	0	1	1	1	5
5	0	0	0	0	0	1	0	0	1	1	1	4
6	0	0	0	0	0	0	0	0	0	1	0	1
7	0	0	0	0	0	0	0	1	1	0	1	3
8	0	0	0	0	0	0	0	0	1	0	1	2
9	0	0	0	0	0	0	0	0	0	0	1	1
10	0	0	0	0	0	0	0	0	0	0	0	0
11	0	0	0	0	0	0	0	0	0	0	0	0
Column sums	0	0	0	2	3	4	0	1	7	5	8	30

For the purposes of the simulation, a complete effects matrix is computed from the valency matrix of direct effects. The *complete effects matrix* C is the same as the total effects matrix defined in Appendix 3, except that the only entries used are $+1$, -1, and 0. If there is imbalance (that is, if the indirect effect of one concept on another is positive through one path and negative through another), then the indirect effect of the shortest path is used as the entry in the complete effects matrix. The imbalance still exists, though, and needs to be considered subsequently in the simulation.

The computation of row and column sums of the absolute values of the elements of R gives other useful measures analogous to the outdegree and indegree of the adjacency matrix. The row sum of R for row i specifies the total number of concepts reachable from concept i, while the column sum for column i gives the total number of concepts from which concept i can be reached.

After the valency reachability and complete effects matrices are constructed, the simulation of a given foreign policy event can begin. The event is input in the form of an initial list of concepts to be highlighted in the cognitive map. From these initially high-lighted concepts, a full *highlight vector* is constructed by the process of indirect highlighting. All concepts from which an initially highlighted concept can be reached lie on potential explanatory *antecedent paths,* and are so identified in the highlighted vector. Similarly, all concepts that can be reached from an initially highlighted concept lie on potential *consequent paths,* and therefore are also indirectly highlighted. These operations are performed by consulting the columns and rows, respectively, of the reachability matrix. Concepts not highlighted, initially or indirectly, in the highlight vector will play no explanatory role in the problem under analysis; such concepts can therefore be eliminated for the time being from both the valency and reachability matrices. Policy concepts will be used in the selection and evaluation of relevant policy options, but do not play an explanatory role; as a result, they are also temporarily removed from the valency and reachability matrices.

If, in the illustrative cognitive map, concept 5 is initially highlighted because it reflects some important aspect of a foreign policy problem under analysis, then concepts 3 and 4 would be indirectly highlighted because they lie on potential antecedent paths and concepts 6, 9, 10, and 11 would be indirectly highlighted because they lie on potential consequent paths. Concepts 7 and 8 are not highlighted, and will therefore not play a role in the explanation-finding process; neither will concepts 1 and 2, which are policy concepts.

The highlighted concepts and the perceived relationships among them form the subset of the decision maker's belief system from which explanations will be deduced; the analysis of this remaining network is the central part of the model. This consists of six phases:

> search for antecedent paths;
> search for consequent paths;
> formulation of alternative explanations;
> selection of the preferred explanation;
> search for relevant policy options; and
> evaluation and ranking of relevant policy options.

The search for antecedent paths involves the identification of the various linear sequences of concepts leading to the concepts externally highlighted. Antecedent paths are located by starting with the initially highlighted concepts and, for each, searching the respective *column* of the valency matrix to identify the immediately antecedent concepts. If there are several immediately antecedent concepts, the one with the highest cognitive centrality is chosen as the best next step in the path; this procedure directs the search to the most complex, and hence most central region of the cognitive map. Once the second concept of the path has been chosen, the valency matrix is searched for the concept directly antecedent to it with the highest cognitive centrality. This procedure is followed until a concept with no antecedents is reached; this concept with an indegree of 0 marks the beginning of this antecedent path. At this point all relationships unique to this antecedent path are removed from the valency matrix. The same procedure is then followed to locate the next possible antecedent path, and so forth, until gradually the entire set of antecedent relationships in the valency matrix is fully reduced.

At this point the full *set of antecedent paths* has been identified. Each path is now tested to ascertain whether at least one of the relationships on the path is perceived as historically supported. If no historical support exists, the path is suppressed. In this manner, the set of antecedent paths is reduced to the *set of plausible antecedent paths,* which is then stored.

Applying this algorithm to the illustrative cognitive map will result in the location of two antecedent paths: (3–4–5) and (3–5), when concept 5 is the initially highlighted concept.

The search for consequent paths is performed in an analogous manner. This time, however, the search begins with the value concepts rather than with the initially highlighted concepts. The columns of the valency matrix are again used to locate directly antecedent concepts, and the choice among several directly antecedent concepts is again resolved by the cognitive complexity criterion. The construction of a consequent path proceeds until either an initially highlighted concept or a concept on an antecedent path is reached. At this point, the relationships unique to this consequent path are removed from the valency matrix and the search procedure is performed iteratively until the full *set of consequent paths* has been identified. The historical support test is not applied to consequent paths, since these reflect conjectures regarding future behavior rather than inferences from past experience. The set of consequent paths is thus identical to the *set of plausible consequent paths.*

The illustrative cognitive map with concept 5 initially high-lighted will yield two consequent paths when this algorithm is applied; these are (5–6–10) and (5–9–11).

From the full set of plausible antecedent and consequent paths, one or more explanations can be derived. The number of explanations available depends on the number of unique, mutually inconsistent sets of antecedent and consequent paths that exist. Inconsistency, in this sense, is identical to imbalance. If the sign of the perceived relationship between two concepts when determined over one path differs from the sign obtained over another path, imbalance is present, and the paths belong to two separate inconsistent explanations, one of which will be accepted and the other suppressed.

Explanation selection is accomplished in the model with the aid of a *path balance matrix* P. If the number of plausible antecedent paths is a and the number of consequent paths is b, then the path balance matrix P is a square matrix of size $c \times c$, such that $c = a + b$. Matrix P is binary with each element $p_{ij} = 1$ if paths i and j are mutually balanced, and $p_{ij} = 0$ if they are imbalanced. Entries on the main diagonal equal 1 by definition. The matrix is symmetric, because the balance relationship is symmetric (that is, if i balances j, then j balances i). The balance relationship is not transitive, however, since, if i balances j and j balances k, it does not necessarily follow that i balances k. For this reason, each element of P above the main diagonal, p_{ij}, has to be uniquely determined by examining the subnetwork of relationships among the shared concepts on paths i and j. If paths i and j share less than two concepts, imbalance is not possible, and p_{ij} is set at 1.

The path balance matrix may then be used to identify all sets of antecedent and consequent paths that form balanced consistent explanations. The model predicts that the explanation that will be preferred by the decision maker will be the one with the highest cognitive centrality. The cognitive centrality of explanation k is defined in the model as

$$cc_k = \sum_{i=1}^{n} (cc(i)\ x_{ik})$$

where n is the total number of concepts, $cc(i)$ is the cognitive centrality of concept i, and x_{ik} is a boolean variable with a value of 1 if concept i is present in explanation k, and 0 otherwise.

356

Operationally, the search for the preferred explanation is accomplished within the model in the following manner: the cognitive centrality for each antecedent and consequent path located is computed as the sum of the total degrees of its component concepts. The path with the highest cognitive centrality is selected as the base of the explanation. All other paths are then examined in order of decreasing cognitive centrality, with the aid of the path balance matrix, to determine whether they are consistent with all paths previously selected as part of the preferred explanation. If so, they are added to the explanation.

When the explanation-finding algorithm was applied to the illustrative cognitive map, four antecedent and consequent paths were located:

1 $(3–4–5); 2+3+4=9$
2 $(3–5); 3+4=7$
3 $(5–6–10); 4+2+1=7$
4 $(5–9–11); 4+4+1=9$

The cognitive centrality of each path is shown following the identifications of the component concepts. From the five paths a 4 x 4 path balance matrix is derived (Figure A4–5). This matrix shows

FIGURE A4–5.

A 4×4 Path Balance Matrix

	1	2	3	4
1	1	0	1	1
2	0	1	1	1
3	1	1	1	1
4	1	1	1	1

that all paths are mutually balanced, with the exception of paths 1 and 2. Paths 1 and 2 are inconsistent, since path 1 yields a positive linkage between 3 and 5, while path 2 yields a negative linkage. Applying the preferred explanation search algorithm to this path balance matrix, an explanation consisting of paths 1, 3, and 4 is selected; this explanation has an overall cognitive centrality of 17.

With the preferred explanation identified, the valency matrix is reduced by removing from it all nonpolicy concepts and relationships that are not present in the explanation; policy concept linkages are restored to the valency matrix at this time. A final reachability matrix can then be computed, and the search for relevant policy options can be performed.

The search for policy options involves the examination of the reachability matrix to determine if, for each given policy concept, one or more concepts that are part of the explanation are reachable. If so, that policy concept is added to the set of relevant policy concepts; otherwise it is discarded as inapplicable.

In our example there are two policy concepts, concepts 1 and 2. Both of these are relevant, since they are adjacent to concepts that are part of the preferred explanation (concept 1 is adjacent to concept 4, while concept 2 is adjacent to concept 9).

The set of relevant policy concepts is evaluated and ranked. Evaluation is performed in terms of the differential impact of the policy concepts on an externally specified and ranked set of high-order value concepts. This operation involves the use of a *policy impact matrix* Q, which is a rectangular matrix of size $p \times s$, where p is the total number of relevant policy concepts and s is the total number of the high-order value concepts. Q is a signed binary matrix where each element q_{ij} specifies the sign of the perceived effect that policy concept i has on value concept j. Essentially, Q is a submatrix of the complete effects matrix C, and is constructed from it.

The ranking of the relevant policy concepts is then done using a lexicographic decision algorithm. Based on the proposition that decision makers do not seek to maximize all of their values simultaneously, but rather pay selective attention to one high-order value at a time, this procedure involves the iterative classification of the policy concepts into three categories (positive impact, zero impact, and negative impact) with respect to each value concept, starting with the most important value first. This is computed by calculating a *policy impact index* N for each relevant policy concept, such that

$$N_i = \sum_{j=1}^{s} (10^{s-j} q_{ij})$$

where the s value concepts are so ranked that value 1 is perceived as more important than value 2, etc. Selection of the preferred

358

policy, then, involves selection of the relevant policy concept with the highest policy impact index.

In our example, the policy impact matrix is of size 2×2 involving 2 policy concepts (1,2) and 2 value concepts (10,11) (Figure A4–6). Policy concept 1 is thus perceived to have a positive effect

FIGURE A4–6.

A 2×2 Policy Impact Matrix

	10	11
1	+1	−1
2	0	+1

on value 10 and a negative effect on value 11; policy concept 2 has no perceived effect on value 10 and a positive effect on value 11. If value concept 10 is deemed more important than value concept 11, policy concept 1 would be preferred. If the value rankings were reversed, then concept 2 would become the preferred policy.

The simulation model has been implemented in FORTRAN IVH for the IBM 370/145 system available at The American University Computation Center, and in its present form is capable of processing cognitive maps involving up to two hundred concepts.

Guide to Source Materials
—Robert Axelrod

This appendix offers suggestions on source materials for the researcher who wishes to employ the cognitive mapping approach. Suggestions are made on how material can be custom made, borrowed from other studies, or located in documentary sources. For the researcher who wants unobtrusive and verbatim records of private meetings, twenty-one specific suggestions are offered, but the point is also made that such strict requirements are not necessary for most research purposes.

This appendix is designed to help a researcher who wishes to use the cognitive mapping approach. In Chapter 11 fifteen projects were suggested, and many others are possible. Most of these projects require the availability of suitable source material to analyze. This appendix is devoted to offering suggestions on source material suitable for the analysis of cognitive maps.

The primary principle in seeking suitable material is that the researcher distinguish between necessary and desirable features of the materials. For example, if the goal is to study the role of new information in decision making, the researcher might be able to find suitable materials in four or five places. If, however, the researcher *also* insists that the documents deal with a particular subject, say, United States-Cuban relations between 1965 and 1970, then no suitable material may be available. If a given subject *is* required, the best information retrieval devices are people who specialize in that subject area, especially librarians, scholars, and practitioners.

CUSTOM-MADE MATERIALS

A tremendous aid to the study of cognition and decision making is that the researcher does not have to rely on previously existing

I would like to thank Margaret Wrightson, my research assistant, for her help in formulating many of the descriptions of the sources cited in this appendix.

materials. For many research topics, generating one's own materials is also possible. This has the advantage of allowing the researcher to have some control over the participants, the subject matter, and the setting. If often has the disadvantage of requiring the generalization of the findings to a different setting, which is not under the control of the researcher.

Gaming provides a fruitful technique to generate suitable source materials. For example, in Chapter 6 Bonham and Shapiro used a political-military game with three players to generate the transcript of a Middle East expert talking about his beliefs in the context of a specific policy problem. Experimental psychologists and sociologists have long done small-group experiments that allow the participants to communicate with each other in more or less structured formats. Dozens, if not hundreds, of these small-group experiments have already been recorded on audio or video tape, and many are probably available for analysis.[1] In some cases, the researcher may be lucky enough to find what he is looking for in a previously conducted experiment for which the authors are willing to make available the tapes or transcripts of the discussions. In any case, the sheer number of such experiments demonstrates that it may not be too difficult to conduct one's own small-group experiment, custom designed to generate source material under suitable conditions. This is especially true if the research goal is to understand the effects of some particular variables that can be readily manipulated or statistically controlled in such laboratory settings.

For those who want more realism, but still want to have some control over the setting, a useful compromise is to use medium-level decision makers from ongoing institutions such as local governments, businesses, and unions. An example of this approach is Barber's (1966) study of local budgeting, in which entire town councils met to consider his own hypothetical budgetary problems. Such ongoing groups may require anonymity, but they make excellent subjects because they can be studied in detail, but still retain the often critical contextual factors of a standing group that are so hard to simulate in an experiment with college students.

Another way in which the experimenter can generate his own material is with the questionnaire method. This method allows the researcher to select his own subject area and his own respondents, and then ask the respondents (or judges, as they have been called) to specify the causal linkage between every ordered pair of varia-

[1] For guides to the small-group literature, see Chapter 11, n. 10.

bles. This is what Roberts did in Chapter 7, with judges giving their judgments about the beliefs of several different actors as represented in a large collection of documents they had read. With such structured questionnaires, one can derive the cognitive maps quite directly, as described in Roberts in Appendix 2. With less structured interviews, one can use the documentary coding technique to derive the maps.

Semistructured interviews are especially helpful when the researcher wishes to control the subject matter, but still allow the respondents to express themselves in their own words. An excellent example is Putnam's (1973) study of Italian and British members of the parliament, which analyzes their cognitive styles as well as their policy preferences. Materials such as this could also be used for cognitive mapping analysis, especially since Putnam found that he was able to tape record more than 95 percent of the interviews. Interviews that guarantee the respondent's anonymity may be better than policy discussions as source materials, if the research goal is to make inferences about beliefs rather than (say) the dynamics of the policy process. The researcher must be careful, however, about his own impact on the message elicited. For example, if the interviewer asks what the respondent means by a certain statement, the respondent is likely to provide more detail on that subject, and this may make his cognitive map have more points and arrows in that neighborhood.

UNOBTRUSIVE MEASURES

For those who want source material uncontaminated by the presence of the researcher himself, unobtrusive measures are needed.[2] For the purposes of cognitive mapping, the main source of such unobtrusive materials is documents generated for purposes other than the researcher's own. The range of such documentary material is almost as great as the collections of major libraries and archives.

If one wants to stay close to the form of the assertions actually made by the actors, one can use the documentary method of coding the documents. This method is not suitable for large collections of documents, bècause of the time it takes to code a long text (see Chapter 10, section B). For documents of limited length, however, the documentary coding method is perfectly suitable.

[2] A wonderful book on this subject is Webb, et al. (1966).

If one is interested in analyzing written words, rather than spoken words, the range of source material is huge. Just go to a library. For example, if one wanted to study Adolph Hitler's early assertions, his *Mein Kampf* is readily available (Boston: Houghton Mifflin, 1943). For assertions made in greater privacy, there are available very rich collections of letters and diaries of many public figures, especially dead ones. There are also some excellent collections of internal governmental memoranda. The origins of World War I provide a wealth of published material from each of the governments involved. For a guide to this material, see Zinnes (1963). An outstanding recent collection is *The Pentagon Papers*.

1. *The Pentagon Papers* (The Senator Gravel edition, 5 volumes, Boston: Beacon Press, 1971–1972); or *U.S.-Vietnam Relations, 1945–1967; Study* (12 volumes of text consisting of the first 43 volumes of the original 47-volume study, Washington, D.C.: Government Printing Office, 1971). This is the leaked Defense Department history of U.S. decision making on Vietnam. It contains the text of numerous classified documents as well as an interpretive history.

For some purposes, spoken words have important advantages over written words. For one thing, spontaneously spoken words may provide a better indication than carefully composed words of how the person thinks about an issue on his own. For another thing, the critical interactions between policy makers are often done through the spoken rather than the written words. For these reasons, all three empirical studies in this volume that used the documentary method used source materials based on spoken words.

Words can be spoken in public or in private. Documentary materials recording words spoken in public are anything but rare. A fascinating early example is the contemporary accounts of Thucydides.

2. Thucydides, *The Peloponnesian War* (Benjamin Javett, trans., New York: Bantam, 1960). Contains Thucydides' reconstruction of many speeches, including some of Pericles and the two debates in Athens on what should be done with the inhabitants of the conquered cities of Mytilene (416 B.C.) and Melos (427 B.C.).

More recently, there are public debates of legislatures. The recent output of the American Congress is awe-inspiring, but for older material the British are unexcelled.

3. *Cobbett's Parliamentary History of England: From the Norman Conquest in 1066 to the Year 1803.* (36 volumes, Lon-

don: Printed by F. Curso Hansard, Peterborough-Court, Fleet Street, published by R. Bagshaw, Brydges-Street, Covent Garden, 1806). Earlier volumes reported speeches in the third person, but later volumes contain many lively debates on political issues. The degree of editing is hard to determine in many cases, due to the formal mode of speech. *Parliamentary Debates* (Hansard's), (London: His/Her Majesty's Stationery Office). There are approximately 1800 volumes of parliamentary debates from 1803 to the present in Hansard's. The earlier volumes contain many one- or two-page speeches followed by some rebuttal. The more recent volumes contain substantial verbatim discussion and disagreement.

In the last few decades the recording of legislative debates, legislative hearings, administrative hearings, speeches, press conferences, interviews, and trials has reached astronomical proportions. If the researcher can employ such public utterances on recent public affairs, there will be no lack of volume. Even TV news coverage is available.

4. *Vanderbilt News Archives.* This archive contains videotapes of the network evening news programs since August 5, 1968. Videotapes and audiotapes are available for rental, either as full programs or compilations of specified items. Some companion materials on major news events are also available. For access to the collection, write The Administrator, Vanderbilt Television News Archive, Joint University Libraries, Nashville, Tennessee 37203.

For some research projects, confidential source material is needed. This would be the case if the researcher wanted to study topics such as how policy-making groups operate in private, or how assertions made to a few close colleagues differ from assertions made to the general public on the same subject. Here is where the shortage of source materials begins to be a problem. The problem arises precisely because the researcher wants to observe behavior that the participants intended to be confidential. The principal method for dealing with this problem is to use source materials that were generated for institutional reasons and that later become available. In searching for such material, the researcher should be aware that such materials can become available in a variety of ways, including:

1. leaks (for example, the *Pentagon Papers,* mentioned earlier);

2. capture (for example, the Nazi archives);

3. release due to legal proceedings (for example, some of former President Nixon's White House tapes);

4. automatic release after a fixed period of time (for example, most of the British documents, including the Eastern Committee transcripts used in Chapter 4); and

5. negotiated release with specific conditions (that the participants' identities will be masked; for example, the publication of transcripts of psychiatric therapy sessions).

Spoken words are not always recorded verbatim. This is especially true when the documents are the institutional records of what happended at meetings. In such case, the available records are usually in the form of more or less detailed minutes. Whether minutes are preferable to verbatim transcripts depends on the purpose of the research. If the goal is to study the stylistic differences between two participants, minutes might not be adequate. On the other hand, if the goal is to study the flow of the argument, then a good set of minutes might well be preferable to a verbatim transcript, because the minutes would be much more concise. Three examples of such minutes of policy meetings are from the American Constitutional Convention, the Munich negotiations, and the Japanese decision to attack the United States in 1941.

5. James Madison, *Journal of the Federal Convention,* ed. E. H. Scott (Chicago: Scott, Foresman, 1898). These are Madison's detailed notes on the Constitutional Convention of 1787, which formed the basis of Ross's study of Gouverneur Morris in Chapter 5 of this volume.

6. E. L. Woodward, Rohan Butler, and Margaret Lambert, eds., *Documents on British Foreign Policy, 1919–1939,* third series, vol. II, 1938 (London: His Majesty's Stationery Office, 1949). Germany, Foreign Ministry, *Documents on German Foreign Policy, 1918–1945,* Series D, Vol. II (Washington, D.C.: Government Printing Office, 1949). The detailed British and German minutes of the Munich negotiations between Hitler and Chamberlain are contained in these volumes. They match very closely.

7. Nobutaka Ike, trans. and ed., *Japan's Decision for War: Records of the 1941 Policy Conferences* (Stanford: Stanford University Press, 1967). These are the records of five imperial conferences and fifty-seven liaison conferences between representatives of the cabinet and the army and navy. They deal with questions of foreign policy, such as the decision to move south against Britain and the United States rather than north against the Soviet Union.

For some research purposes, it is helpful to have verbatim records of meetings that were held in confidence. Having verbatim records is useful to guarantee against distortion and to preserve style. Having records of meetings that were held in confidence is useful to guarantee that the speakers are addressing each other and not some larger audience.

Naturally, verbatim records of meetings held in confidence are not very common. Most meetings held in confidence are kept in confidence, and are not available to the researcher. Moreover, keeping verbatim records is an expensive process, and therefore not usually undertaken. What follows are twenty-two instances of such available verbatim records of nonpublic meetings. The first group is nongovernmental, from a union-management negotiation (number 8) and an academic discussion of programmed learning (9). The next group consists of records of high-level meetings on foreign and military policy from Britain (10), the United States (11), Germany (12–14), and Japan (15–16). Then there are multinational negotiations from the end of World War I (17–19), the depression of the 1930s (20), and the beginning of the Cold War (21–23). The next group deals with the crises in China in 1924 and 1946 (24 and 25), and in Nigeria in 1967 (26). The final group includes domestic American political meetings dealing with federal-state relations (27), rules for affirmative action in the Democratic party (28), and the White House cover-up of Watergate (29).

8. Ann Douglas, *Industrial Peacemaking* (New York: Columbia University Press, 1962.) The first part of the book is an abstract analysis of bargaining styles in industry, while the second part is a 466-page transcript of one labor-management negotiation. The true names of the fifteen participants are not disclosed. The transcript is from the tape recordings of seven sessions held between March 21 and April 18, 1953. The conversations of the negotiating sessions are extremely candid and unedited.

9. Gilbert Teal, ed., *Programmed Instruction in Industry and Education* (Stanford: Public Service Research, Inc., 1963). This books includes the verbatim transcript of the proceedings of a conference on the Institute of Programmed Instruction, July 10–14, 1961. There were thirty participants. Topics discussed include learning theory, principles for programmed instruction, evaluation of programming methods, implications of research in program improvement, and roles of instructors. The editor notes that the comments of the participants are presented almost exactly as spoken, with only minor grammatical changes. The discussions

366

are not argumentative, though differences of opinion are expressed. The transcript is approximately 300 pages.

10. *Eastern Committee, Minutes and Verbatim Annex, Cab 27/24* (London: Public Records Office, 1919–1920, available on microfilm). This is the material used in my study of British neoimperialism in Persia (Chapter 4). Other meetings of the same committee discuss policy toward other regions between the Mediterranean and India, including Palestine, Armenia, and the Caucasus. Altogether, ten meetings in 1918–1919 were recorded verbatim, probably with a small amount of editing to improve the grammar.

11. *The Morganthau Diary. China:* Vols. i and ii, 1965; *Germany:* Vols. i and ii, 1967. (U.S. Senate, 89th and 90th Congresses, Subcommittee on Investigating the Administration of the Internal Security Act and Other Internal Security Laws of the Committee on the Judiciary). Henry Morganthau, President Franklin Roosevelt's trusted Secretary of the Treasury from 1934 to 1945, had transcripts kept of conversations among high-ranking Treasury officials. Together with his files of letters and memos, his "diaries" compose over eight hundred volumes. In the course of the Senate investigations, material dealing with the Treasury Department's involvement in foreign affairs was published in the four volumes cited here. These volumes contain many verbatim records of candid phone conversations and policy meetings, with little editing.

12. Germany, Wehrmacht, Oberkommando, *Hitler Directs His War,* Felix Gilbert, ed. (New York: Oxford University Press, 1950). See also Germany, Wehrmacht, Oberkommando, *Hitlers Lagebesprechungen Die Protokollfragmente seiner militarischen Konferenzen, 1942–1945* (Herausgegeben von Helmut Huber, Stuttgart: Deutsche Verlags-Anstalt, 1962). These are the secret records of Hitler's daily military conferences during World War II. They include very candid discussions. The Gilbert edition contains 150 pages in translation, while the Huber edition contains 900 pages in the original German.

13. Office of the U.S. Chief Council for Prosecution of Axis Criminality, *Nazi Conspiracy and Aggression,* Vols. 1–6. (Washington, D.C.: Government Printing Office, 1946). While not all of the captured Nazi archives have been translated and published, some of the most interesting documents are available through publications related to the Nuremberg trials. Among the transcripts published by the U.S. Chief Council is one of a meeting chaired by

Goering on November 12, 1938, dealing with the Jewish question in light of the massive pogrom that just occurred (Vol. 4, 425–456), and one of a meeting between Hitler and his military aides on the deteriorating military situation as of January 27, 1945 (Vol. 6, 655–717).

14. *International Military Tribunal, Trial of the Major War Criminals before the International Military Tribunal, Nuremberg, 14 November 1945–1 October 1946,* Vols. 1–4 (Nuremberg, 1949). Among the interesting materials in these volumes are transcripts in German of telephone conversations dealing with Austria in 1938 (Vol. 31, 354–384), and the stenographic report of the trial of eight people for the 1944 attempt on Hitler's life (Vol. 33, 299–530).

15. International Military Tribunal for the Far East, *International Military Tribunal for the Far East: Decisions of the Imperial Conference in Prosecutor's Evidence—Exhibits.* Vols. 1–131. (Tokyo, 1946–1947). This huge collection includes many exhibits of the records (most with translations) of high level Japanese policy meetings, largely from the 1930s, including records of the Privy Council and the Imperial Conference meetings. Among the most useful records of meetings are exhibits 241, 492, 527, 528, 552, 787A, 850, 911A, 1030, and 2205A. Unfortunately, these records tend to be short relative to the length of the meetings, indicating that they are probably paraphrased rather than strictly verbatim.

16. Miyoji Ito, *Suiuso Nikki.* (Tokyo: Hara Shobo, 1966). These are the records of a participant in the *Gaiko Chosakai* (Diplomatic Advisory Council) during the period 1918–1919. Among the issues considered by this high level group were the Japanese positions at the Paris Peace Conference and the Japanese role in the Siberian intervention. The records consist of five hundred pages of virtually verbatim notes covering twenty-six meetings, but they are not available in translation. For a discussion of the group and its significance see Morley (1957).

17, Harry R. Rudin, *Armistice 1918.* (New Haven: Yale University Press, 1944). Excerpts of transcripts from a German cabinet meeting on October 17, 1918 (pp. 145–153), the Allied Supreme War Council on November 1 (pp. 276–277), the War Council and a representative of Germany on November 1–2 (pp. 290–302), and an Allied discussion of specific armistice terms on November 4 (pp. 303–317).

18. Great Britain, Foreign Office; Rohan Butler and E. L.

Woodward, eds., *Documents on British Foreign Policy, 1919–1939, First Series, 1919*. (London: His Majesty's Stationery Office, 1948–1954). Transcripts of meetings between Allied leaders at the 1919 Paris Peace Conference (Versailles Conference) are contained in Vol. 2, 914–968), Vol. 3, 348–355, and Vol. 5, passim.

19. U.S. Department of State, *Papers Relating to the Foreign Relations of the United States, The Paris Peace Conference, 1919* (Washington, D.C.: Government Printing Office, 1945–1946). Volume 4, 191–201, contains transcripts of a meeting of the Council of Four (Wilson, Lloyd George, Clemenceau, and Orlando) with the premier of Poland on June 5, 1919. Volume 9 contains transcripts of a series of meetings between representatives of the five major powers (the International Council of Ministers) and representatives of the smaller powers in January 1920. Volume 11 contains transcripts of a series of meetings of the Commissioners and Technical Advisers of the American Commission to Negotiate Peace during the period June to September 1919.

20. Great Britain, Foreign Office; Rohan Butler and E. L. Woodward, eds., *Documents on British Foreign Policy, 1919–1939, Second Series*. (London: His Majesty's Stationery Office, 1947–1948). Volume 2 contains the transcripts of meetings of the London Conference of 1931 with representatives of seven industrial nations discussing the current world economic situation and possible corrective measures. The shortness of the transcripts in relation to the duration of the meetings indicates heavy editing. Volume 3 contains a transcript of a meeting between representatives of Great Britain and Germany in 1932 on the problem of German war reparations.

21. U.S. Department of State, U.S. Congress, House Document No. 154. *Foreign Relations of the United States, 1945. Diplomatic Papers: The Conferences at Malta and Yalta: 1945.* (Washington, D.C.: Government Printing Office, 1955). This volume contains the records of Hess and Mathews. The Yalta Conference brought together Stalin, Roosevelt, and Churchill in February 1945. The records of the meetings (chapter 3, pp. 611–855) consist largely of the notes of Hess and Matthews. The editing is fairly heavy, especially in the longer speeches of the participants.

22. U.S. Department of State. *Foreign Relations of the United States, 1945, Vol. II. The Conference of Berlin (The Potsdam Conference).* (Washington, D.C.: Government Printing Office,

1960). This volume contains approximately six hundred pages of records of the Potsdam Conference. Of the various accounts, only the "Rohen Notes" are written as direct quotes, but the shortness of these notes indicates that they are probably paraphrased.

23. U.S. Department of State. *Foreign Relations of the United States, 1946* (Washington, D.C.: Government Printing Office, 1970). Volume 2 contains transcripts of the meetings of the Big Four foreign ministers discussing provisions of the Rumanian, Hungarian, Bulgarian, and Italian Peace Treaties, July to December, 1946. The transcripts are 3 to 15 pages in length and include approximately 25 meetings, 350 pages in all. There is a moderate degree of editing without damage to the center of the conversations. Volume 3 contains transcripts of the 1946 Paris Peace Conference between representatives of the Big Four, with a moderate degree of editing.

24. Warren Kuo, *Analytic History of the Chinese Communist Party* (Taipai: Institute of International Relations, Republic of China, 1966). This volume contains the record of a conversation of June 25, 1924, on the organization of the Chinese Communist Party and the Kuomintang (pp. 396–400). The participants are Representative Borodin and KMT Central Supervisory Committee Members Hsieh Chih and Chang Chi. In this rare document, the Chinese responses to Borodin are not denoted by speaker, but otherwise the texts seem only lightly edited.

25. U.S. Department of State, *Foreign Relations of the United States, 1945, Volume X–XI, The Far East: China* (Washington, D.C.: Government Printing Office, 1972). These are the records of the Marshall Mission to China in 1946, which aimed to mediate between the forces of the Nationalist government and the Communist forces. They contain the verbatim transcripts of numerous meetings between General George Marshall and Chou En-lai, both alone and with a representative of the Nationalist government. Although the negotiations came to naught, they were vigorously pursued from January to December 1946.

26. Nigeria, Federal Ministry of Information, *Meeting of the Nigerian Military Leaders Held at Peduase Lodge, Aburi, Ghana, 4–5 January, 1967.* This is a verbatim record of the meetings held in Ghana among the Nigerian military leaders in their unsuccessful effort to stave off a civil war. Among the leading participants were the men who later led the opposing sides in the war: Lieutenant-Colonel Gowon and Lieutenant-Colonel Ojukwu.

27. *Proceedings of the Meeting of Joint Federal-State Action Committee. First Session, October 3, 1957* (Chicago: The Master Reporting Company, 1957). This is a stenographic record of discussion between federal and state officials (including several governors) on the following topics: the school lunch program, disaster relief, vocational education, water pollution, and supplementary old age assistance. Editing is slight to moderate in this 102-page transcript.

28. *Democratic Reform Commission Proceedings.* This commission formulated the controversial rules for affirmative action for the 1972 Democratic National Convention. The transcripts are available for inspection at the Democratic National Committee (1625 Massachusetts Avenue, N.W., Washington, D.C. 20036), and excerpts have appeared in Theodore White's *Making of a President, 1972* (New York: Atheneum, 1973).

29. Former President Nixon's White House Tapes. (A definitive edition is not yet available, but transcripts of the tapes have been published by the New York *Times* as they became available.) Former President Nixon arranged the tape recording of virtually every conversation he had in the White House Oval Office and several other selected locations from 1969 to 1974. Apparently, except for H. R. Haldeman, not even his senior advisors knew their discussions with the President were being recorded. It is an understatement to say that these tapes can be a valuable source of insight into high-level decision making under conditions of assumed confidentiality.

Abelson, Robert P., 1968a. "Computer Simulation of Social Behavior," in Gardner Lindzey and Elliot Aronson, eds., *The Handbook of Social Psychology,* Vol. 2, 2nd ed. Reading, Mass.: Addison-Wesley.

———, 1968b. "Psychological Implication," in Robert P. Adelson, *et al.,* eds., *Theories of Cognitive Consistency: A Sourcebook.* Chicago: Rand McNally, pp. 112–139.

———, 1971. "The Ideology Machine," paper prepared for the annual meeting of the American Political Science Association, Chicago, September 1971.

———, 1973. "The Structure of Belief Systems," in Roger C. Schank and Kenneth M. Colby, eds., *Computer Models of Thought and Language.* San Francisco: W. H. Freeman, pp. 287–339.

Abelson, Robert P., Elliot Aronson, William J. McGuire, Theodore M. Newcomb, Milton J. Rosenberg, and Percy H. Tannenbaum, eds., 1968. *Theories of Cognitive Consistency: A Sourcebook.* Chicago: Rand McNally.

Abelson, Robert P., and J. Douglas Carroll, 1965. "Computer Simulation of Individual Belief Systems," *American Behavioral Scientist,* 8, 24–30.

Abelson, Robert P., and David E. Kanouse, 1966. "Subjective Acceptance of Verbal Generalization," in S. Feldman, ed., *Cognitive Consistency.* New York: Academic Press, pp. 171–197.

Abelson, Robert P., and C. M. Reich, 1969. "Implication Modules: A Method for Extracting Meaning from Input Sentences," in Donald E. Walker and Lewis M. Norton, eds., *Proceedings of the International Joint Conference on Artificial Intelligence.* Boston: Mitre Corporation, pp. 647–748.

Abelson, Robert P., and Milton J. Rosenberg, 1958. "Symbolic Psycho-Logic: A Model of Attitudinal Cognition," *Behavioral Science,* 3, 1–13.

Alker, Hayward R., Jr., 1973. "Research Paradigms and Mathematical Politics," paper prepared for the IPSA Roundtable on Quantitative Methods and Political Substance—Toward Better

Research Strategies, Mannheim, Germany. Revised January 1973.

Alker, Hayward R., Jr., and William J. Greenberg, 1971. "The UN Charter: Alternative Pasts and Alternative Future," in E. H. Fedder, ed., *The United Nations: Problems and Prospects*. St. Louis: Center for International Studies, University of Missouri, Monograph #3, pp. 113–142.

Allison, Graham T., 1969. "Conceptual Models and the Cuban Missile Crisis," *American Political Science Review,* 63, 689–718.

———, 1971. *Essence of Decision: Explaining the Cuban Missile Crisis*. Boston: Little, Brown.

Allison, Graham T., and Morton H. Halperin, 1972. "Bureaucratic Politics: A Paradigm and Some Policy Implications," *World Politics,* 24 (Supplement), 40–79.

Almond, Gabriel A., Scott C. Flanagan, and Robert J. Mundt, eds., 1973. *Crisis, Choice, and Change: Historical Studies of Political Development*. Boston: Little, Brown.

Anderson, Joel E., Jr., 1973a. "The 'Operational Code' Approach: The George Construct and Senator Arthur H. Vandenberg's 'Operational Code' Belief System," paper prepared for the annual meeting of the American Political Science Association, New Orleans, September 1973.

———, 1973b. "The 'Operational Code' Belief System of Senator Arthur H. Vandenberg: An Application of the George Construct." Ph.D. dissertation, University of Michigan.

Antle, L. G., and G. P. Johnson, 1973. "Integration of Policy Stimulation, Decision Analysis and Information Systems: Implications of Energy Conservation and Fuel Substitution Measures on Inland Waterway Traffic," in *Proceedings of Computer Science and Statistics: Seventh Annual Symposium on the Interface*. Ames: Iowa State University.

Arnstein, Fred, 1971. "Comment on 'Three Not-so-Obvious Contributions of Psychology to Peace' by Ralph K. White," and "Response to White's Rejoinder," *Journal of Social Issues,* 27, 207–209, 212–220.

Arrow, Kenneth, 1951. *Social Choice and Individual Values*. New York: Wiley.

Art, Robert J., 1973. "Bureaucratic Politics and American Foreign Policy: A Critique," *Policy Sciences,* 4, 467–490.

Ashby, Ned, 1969. "Schumacher and Brandt: The Divergent 'Operational Codes' of Two German Socialist Leaders," mimeographed paper, Stanford University.

Auld, P., and E. J. Murray, 1955. "Content Analysis Studies of Psychotherapy," *Psychological Bulletin,* 52, 377–395.

Axelrod, Robert, 1967. "The Structure of Public Opinion on Policy Issues," *Public Opinion Quarterly,* 31 (Spring), 51–60.

———, 1972a. *Framework for a General Theory of Cognition and Choice.* Berkeley: Institute of International Studies.

———, 1972b. "Psycho-Algebra: A Mathematical Theory of Cognition and Choice with an Application to the British Eastern Committee in 1918," *Papers of the Peace Research Society (International),* 18, 113–131. Published in revised form as Chapter 4 of this volume.

———, 1973. "Schema Theory: An Information Processing Model of Perception and Cognition," *American Political Science Review,* 67 (December), 1248–1266.

———, 1975. "An Experiment on How a Schema Is Used to Interpret Information," in Matthew Bonham and Michael Shapiro, eds., *Thought and Action in Foreign Policy.* Basel: Birkhaüser Verlag.

Bales, Robert F., 1950. *Interaction Process Analysis.* Cambridge, Mass.: Addison-Wesley.

Bales, Robert F., A. Paul Hare, and Edgar F. Borgatta, 1957. "Structure and Dynamics of Small Groups: A Review of the Literature," in Joseph B. Gittler, ed., *Review of Sociology.* New York: Wiley, pp. 391–422.

Ball, Desmond J., 1974. "The Blind Men and the Elephant: A Critique of Bureaucratic Politics Theory," *Australian Outlook,* 28, 71–92.

Barber, James David, 1966. *Power in Committees.* Chicago: Rand McNally.

———, 1972. *The Presidential Character: Predicting Performance in the White House.* Englewood Cliffs, N.J.: Prentice-Hall.

Beaverbrook, William Maxwell Atken, 1956. *Men and Power, 1917–1918.* London: Collins.

Bennett, Stephen Earl, 1971. "Modes of Resolution of a 'Belief Dilemma' in the Ideology of the John Birch Society," *Journal of Politics,* 33, 735–772.

Berelson, Bernard, 1952. *Content Analysis in Communication Research.* Glencoe, Ill.: Free Press.

Blalock, Herbert M., 1964. *Causal Inferences in Non-Experimental Research.* Chapel Hill: University of North Carolina Press.

Bogart, K., 1971. "Preference Structures, I, II," mimeograph ed. paper, Dartmouth College, Hanover, N.H.

Bonham, Matthew, and Michael Shapiro, 1973. "Simulation in the Development of a Theory of Foreign Policy Decision-Making," in Patrick J. McGowen, ed., *Sage International Yearbook of Foreign Policy Studies,* Vol. 1.

———, eds., 1975. *Thought and Action in Foreign Policy.* Basel: Birkhaüser Verlag.

———, forthcoming. "Simulating Foreign Policy Decision-Making: An Application to the Middle East," in Joseph Ben-Dak, ed., *Simulation Yearbook.* New York: Gordon & Breach.

Boulding, Elise, 1972. "Peace Research: Dialectics and Development," *Journal of Conflict Resolution,* 16, 469–475.

Brandon, Henry, 1973. "Were We Masterful . . . ," *Foreign Affairs,* 9 (Winter), 158–170.

Brecher, Michael, 1968. *India and World Politics: Krishna Menon's View of the World.* London: Oxford University Press.

———, 1973. "Images, Process and Feedback in Foreign Policy: Israel's Decisions on German Reparations," *American Political Science Review,* 67, 73–102.

Brecher, Michael, Blema Steinberg, and Janice Stein, 1969. "A Framework for Research on Foreign Policy Behavior," *Journal of Conflict Resolution,* 13, 75–101.

Brenner, Michael J., 1973. "The Problem of Innovation and the Nixon-Kissinger Foreign Policy," *International Studies Quarterly,* 17, 255–294.

Brim, Orville, David C. Glass, David E. Lavin, and Norman Goodman, 1962. *Personality and Decision Processes.* Stanford: Stanford University Press.

Broadbent, D. E., 1971. *Decision and Stress.* London: Academic Press.

Brodin, Katarina, Kjell Goldmann, and Christian Lange, 1972. "Belief Systems, Doctrines, and Foreign Policy," *Conflict and Cooperation,* 8, 97–112.

Brown, B., S. Cochran, and N. C. Dalkey, 1969a. *The Delphi Method, II: Structure of Experiments,* RM-5957. Santa Monica, Cal.: Rand Corp.

———, 1969b. *The Delphi Method, III: Use of Self-Ratings to Improve Group Estimates,* RM-6115-PR. Santa Monica, Cal.: Rand Corp.

————, 1970. *The Delphi Method, IV: Effect of Percentile Feed-back and Feed-In of Relevant Facts,* RM-6118-PR. Santa Monica, Cal.: Rand Corp.

Brown, T. A., F. S. Roberts, and J. Spencer, 1972. *Pulse Processes on Signed Digraphs: A Tool for Analyzing Energy Demand,* R-926-NSF. Santa Monica, Cal.: Rand Corp.

Burgess, Philip M., 1967. *Elite Images and Foreign Policy Outcomes.* Columbus: Ohio State University Press.

Burnstein, Eugene, and Amiram Vinokur, 1973. "Testing Two Classes of Theories about Group Induced Shifts in Individual Choice," *Journal of Experimental Psychology,* 9, 123–137.

Campbell, Angus, Philip E. Converse, Warren E. Miller, and Donald Stokes, 1960. *The American Voter.* New York: Wiley.

Campbell, Donald T., and Julian C. Stanley, 1963. *Experimental and Quasi-Experimental Designs for Research.* Chicago: Rand McNally.

Cartwright, Dorwin, and Frank Harary, 1965. "Structural Balance: A Generalization of Heider's Theory," *Psychological Review,* 63, 277–293.

Choucri, Nazli, and Robert C. North, 1972. "Dynamics of International Conflict: Some Policy Implications of Population, Resources, and Technology," *World Politics,* 24 (Supplement), 80–122.

Coady, S. K., G. P. Johnson, and J. M. Johnson, 1973. "Effectively Conveying Results: A Key to the Usefulness of Technology Assessment," Institute for Water Resources, Corps of Engineers, mimeographed paper delivered at the First International Congress on Technology Assessment, The Hague, May 31.

Cobb, Roger W., 1973. "The Belief-System Perspective: An Assessment of a Framework," *Journal of Politics,* 35, 121–153.

Cole, H. S. D., Christopher Freeman, Marie Jahoda, and K. L. R. Pavitt, eds., 1973. *Models of Doom, A Critique of the Limits of Growth.* New York: Universe Books.

Converse, Philip E., 1964. "The Nature of Belief Systems in Mass Publics," in David Apter, ed., *Ideology and Discontent.* New York: Free Press of Glencoe, pp. 206–256.

Cottam, Richard W., 1973. "Foreign Policy Motivations," *International Studies Newsletter* (Winter), 52–60.

————, forthcoming. *Foreign Policy Motivation: The British in Egypt.*

Cummins, H. W., 1974. "Value Structure and Political Leadership," in Vincent Davis and Maurice East, eds., *Sage Professional Papers in International Studies*. Beverly Hills: Sage.

Cyert, Richard, and James G. March, 1963. *A Behavioral Theory of the Firm*. Englewood Cliffs, N.J.: Prentice-Hall.

Dahl, Robert A., 1967. *Pluralist Democracy in the United States*. Chicago: Rand McNally.

Dalkey, N. C., 1969. *The Delphi Method: An Experimental Study of Group Opinion*, RM-5888-PR. Santa Monica, Cal.: Rand Corp.

Dalkey, N. C., R. Lewis, and D. Snyder, 1970. *Measurement and Analysis of the Quality of Life*, RM-6228-DOT. Santa Monica, Cal.: Rand Corp.

Dalkey, N. C., and D. L. Rourke, 1971. *Experimental Assessment of Delphi Procedures with Group Value Judgments*, R-612-ARPA. Santa Monica, Cal.: Rand Corp.

Dalkey, N. C., D. L. Rourke, and B. Brown, forthcoming. *Effect of Feed-in of Multiple Relevant Facts on Group Judgment*, R-679-ARPA. Santa Monica, Cal.: Rand Corp.

D'Amato, Anthony A., 1967. "Psychological Constructs in Foreign Policy Prediction," *Journal of Conflict Resolution*, 11, 294–311.

Davis, Eric L., 1974. "Presidents' Belief Systems and Decision-Making Processes under Stress," mimeographed paper, Stanford University, June.

de Rivera, Joseph, 1968. *The Psychological Dimension of Foreign Policy*. Columbus, Ohio: Merrill.

de Sola Pool, Ithiel, ed., 1959. *Trends in Content Analysis*. Urbana: University of Illinois Press.

Deutsch, Karl, 1966. *The Nerves of Government*. New York: Free Press.

Douglas, Ann, 1962. *Industrial Peacemaking*. New York: Columbia University Press.

Dye, David R., n.d. "A Developmental Approach to the Political Style of Getulio Vargas," mimeographed paper, Stanford University.

Eastern Committee, *Minutes and Verbatim Annex, Cab 27/24*. London: Public Record Office.

Easton, David, 1965. *A Systems Analysis of Political Life*. New York: Wiley.

Eckhardt, William, 1967. "Can This Be the Conscience of a Conservative? The Value Analysis Approach to Political Choice," *Journal of Human Relations*, 15, 443–456.

378

Eckhardt, William, and Ralph K. White, 1967. "A Test of the Mirror-Image Hypothesis: Kennedy and Khrushchev," *Journal of Conflict Resolution,* 11, 325–332.

Etheredge, Lloyd, 1974. "A World of Men: The Private Sources of American Foreign Policy." Ph.D. dissertation, Yale University.

Etzioni, Amitai, 1969. "Social-Psychological Aspects of International Relations," in Gardner Lindzey and Elliot Aronson, eds., *The Handbook of Social Psychology,* Vol. 5, 2nd ed. Reading, Mass.: Addison-Wesley.

Farrand, Max, 1913. *The Framing of the Constitution of the United States.* New Haven: Yale University Press.

———, 1921. *The Fathers of the Constitution.* New Haven: Yale University Press.

Feigenbaum, Edward A., and Feldman, Julian, eds., 1963. *Computers and Thought.* New York: McGraw-Hill.

Festinger, Leon, 1957. *A Theory of Cognitive Dissonance.* Evanston, Ill.: Row, Peterson.

Flament, Claude, 1963. *Applications of Graph Theory to Group Structure.* Englewood Cliffs, N.J.: Prentice-Hall.

Forrester, Jay, 1971. *World Dynamics.* Cambridge: Wright-Allen.

Frank, Jerome D., 1967. *Sanity and Survival: Psychological Aspects of War and Peace.* New York: Vintage Books.

Frankel, Joseph, 1963. *The Making of Foreign Policy: An Analysis of Decision-Making.* London: Oxford University Press.

Freeman, Christopher, 1973. "Malthus with a Computer," in Donella Meadows, *et al.,* eds., *Models of Doom, A Critique of the Limits of Growth.* New York: Universe Books.

Friedman, M., 1937. "The Use of Ranks to Avoid the Assumption of Normality Implicit in the Analysis of Variance," *Journal of the American Statistical Association,* 32, 675–699.

Garnham, David C., 1971. "Attitudes and Personality Patterns of Foreign Service Officers and the Conduct of American Foreign Affairs." Ph.D. dissertation, University of Minnesota.

George, Alexander L., 1959a. *Propaganda Analysis.* Evanston, Ill.: Row, Peterson.

———, 1959b. "Quantitative and Qualitative Approaches to Content Analysis," in Ithiel de Sola Pool, ed., *Trends in Current Analysis.* Urbana: University of Illinois Press.

———, 1969. "The 'Operational Code': A Neglected Approach

to the Study of Political Leaders and Decision-Making," *International Studies Quarterly,* 13, 190–222.

———, 1972. "The Case for Multiple Advocacy in Making Foreign Policy," *American Political Science Review,* 66, 751–785, 791–795.

———, 1974. "Adaptation to Stress in Political Decision-Making," in G. V. Coelho, D. A. Hamburg, and J. Adams, eds., *Coping and Adaptation.* New York: Basic Books.

George, Alexander L., and Juliette L. George, 1956. *Woodrow Wilson and Colonel House: A Personality Study.* New York: John Day.

Gerbner, George, Ole R. Holsti, Klaus Krippendorff, William J. Paisley, and Philip J. Stone, eds., 1969. *The Analysis of Communication Content: Developments in Scientific Theories and Computer Techniques.* New York: Wiley.

Gibbins, Roger, n.d. "The Political Leadership of William Lyon Mackenzie King," mimeographed paper, Stanford University.

Gilson, Charlotte, and Robert P. Abelson, 1965. "The Subjective Use of Inductive Evidence," *Journal of Personality and Social Psychology,* 2, 301–310.

Glad, Betty, 1966. *Charles Evans Hughes and the Illusion of Innocence: A Study in American Diplomacy.* Urbana: University of Illinois Press.

Goldmann, Kjell, 1971. *International Norms and War between States: Three Studies in International Politics.* Stockholm: Läromedelsförlagen.

Graubard, Stephen, 1973. *Kissinger: Portrait of a Mind.* New York: Norton.

Greenstein, Fred I., 1969. *Personality and Politics: Problems of Evidence, Inference, and Conceptualization.* Chicago: Markam.

Gutierrez, G. G., 1973. "Dean Rusk and Southeast Asia: An Operational Code Analysis," paper prepared for the annual meeting of the American Political Science Association, New Orleans, September.

Haas, Michael, 1967. "Bridge-Building in International Relations: A Neo-traditional Plea," *International Studies Quarterly,* 11, 320–338.

Halperin, Morton H., 1974. *Bureaucratic Politics and Foreign Policy.* Washington, D.C.: Brookings Institution.

Hanrieder, Wolfram, 1967. *West German Foreign Policy, 1949–1963: International Pressure and Domestic Response.* Stanford: Stanford University Press.

Harary, Frank, Robert Z. Norman, and Dorwin Cartwright, 1965. *Structural Models: An Introduction to the Theory of Directed Graphs.* New York: Wiley.

Hare, A. Paul, 1972. "Bibliography of Small Group Research, 1959–1969," *Sociometry,* 35, 1–150.

———, 1962. *Handbook of Small Group Research.* New York: Free Press.

Heider, Fritz, 1946. "Attitudes and Cognitive Organization," *Journal of Psychology,* 21, 107–112.

Heiskanen, Heikki, 1973. "Oikeusoppia Systeemiteoreettisesti Tarkasteltuna," *Eripainos Oikeustiede,* 4, 187–249. English summary: "Jurisprudence from a System-Theoretical Point of View," pp. 249–275.

———, 1974a. "A Systems Theoretical Approach to the Analysis of Social Action and Decisions," Helsinki: Finnish Academy of Sciences, Series B, No. 191.

———, 1974b. "Exercise Course on Content Analysis," Research Report, Helsinki: University of Helsinki, Institute of Social Policy.

Heradstveit, Daniel, 1974. *The Outline of a Cumulative Research Strategy for the Study of Conflict Resolution in the Middle East.* Oslo: Norsk Utenrikspolitisk Institutt.

Hermann, Charles F., 1969a. *Crises in Foreign Policy.* Indianapolis: Bobbs-Merrill.

———, 1969b. "International Crisis as a Situational Variable," in James N. Rosenau, ed., *International Politics and Foreign Policy,* rev. ed. New York: Free Press.

———, ed., 1972. *International Crises: Insights from Behavioral Research.* New York: Free Press.

Hermann, Charles F., and Linda P. Brady, 1972. "Alternative Models of International Crisis Behavior," in Charles F. Hermann, ed., *International Crises: Insights from Behavioral Research.* New York: Free Press, pp. 281–320.

Hermann, Charles F., and Margaret G. Hermann, 1967. "An Attempt to Simulate the Outbreak of World War I," *American Political Science Review,* 56, 400–416.

Hermann, Margaret G., 1972. "How Leaders Process Information and the Effect on Foreign Policy," paper read at the annual meeting of the American Political Science Association, Washington, D.C.

———, 1974. "Effects of Leader Personality on National Foreign

Policy Behavior," in James N. Rosenau, ed., *Comparing Foreign Policies*. New York: Halsted Press.

Hermann, Margaret G., and. Charles F. Hermann, 1974. "Maintaining the Quality of Decision Making in Foreign Policy Crises: A Proposal," Chapter 16 of *Report on Minimizing "Irrationalities,"* prepared under the general direction of Alexander L. George for the Commission of the Organization of the Government for the Conduct of Foreign Policy, December.

Hilton, Gordon, 1969. "The Stanford Studies of the 1914 Crisis: Some Comments," mimeographed paper, London.

Hoffman, Erik P., and Frederick J. Fleron, eds., 1971. *The Conduct of Soviet Foreign Policy*. Chicago: Aldine-Atherton.

Hoffman, Stanley, ed., 1960. *Contemporary Theory in International Relations*. Englewood Cliffs, N.J.: Prentice-Hall.

Holsti, Ole R., 1962. "The Belief System and National Images: John Foster Dulles and the Soviet Union." Ph.D. dissertation, Stanford University.

————, 1967. "Cognitive Dynamics and Images of the Enemy," in David J. Finlay, Ole R. Holsti, and Richard R. Fagen, *Enemies in Politics*. Chicago: Rand McNally, pp. 25–96.

————, 1969. *Content Analysis for the Social Sciences and Humanities*. Reading, Mass.: Addison-Wesley.

————, 1970. "The 'Operational Code' Approach to the Study of Political Leaders: John Foster Dulles' Philosophical and Instrumental Beliefs," *Canadian Journal of Political Science*, 3, 123–157.

————, 1972. *Crisis, Escalation, War*. Montreal and London: McGill-Queen's University Press.

————, 1974. "The Study of International Politics Makes Strange Bedfellows: Theories of the Radical Right and Left," *American Political Science Review*, 68, 217–242.

Holsti, Ole R., and Alexander L. George, 1975. "The Effects of Stress on the Performance of Foreign Policy-Makers," in C. P. Cotter, ed., *Political Science Annual: Individual Decision-Making*. Indianapolis: Bobbs-Merrill.

Horvath, Fred E., 1959. "Psychological Stress: A Review of Definitions and Experimental Research," in Ludwig von Bertalanffy and Anatol Rapoport, eds., *General Systems: Yearbook of the Society for General Systems Research*, 4.

Hveem, Helge, 1972. *International Relations and World*

Images, a Study of Norwegian Foreign Policy Elite. Oslo: Universitetsforlaget.

Ike, Nobutaka, ed. and trans., 1967. *Japan's Decision for War: Records of the 1941 Policy Conferences.* Stanford: Stanford University Press.

Insko, Chester A., 1967. *Theories of Attitude Change.* New York: Appleton-Century-Crofts.

International Military Tribunal for the Far East, 1946–1948. *Decisions of Imperial Conferences in Prosecution's Evidence.* Tokyo, exhibits 552, 911A, and 1030.

Isaak, Robert A., 1975. "Psychosocial Factors in Foreign Policy: The Case of Kissinger," paper read at the annual meeting of the International Studies Association, Washington, D.C., February.

Janis, Irving L., 1972. *Victims of Groupthink: A Psychological Study of Foreign-Policy Decisions and Fiascoes.* Boston: Houghton Mifflin.

Janis, Irving L., and Howard Leventhal, 1968. "Human Reaction to Stress," in Edgar F. Borgatta and William W. Lambert, eds., *Handbook of Personality Theory and Research.* Chicago: Rand McNally.

Jensen, Lloyd, 1966. "American Foreign Policy Elites and the Prediction of International Events," *Peace Research (International) Society Papers,* 5, 199–209.

Jervis, Robert, 1968. "Hypotheses on Misperception," *World Politics,* 20, 454–479.

———, 1969. "The Costs of the Quantitative Study of International Relations," in Klaus Knorr and James N. Rosenau, eds., *Contending Approaches to International Politics.* Princeton: Princeton University Press.

———, 1970. *The Logic of Images in International Relations.* Princeton: Princeton University Press.

———, forthcoming. *Perception and Misperception in International Politics.* Princeton: Princeton University Press.

Johnson, Loch, 1973. "Operational Codes and the Prediction of Leadership Behavior: Senator Frank Church at Mid-Career," paper prepared for the annual meeting of the American Political Science Association, New Orleans, September.

Jones, Edward E., *et al.,* eds., 1971. *Attribution Theory, Perceiving the Causes of Behavior.* Morristown, N.J.: General Learning Press.

BIBLIOGRAPHY

Joxe, Alain, 1966. "Analyse d'un Systeme d'Objectifs Nationaux," *Journal of Peace Research,* 3, 244–256.

Kane, J., 1972. "A Primer for a New Cross-Impact Language— KSIM," *Technological Forecasting and Social Change,* 4, 129– 142.

Kane, J., W. Thompson, and I. Vertinsky, 1972. "Health Care Delivery: A Policy Simulation," *Socio-Economic Plann. Sci.,* 6, 283–293.

Kane, J., I. Vertinsky, and W. Thompson, 1973. "KSIM: A Methodology for Interactive Resource Policy Simulation," *Water Resources Research,* 9, 65–79.

Kaplan, Abraham, 1964. *The Conduct of Inquiry.* San Francisco: Chandler.

Kaplan, Morton A., 1968. "A Psychoanalyst Looks at Politics: A Retrospective Tribute to Robert Waelder," *World Politics,* 20, 694–704.

Kavanagh, Dennis A., 1970. "The 'Operational Code' of Ramsey MacDonald," mimeographed paper, Stanford University.

————, 1973. "Crisis Management and Incremental Adaptation in British Politics: The 1931 Crisis of the British Party System," in Gabriel A. Almond, Scott C. Flanagan, and Robert J. Mundt, eds., *Crisis, Choice, and Change: Historical Studies of Political Development.* Boston: Little, Brown.

Kelley, Harold H., 1971. "Causal Schemata and the Attribution Process," in Edward E. Jones, *et al.,* eds., *Attribution: Perceiving the Causes of Behavior.* Morristown, N.J.: General Learning Press.

Kelley, Harold H., and John W. Thibaut, 1969. "Group Problem Solving," in Gardner Lindzey and Elliot Aronson, *Handbook of Social Psychology,* Vol. 4, 2nd ed. Reading, Mass.: Addison-Wesley, pp. 1–101.

Kelman, Herbert C., ed., 1965. *International Behavior: A Social-Psychological Analysis.* New York: Holt, Rinehart and Winston.

Kemeny, J. G., and J. L. Snell, 1973. *Mathematical Models in the Social Sciences.* Cambridge, Mass.: M.I.T. Press.

Kendall, M. G., 1962. *Rank Correlation Methods.* New York: Hafner.

Kirkpatrick, Samuel A., 1975. "Psychological Views of Decision-Making," in Cornelius P. Cotter, ed., *Political Science Annual: Individual Decision-Making.* Indianapolis: Bobbs-Merrill.

Klineberg, Otto, 1964. *The Human Dimension in International Relations.* New York: Holt, Rinehart and Winston.

384

Knutson, Jeanne N., 1972. *The Human Basis of the Polity: A Psychological Study of Political Men.* Chicago: Aldine, Atherton.

Krantz, D. H., R. D. Luce, P. Suppes, and A. Tversky, 1971. *Foundations of Measurement, I.* New York: Academic Press.

Krasner, Stephen D., 1972. "Are Bureaucracies Important?" *Foreign Policy,* 7, 159–179.

Kruzic, P. G., 1973a. "A Suggested Paradigm for Policy Planning," TN-OED-016. Menlo Park, Cal., Stanford Research Institute.

———, 1973b. "Cross-Impact Analysis Workshop." Menlo Park, Cal.: Stanford Research Institute Letter Report, June 23.

Lambert, Robert M., 1966. "An Examination of the Consistency Characteristics of Abelson and Rosenberg's 'Symbolic Psychologic'," *Behavioral Science,* 11, 126–130.

Lampton, David M., 1973. "The U.S. Image of Peking in Three International Crises," *Western Political Quarterly,* 26, 28–50.

Landau, David, 1972. *Kissinger: The Uses of Power.* Boston: Houghton Mifflin.

Lawrence, Donald A., forthcoming. "The Operational Code of Lester Pearson." Ph.D. dissertation, University of British Columbia.

Lazarus, Richard S., n.d. "The Self-Regulation of Emotion," mimeographed paper, University of California at Berkeley.

Lazarus, Richard S., James R. Averill, and Edward M. Opton, Jr., 1969. "The Psychology of Coping: Issues of Research and Assessment," paper prepared for a conference on "Coping and Adaptation," Stanford University, Department of Psychiatry, March 20–22.

Lazarus, Richard S., James Deese, and Sonia Osler, 1952. "The Effects of Psychological Stress upon Performance," *Psychological Bulletin,* 49, 293–317.

Leites, Nathan, 1951. *The Operational Code of the Politburo.* New York: McGraw-Hill.

———, 1953. *A Study of Bolshevism.* Glencoe, Ill.: Free Press.

Lenczowski, George, 1949. *Russia and the West in Iran, 1918–1948: A Study in Big-Power Rivalry.* Ithaca, N.Y.: Cornell University Press.

Levins, R., 1974. "The Qualitative Analysis of Partially Specified Systems," *Annals of the N.Y. Academy of Sciences,* 231, 123–138.

———, forthcoming. "Evolution in Communities near Equilibrium," in J. Diamond and M. Cody, eds., *Ecology of Species and Communities.* Cambridge, Mass.: Harvard University Press, Belknap Press.

Lipset, Seymour Martin, 1960. *Political Man.* Garden City, N.Y.: Doubleday.

Lowenthal, Abraham F., 1972. *The Dominican Intervention.* Cambridge, Mass.: Harvard University Press.

Lowi, Theodore J., 1969. *The End of Liberalism: Ideology, Policy, and the Crisis of Public Authority.* New York: W. W. Norton.

Luce, R. Duncan, and Howard Raiffa, 1957. *Games and Decisions.* New York: Wiley.

Madison, James, 1898. *Journal of the Federal Convention,* edited by E. H. Scott. Chicago: Scott, Foresman.

————, 1966. *Notes of Debates in the Federal Convention of 1787.* New York: Norton.

Malone, Craig S., 1971. "The Operational Code of Lyndon Baines Johnson," mimeographed paper, Stanford University, July.

March, James G., and Herbert Simon, 1958. *Organizations.* New York: Wiley.

Marsden, G., 1965. "Content Analysis Studies of Therapeutic Interviews: 1954 to 1964," *Psychological Bulletin,* 63, 298–321.

Maruyama, Magoroh, 1963. "The Second Cybernetics: Deviation-Amplifying Mutual Causal Processes," *American Scientist,* 51, 164–179.

May, Ernest R., 1973. *"Lessons" of the Past: The Use and Misuse of History in American Foreign Policy.* New York: Oxford University Press.

McClosky, Herbert, 1956. "Concerning Strategies for a Science of International Politics," *World Politics,* 8, 281–295.

————, 1964. "Consensus and Ideology in American Politics," *American Political Science Review,* 58 (June), 361–379.

McGuire, William J., 1969. "The Nature of Attitude and Attitude Change," in Gardner Lindzey and Elliot Aronson, eds., *The Handbook of Social Psychology,* Vol. 3, 2nd ed. Reading, Mass.: Addison-Wesley, pp. 136–314.

McLellan, David, 1971. "The 'Operational Code' Approach to the Study of Political Leaders: Dean Acheson's Philosophical and Instrumental Beliefs," *Canadian Journal of Political Science,* 4, 52–75.

Meadows, H. Donella, Dennis L. Meadows, Jorgen Randers, and William W. Behrens III, 1972. *The Limits of Growth.* New York: New American Library.

Mennis, Bernard, 1972. *American Foreign Policy Officials: Who They Are and What They Believe Regarding International Politics.* Columbus: Ohio State University Press.

Milburn, Thomas W., 1972. "The Management of Crisis," in Charles F. Hermann, ed., *International Crises: Insights from Behavioral Research.* New York: Free Press, pp. 259–280.

Minsky, Marvin, ed., 1968. *Semantic Information Processing.* Cambridge, Mass.: M.I.T. Press.

Mintz, Max M., 1970. *Gouverneur Morris and the American Revolution.* Norman: University of Oklahoma Press.

Morgenthau, Hans J., 1968. "Common Sense and Theories of International Relations," in John C. Farrell and Asa P. Smith, eds., *Theory and Reality in International Relations.* New York: Columbia University Press.

Morley, James, 1957. *The Japanese Thrust into Siberia, 1918.* New York: Columbia University Press. Reprinted Freeport, N.Y.: Books for Libraries, 1972.

Mueller, John, 1969a. "Deterrence, Numbers and History," Security Studies Project, University of California at Los Angeles.

Mueller, John, 1969b. "The Uses of Content Analysis in International Relations," in George Gerbner, *et al.,* eds., *The Analysis of Communication Content: Developments in Scientific Theories and Computer Techniques.* New York: Wiley.

Murstein, Bernard I., 1965. *Handbook of Projective Techniques.* New York: Basic Books.

Nazi Conspiracy and Aggression, Vol. 6 (1946). Washington, D.C.: U.S. Government Printing Office, pp. 425–457.

Nigeria, Federal Ministry of Information, 1967. *Meeting of the Nigerian Military Leaders Held at Peduase Lodge, Aburi, Ghana, 4–5 January, 1967. Minutes.* Lagos.

North, Robert C., Ole R. Holsti, M. George Zaninovich, and Dina A. Zinnes, 1963. *Content Analysis: A Handbook with Applications for the Study of International Crisis.* Evanston, Ill.: Northwestern University Press.

Organization for Economic Cooperation and Development, 1974. "The Slowdown in R&D Expenditure and the Scientific and Technical System," Report SPT 1, Paris.

Osgood, Charles E., 1959a. "The Representational Model and Relevant Research Methods," in Ithiel de Sola Pool, ed., *Trends in Content Analysis.* Urbana: University of Illinois Press.

———, 1959b. "Suggestions for Winning the Real War with Communism," *Journal of Conflict Resolution,* 3, 311–325.

————, 1962. *Alternative to War or Surrender*. Urbana: University of Illinois Press.

Osgood, Charles E., Sol Saporta, and Jum C. Nunnally, 1956. "Evaluative Assertion Analysis," *Litera*, 3, 47–102.

Osgood, Charles E., and Percy H. Tannenbaum, 1955. "The Principle of Congruity in the Prediction of Attitude Change," *Psychological Review*, 62, 42–55.

Page, William, 1973. "The Population Subsystem," in H.S.D. Cole, *et al.*, eds., *Models of Doom: A Critique of the Limits to Growth*. New York: Universe Books.

Paige, Glenn D., 1968. *The Korean Decision*. New York: Free Press.

Prescott, Arthur Taylor, 1941. *Drafting the Federal Constitution*. Baton Rouge: Louisiana State University Press.

Putnam, Robert D., 1973. *The Beliefs of Politicians: Ideology, Conflict and Democracy in Britain and Italy*. New Haven: Yale University Press.

Raiffa, H., 1969. *Preferences for Multi-attributed Alternatives*, RM-5868-DOT/RC. Santa Monica, Cal.: Rand Corp.

Raser, John, 1966. "Personal Characteristics of Political Decision-Makers: A Literature Review," *Papers of the Peace Research Society (International)*, 5, 161–181.

Roberts, F. S., 1971. "Signed Digraphs and the Growing Demand for Energy," *Environment and Planning*, 3, 395–410; also R-756-NSF, Santa Monica, Cal.: Rand Corp., 1971.

————, 1972a. *Building an Energy Demand Signed Digraph I: Choosing the Nodes*, R-927/1-NSF. Santa Monica, Cal.: Rand Corp.

————, 1972b. *Building an Energy Demand Signed Digraph II: Choosing Edges and Signs and Calculating Stability*, R-927/2-NSF. Santa Monica, Cal.: Rand Corp.

————, 1973. "Building and Analyzing an Energy Demand Signed Digraph," *Environment and Planning* 5, 199–221.

————, 1974. "Structural Characterizations of Stability of Signed Digraphs under Pulse Processes," in R. Bari and F. Harary, eds., *Graphs and Combinatories*, Springer Verlag Lecture Notes in Mathematics, No. 406. New York.

————, forthcoming a. *Discrete Mathematical Models, with Applications to Social, Biological, and Environmental Problems*. Englewood Cliffs, N.J.: Prentice-Hall.

————, forthcoming b. *Weighted Digraph Models for Energy Use and Air Pollution in Transportation Systems,* R-1578-NSF. Santa Monica, Cal.: Rand Corp.

Roberts, F. S., and T. A. Brown, 1974. "Signed Digraphs and the Energy Crisis," submitted to *American Mathematical Monthly.*

Robinson, W. S., 1957. "The Statistical Measure of Agreement," *American Sociological Review,* 22, 17–25.

Rokeach, Milton, 1968. *Beliefs, Attitudes and Values.* Washington, D.C.: Jossey-Bass.

Rosenau, James N., 1966. "Pre-Theories and Theories of Foreign Policy," in R. Barry Farrell, ed., *Approaches to Comparative and International Politics.* Evanston, Ill. Northwestern University Press.

———, 1967. "The Premises and Promises of Decision-Making Analysis," in James C. Charlesworth, ed., *Contemporary Political Analysis.* New York: Free Press.

———, 1968. "Private Preferences and Political Responsibilities: The Relative Potency of Individual and Role Variables in the Behavior of U.S. Senators," in J. David Singer, ed., *Quantitative International Politics.* New York: Free Press.

———, 1970. *The Adaptation of National Societies: A Theory of Political System Transformation.* New York: McCaleb-Seiler.

———, 1971. *The Scientific Study of Foreign Policy.* New York: Free Press.

Rosenau, James N., Philip M. Burgess, and Charles F. Hermann, 1973. "The Adaptation of Foreign Policy Research: A Case Study of an Anti-Case Study Project," *International Studies Quarterly,* 17, 119–144.

Rosenau, James N., and Charles F. Hermann, 1973. *Final Report to the National Science Foundation on Grant GS–3117,* mimeographed, Columbus, Ohio, June 15.

Rothstein, Robert L., 1972. *Planning, Prediction, and Policymaking in Foreign Affairs: Theory and Practice.* Boston: Little, Brown.

Schank, Roger C., 1973. "Identification of Conceptualizations Underlying Natural Language," in Roger C. Schank and Kenneth M. Colby, *Computer Models of Human Thought and Language.* San Francisco: W. H. Freeman, pp. 187–248.

Schelling, Thomas C., 1963. *The Structure of Conflict.* Cambridge, Mass.: Harvard University Press.

Schick, Jack M., 1975. "Cognitive Dissonance and Competitive Assumptions: Naval Leaders and the Arms Race," paper prepared for the annual meeting of the American Political Science Association, San Francisco, September.

Schneider, Barry R., 1972. "Danger and Opportunity." Ph.D. dissertation, Columbia University.

Semmel, Andrew, 1972. "Some Correlates of Foreign Policy Attitudes among Foreign Service Officers." Ph.D. dissertation, University of Michigan.

Sen, A. K., 1970. *Collective Choice and Social Welfare*. San Francisco: Holden-Day.

Shapiro, David, and Andrew Crider, 1969. "Psychophysiological Approaches in Social Psychology," in Gardner Lindzey and Elliot Aronson, eds., *The Handbook of Social Psychology*, Vol. 3, 2nd ed. Reading, Mass.: Addison-Wesley.

Shapiro, Michael J., and G. Matthew Bonham, 1973. "Cognitive Processes and Foreign Policy Decision-Making," *International Studies Quarterly*, 17, 147–174.

Shneidman, Edwin, 1961. "A Psychological Analysis of Political Thinking: The Kennedy-Nixon 'Great Debates' and the Kennedy-Khrushchev 'Grim Debates'," mimeographed paper, Cambridge, Mass.

————, 1963. "Plan II. The Logic of Politics," in L. Arons and M. A. May, eds., *Television and Human Behavior*. New York: Appleton-Century-Crofts.

————, 1966. *The Logics of Communication*. China Lake, Cal.: U.S. Naval Ordnance Test Station.

————, 1969. "Logic Content Analysis: An Explication of Styles of Concludifying," in George Gerbner, *et al., The Analysis of Communication Content*. New York: Wiley.

Simmons, Robert F., 1970. "Natural Language Question-Answering Systems: 1969," in Tefko Saracevic, ed., *Introduction to Information Science*. New York: R. R. Bowker, pp. 467–484.

Simon, Herbert, 1947. *Administrative Behavior*. New York: Macmillan.

————, 1957. *Models of Man*. New York: Wiley.

————, 1969. *The Sciences of the Artificial*. Cambridge, Mass.: M.I.T. Press. Chapter 4 reprinted from "The Architecture of Complexity," *Proceedings of the American Philosophical Society*, 106 (1962), 467–482.

Singer, J. David, 1961. "The Level-of-Analysis Problem in International Relations," *World Politics*, 14, 77–92.

————, 1968. "Man and World Politics: The Psycho-Cultural Interface," *The Journal of Social Issues*, 24, 127–156.

————, 1971. *A General Systems Taxonomy for Political Science.* New York: General Learning Press.

Slovic, Paul, and Sarah Lichtenstein, 1971. "Comparison of Bayesian and Regression Approaches to the Study of Information Processing in Judgment," *Organizational Behavior and Human Performance,* 6, 649–744.

Snyder, Richard C., H. W. Bruck, and Burton Sapin, 1962. *Foreign Policy Decision Making.* New York: Free Press. Original monograph published in 1954.

Snyder, Richard C., and Glenn D. Paige, 1958. "The United States Decision to Resist Aggression in Korea: The Application of an Analytical Scheme," *Administrative Science Quarterly,* 3, 341–378.

Stagner, Ross, 1967. *Psychological Aspects of International Conflict.* Belmont, Cal.: Brooks/Cole.

Stassen, Glen H., 1972. "Individual Preference versus Role-Constraint in Policy-Making: Senatorial Response to Secretaries Acheson and Dulles," *World Politics,* 25, 96–119.

————, 1973. "Revising the 'Operational Code' Method," paper prepared for the annual meeting of the American Political Science Association, New Orleans, September.

Stein, Janice Gross, 1968. "Krishna Menon's View of the World: A Content Analysis," in Michael Brecher, ed., *India and World Politics: Krishna Menon's View of the World.* New York: Frederick A. Praeger.

Steinbruner, John D., 1968. "The Mind and the Milieu of Policy-Makers: A Case History of the MLF." Ph.D. dissertation, M.I.T.

————, 1970. *Some Effects of Decision Procedures on Policy Outcomes,* Arms Control Project, M.I.T. Center for International Studies, C/70–9. Cambridge, Mass.

————, 1974. *The Cybernetic Theory of Decision.* Princeton: Princeton University Press.

Stevens, S. S., 1946. "On the Theory of Scales of Measurement," *Science,* 103, 677–680.

————, 1951. "Mathematics, Measurement and Psychophysics," in S. S. Stevens, ed., *Handbook of Experimental Psychology.* New York: Wiley.

————, 1957. "On the Psychophysical Law," *Psychological Review,* 64, 153–181.

————, 1968. "Measurement, Statistics, and the Schemapiric View," *Science,* 161, 849–856.

Stone, Philip J., Dexter C. Dunphy, Marshall S. Smith, and Daniel

M. Ogilvie, 1966. *The General Inquirer: A Computer Approach to the Analysis of Content in the Behavioral Sciences.* Cambridge, Mass.: M.I.T. Press.

Stone, Philip J., *et al.,* 1969. "Improved Quality of Content Analysis Categories: Computerized Disambiguation Rules for High Frequency English Words," in George Gerbner, *et al.,* eds., *The Analysis of Communication Content.* New York: Wiley.

Strausz-Hupé, Robert, William R. Kintner, James E. Daugherty, and Alvin J. Cottrell, 1959. *Protracted Conflict.* New York: Harper.

Stupak, Ronald J., 1971. "Dean Rusk on International Relations: An Analysis of His Philosophical Perceptions," *Australian Outlook,* 25, 13–28.

Suppes, P., and J. L. Zinnes, 1963. "Basic Measurement Theory," in R. D. Luce, R. R. Bush, and E. Galanter, eds., *Handbook of Mathematical Psychology, I.* New York: Wiley, pp. 1–76.

Taylor, Michael, 1969. "Influence Structures," *Sociometry,* 32, 490–502.

————, 1970. "The Problem of Salience in the Theory of Collective Decision-Making," *Behavioral Science,* 15, 415–430.

Thordarson, Bruce, 1972. *Trudeau and Foreign Policy: A Study in Decision-Making.* Toronto: Oxford University Press.

Thucydides, 1960. *The Peloponnesian War,* Benjamin Jowett, trans. New York: Bantam.

Trotter, R. G., 1971. "The Cuban Missile Crisis: An Analysis of Policy Formulation in Terms of Current Decision-Making Theory." Ph.D. dissertation, University of Pennsylvania.

Tweraser, Kurt, 1973. "Senator Fulbright's Operational Code as Warrant for His Foreign Policy Advocacy, 1943–1967: Toward Increasing the Explanatory Power of Decisional Premises," paper prepared for the annual meeting of the American Political Science Association, New Orleans, September.

Ullman, Richard, 1968. *Britain and the Russian Civil War,* Vol. 2 of *Anglo-Soviet Relations, 1917–1921.* Princeton: Princeton University Press.

Verba, Sidney, 1961. "Assumptions of Rationality and Non-Rationality in Models of the International System," *World Politics,* 14, 93–117.

Vickrey, W. S., 1968. "Pricing in Urban and Suburban Transportation," in G. M. Smerk, ed., *Readings in Urban Transportation.* Bloomington: Indiana University Press.

Walker, Donald E., and Lewis M. Norton, eds., 1969. *Proceedings of the International Conference on Artificial Intelligence.* Boston: Mitre Corp.

Walker, Stephen G., 1975. "Cognitive Maps and International Realities: Henry A. Kissinger's Operational Code," paper prepared for the annual meeting of the American Political Science Association, San Francisco, September.

Waltz, Kenneth N., 1959. *Man, the State and War: A Theoretical Analysis.* New York: Columbia University Press.

Webb, Eugene J., Donald T. Campbell, Richard D. Schwartz, and Lee Sechrest, 1966. *Unobtrusive Measures: Nonreactive Research in the Social Sciences.* Chicago: Rand McNally.

White, Gordon, 1969. "A Comparison of the 'Operational Codes' of Mao Tse-tung and Liu Shao-chi," mimeographed paper, Stanford University.

White, Ralph K., 1951. *Value Analysis: The Nature and Use of the Method.* Glen Gardiner, N.J.: Liberation Press.

————, 1970. *Nobody Wanted War: Misperception in Vietnam and Other Wars.* Garden City, N.Y.: Anchor.

————, 1971. "Rejoinder" and "Counter Response," *Journal of Social Issues,* 27, 209–212, 220–227.

Wilensky, Harold L., 1967. *Organizational Intelligence: Knowledge and Policy in Government and Industry.* New York: Basic Books.

Zacher, Mark W., 1970. *Dag Hammarskjold's United Nations.* New York: Columbia University Press.

Zinnes, Dina A., 1963. "Documents as a Source of Data," in Robert C. North, *et al.,* eds., *Content Analysis: A Handbook with Applications for the Study of International Crises.* Evanston, Ill.: Northwestern University Press, pp. 17–36.

————, 1966. "A Comparison of Hostile Behavior of Decision-Makers in Simulated and Historical Data," *World Politics,* 18, 474–502.

Zinnes, Dina A., Joseph L. Zinnes, and Robert D. McClure, 1972. "Hostility in Diplomatic Communication: A Study of the 1914 Crisis," in Charles F. Hermann, ed., *International Crisis: Insights from Behavioral Research.* New York: Free Press.

Library of Congress Cataloging in Publication Data

Main entry under title:

Structure of decision.

    Bibliography: p.
    Includes index.
    1. Decision-making in public administration.
2. Choice (Psychology)   3. Cognition.   I. Axelrod,
Robert M.
JF1525.D4S77   350   76–3242
ISBN 0–691–07578–6
ISBN 0–691–10050–0pbk.